Hospital and Healthcare Facility Design

THIRD EDITION

Hospital and Healthcare Facility Design

THIRD EDITION

Richard L. Miller, FAIA

Earl S. Swensson, FAIA

J. Todd Robinson, AIA

W. W. NORTON & COMPANY
NEW YORK · LONDON

Copyright © 2012 by Richard L. Miller, Earl S. Swensson, and J. Todd Robinson
Copyright © 2002, 1995 by Richard L. Miller and Earl S. Swensson

First edition published as NEW DIRECTIONS IN HOSPITAL AND HEALTHCARE FACILITY DESIGN

Manufacturing by KHL Printing Co. Pte Ltd
Book design by Abigail Sturges
Production manager: Leeann Graham

Library of Congress Cataloging-in-Publication Data

Miller, Richard L. (Richard Lyle)
 Hospital and healthcare facility design / Richard L. Miller, Earl S. Swensson, J. Todd Robinson. — 3rd ed.
    p. cm.
 Includes bibliographical references and index.
 ISBN 978-0-393-73309-9 (hardcover)
 1. Hospital buildings—Design and construction.
 I. Swensson, Earl S. II. Robinson, J. Todd. III. Title.
 RA967.M487 2012
 725'.51—dc23

2011038054

ISBN: 978-0-393-73309-9

W. W. Norton & Company, Inc.,
500 Fifth Avenue, New York, N.Y. 10110
www.wwnorton.com

W. W. Norton & Company Ltd.,
Castle House, 75/76 Wells Street, London W1T 3QT

0 9 8 7 6 5 4 3 2 1

Contents

Foreword

Earl Swensson's reputation as one of the most distinguished architects in his field preceded him before I was introduced to him in person a few years ago. We met at an awards ceremony during which we were both honored as alumni of Metro Nashville Public Schools. Having grown up and gone to college and medical school in Nashville, Tennessee, I was well aware of the impact that his design firm, Earl Swensson Associates, has had on the city. Whenever I return to Nashville, I am greeted by the now-familiar outlines of the AT&T "Batman" Building and the Gaylord Opryland Hotel and Convention Center, among others. What Earl Swensson Associates is perhaps most renowned for, however, is its work in healthcare design, a field that overlaps my own.

As a physician and dean of a medical school, I am very comfortable in hospitals, doctors' offices, and other medical facilities, but I recognize that for many people, this is not the case. The concept that animates the approach of the authors—Richard Miller, Earl Swensson, and J. Todd Robinson—to healthcare architecture, which they term "Synergenial," is the creation of "functional environments that evoke positive responses from their users on physical, intellectual, and emotional levels." Positively engaging patients with their surroundings reduces stress and, ideally, enhances healing and overall well-being. *Hospital and Healthcare Facility Design* showcases beautiful examples of projects by Earl Swensson Associates and more than 30 other architectural firms that thoughtfully integrate design elements, patient amenities, and support services into clinical facilities of varying sizes. These buildings and treatment units from around the United States are helping to shape the future of healthcare delivery. At the same time, they reflect developments that have transformed the practice of medicine over the past 50 years.

Since I first entered medical school in the 1960s, advances in technology and drug development have led to improved diagnosis and treatment across the spectrum of disease. Life expectancy in the United States has increased steadily, driven largely by improvements in the prevention and treatment of heart disease and stroke. Sophisticated imaging techniques now allow physicians to visualize the body's tissues and organs with a high degree of specificity, although there remain areas where early diagnosis is rare, such as prostate cancer. Surgical interventions have become less invasive and more refined, while newer, nonsurgical procedures have emerged as therapeutic options for many patients. Perhaps in the not-so-distant future, genetic approaches to prevention and treatment, including personalized medicine, and the potential applications of stem cell research will further revolutionize the way that medicine is practiced.

These scientific and technological breakthroughs in modern medicine have occurred at the same time that the healthcare delivery system has undergone fundamental changes. Hospitals have shifted from being the primary site of healthcare delivery for acutely ill patients to being part of a treatment network that often includes outpatient or ambulatory care facilities, long-term care facilities, and home healthcare. This trend has emerged in part due to the high costs associated with modern healthcare, which is one of the major challenges currently facing our nation, and in part because of the aging patient population, now increasingly prone to chronic diseases.

This third edition of *Hospital and Healthcare Facility Design* clearly captures how these and other forces have coalesced to impact the field of healthcare architecture and design. Instead of massive structures that can often be perceived as cold and sterile, contemporary healthcare design calls for flexible, patient-centered spaces that inspire overall healthy living and can be adapted to emerging technologies and changing institutional needs. Illustrated with numerous case studies, this book describes how the shift toward shorter hospital stays, a greater reliance on disease prevention and self-care, and the increasing demand for sustainable and cost-effective building solutions have shaped the settings in which modern medicine is practiced. It is a valuable resource for the healthcare design community as our healthcare system continues to evolve.

Antonio M. Gotto, Jr., MD, PhD
Stephen and Suzanne Weiss Dean
Weill Cornell Medical College
New York, NY

Preface

Much has changed in the healthcare field since the second edition of this book was published, and even more since the first, which only underscores what we have said all along when it comes to healthcare: writing about the future can be a tricky business, especially in a field where the politics are volatile, the issues complex, and the economics daunting. In the healthcare arena, changes have been occurring so rapidly for so long that what once might have seemed a dramatic change often appears these days to be routine development. None of this, of course, changes the need to make sure the designs of our facilities stay fluid and flexible and include strategies for future use, strategies that differ from the way we use our designs today.

Again in this edition, we need to make clear from the beginning that we are not writing about the vicissitudes of healthcare financing and the politics of healthcare reform. Nor have we produced a book about the varying impact of new technologies on the current practice of medicine, except as it affects design and the need to plan for its accommodation. And we are certainly not attempting to provide here a comprehensive discussion about the future of healthcare itself. Instead, we are writing about new directions in hospital and healthcare facility designs—new directions that we, as designers of healthcare facilities, recognize and can document, new directions that have an impact on how we plan and build today—the move toward "green" design strategies, for example, toward evidenced-based design, and toward sustainable architecture. These are directions currently underway, and they are directions away from the past and toward the future, but they are after all only directions.

Our modest hope is that by observing various trends and discussing them, we can offer some practical aid to architects and healthcare administrators who must plan and design and build today for a future that none of us in the end can know in all its specific and detailed splendor. Our methods are not those of crystal ball gazers or biblical prophets. They are more down to earth: research and analysis; observation and reasonable inference; practical experience and learning. We provide a historical perspective about hospitals and their design in the past and discuss what types of considerations ought to go into design to meet today's needs and future concerns. We discuss specific trends in the design of healthcare facilities recently built or in the planning stages. Finally, we proffer our observations on a wide range of design concerns and specific structures.

Indeed, many of the changes that occurred in the past, some of which rose to the level of what we called paradigm shifts that we discussed in the earlier editions, have had pretty much the effect we suggested. And for that reason, too, we have been led to produce this revised third edition. To cite one example, the shift from a provider-driven to a user-driven system has become so pronounced that, today, it is almost conventional wisdom. Yet as part of the movement toward evidence-based design, it continues to change the way in which facilities are planned and designed. Hospitals today strive to be user-friendly, to focus on the needs of the patients, of their families, and of the professionals who care for them and serve them. This revision reflects, then, both the ubiquity of the user-driven paradigm and the changes it continues to promote in healthcare facility design. Then, too, consider the growing number of hospitals that focus on women's health and on caring for children, which has led us to expand the chapter dealing with these subjects. And think of the paradigm shift we discussed in the first two editions that was created by the aging of the American population, from designing for a healthy thirty-year-old man to designing for a less-than-healthy seventy-year-old woman. Today, the implications of that shift are even more evident than they were in the second edition, and we have expanded the chapter on long-term care and designing for the elderly that we added last time. We also updated the case studies we kept from previous additions, though a great number of the case studies included are entirely new, and all the case studies are intended to illustrate our discussion of hospital and healthcare design.

However, the book's focus has not changed. It remains a place to start, not a primer but an introduction, yet still a book more for practitioners than for theorists, more for those looking to build than for those looking to predict, and a book for practitioners and builders who know that what they practice and what they build must be thoroughly informed by clear-headed theories about, and sober-eyed looks at, both the world around them and the road to the future.

Acknowledgments

No book—especially a book about a subject so complex as healthcare facility design—can be written without help from others, and we wish to recognize all those who participated in producing this third edition, as well as those who helped on our two previous endeavors.

First, there is writer and wordsmith Charles Phillips of Zenda, Inc. He built on the work he did for the second edition and on that he and his coworkers at Zenda—Alan Axelrod and Patricia Hogan—did on the first, helping us string words together and editing the manuscript for clarity and precision. For this new edition, Phillips once again provided us not only with his skills as a writer and editor, but he once again deployed his talent for listening to those with whom he works, a talent essential to bringing our ideas into the public space of the printed page.

First and foremost, those he listened to were not only the authors of the book, but the employees of Earl Swensson Associates. Crystal Ullestad, our liaison with Phillips and Zenda, coordinated the project from start to finish. For this edition, she coordinated all efforts on the project, made sure the revision remained on track, traced down new images, badgered the slow and the recalcitrant for materials, case studies, and artwork, and spent hours making sure the new text was not just new, but right. Just as Crystal was aided in the first edition by Don Zirkle, and the second by Karen Edlund, this time out she found help again from Karen Edlund and also from Sue Halford.

In the first edition, Phillips, the folks at Zenda and Crystal and ESa staff were guided by an outline of topics to be covered and a list of case studies to be included put together by Harold Petty, Todd Robinson, Sam Burnette, and Don Zirkle, all of whom read and critiqued the manuscript, while Kathy Carr reviewed the text for accuracy, especially from the viewpoint of interior design. For the second edition, the group—Harold, Todd, Sam, and Don—got together again, and—joined by David Minnigan—reviewed the first edition, broadly outlined the changes and updating needed, and suggested new information, images, case studies, and new chapters. For this third edition Sam Burnette and Misty S. Chambers and other ESa staff fulfilled that function, while Todd Robinson signed on again, this time as coauthor. We wish to thank those on ESa's staff who helped make this book work: Sandy Dickerson, who helped on previous editions, was also deeply involved this go-around, especially in dealing with photographs. Shali Nelson, too, once again helped with photos and images. Kerry Foth also helped again this time. Other ESa employees who provided support and technical assistance, from producing graphics to typing correspondence on one or more of our three editions include: Lisa Chumbler, Shirley Condra, Rhonda Conner, Ginger Schaffer, and Laurie Stanley.

In creating this book, it was not only ESa staff who participated in that now long ago, initial day-long retreat and brainstorming session that kicked off the project. There, too, as we have said before, gathered around the room to share their knowledge and their insight were William W. Arnold, III, Kenneth N. Barker, PhD, Michael Boroch, Gene Burton, Donna Finney, Jeff Hardy, Teri Louden, and Charles Phillips. The discussions they participated in, the criticisms they offered, the general information they provided, and the concerns and issues they raised were key to the success of the book, and they are a large part of the reason it has gone through three major editions.

If the day-long retreat was the first stage of the process, the necessary final stage was the reading and review of the completed manuscript for that first edition by those who knew the field, and some who might be expected to use the published book. They included: Kenneth N. Barker, Michael Boroch, Gene Burton, Dan Buxbaum, Donna Finney, Elbert Garner, Teri Louden, Clayton McWhorter, Roscoe R. Robinson, MD, Dick Rosenvold, and Bob Vraciu. For the second edition, Gene Burton of Gene Burton & Associates and Mary Huston McClendon of The Centre for Health Care Planning read the manuscript and brought to bear on it their immense experience in and knowledge of the healthcare field. And for this third edition, once again Gene Burton & Associates, this time led by Terry Miller, reviewed the manuscript and made handy their advice, which we in almost every case followed.

Finally, we wish to thank Antonio M. Gotto, who has honored us with an elegant and inspiring foreword for this, our third, edition.

We thank all these, and others too numerous to mention, for helping us once again to create a work of which we are proud. As before, what you will find of the good and the true in the following pages is in no small part their doing—only the errors and mistakes do we, the authors, alone assume as our own.

Richard L. Miller, FAIA
Earl S. Swensson, FAIA
J. Todd Robinson, AIA

CHAPTER 1

Principles

New Paradigms in a New Century

We have been raised to believe in medical miracles. And with good reason. In the last century medicine evolved from the relatively ineffectual—and often downright harmful—study and palliation of illness and injury to a system of positive, effective, life-prolonging intervention. That intervention has increasingly emphasized the component of diagnosis, so that the trend has been toward earlier intervention and, most recently, prevention or, as it is more accurately termed, "wellness." Today's medical technology, genetic research, and drug therapies hold the promise of not merely alleviating much suffering but also of avoiding it altogether—provided we can find a way to pay for the diagnostics, the treatments, and the drugs they introduce.

But today, despite some healthcare reforms, most people fear the cost of illness almost as much as illness itself. Healthcare costs have persistently greatly exceeded general inflation, and, as many employers found it increasingly difficult or impossible to continue providing the level of healthcare insurance American workers had long taken for granted, more and more Americans found themselves with inadequate insurance or none at all. Healthcare reform, considered impossible after its utter collapse during the Clinton administration, has become a top national political priority again, despite worldwide economic woes. Once it passed, however, healthcare reform itself became a source of economic worry, and the debate over who should pay for what continues.

Not so long ago attempts to contain the spiraling costs of healthcare in America and the unprofitability, impracticality, even impossibility of insurance ever fully funding these costs led to the advent of managed care and the introduction of diagnosis-related groups (DRGs) by the federal government. Indeed in the 1980s, managed care and related cost-containment programs were heralded as waves of the future, despite much grumbling among professionals and even the occasional public outrage at the callousness of the hybrid managed-care system that soon developed in a political vacuum, especially as such programs became increasingly stringent in the controls they applied.

But a more basic change was underway as well. A population regarded traditionally as a pool of patients and potential patients had come to be viewed as a target audience of "healthcare consumers" participating in a "healthcare marketplace." Healthcare providers, including those responsible for planning and running hospitals and healthcare facilities, were understandably anxious about the growing impact of managed care and cost containment, but it was the startlingly rapid transition from the provider-dominated payment systems of the mid- to late-twentieth century to the turn-of-the-century consumer-centered marketplace that proved the more profound paradigm shift.

Since Thomas S. Kuhn's groundbreaking book, *The Structure of Scientific Revolutions*, many of us have learned to think not in terms of an era's zeitgeist, but in terms of changing paradigms: models, patterns, sets

Atrium Medical Center, Middletown, Ohio. The center marks a new era of healthcare delivery. *Photo Jeff Millies © Hedrich Blessing.*

West Houston MOB, Houston, Texas. Glazing makes the West Houston facility energy-efficient. Patients enter the MOB through a doorway separate from the physicians' entrance. *Photo Bill LaFevor.*

of assumptions about a field, profession, or society that explain that field, profession, or society to us and thereby guide our thinking and behavior in relation to the field, profession, or society. In *The Social Transformation of American Medicine*, Paul Starr traced the accumulation of economic, social, and political power by American physicians and chronicled the evolution of the hospital, which is intimately bound up with the elevation of the physician. Starr outlined three phases in the evolution of the American hospital.

The first, spanning from 1750 to 1850, witnessed the development of two kinds of institutions: voluntary hospitals, which were operated by charitable lay boards, though usually affiliated with some Protestant religious body; and public hospitals, operated by municipal or county governments and developed from the almshouses maintained by many colonial communities. The second phase, which began during the mid-nineteenth century and ran to its end, saw the formation of "particularistic" hospitals funded by religious or ethnic institutions. The period also witnessed the growth of specialized hospitals for women and for treating certain diseases. In addition, homeopaths and other members of medical sects opened their own specialized hospitals. Finally, from 1890 and into the first three decades of the twentieth century, profit-making hospitals came into operation, funded and run by corporations or by physicians.

This development reflected the emergence of a paradigm shift from a healthcare system controlled by religious, charitable, and governmental authority to a system centered on and controlled by the healthcare providers themselves, chiefly physicians. By the first quarter of the twentieth

Spotsylvania Regional Medical Center, Fredericksburg, Virginia. A two-story atrium welcomes visitors. *Photo © Kyle Dreier Photography.*

century, physicians had focused the practice of medicine on the hospital institution, much as the clergy had for centuries focused the practice of religion on the church. Moreover, physicians structured payment systems in such a way that the doctor-patient relationship was free from "lay" interference, with the healthcare provider setting fees and enjoying unrestricted and sovereign discretion in using the hospital's resources to resolve his or her patient's problem.

To be sure, the wealthy could afford to buy more—and often better—medical care than the less fortunate. However, as Starr pointed out, even the elite voluntary and municipal hospitals, as well as the most prestigious private hospitals, which were teaching hospitals associated with universities and medical schools, actually brought together the top and bottom strata of society. Physicians needed patients who could afford to pay, but they also needed poorer patients for research and teaching purposes. For some five decades, this provider-centered paradigm not only worked but was accepted uncritically. Like the hospital itself, it had become an "institution" in the social sense. Then, by the middle of the 1980s, apparently in direct response to a faltering economy, reduction in insurance benefits, and sharply rising healthcare costs, this paradigm shifted rapidly from those who provide the care to those who pay for the care.

The shift came with such apparent suddenness that it was perceived as a crisis, not only by financially beleaguered patients ("consumers"), but also by healthcare providers and by those who plan and administer hospitals. By the close of the 1980s, the hospital industry profit margins sharply declined, beds

Johns Hopkins Hospital Outpatient Center, Baltimore, Maryland. The center, with its light, airy appearance, features clear signage to assist patients in wayfinding and in identifying departments. *Courtesy Payette. Photo Dan Forer.*

were empty, the product portfolio had matured, administration became an entrenched and coagulated bureaucracy, CEOs were hired and fired at a rate outpaced only by the entertainment industry, and—in desperation—management embarked on an epidemic of poorly thought-out attempts at diversification into other industries, some related to healthcare, many totally unrelated.

In 1985, for example, inpatient hospital use declined by almost 20 percent, while profit margins remained high. Two years later, even in the face of declining inpatient population, hospitals enjoyed revenues 100 percent above 1980 levels. Yet, after another two years, by the end of 1989, the record-setting margins had evaporated, and it was administrator turnover, at 25 to 30 percent annually, that broke all records.

Administrators perceived all of this as a crisis and feared for the survival of not only their particular hospital but also of all hospitals. The crisis mentality was only fed by the growing power of managed-care programs in the 1990s. When the insurance companies took increasing control of healthcare decision making—from dictating when their policyholders could see specialists, to which specialists they could see, to which treatments they would allow the specialists to prescribe—that frustrated medical professionals who saw the system as breaking down rather than undergoing a paradigm shift.

Such a notion provided little comfort as insurers, responding to their primary customers in corporate America, began to squeeze those who provided healthcare services. Under this pressure, hospitals began to reduce the lengths of stay and increasingly to move patient care to ambulatory settings. They grew more aggressive about their reimbursement arrangements as they, rather than the insurance companies, assumed more of the cost-of-care risks, and they lost market clout as they lost the ability to charge freely for their services to a third party. Many other traditional acute-care hospitals began closing and others, to survive, branched out from inpatient care to offer a wide spectrum of services, focusing on early diagnosis, wellness, outpatient treatment, and the management of chronic illnesses, and providing ambulatory care, home care, and extended care for aging and chronically ill patients.

To keep down the cost of caring for aging populations, savvy institutions created integrated delivery systems (IDSs) aimed at providing vertically integrated services—from healthcare for individuals and groups to proprietary managed-care networks, from home care to hospital inpatient and extended-care services. IDSs turned the local healthcare institution into an established brand name providing a recognizable consumer product; they stabilized costs and promised to increase profits by keeping care within set budgets; and they made patients healthier. Indeed, for a while, with healthcare costs per capita falling to a thirty-year low, with physician salaries stabilizing, and with insurance premiums actually decreasing, it seemed as if managed care might work. Physicians had come up with their own response to the HMO (health management organization), the physician practice management (PPM) organizations; the aging population promised great potential for growth; and hospital profits continued to climb through the 1990s.

St. Luke's Hospital at The Vintage, Willowbrook, Texas. The gift shop, designed by ESa, sits off an entrance bathed in natural light. *Photo © Michael Peck.*

Then it all fell apart. The gain in market share for HMOs turned out not to be a cure-all. The IDSs ultimately realized few of the expected economies of scale, their costs consequently proved higher than fees and charges could cover, and they ran into debilitating cash-flow problems. Staff morale deteriorated and productivity suffered. As a result caregivers and management squabbled, and nurses, medical technicians, and even doctors turned to labor unions for help. Worst of all, having transformed their patients into consumers, hospitals failed to satisfy their customers. The healthcare industry had mistaken a paradigm shift for a management crisis. They fixed their businesses; they did not address the change—the new link between satisfied patients and profits. Some healthcare facilities are now hiring physicians as hospital employees, which protect doctors against some of the risks of

business and medical care, the increasing costs of malpractice insurance, and so on. Indeed, it seems many physicians do not want to manage healthcare anymore but simply to practice medicine again.

The Reality of Paradigm Shift

The perception of crisis is the product of an exclusive focus on the short term. Unfortunately, the term "paradigm" itself has become such a buzzword among management consultants that the concept it connotes—the very assumptions by which we structure our reality—may also be confused with the paraphernalia of crisis and quick fix. Analyzing, understanding, adapting to, and, finally, anticipating paradigm shifts are essential to seeing beyond—and getting beyond—immediate crises to seize the larger, longer-term opportunities for which a crisis often serves as a messenger.

The consumer backlash against managed care was fueled by limited choices, poor access, excessively increasing costs, bad service, and a growing awareness of health issues. In this new era, patients demand the basics they would demand of any good service or product: sufficient and accurate information about the product, a right to participate in the decision making about its purchase; open and direct communication with the provider; a greater choice of providers; timely, convenient, and reliable services; a high-quality, friendly environment; and respect for their dignity, compassion for their conditions, and empathy for their suffering from the people they pay to care for them. And the transition from a provider-centered to a patient (consumer)-centered healthcare system is only one among a number of profound and interrelated paradigm shifts currently active and shaping the emerging social and technological climate in which architects, healthcare and hospital administrators and planners, healthcare providers, and public policymakers must collaborate to create hospital and healthcare facilities with the quality, cost-effectiveness, and flexibility sufficient to carry them

St. Luke's Hospital Medical Tower, Houston, Texas. St. Luke's futuristic design signals to its patients that they will receive the best care possible at this state-of-the-art medical facility and teaching hospital. The medical tower features thirteen floors of medical offices and, reflecting the trend away from inpatient care, devotes one entire floor to ambulatory surgery. Courtesy Cesar Pelli & Associates. Photo Paul Hester/Lisa Hardaway & Paul Hester, Photographers.

through the twenty-first century. As architects who design extensively for the healthcare industry, we have been struck by the profound and governing presence of four major paradigm shifts and a welter of less sweeping, but still significant, minor shifts listed below:

• *From youth to maturity.* Since the beginning of the industrial age, we have preferred to abandon what is old or outdated, whether things or people. Now that paradigm is changing and giving way to maturity, which means neither young nor aged, new nor old. Maturity entails the acquisition of an evolving wisdom that transcends either-or stereotypes. More importantly for our purposes here, it has a profound impact on the architecture of healthcare itself. The percentage of Americans over age seventy-five keeps climbing. Ironically, as folks live longer, the healthcare system can become a victim of its own success. The elderly are much more likely to get sick, which puts greater pressure on traditional healthcare facilities. But it has also spawned a range of alternate facilities designed for varying needs of the independent elderly.

• *From remediation to health.* Contemporary American medicine is undergoing a dramatic shift from remediation (the pure art of healing) to health—an art of well-being and health maintenance. The new paradigm has greatly affected hospital architecture and also figures in the needs of those who use virtually every other type of building as well.

• *From specialization to wholeness.* Today we look to the whole of the healthcare environment. The idea, backed by much research, is that a pleasant,

New Medical Center/Kaiser Foundation Health Plan, Inc., Fresno, California. Floor plan, first floor. The plans for this facility feature the flexibility for future expansions. The building is arranged along a mall that separates inpatient and outpatient services. *Courtesy Ratcliff.*

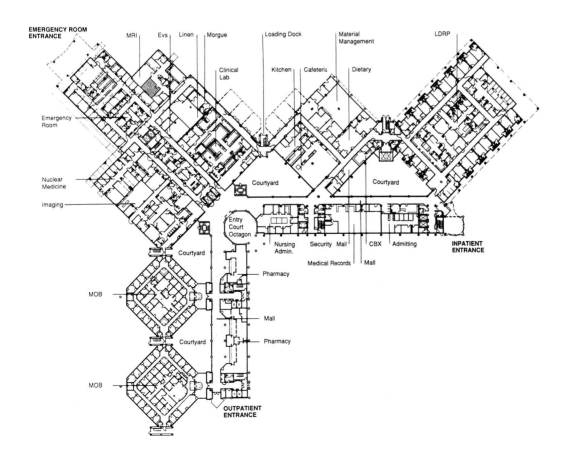

The Heart Center of Western Baptist Hospital, Paducah, Kentucky. *Photo © Sam Fentress.*

stress-free environment, both architectural and landscape, helps heal the patient. Color, finishes, indirect lighting, fine furniture, ample daylight, and views all constitute the healing environment, and they all have their price.

• *From reaction to anticipation.* It is no longer sufficient for a facilities planner, hospital administrator, healthcare policymaker, or architect to recognize a need and respond to it. Human needs are by their nature dynamic; contemporary technology has accelerated that dynamism. Structures—whether social or physical—designed for human beings must, therefore, emulate that dynamism by anticipating evolving needs.

In addition to getting in sync with these major paradigm shifts, hospital planners and designers also need to recognize the following transitions:

• *From exclusivity to system.* The traditional definition of the "healthcare system" does not define a healthcare system at all, but, rather, a disease-care system. And "system," by this definition, encompasses only that portion of the population actually and currently receiving professional treatment. The rest of the population remains outside the "system." Therefore, taking the larger view, this traditional definition emphasizes fragmentation rather than a genuine system. The current paradigm shift places the entire population within a healthcare system. At any particular time, any individual may be located along a continuum within a whole system of healthcare. The hospital or healthcare facility must learn to serve those in the community who currently require treatment as well as those healthy individuals who may benefit from wellness programs. Architects will be called upon to plan facilities that provide for extensive community outreach and that overcome the image of the hospital as an isolated fortress.

• *From a focus on sickness to wellness.* Intervention exclusively during illness or injury makes for fragmented, episodic care. Emerging healthcare delivery systems will focus on wellness and health maintenance. In accommodating this shift, hospitals will undoubtedly become more closely integrated into the community.

• *From fragmentation to integration.* In the past, integration of medical care meant gathering a panoply of doctors and a warehouse full of equipment under one enormous roof and calling the result a hospital. In fact, in the early Industrial Age, such an arrangement was less fragmented and more efficient than if physicians had labored independently. In the Information Age, however, it is no longer sufficient—and no longer always necessary—to gather personnel and equipment into a single building or complex. The technology now exists for deep integration of treatment among any number of healthcare professionals. Care delivery functions, finance, and administration can be thoroughly integrated, and data can be disseminated communitywide, statewide, nationwide, and internationally. On the simplest level, planning and designing a hospital will involve accommodating information technology. More significantly, this technology provides further incentive for decentralizing healthcare facilities. For example, a physician will be able to transmit data from his office to the hospital rather than compel his patient to visit the hospital in person.

Katz Women's Hospital—Long Island Jewish Medical Center. This new building, designed by Skidmore, Owings & Merrill (SOM), is both a medical facility and the centerpiece of a revitalization plan. Acting as a new front door to the hospital's main tower, the 250,000-sq.-ft. structure aims to consolidate women's services and provide healthcare to expectant mothers. *Courtesy Skidmore, Owings & Merrill. Photo SOM | © studioamd.*

• *From hierarchical to functional.* Traditional hospitals are organized according to management hierarchies. Like many large corporations, hospitals tend to suffer from bloated layers of management, which mask the fact that, at its most basic and essential, a hospital is a "neighborhood" business centered on a relationship between the doctor and the patient. The shift toward the functional reduces management hierarchies and calls for building designs that are less corporate and more humanly scaled, that are flexible enough to treat a patient's condition rather than fit a patient into a particular department, and that are generally less monolithic in concept as well as appearance.

• *From passive participation to active participation.* Along with a healthcare marketplace that was wholly

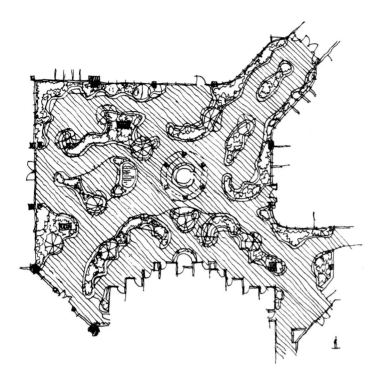

Centennial Medical Center/Garden Court, Nashville, Tennessee. Floor plan, main level (first floor). The eight-story atrium, which connects the facility's MOB with its hospital, offers soothing running waters, a pleasing array of plantings, and private seating areas for families and visitors. Some of the patient rooms overlook the atrium. *Sketch by Earl S. Swensson.*

provider-centered came the doctor-patient relationship in which the patient was expected to put himself in the physician's hands. Now that the market has shifted from the provider to the patient, the patient expects—and is expected—to take a more active role in treatment, making informed choices and collaborating with, rather than submitting to, health professionals. Hospital and health-facility architecture can accommodate this shift by drawing more extensively on retail and hospitality models of design and by including in their designs information-access facilities open to patients.

• *From institutional to noninstitutional.* This may be the single most visible shift, so far as design is concerned. The architecture of traditional hospitals invokes the overwhelming and oppressive majesty of the institution and is aimed at impressing the individual with his comparative insignificance. The new, noninstitutional paradigm seeks, through design, to empower the individual, not to debilitate him. Architects are turning from the traditional institutional models to retail, hospitality, and residential models of design to create friendly, nonthreatening hospital environments.

These are the broadest of the paradigm shifts that place hospital and healthcare facility design on the cutting edge. From these grow the following specific trends:

• *From inpatient to ambulatory care.*

• *From freestanding community hospitals to large regional, religious-based, or mega-corporation-owned facilities.*

• *From urgent care to primary care.* Traditionally, patients with urgent (but nonemergency) medical needs entered the hospital emergency department if they had not established a relationship with a family physician. Increasingly, ambulatory care centers, conceived along the lines of a retail model, have replaced the hospital emergency room (and even the personal physician) for urgent care. These days, even retail drugstores have instant-diagnosis minute clinics, attractive as alternatives to the long waits elsewhere, including in many physicians' offices. To remain competitive in this environment, hospitals are sponsoring primary-care centers distinct from the traditional emergency room.

• *From nursing home to subacute center.* Long-term-care facilities may be integrated with hospitals and will emphasize rehabilitation over warehousing or maintenance. Instead of the patient being consigned to a nursing home, the hospital-based nursing home cares for a patient for shorter periods of time, fostering more extended periods of home care, self-care, or semi-sheltered care. In general, medicine will see a shift from institutional dependency to self-care. Architects will work with administrators and facilities planners to create design strategies to enable the hospital to participate in and foster this movement toward self-care.

Other Trends

Several other related trends affect or promise to affect hospital and healthcare design. The quality and the safety of healthcare facilities have of course always been paramount design concerns, but these days heightened attention is being paid to measuring the quality of care and to publishing the results. Hospitals are expected to track everything from an individual physician's work to the number of accidents, medication errors, and other mistakes that occur in a given institution. Federal, state, and local governments as well as federal and private insurers and other payers issue their own reporting requirements. Such accountability, while it irritates administrators and sometimes angers doctors and surgeons, has led to an emphasis on evidence-based care.

Evidence-based care—and the concomitant evidence-based design (EBD)—demands that care and treatment guidelines be based on empirical data that show why one treatment or care option is superior to other forms of care. This information is then used to develop care mapping to define the best care delivery.

Indeed, some clients now ask architects to provide evidence that certain design features improve the quality of patient care. Most often clients demand evidence that the physical environment—the facility itself—reduces stress and aids healing. Many firms have developed research operations specifically to provide such evidence and many conduct tests in a variety of venues. They are also testing some facility designs aimed at creating safer, more efficient environments, as well as "healthy" spaces. Clearly architects need to be aware that the environments they build are going to be measured as part of the quality of caregiving.

So key is this current trend that it has become a national focus for architects, some of whom have established the Center for Health Design (CHD), a nonprofit research, education, and advocacy organization dedicated to EBD. It offers the Evidence-Based Design Accreditation and Certification (EDAC) program, begun in 2005 with funds from the Robert Wood Johnson Foundation, and maintains a growing list of advocate firms who are dedicated to using an evidence-based design process in healthcare facilities and who commit to having 25 percent of their professionals go through the accreditation process.

All of this—evidence-based design, care mapping, and tracking the impact of the healthcare environment on patients—places greater emphasis on information management. Add to that the demands of the Health Insurance Portability and Accountability Act (HIPAA), which requires that more diligence be paid to patient-record privacy and data collection. Throw in the burgeoning population of doctors and nurses using—no, *relying* on—personal digital assistants (PDAs), mobile workstations, wireless notebooks, and

Critical Care Tower at Vanderbilt University Medical Center, Nashville, Tennessee. With its skylights, the airy central atrium offers respite for patients and visitors. *Courtesy Earl Swensson Associates and Don Blair & Partners Architects, LLP. Photo © Kyle Dreier Photography.*

smart phones. Clearly, to provide quality care medical professionals must be able to manage data from varying sources for each patient, and healthcare designs must accommodate their growing demand to do so.

Of course, information technology is not the only kind of technology whose presence continues to flourish in the current healthcare environment. Diagnostic imaging; genetics-based testing and treatments; and proteomics are all becoming standard. And therapeutic technology is transforming hospital care.

Take the most obvious example—the cardiac stent. Despite some worries about the long-term safety of these devices, they have dramatically reduced the amount of cardiac bypass surgery that occurs. Then there are the statin-based pharmaceuticals, which have reduced the frequency of cholesterol-related, cardiologic, and vascular conditions. Cancer therapies are shorter, better targeted, and guided by technology. Joint replacements have become commonplace. So, too, have therapeutic interventions for neurological and gastrointestinal diseases.

At the same time these advances are increasing the average lifespan, hospitals are being hit by a tsunami of elderly patients that threatens to overwhelm healthcare facilities. Staffing shortages and rising costs drive hospitals to seek greater efficiencies, which leaves providers feeling they have less time to spend with patients, and patients anxious about their health concerns, their therapeutic options, and their lives.

Taken together, these trends in staffing and operations play a powerful role in shaping the design of new healthcare facilities. The rising cost of construction further obligates hospitals and architects to look at options such as lean design and lean construction. Pioneered by Toyota Motor Company in the 1970s, lean design has since become common in many other industries. Its chief idea is to provide workers all they need to do their jobs as close as possible to their work sites. Doing so cuts down repetitive motions, shortens distances between tasks, and eliminates wasted time and resources. This, in turn, increases productivity, produces cost savings, and improves an outfit's competitive edge. For hospitals, lean design aims at improving both the efficacy and efficiency of care.

Traditional nursing stations have been getting smaller, moving toward keeping the caregiver closer to the patient and materials closer to the point of care. Nursing units, then, are designed to minimize the distance between the nurses' station and patient rooms, and between the nurses' station and the supplies and medications nurses need to treat their patients, all of which, along with computers in patient rooms, is improving a hospital's operational efficiency and the experiences of its patients.

These trends all increase the architect's responsibility for his or her design, since hospitals and other healthcare clients are increasingly unwilling to accept the architect's mere assertion that this or that design feature improves patient care. They want the facts, they want proof, and the architect needs the research at hand.

Speaking the Language of Business

In the pages that follow, we consider strategies for accommodating and anticipating the paradigm shifts and trends just outlined. All of the traditional concerns of the architect still apply, and the architect or facilities planner also needs to be sensitive to the social, economic, and technological issues that impact healthcare today. In the new market-driven healthcare climate, however, all of those involved in planning, designing, and allocating resources for hospitals and healthcare facilities must become fluent in the language of business if they are to be heard.

The language of business used to require simply stating matters in terms of dollars and cents but now requires expressing oneself in terms of cost-effectiveness. The purchasers of healthcare were once obliged to assume all economic risks; now, providers take on more of the risk. Consumers have learned to differentiate—rather than equate—high cost and high quality and, formally or informally, evaluate the services they choose by applying this equation: Value = Cost + Quality. Along with this comes a questioning of the appropriateness of the cost and quality offered by the healthcare provider due to the fact that consumers shop for value. Healthcare providers must also look for value.

This is what it means to design cost-effective structures, and doing so entails some very difficult choices. In the recent past, healthcare providers worked in a culture of healthcare entitlement. The predominant culture still endorses healthcare for everyone but necessitates rationing of technology. In the recent past, healthcare providers were mission-oriented. Today, that mission is to varying degrees defined as delivering value to market. In the past, purchasers of healthcare services focused on episodic costs. Today, the trend is toward a focus on the cost of caring for a defined population, and, whereas healthcare providers have been accustomed to emphasizing services and procedures—the hospital was where you went when you were sick—the trend now is promoting, managing, and maintaining the health of the community.

Finally, healthcare providers have resisted any policy that questions the cost of sustaining life. "Life at any cost" is, after all, as old as the Hippocratic Oath. Today, healthcare providers at every level are questioning those costs.

Architecture and Medicine

Learning the language of business is invaluable for planning and communicating design strategies in the field of healthcare. But, in speaking this language, we must never forget that hospitals are more than businesses. They reach to the very core of society and civilization as expressions and instruments of our deepest humanity and compassion.

The architect's role in shaping these expressions and instruments is a socially crucial one. Indeed, the practice of medicine and the practice of architecture are more intimately related than may be superficially apparent.

St. Luke's Hospital at the Vintage, Willowbrook, Texas. *Photo © Michael Peck.*

When the social-reform-minded dramatist Henrik Ibsen wrote *The Master Builder* in 1892, it was natural for him to choose as his hero—and the ideal of the socially responsible man—an architect. Since ancient times, the vocation of architecture has been seen as nothing less than the vocation of building, shaping, and rebuilding the human world. Beset with the burgeoning urban squalor of the Industrial Revolution at full tilt, no era turned more earnestly to the architect than the age of Ibsen. From the late-nineteenth to the mid-

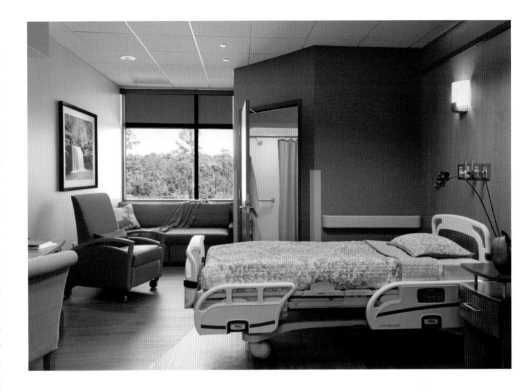

St. Luke's Hospital at the Vintage, Willowbrook, Texas. Natural lighting benefits patients' rooms and staff work areas as well as the public spaces. *Photo © Michael Peck.*

twentieth century, social thinkers looked to the architect for society's salvation. In a different play, *The Enemy of the People*, Ibsen found another metaphorical figure to represent the socially responsible man: the physician.

That the playwright should have chosen an architect and a physician to represent essentially the same thing makes perfect sense. At its best, architecture is a profession of wellness—a sister, in fact, to the medical profession. Our firm, Earl Swensson Associates (ESa), has coined a term to describe this approach to architecture. Synergenial® design was created from *synergism* and *geniality* to describe a design approach that acknowledges both the synergistic nature of the problem-solving process and the congenial, user-sensitive attributes of a successfully designed solution. Synergenial buildings are functional environments that evoke positive responses from their users on physical, intellectual, and emotional levels.

The synergism comes from combining state-of-the-art technology and sound economics with the information—scientific and functional—at the contemporary architect's disposal to produce an effective design inspired by the people who are going to use it. The hope is that a design so inspired will appeal to all the human senses all the time, making its attraction subtle, sophisticated, even subconscious—genial rather than critical. However, "Synergeniality" can be evaluated in terms of the five Ps.

PEOPLE

• *The test of synergism.* Time management: The management technique for accomplishing a proposed design.

• *The test of geniality.* Senses: Eliciting desired human responses from all aspects of a proposed design.

PURPOSE

• *The test of synergism.* Client/User: Determining the desires of the client and the needs of the users of a design to satisfy them.

• *The test of geniality.* Task performance: Establishing the ergonomic and psychological conditions that optimize a proposed design's effectiveness.

PRICE

• *The test of synergism.* Financing: Identifying all factors affecting the financing of a proposed design, as well as any financial limits, conditions, and time restrictions.

• *The test of geniality.* Lifetime cost: Anticipating total financial ramifications during the lifetime of a design, from initial investment to future returns.

PLACE

• *The test of synergism.* Locale: The accurate report of existing physical and legal conditions that affect a proposed design and the acknowledgment of anticipated changes.

• *The test of geniality.* Climatic setting: Acknowledging the atmospheric conditions of a design that affect the senses and emotions.

PERSPECTIVE

• *The test of synergism.* Technology: Utilizing technical advances to execute a proposed design.

• *The test of geniality.* Historical/cultural setting: Cultivating the proper appreciation for a design's cultural context.

If there is any single yardstick to apply in evaluating the buildings discussed in this book, always in the context of the emerging paradigms governing society in general and the healthcare industry in particular, it is the concept of Synergenial design. This approach grew primarily from almost fifty years of practice rather than from a predisposition to develop a comprehensive, all-encompassing theory; it is no accident that its most intensive development came in connection with our firm's extensive work in the healthcare field. We witnessed firsthand the shift away from acute-care hospitals. In the early 1980s, our hospital clients asked us to develop a panoply of new types of facilities: outpatient clinics, wellness centers, and medical office buildings with ambulatory surgery capabilities.

As we—and others—studied the changing nature of medical care and the effect it was having on architecture, we began to discover just how much effect architecture had on medicine. Patients exposed to noise or stuck in windowless rooms required stronger painkillers, became anxious or even delirious more readily, and more often fell into depression. When a patient could gaze out a window for even a few minutes at trees, water, or gardens, his blood pressure dropped. Clearly, there were healthy rooms and unhealthy rooms, and we began to extrapolate from there, cautiously working toward the somewhat dangerous notion of a healthy architecture—one that, like

St. Vincent's North Tower, Birmingham, Alabama. The three-story entry lobby designed by Earl Swensson Associates. *Photo © Kieran Reynolds Photography.*

contemporary medicine, seeks to be preventive, to promote health, rather than to be remedial, to cure ills already present.

Now, as an aesthetic category, "health" has a long pedigree. The notion of health was basic to Aristotle's *Poetics*, a fact recognized and exploited by the University of Chicago's "New School" of literary criticism back in the 1950s. Opponents of the so-called Chicago school found the pronouncing of this or that work of literature or art healthy or unhealthy not merely irresponsible exegesis but intellectually quite dangerous, no doubt hearing in the word the echoes of Nazi aesthetics. The idea of health as a normative value has been so abused that one could easily be leery of applying it—even when appropriate. Yet, undeniably, there are healthy buildings and unhealthy ones, and a responsible and judicious approach to the concept should not be dismissed simply because the term was misused politically in the past.

LeConte Medical Center, Sevierville, Tennessee. The lobby, like much of the replacement medical campus, was designed to be aesthetically compatible with the architecture of the historic town in the foothills of the Great Smoky Mountains. *Courtesy Earl Swensson Associates and BarberMcMurry architects. Photo © Kyle Dreier Photography.*

Nothing would seem more natural than to look to hospitals themselves for examples of healthy architecture, since, by definition, they should be structures intended primarily to promote the good health of their users. Yet, as everyone knows, hospitals have traditionally been distinctly unhealthy environments, places to avoid unless you are so ill that you cannot do so. Not only are many hospitals unhealthy in the strictest sense of the word, they are far too often inhospitable.

So far as existing hospitals are concerned, this is the rule rather than the exception: Sick men and women, accompanied by anxious and worried families, arrive at most hospitals only to be greeted by harsh lights, stark corridors, noisy equipment, acrid and unpleasant smells, and a cold, soulless expanse of marblelike hardness and stainless steel. Not only are patients denied access to medical information, they are stripped of their privacy upon arrival and given no opportunity or space for intimate talks or private grief. Under the acceleration of medical technology, many hospitals became huge machines, built—or, more often, awkwardly retrofitted—to accommodate rapidly changing equipment and ever more bureaucratic staffs. In the name of technology a host of dehumanizing structures were built, and, in the name of sanitation, sterile environments were created.

Far from promoting health, hospitals can actually make sick people unhealthier. As Wayne Ruga, who has organized the annual Symposium on Healthcare Design, once said: "When a patient's anxiety increases, the immune system is suppressed, and the body is weakened in its ability to fight disease." There is actually a phenomenon known as ICU syndrome, which occurs when a critically ill patient is subjected twenty-four hours

St. Louis Children's Hospital, St. Louis, Missouri. This light, airy, playful, and healthy design appeals to children. *Courtesy HOK. Photo Alise O'Brien.*

a day to harsh and unvarying fluorescent light, the incessant beep of monitors and thump of respirators, and the disorienting sameness of the stark white or sickly colored walls still typical of many intensive care units. The syndrome consists of sleep disturbances, hallucinations, and, on occasion, mild psychosis.

These sick buildings have not only harmed those who used them, but they have also injured, perhaps fatally, the institutions of which they are the physical expression. They cannot compete in the emerging healthcare marketplace. The new consumer will not tolerate, let alone choose, them.

Undeniably, the role of the traditional, acute-care hospital has diminished. In the language of business, its market share keeps decreasing. Is this, then, a singularly inopportune time to promote new construction? Hardly. For it is not that the hospital is dying. Rather, it is being redefined in the name of survival as well as service—by physicians, researchers, technologists, politicians, insurance providers, government bureaucrats, and patients. Working with and among all of these people, the architect gives form to the emerging redefinitions. In the hospital project, the architect faces the opportunity and challenge of creating new, exciting, useful, and humane structures—"healthy" buildings—in the new paradigm.

CHAPTER 2

Traditional Hospital

A Warehouse for the Sick

Architects pride themselves on the conviction that the spaces they design profoundly affect the people who use the buildings. The hospital—whose linguistic roots, not coincidentally, are the same as those of *hotel, hostel, hospitable,* and *hospitality*—should connote the qualities and emotions embodied in the names the U.S. Navy has traditionally assigned to its hospital ships: hope, solace, repose. Instead, the hospital often evokes emotions that range from discomfort to anxiety to outright phobia in people who say they simply "cannot stand hospitals." There was a time, of course, when such a response would have been perfectly reasonable. In the days before antisepsis and anesthesia, let alone antibiotic drugs and X-ray machines, hospitals were indeed places to be avoided. You generally went to a hospital only if you could afford nothing better—that is, physician-attended home treatment—and, if you did go to a hospital, it was very likely that you would not leave it alive.

Although those days are long past and most people enter the hospital with every expectation of emerging with their condition cured, improved, or at least palliated, Rodney M. Coe's summation of the "meaning of hospitalization" in his *Sociology of Medicine* (1970) still hits home, some thirty years later:

> Many . . . attributes of illness may be carried over to the hospital situation and, perhaps, even exaggerated by some features of the hospital. In the first place, the hospital is a strange environment for most people. It has different sounds and smells than the environments to which most of us are accustomed. There is a sort of "air of emergency" about the place as doc-

THE HEALING TEMPLE OF ASCLEPIOS AT EPIDAURUS, GREECE - 5TH CENTURY B.C.

tors, nurses, and other uniformed personnel move rapidly from one place to another. . . . [There is also] the threatened disruption of normal roles—particularly separation from the family and from the work role.

The onset of illness is . . . an intensely personal matter calling for personalized or supportive responses from the personal community in the form of expressed concern and succorant behavior. Under ordinary circumstances, this would likely be the type of response elicited from family members and friends. When the sick person is removed from the home setting and admitted to the hospital, he is not only deprived of these primary-oriented responses, but also exposed to a series of interactions with others which are characterized as objective and impersonal. They may range from the somewhat bureaucratic, officious behavior of admitting clerks and other administrative personnel to the professional scientific aplomb of nurses and examining physicians.

The architect may well protest that none of this is her fault. Illness is anxiety provoking, and if medical personnel are officious, bureaucratic, and impersonal, well, it is hardly the doing of hospital architecture. But the architecture of the hospital is an expression of the cultural and emotional dynamics of the institution. It is as much an expression of these dynamics as the words and demeanor of the medical professionals and others who attend patients. Folk wisdom, mother wit, common sense, and a burgeoning volume of scientific studies argue that emotional stress tends to exacerbate physical illness, whereas environmental factors that contribute to a sense of emotional well-being tend to ameliorate physical conditions. Unfortunately,

Temple of Asclepios, 400 B.C., Epidauros, Greece. By the time of Hippocrates, the temples of Asclepios offered a place of worship and shelter for the sick. Healing temples resembled spas, emphasizing exposure to fresh air, sunlight, rest, baths, exercise, and reasonable diet. *Sketch by Earl S. Swensson.*

Pennsylvania Hospital. The Palladian model dominated hospital design in the eighteenth and nineteenth centuries. These charitable institutions almost exclusively dealt with the sick who were too poor to have personal physicians tend to them in their homes.

there are two major reasons why architects, planners, and hospital administrators cannot simply decide to humanize hospital design.

The first reason involves areas in which technological needs conflict with patients' needs. No matter how well designed a hospital is, it must compromise between these two sets of needs. The most humane environment for a sick person is the home, and, indeed, many medical futurists see an increasing trend away from hospital care to home care. But, for the immediate future and certainly for individuals requiring advanced diagnostic, surgical, or life-support treatment, it is necessary for the patient to leave the home environment and come to a central location in which the necessary personnel and equipment are assembled and available. The very fact that the patient must be brought to the physicians and the technology rather than these being brought to the patient at home is a compromise.

The second reason involves the conflict between the efficiency needs of care providers and the social and psychological needs of patients. In the 1970s, for example, there was great interest in hospital plans that designed nursing units in a circular fashion, with the nursing station located centrally within the unit. Nurses who worked in circular units reported that patient supervision was much easier and that they could even spend more time with individual patients than was possible in layouts of more conventional double-loaded corridors. One researcher, however, went beyond surveying the nurses to asking patients what they thought of the design. Overwhelmingly, patients complained that the design cost them their privacy.

How important is a sense of privacy to the emotional state of a hospitalized person? This depends largely on the length of the hospitalization and the nature of the illness. However, among patients hospitalized with psychiatric disabilities, loss of privacy can be frankly traumatic, and many studies demonstrate the importance of territory and personal space in the hospital environment. Yet no one would deny the desirability of making the nurse's demanding job less arduous and more efficient. These conflicting needs demonstrate that designing humane hospitals is a desirable goal, but it is not the only goal, and, like all design tasks, that of designing a hospital requires a thoughtful balancing of various needs. The trouble is that what we are calling the traditional hospital—and, as we shall see, that tradition actually takes many forms and is enacted in a range of degrees—tends to resist compromise and ignore the difficult question of balance. Hospitals of the old paradigm are, in varying attenuated degrees, what the great sociologist Erving Goffman characterized as "total institutions."

Total Institutions

Total institutions are organized to provide for *all* the basic needs of the people who live in them. As Goffman wrote in his seminal *Asylums: Essays on the Social Situation of Mental Patients and Other Inmates* (1961):

> All aspects of life are conducted in the same place and under the same single authority. Second, each phase of the member's daily activity is carried on in the immediate company of a large batch of others, all of whom are treated alike and required to do the same thing together. Third, all phases of the day's activities are tightly scheduled, with one activity leading at a prearranged time to the next, the whole sequence of activities being imposed from above by a system of explicit formal rulings and a body of officials. Finally, various enforced activities are brought together into a single rational plan, purportedly designed to fulfill the official aims of the institution.

There is also a castelike split between those who administer the institution and those to whom they minister. Patients entering the old paradigm hospital are subjected to "stripping"—something like the process a Marine inductee undergoes when exchanging distinctive civilian clothes for a nondescript uniform; patients must submit to a system that more or less strictly controls resources as well as authority. One resource that old-paradigm hospitals tend to dispense in parsimonious fashion is information, and not surprisingly a lack of information is one of the major complaints patients make about hospitals.

Finally, the total institution exerts control on the patient by restricting her mobility, a factor that not only makes it easier for medical staff to attend to the patients, but also intensifies (for better or, more certainly, for worse) the status of being ill.

All of these measures of control at once depersonalize the patient and segregate her from the general population, intensifying the anxiety, shame, guilt, and fear that often accompany illness and injury. Again, the architect may ask: What has this to do with me and my job?

A nineteenth-century wood engraving of Napoleon III at a hospital in Lyons, France, shows the typical warehouse approach to hospital design. *Courtesy CORBIS.*

The architecture of the old-paradigm hospital grows from the idea of a total institution. The older hospitals, those from 1930 and earlier, may inspire awe, but it is the awe evoked by a cathedral or prison. These hospital buildings are characteristically monumental, often employing neo-Gothic decorative elements and relying on hard, unyielding materials, including cold marble that, unfortunately, bespeaks a mausoleum rather than a place of comfort and healing.

Many hospitals built during the 1950s and 1960s partake more of a functional modernism, deliberately stripping away such ecclesiastical reminders as Gothic ornamentation to present a front that is efficient, professional, and sterile—figuratively as well as literally. Where marble and granite predominate in the public areas of the earlier buildings, stainless steel and glass are more common in the later structures. The style of both types of building, however, communicates an allegiance to the totality of the institution. That is, though the hospital building of the 1920s is likely to look very different from that of the 1950s, a casual observer—or user—is apt to describe both as *institutional*.

The History of an Institution

Grim as it may be, the design of the traditional or old-paradigm hospital is neither an accident nor a mistake. It is the product of ever-evolving ideas of society, science, and the status of the medical community.

The first evidence of something resembling a hospital—that is, institutionalized care for the sick—may be found as early as 1200 B.C.E., when patients were cared for in Greek temples. By 400 B.C.E., the time of Hippocrates, the temples of Asclepios appeared. These were structures devoted not only to worship but specifically to sheltering the sick. Most historians consider these the first hospitals of the Western world. They were not primarily inpatient institutions, but more closely resembled spas, emphasizing exposure to fresh air, sunlight, rest, baths, exercise, and a reasonable diet. Medication was prescribed, apparently, but in moderation.

In Egypt, priest-physicians administered medical care, including the prescription of drugs and the performance of some surgery, in temples by 600 B.C.E. By far the most advanced hospitals of the ancient world seem to have been the *cikistas* of India, built between 273 and 232 B.C.E. There, Hindu physicians brought surgery to a highly developed degree and administered efficacious medicines. Moreover, cleanliness was the hallmark of the cikistas, and, as in the modern hospital, patients stayed overnight and attendants ministered to them.

During medieval days, classical medical knowledge was largely forgotten. However, ecclesiastic "hotels" were erected beside many churches to shelter the sick, who were cared for by priests. Treatment was very limited; instead, caring, compassion, and spiritual comfort were emphasized. The religious aspect of the ecclesiastical hotel increasingly displaced the succorant functions of these institutions throughout the course of the medieval period in Europe, and they developed into buildings with large open wards featuring an altar and sometimes a chapel at the end or in the middle. The layout of the ward was meant to ensure that patients could hear and see religious services.

During this same time in the Middle East, efficacious physical medicine evolved into a sophisticated art. There is evidence that Muslim physicians used inhalant anesthetics and had at their disposal a wide range of drugs. Thirteenth-century Cairo's Al-Mansur Hospital had separate wards for serious illnesses, outpatient clinics, and homes for long-term convalescence.

It was during the early Renaissance that the word "hospital" came into being (derived from the Latin *hospes*, meaning "host" or "guest") and that hospitals began to exist separately from churches. The oldest hospital in Western Europe is the Hotel Dieu in Paris, which was built in 550 C.E. and rebuilt during the thirteenth century. By the early Renaissance, it functioned in a manner strikingly similar to that of a modern hospital. Patients were classified and separated according to type and severity of illness, and there was a separate unit for women recovering from childbirth. The hospital was divided into various departments, each governed by a head; a board of provisors directed the entire institution, and patients who could afford to pay for services rendered.

The Protestant Reformation closed many of the Catholic hospitals in Protestant countries, and these were taken over or replaced by privately financed and conducted institutions. In Catholic France, prior to the Revolution, hospitals remained essentially religious, with wards laid out to provide patients with an opportunity to hear and see religious services. Secularization proceeded rapidly following the French Revolution, however.

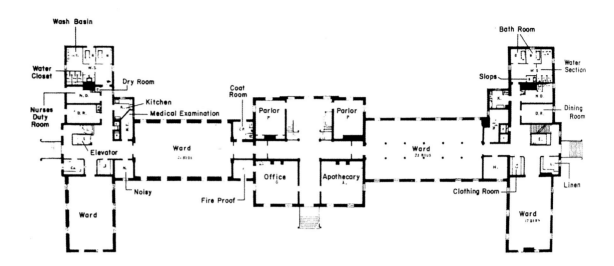

Pennsylvania Hospital. Floor plan, first floor. The Palladian design conveyed control and authority over the patients within. This early American hospital sought to regulate the moral behavior of the sick poor as much as to care for their ailments.

Despite secularization, many hospitals retained the look of religious structures, indicating the institution's former affiliation with the Church. In England, however, the characteristic eighteenth-century hospital came to resemble a Palladian mansion, except that the heights of the various stories were equal whereas the domestic Palladian model varied story height as a reflection of the differing social functions of each floor. The eighteenth century was a boom time for English hospitals, in part due to the military, which built facilities to promote the maintenance of adequate manpower in the army and navy. One military hospital at Stonehouse, Plymouth, built in 1762, actually embodied in its design the most advanced medical thinking of the period. In the mid-eighteenth century, the prevailing theory of the causality of disease was the miasmatic or zymotic theory, which held that illness was the result of miasma or "bad air" (witness the term *malaria*, literally "bad air") and that an effective deterrent to miasma was the circulation of plenty of fresh air. With this in mind, the Admiralty hospital was built as a series of detached pavilions connected by an open arcade, to expose patients to the maximum amount of natural ventilation.

Stonehouse was precocious, however, since the pavilion plan, endorsed by the medical profession, would not come into its own until well into the nineteenth century. Most eighteenth-century hospitals adhered to the Palladian model, which befitted their dignified status as charitable institutions and pleased the subscribers and boards of governors, who were gentlemen accustomed to the elite gentility implied by the Palladian form.

Significantly, the imposing, mansionlike edifice functioned almost exclusively as a means of dealing with the sick poor. Well-to-do and middle-class persons preferred home treatment. The baronial architecture conveyed authority and control, and, indeed, the hospital institution was aimed at regulating the sick poor as much as caring for them. Concentrating the needy in a central location made treating them a more economical proposition, allowed staff to supervise moral conduct, and discouraged malingering. It also firmly controlled resources, changing the basis of poor relief from cash to food, medicine, and medical attention.

Many early twentieth-century hospitals featured architectural elements that decried their distant ecclesiastical ancestry, but the architectural and bureaucratic roots of the modern hospital as a total institution are to be found in eighteenth-century England. Like most old-paradigm hospitals, some of them still in use in the late twentieth century, those eighteenth-century buildings featured corridor plans that reflected and reinforced rigid social organization, a hierarchy extending down from the board of governors and their customary resident member—called the house visitor—progressively downward to the medical staff, the pharmacist (apothecary), the nursing staff, servants, and, last, the patients. Significantly, at London Hospital, the administrative committee room occupied the most prominent space in the middle of the first floor. This prominence foreshadowed late-twentieth-century practice, where administrative and bureaucratic bloat became the norm (a study published in *The New England Journal of Medicine* in 1993 linked 25 percent of hospital costs to paperwork).

In London Hospital, the staff rooms were arranged along two corridors leading out from the committee room. Occupants were placed in diminishing social order, beginning with the physicians, who were closest to the committee room, and terminating with the nurses, who were farthest from it. The patient wards were located on the building's south side. Access to each ward was by a single door on either end of a corridor. Each door opened onto a ward lobby, from which three fifteen-bed wards radiated, allowing nursing staff to supervise the ward simultaneously and control entry to and exit from them. Rules of the London Hospital did not permit a patient to come and go of his own volition.

By the late-eighteenth and early-nineteenth centuries, hospitals had shed their Palladian pretensions, along with most other ornamentation, to become increasingly austere and—there is no other word for it—institutional. Some buildings combined gracious detail with lines and proportions more suited to a penal institution, which, as architectural historian Adrian Forty points out in his *Objects of Desire: Design and Society Since 1750* (1986), was the result of the governors' own conflicting motives. On the one hand, he said, they desired a fine building, some noble institution that would decorate the town, trumpet their philanthropy, and attract contributions. On the other, they wished to deter those who did not "deserve" care, reduce the costs of sick relief, and preach to the poor about their reliance on charity.

During the transition from the eighteenth to the nineteenth century hospitals played a key role in the development of medicine as a sovereign profession even as they were transformed by it. Eighteenth-century physicians were classed with tradesmen and, indeed, servants. Generally speaking, they put themselves at the beck and call of their wealthier patients, whom they visited and treated at home. In contrast, hospitals, which were mainly patronized by the poor, concentrated patients for the convenience of the physician.

The distinction went even deeper. The eighteenth-century physician's paying clients, treated at home, exercised a great deal of authority over the physician as well as prescribed treatment. Moreover, physical examination involving actual contact between the doctor and his patient was a rarity discouraged by the social gulf that separated the practitioner from his client.

Johns Hopkins University Hospital, Baltimore, Maryland. The impractical pavilion plan of hospital design long outlived the miasmatic or zymotic theory of disease that encouraged open arcades and maximum ventilation as a means of curing the sick. *Courtesy CORBIS.*

Instead, the physician listened as the patient described symptoms, observing what he could, and prescribed a course of treatment accordingly. In the hospital, however, where poor patients were more or less captive and, in any case, were of lower social caste than the physician, actual physical examination was possible. Since the physician had far more control over the patient in the hospital setting, medical science progressed more rapidly there.

With the gradual development of empirical medicine, made possible in large measure by the hospital setting, physicians slowly gained a measure of respect and social position as well as authority in decisions affecting hospital design. As early as 1752, Sir John Pringle promoted the salutary effects of ample ventilation, an issue that soon came to figure in discussions of the design of hospitals as well as prisons. It was not until the mid-nineteenth century, however, that medical theories of fresh air and ventilation to combat the evil effects of stagnant air and miasma began to exert practical influence over new hospital construction. But even before this time, physicians were concerned about cross-infection, which, they believed, resulted from massing patients in large, undifferentiated wards. Advanced hospitals, therefore, began to segregate surgical from nonsurgical cases and even attempted to divide and isolate patients according to symptoms.

Along with smaller wards and segregation came ever-increasing control emanating directly from medical staff as opposed to the institutional administrators and governors. One early-nineteenth-century French observer, according to Forty, pointed out that at Parisian hospitals severe punishments, such as privation of food or wine, even prison itself, were inflicted on any patients who disrupted the established order or who resisted the will of the doctor, even if the patients' demands were not relevant to the treatment of their illnesses.

The physicians' power over patients was reinforced by architecture and by hospital furnishings, which became less generally institutional and more specifically clinical. Austerity of furnishings, which had been supported on moral grounds, was now endorsed for medical reasons: the fewer the items present in a ward, the fewer there would be to keep clean. Bed curtains, long regarded as a necessity in the drafty interiors of the days before central heating, were dispensed with in an effort to promote ventilation, despite the total sacrifice of privacy this entailed. Patients were also discouraged or prevented from bringing personal belongings into the hospital setting, since these were considered unhygienic. Thus, hospital patients became wards of a total institution, but less under the moral authority of a charitable board of governors than under the medical authority of physicians.

The mid-nineteenth century saw the triumph of the pavilion-plan hospital in France and England. This hospital type, adumbrated in Stonehouse and the Hotel Dieu (as rebuilt after a fire in the 1780s), consisted of what were in effect separate buildings joined by a single arcade or corridor. The design grew directly out of physicians' recommendations to provide maximum exposure to fresh air in an effort to dispel miasma.

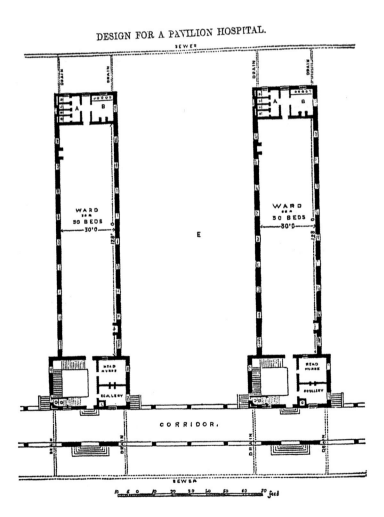

DESIGN FOR A PAVILION HOSPITAL.

The Nightingale ward, a rectangular space with fifteen beds arranged along two long walls, austere furnishings, and a single entrance adjacent to the nurses' station, sacrificed patient privacy for nursing efficiency.

During the height of popularity of the pavilion-plan hospital, the single most influential medical professional, in terms of hospital design, was neither a doctor nor an architect but a nurse—Florence Nightingale. Her mission of reform, which encompassed the establishment of hygiene as well as the promotion of nursing as a respectable profession, dovetailed perfectly with the trend toward larger wards, ample ventilation, and interior austerity. Her design for the ideal ward—a long rectangular space with fifteen beds arranged along long walls and a single entrance adjacent to the nurse's station—was widely adopted and christened the "Nightingale ward." Privacy was entirely sacrificed for nursing efficiency and the ability to regulate entry to and exit from the ward. Nightingale advocated plans that eliminated small spaces, including closets, sculleries, and lobby areas, which she believed were not only unhygienic but functioned as a hiding place where patients or servants, disposed to wrongdoing, might hide or skulk.

The triumph of the pavilion plan may have been associated with the miasmatic or zymotic theory of disease, but the continued dominance of this building style long outlasted belief in the scientific basis for it, persisting well after the zymotic theory was displaced by the modern germ theory and after numerous studies showed the pavilion plan to be no more conducive to patients' health than any other hospital layout. The persistence of the pavilion plan is even more remarkable when its disadvantages are taken into account.

The footprint of such structures is very large, claiming extensive tracts of expensive urban real estate. Construction and maintenance costs are also considerable, since the pavilion-style hospital is really a complex of individual structures linked together. Forty claims that the pavilion plan persisted mainly because the imposing style endowed the physician's role with an added measure of magnificence, justifying his social elevation and providing a rationale for ever-increasing professional fees. Thus the dominant form of the general hospital at the end of the nineteenth century was more expressive of social, cultural, and professional values and motives than of perceived functional medical needs, let alone the human needs of the patient.

As physicians consolidated their prestige, both socially and scientifically, at the start of the twentieth century, the reputation of the hospital also greatly improved from its image as a place for the hopeless poor to linger before death to a center for possibly efficacious treatment. With this amelioration of image, the hospital began to attract paying patients from all social classes. In effect, this was the hospital's first brush with something conventionally definable as a marketplace, and, albeit slowly, hospitals began to cater to that marketplace. For the first time in the history of the institution, patients' needs were directly addressed and gestures toward creating a more humane environment were made. Among these gestures were improved food, more liberal visiting hours, and less arbitrary and absolute issuance of orders; patients were now routinely better informed of schedules and treatment decisions. Design changes were not dramatic, but efforts were made to improve lighting, reduce noise, arrange beds more comfortably, and even to relieve the universal whitewash typical of the Nightingale ward with domestically toned colors.

At about the time that patients gained a significant influence on hospital design, the apparatus of a growing medical technology also began to assert its demands. In fact, the scientific advances in medicine in the early years of the twentieth century promoted massive growth in healthcare. The invention of the X-ray in 1895 made the inner workings of the body visible without surgery. In 1896, almost immediately after Wilhelm Roentgen in Germany discovered he could use electromagnetic radiation to create an image of the body on a photographic plate, known as a radiograph, the Glasgow Royal Infirmary established an X-ray department. And then there was the modern research on antibiotics, which also began in Germany with the 1909 development of the drug salvarsan by Paul Ehdich, the first truly effective treatment of syphilis. By the 1920s other antibiotics were introduced, penicillin by Alexander Fleming and streptomycin by Selman Waksman, who actually coined the term "antibiotics." These advances—especially the growing understanding of infection control—naturally focused more attention on the design of healthcare facilities.

The first modern operating room complex—the Syms operating pavilion at Roosevelt–St. Luke's Hospital in New York—was built in 1891 and modernized in the 1930s when it was expanded into the first major operating suite. Meanwhile, the grim influenza pandemic of 1918 to 1920 destroyed forever the long-held and lingering notion of miasma as the source of disease as researchers slowly discovered the viruses causing such plagues and learned to battle their spread through respiratory isolation. Such major medical research

New York Hospital, New York. Massive hospital buildings dominate the urban landscape. Imposing structures endowed the physician's role with a measure of magnificence, elevated his social position, and justified his increase in fees. *Courtesy CORBIS.*

facilities as Johns Hopkins University and the newly formed Rockefeller University Hospital came into prominence fighting the deadly flu.

Technology and drug treatments increased dramatically after World War II. Consider that in 1950 alone doctors performed a human aorta transplant, researchers isolated the hepatitis-A virus, and drug companies synthesized penicillin for wide-scale production and distribution. Two years later we saw the first heart-lung machine arrive in hospitals, electric shock used to revive a cardiac-arrest patient for the first time, an artificial heart valve inserted into a human being, and an artificial pacemaker regulate heart rhythm. By 1953 doctors were using heart-lung bypass machines, and in 1954 they performed the first full-scale open heart surgery and the first successful kidney transplant. At mid-century psychiatric drugs such as Thorazine and new tranquilizers had become commonplace for the treatment of psychiatric patients. Intensive care medicine in Europe had developed in response to an epidemic of polio. The first intensive care unit (ICU) was established in Copenhagen, Denmark, in 1953, at the *Kommunehospitalet* or Municipal Hospital. In 1962 the first neonatal intensive-care unit (NICU) opened at Children's Hospital of Philadelphia and the University of Pennsylvania. A year later, the first human liver and lung transplants were performed. The first computed tomography machine came in 1970, and magnetic resonance imaging shortly thereafter. The concept of a trauma center developed in the 1960s and 1970s. (Many think Cook County Hospital in Chicago, opened in 1966, was the first trauma center in the United States.)

The needs of patients—once perceived as primarily emotional, now seen as psychosomatic, tightly bound to overall well-being—have come to coexist (often uneasily) with the design demands of technology, the design demands for the efficient working of personnel, and the institutional agenda that persists to a greater or lesser degree in most hospitals. Indeed, the growth of technology and the further development of the germ theory, antisepsis, and heroic surgical procedures coalesced with the modernist movement in architecture to create, by the early 1950s, sleek structures shorn of ornament that suggested a hybrid between high-tech functionalism and a style suited to a downtown corporate headquarters. Many patients found—and find—such a style dehumanizing.

New Directions

Our object is not to condemn the majority of hospitals built before the first edition of this book appeared, but to understand the compelling cultural forces that have shaped them and, where appropriate, to suggest alternatives. Even what we would call old-paradigm hospitals do address some still-useful and valid emotional needs. The monumental and ecclesiastical echoes in some of these structures are not only beautiful in and of themselves, but they may actually inspire and encourage some patients rather than depress them or increase their level of anxiety. The functional modernist approach may not strike all users as inhuman; it may impress some as scientific and efficient,

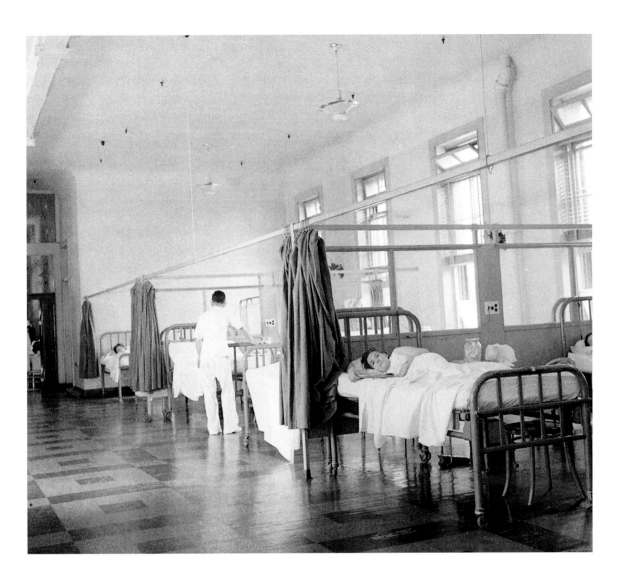

imparting confidence in the healing technology hospitals offer. Yet, as the paradigms enumerated in Chapter 1 continue shifting, we believe these views will diminish in relevance commensurately.

It is not sufficient to change hospital design only to improve the physical plant or even to accommodate new technologies, but to recognize that many of the cultural reasons for the old-paradigm hospital are no longer valid. Patients are still generally cast in a submissive role. Authoritarian— "institutional"—architecture is perceived as depressing, and depression is a definite negative influence on patient health. Depression may well be aggravated by the sense of isolation most old-paradigm hospitals foster. Even institutions that may have extended visiting hours may not make any design provision for family or companions. Finally, traditional designs tend to be rigid and difficult to adapt to expansion, renovation, and the installation of new equipment. It is clear from the literature of hospital design, patient care, and the sociology of medicine that ideas have changed. It is equally clear from most existing hospital and healthcare facilities that, unlike the ideas, which have changed dramatically in the last few decades, the buildings themselves have only begun to change.

CHAPTER 3

Changing Needs, New Directions

The healthcare landscape is changing, and not just because healthcare reform is back on the political agenda. Old-paradigm medical services and hospital structures have failed not only to serve patients and families adequately, but the hospital administrators and medical professionals who use them as well. They have not kept abreast of the medical marketplace. So hospital and healthcare facility design is now moving toward evidenced-based and green design.

Just as green technology in the automobile industry is both a response to a change in the marketplace and an urgent need to protect the natural environment, today's green design seeks to make hospitals more sustainable businesses as well as buildings, healthier places to visit in every sense. This chapter considers the new design trends shaped by the changes in our needs and in the market for healthcare.

Flexibility

By this point in our discussion, at least one principle should have emerged clearly: hospital and healthcare facility design must be sensitive to and responsive to change; that is, it must be, above all, flexible. As the recent economic woes make clear, retailers and manufacturers of consumer goods have always lived and died by the dictates of the marketplace, and when the market changes, a flexible, responsive manufacturer who can change with it may be the only business that can hope to prosper.

But what about healthcare providers, hospital administrators, facility planners, and architects? How feasible is it to be responsive to a marketplace when you deal with a multimillion-dollar building program? It usually is not possible to start building one kind of facility, and then change it into another, let alone finish a building only to turn around, tear it down, and start over again. For while the marketplace paradigm is seductive, and failure to anticipate or respond to the marketplace spells disaster, it is also a fact that it is far more difficult to anticipate or respond to the terms of the market if your product is big, complex, culturally freighted, and staggeringly expensive.

Even beyond that inability to turn on a dime because of its size and complexity, healthcare design's need for flexibility is further intensified by the technological nature of the healthcare industry. Not only must facilities adapt to changing patient populations and changing patient needs, but they must also anticipate the physical demands new technologies may make. Hospitals built in the age of the X-ray machine sometimes have difficulty accommodating the size of today's diagnostic and treatment capital equipment, including the surgical gamma knife and MRI, let alone advanced PET technology. Some trend predictors have suggested that such equipment may become even larger—for example, dedicated MRI units specifically built for operating rooms.

On the other hand, other medical futurists predict that nanotechnology and other trends toward electronic subminiaturization—not to mention the revolution in communications technology and in radiology, thanks to digital imaging—will instead reduce the structural space required for diagnostic

St. Anthony Hospital, Lakewood, Colorado. Main lobby.
Photo © Michael Peck.

hardware. To be sure, it is possible, if costly, to anticipate such a technological contingency and to design and build accordingly. Hence the need for flexibility in design, for spaces that can be expanded—or shrunk—as needed.

How fast are major technological changes evolving? The useful lives of equipment and facilities are contracting, and two or three years can be a long time to remain on the cutting edge. Flexible design means creating facilities that can be quickly, economically, and repeatedly retrofitted and reconfigured—a design task challenging enough, in and of itself, but that may be made more difficult by outmoded building codes.

Flexible design has long been a hallmark of office and commercial spaces, for example, where it presents a relatively easy goal that is primarily a matter of erecting or eliminating partitions. In contrast, hospitals and healthcare facilities make more complex demands on electrical/mechanical systems and, therefore, present greater challenges to achieving flexible design. Moreover, as new monitoring and filtration technologies are developed and become desirable or perhaps even required to ensure air quality and prevent toxicity, these demands will become even more complex.

In old-paradigm designs, the mechanical core was designed more rigidly than any other aspect of a building. It was perceived as a highly durable, virtually permanent component—a good thing, too, since, in hospitals, the mechanical core and electrical core account for 40 to 45 percent (or more) of construction costs. In sharp contrast, new-paradigm thinking calls for mobile, portable, and/or modular multiple HVAC systems designed in relatively small zones that can be easily changed and upgraded. Along with this, construction will use moment-resistant steel frames instead of braced frames or concrete, and floor systems will incorporate a systematic redundancy of penetrations to allow additional service changes as they may be called for in the future.

By the late 1960s, several architectural firms designing hospitals developed variations on a basic structural-mechanical concept aimed at addressing what Eberhard Zeidler, of Craig, Zeidler & Strong, called "a fifth dimension in architecture—the change of space-function due to the lapse of time." Zeidler's firm designed the Health Sciences Center for McMaster University (Hamilton, Ontario), which was among the first hospital structures to use the principle of "interstitial space." The phrase was an apt one for hospital design, since interstitial space was a term borrowed from medicine itself, where it is used to describe the spaces between layers of the skin.

Interstitial spaces are intermediate service floors inserted between primary floors. Within these intermediate floors are all the mechanical, HVAC, and electrical components of the building. Granted their own space, these vital building elements become totally accessible for maintenance, upgrading, retrofitting, and other adaptations without having to invade or close down primary spaces. Not only was the mechanical core rendered more flexible, the primary spaces required fewer fixed vertical obstructions and therefore could be larger, more open, and more easily and quickly renovated and redesigned as needed. By the late 1980s, the interstitial concept had evolved into the Integrated Building System (IBS), first developed for the Veterans Administration hospitals by the firm of Stone, Marraccini, and Patterson.

In IBS designs, the intermediate service (or M/E, mechanical/electrical) floors, separated from primary floors by a fireproof walking deck, were divided into repetitive M/E modules, each with its own utility room, to which all vertical utility runs go. The layout was duplicated on each floor, but each individual module was designed specifically to accommodate the particular department's needs, and, of course, each module could be readily altered or upgraded to meet changing needs.

The triangular design of the inpatient area allows the nursing staff to tend to patients efficiently.

1. Nurses' station
2. Dictation
3. Support
4. Patient rooms

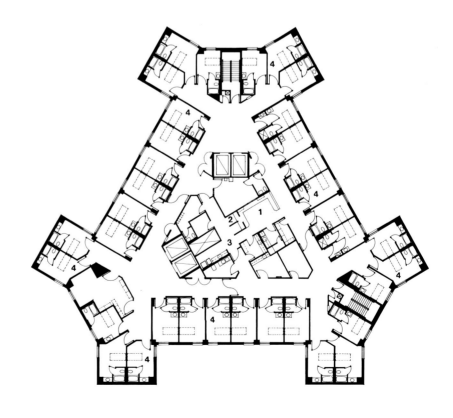

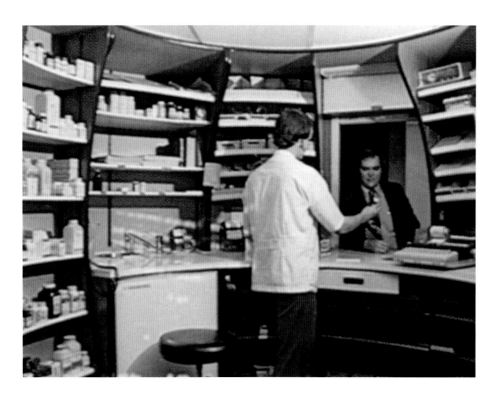

A highly efficient modular pharmacy, the SystaModule offers the flexibility of modules in as many configurations as needed. *Photo Alan Karchmer.*

Interstitial design was never widely accepted because of the high cost of what is essentially a strategy of duplicating floors. Nowadays, architects are more inclined to devote an entire floor for mechanical services, which is a better design because they can keep a consistent skin on the exterior of the building; since they do not have to deal with what in effect amounts to a smaller floor in between others. Currently architects need to be familiar with interstitial floors mostly because they may come in contact with them during renovations.

While many architects and their clients were concerned by the expense of an interstitial strategy, the underlying principle—flexibility of design—emerged as vital in creating cost-effective healthcare facilities.

Flexibility is crucial in planning the layout of the facility space. The traditional "racetrack" corridor design does have a certain flexibility, in that it can often be added to and modified with some ease. However, it is an often inefficient and uncomfortable layout. Long corridors are difficult for nurses to monitor and require many footsteps for physicians as well as nurses, who are obliged to spend more time walking than attending to patients. Similarly, supplies and equipment must be transported long distances. Patients' stress levels might also be increased by long corridors, which are, of necessity, active, bustling, and noisy. Finally, the racetrack plan is inefficient in terms of energy—difficult to heat, to cool, and even to wire cost-effectively.

As noted earlier, circular plan alternatives to the racetrack enjoyed some popularity in the 1970s and were often welcomed by nurses, who saved steps and could more effectively attend to patients' needs. In the 1980s, when ESa was assigned the task of creating a basic hospital plan for the Hospital Corporation of America (HCA), we considered the circular design, but found that it requires too much square footage per bed and wastes space in the central nursing core. The size of the circular floor requires two nursing stations per floor, thereby increasing construction costs and multiplying staffing needs. Finally, the circular plan is inherently less flexible than even the racetrack plan.

So ESa instead moved toward a modified racetrack design (see Chapter 9) that uses a support core to shorten the length of corridor that needs monitoring and cuts down the number of steps nurses and physicians have to take to care for patients.

The idea of flexibility also extends to the range of finishes chosen for buildings, with the most permanent infrastructures—pathways and vertical circulations, for example—finished in high-quality, long-lasting materials, and other areas, subject to shorter life spans, finished with less expensive, less durable, even disposable materials. World War II made heroic demands upon the building industry, greatly accelerating the development of prefabricated structures. By the late 1960s, some hospitals created prefabricated patient rooms out of standard modular units developed by the Research and Graduate Center of Texas A&M's School of Architecture. The Adaptable Building System (ABS) was intended for loftlike spaces and consisted of four basic components: a raised floor, a modular partition panel system, a perforated suspended ceiling unit, and a one-piece molded glass-fiber "hygiene component."

These experiments did not give rise to large-scale use of prefabricated hospital rooms, however. They had potential in situations where substantial undifferentiated and unimpeded open interior space was available, as in a handful of facilities built with deliberately unused expansion ("shell") areas. But few hospitals are planned this way, and therefore the market for prefabricated patient rooms remains small. However, the gains in cost-efficiency and in accuracy of fabrication offered by premanufactured building modules show promise in more specialized hospital and healthcare facility applications.

Beginning in 1969, ESa collaborated with the Research Institute of Pharmaceutical Sciences at the University of Mississippi and General Equipment Manufacturers of Crystal Springs, Mississippi, to develop and manufacture "SystaModule," a self-contained, premanufactured pharmacy unit for a hospital setting. The SystaModule was the result of listening to the needs of hospital pharmacists, a group of professionals whom traditional designs had largely ignored. ESa designed task-oriented units based on human engineering principles, using Le Corbusier's "Modular," a design concept by which man is made the measure in a system of rhythmic harmony, elegant proportion, and maximum efficiency. We designed the modules to accomplish specific tasks and to be assembled, as required, to create a complete pharmacy service unit. Tasks included outpatient dispensing, sterile extemporaneous preparation (including IV admixture), medication order review, and inpatient dispensing—basic, crucial tasks accommodated by no existing design.

SystaModule proved a highly efficient work environment. Whereas preparing each medication in the traditional pharmacy work area took 28.0 seconds, the SystaModule environment required only 7.18 seconds per medication. Beyond this gain in productivity—not only important for patient welfare but also vital to any industry operating in a competitive market—the SystaModule offers great flexibility, since the various modules can be configured and reconfigured as needed and as available space allows.

What Socially Responsible Design Is

Flexible design begins at the planning stage, but it does not end there, nor even after construction is complete. Flexible design, by definition, is dynamic design, a process that is part of what Janet R. Carpman back in 1991 called socially responsible health facility design, which she identified as a major new direction for the industry.

> Socially responsible design has five characteristics:
> 1. It is based on an explicitly understood shared value system.
> 2. It is based on information.
> 3. It is the product of a participatory design process.
> 4. It incorporates periodic, systematic design review.
> 5. It incorporates periodic evaluation of the finished project.

The first three factors ensure that the proposed design is politically, economically, and physically feasible, while placing greatest emphasis on the social, psychological, and physical needs of patients, visitors, and staff. These needs are paramount in socially responsible health facility design. Before design work begins, information is gathered, based on review of pertinent literature, facility visits, interviews and surveys among facility users, and simulations (which these days at ESa means Building Information Modeling, or BIM). This information is used to formulate design guidelines or performance criteria.

During the design process itself, the participation of the users of the facility needs to be sought. This helps to clarify design objectives and to ensure that the objectives of the primary project planners, the architects, and the users mesh. Carefully considered and evaluated, participatory design leads to better design decisions while evoking positive behavior and attitudes from clients and users and creating a community of common interest. Insofar as participatory design averts errors and the necessity for costly modifications, it also has the potential for lowering construction costs. Finally, participatory design provides an opportunity for dynamically assessing design-related organizational policies.

The last two components of the socially responsible model of design are the most relevant to ensuring the ongoing flexibility of the design, because they establish a system in which design is subject to evaluation and reevaluation, both during the design process and after the project ostensibly has been completed. We say "ostensibly," since, in an environment as dynamic as that of the hospital or healthcare facility, the project is never really complete. In today's healthcare environment, a completed project is, truly, a *finished* project: done for, and doomed to, the briefest useful life. In contrast, a project in which the process is built-in stands the greatest chance of enduring.

What Dynamic Design Is

The dynamic approach implied by the goal of socially responsible design is encompassed in what ESa has called "Synergenial Design," a concept discussed in the opening chapter of this book. Synergism and geniality—the component terms of the concept—are the key elements of a design approach that acknowledges both the synergistic nature of the problem-solving process and the congenial, user-sensitive attributes of a successfully designed solution.

An ESa BIM (building information modeling) image created using REVIT.

Synergenial buildings are functional environments that evoke positive responses from their users on physical, intellectual, and emotional levels. To achieve this level of dynamic design requires a high level of responsiveness from architects and designers. The trend in hospital and healthcare design is to bring architects and designers in at the earliest possible stages of a proposed project and then retain them through the life span of the building. In this sense, the building is a dynamic project, as architects and designers strive to meet changing needs.

Patient-Centered Design

Participatory design does have its limitations. Of necessity, those who have the opportunity to participate most fully in the process are planners, administrators, architects, and care providers, including physicians, nurses, and physical plant staff. It is possible and desirable also to gather information from and about the other users of the proposed structure, the patients, who can participate in the design process through a patient advisory council (PAC) or family advisory council (FAC).

Even if patient participation is less formal, the needs and preferences of patients can still inform the design. A retail establishment does not hire custom-

The Heart Center of Western Baptist Hospital, Paducah, Kentucky. *Photo © Sam Fentress.*

ers to serve as merchandise buyers, but the buyer who allows himself to get out of touch with a store's—or Web site's—customers is soon out of a job. The successful retailer does not begin by asking what seems an obvious question: "What merchandise is proper and appropriate for a store to stock?" Instead, he begins by asking, "What do my customers want?" And it is a question he must ask and answer not once, but dynamically, each and every day.

Hospitals and healthcare facilities of the old paradigm "establish" themselves by asking: "What services are proper and appropriate for a hospital to offer?" And this is a step made all the more rigid by being a question to which many planners and administrators believe they already have the answers. In contrast, new-paradigm medical facility planners begin by assessing what their patients want.

Once this kind of questioning begins, an important market distinction emerges. At the most basic level, the traditional general hospital serves two distinct markets:

1. Patients requiring acute care, which includes trauma (emergency); burns; high-risk obstetrical and neonatal care; intensive care; neurological or cardiac surgery; multi-organ failure; organ transplantation; and other life-threatening situations.

2. Patients with chronic conditions or subacute conditions requiring inpatient or ambulatory care. This includes such services as ambulatory diagnostics and surgery; chronic-care screening and maintenance; day treatment and recovery care; routine childbirth; and routine inpatient surgery. Nonurgent emergency room services should be included in this market segment, which may (and, in many communities, should) be expanded to include the primary care network and private practice base. Other community-oriented services include health education, disease prevention, and homecare networks.

Incredibly, by tradition, hospitals have failed to distinguish between these two basic markets. The result, back in the days of full insurance reimbursement, was financial waste and inefficient, inconvenient, and often anxiety-generating care for the patient. In today's more consumer-driven medical marketplace, where costs are contained through systems based on the Diagnostic Related Groupings (DRG) introduced by Medicare in 1983, failure to understand the marketplace structure is likely to result in failure to survive.

The DRG radically altered the way reimbursements were paid. Under the old total-reimbursement system, insurance paid for virtually all tests and procedures that physicians saw fit to order, and hospital stays were reimbursed on a per diem basis. The introduction of DRG, however, meant that, for the most part, insurance paid a lump sum for a given condition, based on the usual and customary cost of treatment for the problem. In cases where hospitals and physicians accepted insurance assignment, the motive for increased efficiency was obvious. The less time and resources expended to resolve a problem, the greater the profit; the more expended, the less the profit—or the greater the loss. In cases where hospitals and healthcare providers depended on the patient to pay, that individual, knowing that his or her reimbursement was capped, was likely to shop around for the best value.

In and of itself, the DRG system was a strong impetus to shorten hospital stays and to transfer as much care to ambulatory departments as possible. Yet, for hospitals designed under the old total-reimbursement rules, this kind of turnover created empty hospital beds. What does an industry do when supply exceeds demand? If you're a flexible manufacturer, you can shift your production to other product lines or you can reduce production and lay off employees. These steps are not as feasible for a hospital, however, and the better solution to empty beds is to fill them through aggressive marketing. (How much healthcare reform will eventually change all this is unclear. Even given extensive changes, the incentives for cost savings are likely to be greater rather than diminished.)

Ultimately it comes down to the question: What does a hospital have to market? The most obvious product is excellence in healthcare, and, to be sure, a facility's reputation for excellence is a strong incentive for patients to select that institution over another. Although, with new results reporting requirements, consumers can look up the data on medical outcomes online, they still find it difficult to judge a hospital on medical standards. The "packaging" of architectural design and the patient amenities that design offers continue to have a direct influence on potential consumers.

Focusing on the patient and on patient care, which we marked as a trend in earlier editions, has endured. An associated trend is vertical integration and work redesign: rethinking the traditional departmental organization of the hospital so as to maximize caregiver contact with patients and to promote continuity of care by making a team of caregivers responsible for each patient from admission to discharge. In vertically integrated hospitals, the multiplicity of departments and bureaucratic fiefdoms is reduced to a few general, integrated areas of responsibility, such as patient services, support services, and patient care.

The following outline suggests some work and design implications of vertical integration for smaller healthcare facilities and indicates how facilities, equipment, and staff may be effectively shared across what once were the barriers of traditional departments.

Patient Services. The combination of business and administrative services allows cross-trained employees to work in a barrier-free environment to minimize duplication of effort and maximize time efficiency. Design should help facilitate streamlined patient processing, a smoother flow of information, and reduced paperwork.

1. A single entry area, under a canopy and adjacent to parking, conveniently serves outpatients, inpatients, emergency walk-ins, and those visiting physicians' offices.

2. Registration processes are centralized at the main entry. These include:
    a. Cross-trained personnel working among centralized scheduling, coding, emergency registration, and reception areas, helping to minimize duplication and assist in wayfinding.
    b. Scheduling for all departments.
    c. Registration to support physicians' offices.
    d. A PBX positioned adjacent to emergency department registration, which allows twenty-four-hour observation of security monitors.
    e. Fast-track registration (registration and cashier combined), a sit-down area for handicapped registration, and a private office for financial counseling.
    f. A shared role of receptionist among volunteers and a facility directory at reception.

3. The medical records, business office, accounting, and information services are within a modular setting with computer flooring to aid cross-training among staff and flexibility to adapt to change; many times records staff can be cross-trained to back up registration.
    a. Medical records and business office records are combined in fixed files to allow several staff members to access information at the same time.
    b. Information systems allow for decentralization and ready availability of records in the future.

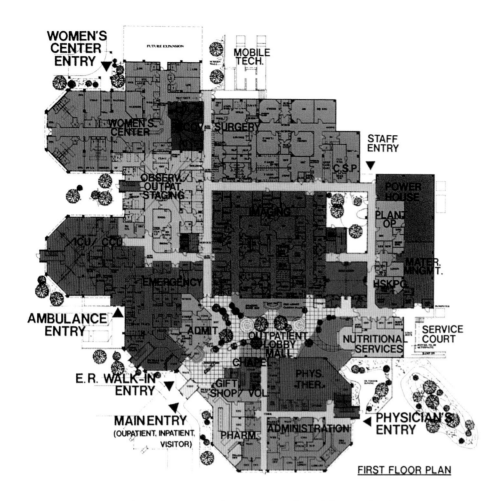

WOMEN'S CENTER ENTRY

FUTURE EXPANSION

MOBILE TECH.

WOMEN'S CENTER

SURGERY

STAFF ENTRY

C.S.P.

OBSERV. OUTPAT. STAGING

IMAGING

POWER HOUSE

PLANT OP.

ICU/CCU

MATER. MNGMT.

HSKPG.

EMERGENCY

AMBULANCE ENTRY

ADMIT

OUTPATIENT LOBBY MALL

NUTRITIONAL SERVICES

SERVICE COURT

CHAPEL

E.R. WALK-IN ENTRY

GIFT SHOP/VOL.

PHYS. THER.

MAIN ENTRY
(OUPATIENT, INPATIENT, VISITOR)

PHARM.

ADMINISTRATION

PHYSICIAN'S ENTRY

FIRST FLOOR PLAN

This plan reflects the vertical integration of services at a full-service community facility.

c. Social services are decentralized and located adjacent to inpatient beds on the nursing floor for the convenience of patients and their families.

4. Administration, nursing administration, medical staff lounge, and human resources work areas are efficiently shared. Human resources has an independent entry located near the main entry, which allows physicians and administration convenient access for communications.

Support Services. Support services create a center for all support requests (such as meals, supplies, mail service, housekeeping services, plant operations support, patient transport, etc.). This center improves communications as well as reduces duplication and supports nursing staff by providing proper training and cost-effective staff to assist in support duties, thereby allowing higher-paid nursing staff to deal with higher-level nursing issues.

1. Pharmacy
    a. Outpatient and inpatient services are combined to minimize pharmacy staff. The outpatient dispensary is located near the front door for the convenience of medical office patients, emergency department patients, and inpatient discharges.
    b. Modular shelving is used for flexibility.

c. Pneumatic tubes reduce the need for couriers to deliver medications to inpatient locations, although some dispensers are located in the inpatient units.

2. Laboratory
   a. A modular design ensures future flexibility.
   b. Pneumatic tubes connect to all patient areas, greatly reducing the need for couriers and expediting processing.
   c. Staff does not draw all blood; staff in patient-care areas is cross-trained to draw blood.
   d. It is located near the materials management area for expedient supply delivery.
   e. The frozen-section function is adjacent to surgery.

3. Support Center
   a. This contains an area for secretarial support and vendor waiting.
   b. It provides a "one-stop-shopping" distribution area for all support services.
   c. Housekeeping, plant operation, materials management, dietary, and mail distribution departments are based here and share secretarial support.

4. Materials Management is positioned ideally to receive and distribute materials.

5. Housekeeping is accessible to all areas but separate from public traffic.

6. Plant Operations/Powerhouse is adjacent to the powerhouse service area for equipment repair.

7. Dietary
   a. This is serviced by the support core.
   b. It is adjacent to the conference center for ease of catering service.
   c. It is located convenient to the outpatient area for dietary counseling.
   d. It is positioned to provide efficient inpatient service.
   e. Nourishment areas are provided on patient floors.
   f. There is a pleasant dining area for inpatients, outpatients, and others located in the outpatient mall.
   g. Outdoor dining is available.

8. Education
   a. This department occupies a prominent position in the outpatient mall for community education.
   b. It is accessible for internal staff education as well as for in- and outpatient education.
   c. A flexible, subdividable conference facility is available.

Patient Care. With facility-wide support systems provided by support services and patient services, optimal use of professional staff is possible. Many traditional areas are combined, through both physical construction and staff cross-training. Flexibility is the key design ingredient.

1. Diagnostic services include imaging, cardiopulmonary assessment, preadmission and lab testing, and drug screening.

    a. Many support staff and areas are shared among the services.

    b. Staff work areas are separated to minimize patient/staff conflicts.

    c. Exam rooms for preadmission testing and cardiopulmonary assessment are not designated for specific functions and are shared among both services for flexibility of use. Staff is cross-trained in multiple tasks.

    d. Imaging is located for easy accessibility from emergency, with heavy-use diagnostic services near the emergency area.

2. Emergency services/critical care includes emergency and ICU/CCU as a combined area.

    a. Emergency shares central registration with all other services.

    b. Triage is adjacent to central registration and visible from the nurses' station.

    c. Fast-track registration expedites minor cases.

    d. Emergency department walk-ins and critical-care cases are separate from trauma cases for the patients, yet shared by staff.

    e. Two areas within the department—trauma and critical care—share support areas and staff.

    f. Adjacent trauma rooms and ICU/CCU rooms provide back-up for one another.

PineLake Medical Center, Mayfield, Kentucky. In this design of unbundled services, separate entrances lead patients and visitors directly to emergency, the MOB, and the women's center. Distinctive entrances minimize, to an extent, wayfinding problems.
Photo Gary Knight.

g. Emergency and ICU/CCU share support and allow for the overflow of staff and rooms from ICU/CCU, if necessary.

h. Outpatient pharmacy is located near the critical-care portion of the emergency department.

i. Waiting area for ICU/CCU is adjacent to patient mall, so that families can use dining facilities and overflow into more comfortable waiting and dining areas.

j. Observation is shared with emergency department and obstetrics.

Massachusetts General Hospital, Center for Aging and Neurodisorders-Building 114, Charlestown, Massachusetts. Payette designed this Center for Aging and Neurodisorders with "neighborhood" laboratories, based on the ratio of six researchers per faculty, creating twelve bench neighborhoods in a continuous open laboratory. *Courtesy Payette. Photo © Bruce T. Martin.*

3. Recovery/Same-Day Surgery/Observation

a. During the daytime, surgery staff monitors the observation area as well as the same-day surgery staging areas.

b. Recovery cross-trains its staff to back up these adjacent areas.

4. Obstetrics

a. This has a distinct entryway to provide patients with privacy and direct attention.

b. This offers one-room birthing (for labor, delivery, recovery, postpartum), where family members and patients can experience the comforts of home in a residential setting.

c. It shares its support areas (soiled utility, dietary, etc.) with recovery/same-day surgery/observation areas.

d. C-sections are performed in the adjacent surgery department.

e. There is a dedicated education area for Lamaze classes, etc.

f. A nurses' station is positioned to monitor the entryway, nursery, corridors, and observation unit.

5. Surgery

a. Its central sterile supply is managed by the support center.

b. Anesthesia is available to surgery suites as well as the obstetrics unit.

6. Physical Therapy

a. Inpatient physical therapy is adjacent to skilled nursing units and medical/surgical units.

b. Outpatient physical therapy is located on the main level for easy access, and it is visible and accessible from the outpatient mall, for sports medicine and wellness marketing aspects.

7. Inpatient Medical/Surgical Care:

    a. The visitors' elevator is separate from the service elevator.

    b. Patient services staff act as receptionists, coders, and unit secretaries; they also monitor the family waiting area.

    c. Nursing substations within the care units bring nursing staff and supplies closer to patients.

    d. Patient rooms are designed in pods for closer, focused monitoring. The pods' modular design enables them to be converted to special-care units. Visual contact with patient beds is possible as in the ICU/CCU.

    e. If toilets are located on the exterior walls, rooms can be converted to intensive-care units by adding glass at the corridor wall.

    f. The support core provides shared restocking areas and support for all pods. The key to this area is adaptability to whatever special-care needs might develop.

8. Physicians' offices are integrated with the hospital for convenient, one-stop access for both patients and physicians.

    a. This design minimizes the duplication of diagnostics and accesses the hospital's laboratory through an integrated pneumatic-tube system.

New Cancer Treatment Center, Kaiser Foundation Health Plan, Inc., South San Francisco, California. Daylight plays a distinct role at this Kaiser treatment center, which is unusual for radiation departments. *Courtesy Ratcliff. Photo © 2009 Tim Maloney, Technical Imagery Studios.*

b. These offices share in the business/medical records/information systems functions of the hospital.

c. Physicians' time use is maximized through proximity to the hospital.

KIRBY MEDICAL CENTER
Monticello, Illinois

ESa designed this sixteen-bed, replacement critical access hospital that includes an integrated physicians' office building. The hospital includes an emergency department; diagnostic imaging; a surgery/gastrointestinal lab; a sleep lab; and a rehabilitation, pharmacy, and support space (which includes environmental services, information services and medical records, materials management, facilities management and laundry, ambulance garage, administration, business office, risk management, social services, and food services).

The structure is oriented toward the public park that borders the back of the property. Patient-focused, the facility's transparent structure offers tranquil views of the park, so that the hospital seems almost an extension of its setting. Outdoor dining also helps meld the hospital to the site, and the architecture of the two-toned exterior mimics that of Monticello's historic district.

Easy wayfinding begins with the vestibule in the tower and runs through the outpatient concourse and a separate corridor for inpatients. Access to nature helps orient patients and visitors. The diagnostic services and medical office building are visible from and accessed off the concourse. A window wall looks out on the park.

Kirby Medical Center,
Monticello, Illinois. Site plan.

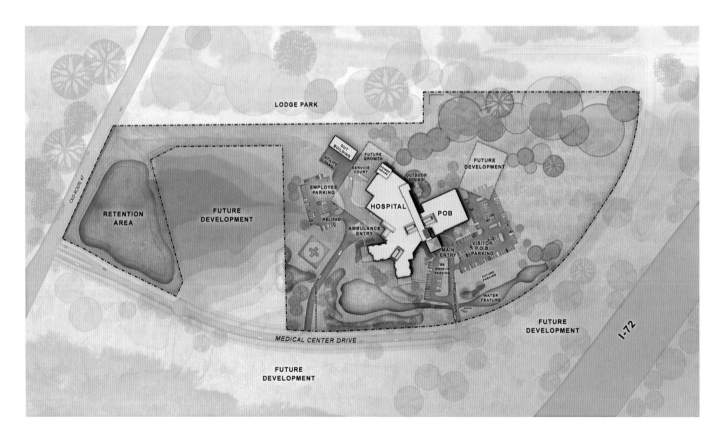

What Healthcare Consumers Look For

Studies conducted by Carpman Grant Associates, environmental design consultants in Ann Arbor, Michigan, suggest that all hospital patients (and visitors) share four basic design-related needs: physical comfort, social contact, symbolic meaning, and wayfinding.

Among the most intimidating aspects of large hospitals are the obstacles they present to wayfinding. Patients, already under stress, can easily feel buried or lost in a forbidding technological maze of equipment and hallways, while visitors are fearful of inadvertently wandering into some restricted,

Mt. Sinai Integrated Medical Campus MOB, Beachwood, Ohio. The attractive atrium area, which links the MOB to a bedless hospital, features dining tables, sculpture, an outpatient pharmacy, and a gift shop. *Photo Gary Knight.*

embarrassing, or even frightening space. In the mid-1980s, ESa conducted research with the assistance of Professor Ken Barker of the Department of Pharmacy Care Systems at Alabama's Auburn University to project the future of healthcare and the role of architecture within it. They created a typical twenty-first-century patient, eighty-six-year-old Edna Johnson, and imagined her involvement with the healthcare system as she coped with a myocardial infarction. Many technological innovations were predicted, but large, home-like patient rooms within structures that featured a similarly homelike scale with plenty of cues to wayfinding and design features intended to make life easier for an aged, frail woman were key to future hospital and healthcare facility designs.

Later, a 1992 survey by Press, Ganey Associates, Inc., showed privacy to be the primary concern of 140,000 hospital patients. Accordingly, Ratcliff Architects of Emeryville, California, and H.O.M. Group, Inc., of San Francisco, developed a prototype of a patient-centered hospital that, in the interest of maximizing privacy, featured all private rooms, all larger than what was typical of most community hospitals—the bed area was 35 percent larger—with each offering the option of family living space. The enlarged rooms also made the space more flexible, assuming that technologies for bedside recording and medication would minimize patient movement from one department to another. Moreover, the patient rooms were grouped into "care suites," each of which accommodated a lounge, library, kitchenette, and conference area for patients, family, and caregivers.

Designs that address the four basic needs outlined above are of paramount importance in the pages that follow, and we explore them in detail. Generally, the overriding patient need that ties these needs together is, in the phrase that futurist John Naisbitt made famous in his classic *Megatrends*, a desire for a "high-tech, high-touch" environment. Patients want the best that technology can offer, administered by the best people, but with this high technology they also want a humanized environment that is comfortable and aesthetically pleasing.

Facilities that lured patients because of their emphasis on comfort began to appear in the mid-to-late 1980s. The Portland-based firm of Broome, Oringdulph, O'Toole, Rudolf, Boles & Associates completed in 1985 the Kaiser-Rockwood Medical Office in Portland, Oregon, deliberately meant to counter the bland anonymity previously associated with that HMO's "no-nonsense" buildings. Set in a beautiful rural landscape and making many references to the area's wood-based architectural traditions, the Rockwood facility—according to the firm's literature on the project—exemplified what John W. Grigsby, a physician and ambulatory care–center developer, described in 1987 as a consumer-driven trend "away from stainless steel, metal doors, linoleum, insensitive lighting, and bland institutional color schemes. The emphasis on 'high touch' means that physician-administrators are asking their architectural consultants to help them de-institutionalize, de-stress, and dress up their waiting rooms, clinics, and hospital service areas. . . . We've even gone as far as trying to duplicate the living room in our very own homes."

The Rockwood facility is a good example of how to add humanizing

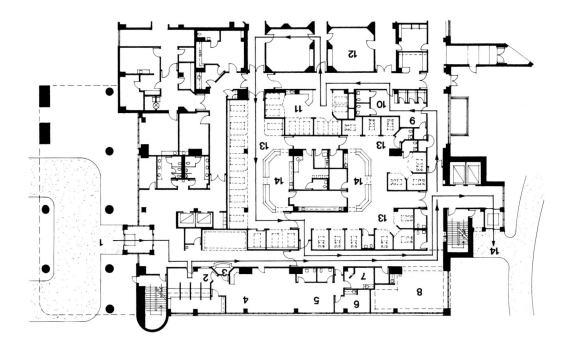

elements through thoughtful reference to the community. As Gideon Bosker related—again, according to the firm—in a 1987 discussion of the building, "The strong emphasis on squares, rectangles, and figural setbacks imparts a high-tech image, while the formidable porte cochere, with its large fir beams and seamed sheet metal roof, conveys the high-touch ambiance of mountain lodges that dot Mt. Hood just down the road."

The health facility does not have to be in scenic Washington state to make meaningful and aesthetically pleasing references to familiar, humanizing surroundings. During the late twentieth century, the hotel became one of the most popular models for new-paradigm hospitals and healthcare facilities.

The Hospitality Model

Some medical complexes incorporate hotels either as part of the complex or adjacent to it. Hotels associated with hospitals serve two purposes. They provide convenient and profit-generating lodging for members of patients' families, and, when thoughtfully configured in relation to the main hospital complex, they can also provide convalescent housing for patients who are not so acutely ill that they must occupy a hospital bed, yet for whom home care is impractical (for instance, because of distance from the healthcare facility) or inappropriate (no caregiver at home or a need for more medical supervision than is available in the home setting).

Even the inpatient hospital itself is learning from the hotel model. Hospitals and hotels share more than a linguistic root connoting the concept of "guest." They both take responsibility for the welfare of a great number of people. Hospitals are beginning to realize the market advantage in treating consumers as guests rather than patients. Houston's Methodist Hospital,

The arrows of this pre-admissions testing area indicate traffic flow through the facility, which has been designed to eliminate the need for crossovers and back-tracking. Patients using the testing area need never enter the hospital proper.

1. Entrance/drop-off
2. Outpatient admitting
3. Reception area
4. Subwaiting room
5. Interview room
6. Blood-drawing room
7. Chest X-ray
8. Waiting room
9. Subwaiting room
10. Patient dressing room
11. Patient holding room
12. Operating room
13. Recovery rooms
14. Patient pick-up

for example, has developed a joint program with the Marriott Corporation to create a hybrid of hotel and hospital services. Incoming patients—or guests—are greeted by doormen, and a bellman takes the patient's luggage to his room. In most cases, the institutional formalities of admitting are handled by telephone before the patient actually enters the hospital. As in a first-class hotel, the hospital is staffed by a concierge, who takes care of special needs and requests—though, in contrast to the conventional hotel, a large part of the concierge's job is to assist patients' families. Valet parking and laundry services are available, as are upgraded rooms, which include gourmet food service.

Even conventionally designed hospitals can, to a degree, incorporate operational policies based on the hospitality model. But these policies are greatly enhanced by design features based on hospitality rather than conventional hospital models, not only in patient rooms but in waiting and lobby areas.

Residential Models

The next logical leap from the hospitality-based model of patient-centered design is to make aspects of the hospital—particularly the patient room—seem homelike. The origin of this design movement was the Planetree organization, founded in 1978 by Angelica Thieriot. A medical lay person—that is, a patient—Thieriot was so horrified by her experience with conventional hospitalization that she created a nonprofit organization to provide the public with medical information and to humanize the quality of patient care. Named for the plane tree under which Hippocrates was supposed to have sat as he lectured his students, the organization developed a thirteen-bed model unit at San Francisco's Pacific Medical Center in 1985.

In addition to such policy innovations as open charts (patients had total access to their own records), an active give-and-take exchange of questions with caregivers, unlimited visitation, and so on, rooms were designed like domestic environments, with plenty of wood, subtle lighting, plants, and even paintings on loan from a local museum. There was a patient lounge with a VCR, a videocassette library, a library of books, and a kitchenette, where patients could prepare their own food if they wished. In the last two decades, other hospitals across the country have implemented the Planetree model, and the organization itself has become an internationally recognized leader in patient-centered care in Canada, the Netherlands, Japan, and Brazil, as well as the United States.

More recently, the organization has established the Planetree Visionary Design Network to certify qualifying firms who follow the Planetree philosophy. Through a rigorous application process, the certification formally recognizes a firm's commitment to the design of healing environments, to evidence-based designs, and to sustainable environments in keeping with now long-standing Planetree efforts to personalize, humanize, and demystify the healthcare system. The program identifies architectural firms—for hospitals planning construction or renovations—that are committed to patient-centered care.

According to Planetree's guidelines, the firm must be committed at all levels (board of directors, administration, management, staff), must ensure that community needs and patient perceptions are incorporated in the planning and implementation of its patient-centered designs, and must also involve hospital staff, medical staff, and volunteers in the process. Elements of this model so closely resemble our Synergenial design long advocated by ESa (and in previous editions of this book), it is little surprise that the firm

Baptist Memorial Hospital-DeSoto, Southaven, Mississippi. The hospitality features of Baptist Memorial's main lobby play off of Mississippi's antebellum architecture. *Photo © Kieran Reynolds Photography.*

Eisenhower George and Julia Argyros Health Center, La Quinta, California. References to the light, color, and texture of the desert are woven into the finishes and design features of the Ambulatory Care Center. *Courtesy Jain Malkin Inc. Photo Ed LaCasse Photography.*

became in October 2009 one of only five firms nationally at that time (and the only one in the Southeast) to be certified as a charter member of the Visionary Design Network.

Hospitality- and home-inspired design programs spring from a conviction that familiar environments are less stressful than unfamiliar environments and, therefore, promote healing. Such programs, however, also make marketing sense, as hospitals use elements of hotel and home to retain medical consumers who might choose a competitor or, under certain circumstances, opt for home care.

The Need for Balance and the Use of Demographics

Hospitality and domestic design models garnered their critics. At the very least, objections were raised that materials and finishes appropriate to hotels and homes do not stand up well to the heavy-duty use they receive in a hospital setting. In some cases, hospitals that contracted with outside providers for upgraded food service, ranging from familiar fast foods to gourmet dinners, found their nonprofit tax status in jeopardy.

Some objections are more profound. Architect Henry Stolzman, writing in *Aesclepius* in 1993, objected that it is a mistake to "disguise" hospitals as "places we associate with comfort":

At worst, this has produced hospitals as sterile and disorienting as ever, with a few cosmetic trappings. At best, it has produced facilities that are well decorated and cleverly planned, but are based on the wrong prototypes.

Hospitals should not look like homes. People are often reluctant to leave their homes for hospitals, but when they do, it is to get a level of technical expertise and intense care that they cannot get at home. A "homey" design, standardized to fill thousands of square feet of rooms and corridors, is never going to be close to what a patient thinks of as home; it will be more hotel or motel. And hotel/motel-like hospitals are antithetical to the idea of home....

He also suggested that it was wrong to "conceal and demean" the realities of caregiving and suggested that a better alternative to the hospitality model could be found in the tradition of the sanitarium and spa of the nineteenth century, which suggested a "more majestic stature, serenity, solidity, and honesty toward function."

Whether one agrees with Stolzman or not, it is clear that flocking to design strategies without regard for the community—the community of healthcare providers, of patients, and of neighbors—is thoughtless. It is important to strive for a sense of balance, in which the needs of no group of users are slighted. It is also important to see beyond the general market trends—the trends to which the approaches outlined above are responses—and examine the more immediate and particular community the hospital or healthcare facility is intended to serve.

Computer-aided demographic studies can assess the nature of the market in the community surrounding the facility. Demographic studies identify communities that are medically underserved and detail such factors as age, incidence of

Shady Grove Adventist Hospital, Rockville, Maryland. Designed by Wilmot Sanz, Inc. *Courtesy Wilmot Sanz, Inc. Photo Michael Dersin.*

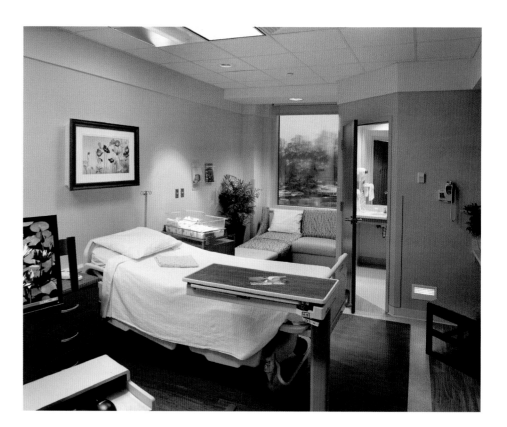

Shady Grove Adventist Hospital, Rockville, Maryland. With private patient rooms, a staff-patient core without the traditional nurses' station, and residential-like family spaces, this expansion, designed by Wilmot Sanz, Inc., follows the Planetree model of patient-focused design. *Courtesy Wilmot Sanz, Inc. Photo Michael Dersin.*

injury, traffic accidents, violent crime, and, using mortality and morbidity data, the incidence and nature of disease. When these medical data are correlated with socioeconomic and environmental conditions, a profile of the type of healthcare facilities required in a community emerges. In specific circumstances, planners may determine that a given market is strongest for specialized medical services, including birthing centers, clinics that treat stress-related disorders, emergency-care centers, immediate-care centers (freestanding facilities once popularly called "doc-in-a-box"), sports medicine facilities, eating-disorder units, long-term-care facilities, and home-health services.

By the late twentieth century, "Centers of Excellence" became the catchphrase to describe services and programs that certain hospitals undertook in response to a perceived market need, to concentrate on providing particular medical services. They usually shared many of the same characteristics, including strong reputations and the most up-to-date clinical resources. The idea was to create a facility of a caliber that would attract the best and most productive specialists in the field, whose presence would, in turn, draw a specifically defined segment of the patient population.

In the Salt Lake Valley of Utah, Cottonwood Hospital assessed community interest in the alternative birthing movement and commissioned the firm of Kaplan McLaughlin Diaz to design a Center for Women's Health, which rapidly increased Cottonwood's market share by 30 percent. West Side Hospital, in Nashville, Tennessee, had no births before 1985, the year it inaugurated a new women's services program, when West Side became part of the new Centennial Medical Center campus. Ultimately, ESa transformed West

Side into the Women's Hospital, a center of excellence for women's care. The hospital offers a full range of women's services, with particular emphasis on education and a family-oriented, homelike birthing environment (see Chapter 11; its neonatal intensive care unit [NICU] is described in Chapter 8). By 1989, the number of births had risen to 2,000; in 1993, it was 2,645. Since then the Women's Hospital has seen around 3,000 births annually.

Aging Population

Direction of design and services offered must, of course, be determined on a community-by-community basis. However, certain market trends are general. Chief among these are the decline in inpatient population and a concomitant rise in demand for outpatient or ambulatory services. Additionally, for inpatients, the length of stay has steadily decreased. Demographically, the population of America is aging, with important implications for the healthcare market and for the design of healthcare—and, for that matter, many other—facilities.

Traditionally, the healthy thirty-year-old man has served as the ideal user of any facility—he was the standard, the yardstick, for architectural design. But the demographic trend toward an aging population, coupled with new building codes stemming in large part from federal legislation in the form of the Americans with Disabilities Act, means that architects should be standardizing public facilities for the ideal of a seventy-year-old woman.

This is especially important in healthcare-related design, since an aging population will make increasingly extensive use of health and hospital facilities.

Guidelines include:

1. using large, clear letters for signs;
2. avoiding lighting the backgrounds of signs;
3. avoiding blues, greens, and neutral colors, among which the aging eye may have trouble distinguishing, for color-coding;
4. providing higher illumination levels and diminishing glare;
5. avoiding uneven lighting;
6. designing acoustically optimal environments that incorporate sound-absorbing materials; acuity of hearing tends to diminish with age, and some persons have difficulty distinguishing speech from background noise;
7. providing ample seating, with chair arms that assist in sitting and rising;
8. enhancing wayfinding and orientation;
9. providing ample handrails;
10. providing adequate door widths for wheelchair use;
11. using easily operated lever-type door hardware;
12. ensuring adequate wheelchair turnaround space in small rooms;
13. ramping throughout for wheelchair access;
14. using surface texture changes on walks adjacent to hazard areas (tactile warning strips).

Design for an aging population is a complex subject, which we explore in Chapter 12. As a design principle, however, it should be recognized that this population trend poses challenges yet also presents medical market opportunities and, therefore, market opportunities for designers and architects as well.

Susan Behar, an interior designer with the firm Universal Design, has described design for aging (and/or disabled) users as "universal design (UD)." The objective of UD is to enhance and promote independence by emphasizing the "Four A's": aesthetics, accessibility, adaptability, and affordability.

For example, the Morton Plant Hospital Family Care Center in Clearwater, Florida, includes a 2,400-sq.-ft. outpatient clinic with wide 36-in. doorways and 5-ft.-wide hallways to accommodate wheelchair users. Similarly, all offices provide a 60-in. turning area for wheelchairs. Door hardware consists of lever handles and U-pulls. Signage, at eye level, is large with clear lettering, carpeting reduces noise, and, where carpeting abuts tile, the two are installed at the same height level for easier mobility. Grab bars are provided throughout—meaning that walls must be properly reinforced—and the bars are brightly colored, not only to enhance visibility, but to make them aesthetically attractive design elements rather than clinical-looking additions. Lighting is designed to help define surfaces more clearly for persons with visual disabilities. In varying degrees, such aspects of universal design are becoming the norm for hospitals and healthcare facilities.

"God," Mies van der Rohe said, "is in the details," and this is, to a great extent, true of design for an aging population. However, with retirement communities, a well-established building and development market, design for an aging population also presents some of the most exciting prospects for creating community-integrated healthcare facilities and for designing entire communities, around healthcare. This achieves a level of coordination and integration impossible in the traditional hospital setting and in the context of traditional relations between hospital and community.

Green Design

Finally, there is a major movement toward "green" design, that is, architecture that, while human-centered, also meets certain standards for environmentally sustainable construction. Green design is at least in part the brainchild of Robert K. Wilson, who as a senior scientist at the Natural Resources Defense Council (NDRC) in 1994 became founding chairman of the Leadership in Energy and Environmental Design (LEED) Steering Committee. As such, he led several disparate nonprofit organizations, government agencies, architects, engineers, developers, builders, product manufacturers, and others, to a broad consensus for certifying environmentally healthy buildings.

This certification system, the LEED Green Building Rating System—promulgated by the U.S. Green Building Council (USGBC)—had grown by 2010 to cover more than 14,000 projects in fifty states and some thirty other countries.

LEED was created to:
- define "green building" by establishing a common standard of measurement;
- promote integrated, whole-building design practices;
- recognize environmental leadership in the building industry;
- stimulate green competition;
- raise consumer awareness of green building benefits; and
- transform the building market.

LEED-certified buildings use key resources more efficiently than conventional buildings simply built to code. And LEED-certified buildings enjoy healthier work and living environments, which, in turn, contributes to higher productivity and better health and comfort for employees. The USGBC has also compiled a list of the benefits of following a LEED strategy, ranging from improved air and water quality to reduced solid waste, all of which benefit the building's users and society at large.

In some cases LEED-certified buildings cost more to design and construct, partly because sustainable construction principles call for better building products. Also the details of LEED certification demand more of construction crews and closer coordination among designers, builders, and clients. Then, too, there are the application costs—registering the project with USGBC, hiring LEED design consultants, and paying the necessary Commis-

Rockingham Memorial Hospital, Harrisonburg, Virginia. Earl Swensson Associates designed this LEED-gold-certified facility in the Shenandoah Valley. *Photo Scott McDonald © Hedrich Blessing.*

sioning Authority, none of which are required for a non-LEED building. But like a lot of things "green," hospitals can earn it all back over time in lower operational costs and increased employee productivity, and the increased marketability as a truly healthier building, which a hospital, perhaps above all other buildings, should strive to be.

ESa incorporated sustainable, green building initiatives in its designs well in advance of industry trends. As a member of the U.S. Green Building Council (USGBC), we support the concept of creating spaces that are sustainable (that is, environmentally responsible), high performance, profitable, and healthy. We feel that sustainability and the basic principles of good design are synonymous and, therefore, we use them as a basis for design in our projects—from front-end site selection and building placement to the final selection of finishes and furniture.

Sustainable design is important to ESa because it improves human performance. We believe environments should be safe and comfortable, yet stimulating, so they enhance the lives of their inhabitants. Such designs result in, for example, improved patient outcomes and healing rates. Sustainable design also can lead to significant cost reductions in utility bills and energy consumption, in overall maintenance, and in staff sick days. And finally, sustainable design helps to achieve a balance in the relationship between the built and natural environment. It makes for good stewardship of natural

resources; it creates an awareness of construction processes and their impact on the world around them that leads, for example, to minimum construction waste; it improves a community's overall infrastructure; and it helps reduce our carbon footprint.

LEED underscores our vision on sustainability, and the following projects showcase a selection of those that have sought and achieved certification.

Rockingham Memorial Hospital, Harrisonburg, Virginia. *Photo Scott McDonald © Hedrich Blessing.*

ROCKINGHAM MEMORIAL HOSPITAL

Harrisonburg, Virginia

Taking the green path in architecture is, in many aspects, synonymous with creating a healing environment through provision of healthy indoor air quality, access to nature, and improved energy performance. The LEED Green Building Rating System awards points based on a facility's adherence to guidelines in five categories: sustainable sites, water efficiency, energy and atmosphere, materials and resources, and indoor environmental quality. The four levels of certification—certified, silver, gold, and platinum—are awarded based on the number of points accrued.

Rockingham Memorial Hospital (RMH), a LEED-gold-certified hospital located in the pastoral, gently rolling hills of Virginia's Shenandoah Valley, made the commitment to go green when early in the conceptual stage, the hospital's board of directors made the decision to build its new, 610,000-sq.-ft., 238-bed

Rockingham Memorial Hospital, Harrisonburg, Virginia. This cardio ambulatory waiting area leads off the main lobby. *Photo Scott McDonald © Hedrich Blessing.*

replacement hospital and health campus as environmentally friendly and sustainable as possible and become the first LEED-certified hospital in Virginia.

Some green aspects of the project that garnered LEED points, such as a highly sophisticated HVAC system, are inherent in any healthcare facility; hospitals normally have more air turnover than in offices or schools, due to infection control. Other much more visible health-related aspects that also score LEED points, such as bicycle racks and low-VOC paints, appeared when the facility neared completion. As part of going green, for example, RMH encouraged employees to use alternate transportation and installed showers for employees who want to ride bikes and run on-site.

"There are a lot of good intuitive design considerations we've followed that lead us to a good building," according to the principal-in-charge, Harold D. Petty of ESa. "These considerations don't necessarily cost more money, but are just good design." However, the biggest cost saver of all is early planning. For example, RMH recycled on-site concrete barn and farmhouse foundations by crushing them into gravel to be used during construction. Subcontractors recycled nine materials—metal, drywall, glass, paper, cardboard, plastic, brick and rubble, concrete, and masonry—that on a normal site would have been thrown into a dumpster. RMH also documented the subcontractors' compliance with LEED emissions standards for building materials.

Any facility seeking LEED certification must meet or exceed the requirements of the latest version of ASHRAE 90.1, an energy guideline, which establishes energy use thresholds for HVAC equipment, lighting, and domestic hot water heating, as well as building envelope requirements based on the climate zone in which the facility will be built. The designers achieved credits for energy efficiency in various ways, the most compelling of which was using methane gas from a nearby landfill in Rockingham County for some of the building's heating requirements.

The hospital selected the new 234-acre site precisely to maintain the integrity of the pastoral setting and to achieve LEED certification. One of the biggest design obstacles was situating the building to avoid wholesale excavations and instead working with natural contours of the land. Part of this involves capturing rainwater runoff in a containment pond flowing into a lake and filtering it before it reaches the ecosystem.

In the end, the hospital layout and design took advantage of the rolling terrain by creating a split-level of public spaces so that patients, families, and staff could enjoy views of the Shenandoah Valley. Upon entry at the first level, a visitor can see through the building.

Exterior building products were chosen to meet the LEED requirements without driving up construction costs. Most products used—sealants, paints, carpets, and flooring—were chosen for the right chemical make-up so as to not emit pollutants.

Collecting data after the new RMH facility became operational was crucial to ensuring other healthcare institutions seeking LEED certification will benefit from RMH's learning process.

CISCO LIFECONNECTIONS HEALTH CENTER
San Jose, California

With the help of Jain Malkin Inc., Cisco Systems is seeking the lofty but achievable goal of improving the health status of employees in its new 24,000-sq.-ft. health center. Cisco's leadership was committed to the benefits of a wellness philosophy and the convenience of having a health center on campus for employees and their families at the corporate headquarters. The median age of Cisco employees is forty; therefore, most of their healthcare experiences have been outpatient. The goal for the new center, or clinic, was to create a healthcare experience that is more in sync with how they do their jobs, which involves the use of leading-edge technologies. Although the staff is diverse, the largest contingent is from India and Asia.

Cisco wanted the clinic to be a place where employees could connect to manage their health, not just get healthcare, thus the focus on wellness and health management. To that end, the building includes a large fitness center and a daycare center. The clinic offers primary and pediatric care along with acupuncture, travel medicine, mental health and nutrition counseling, chiropractic, physical therapy, pharmacy, lab, and radiology.

Specifically Cisco wanted designers to create a facility that would focus on the optimal patient experience, one enabled by technology; provide care in a quiet and private environment; improve the productivity of the clinical staff by making it easy to move back and forth with few steps; create a larger "showcase" care suite that allowed Cisco to promote this concept with other large companies and partners; and embrace sustainability with the goal of LEED gold certification.

At the start of the project, the Cisco planning team created a template for mapping every aspect of the patient experience. For example, patients can log-in on the Internet and schedule their own appointments. Patients have a choice of four options for confirming the appointment or canceling or changing it, including email, phone, text message, or secure messaging. Patients may drive to the clinic, or use a shuttle or light rail from the various campus buildings.

Patients check in using an electronic wireless tablet or wall-mounted kiosk and are directed to the next available care suite. The receptionist or "health ambassador" hands the patient a wireless tablet PC. The goal is no time spent waiting in the reception room, which reassures patients that the clinic respects their time and that it has been expecting them. Patient surveys after the first six months of operation indicated that patients were waiting fewer than three minutes.

Tests are as nonintrusive as possible with blood draw, radiology, and procedure rooms nearby. Vital signs are captured and automatically uploaded to the electronic health record. There is total transparency with all information shared with patients on the forty-two-inch wall monitor. The care providers' badges activate the screen system and log them onto the system. After the provider logs onto the system, even the patient's fitness center data can be reviewed as can various types of diagnostic test results; the Internet can be searched for periodical journal articles; the patient's medical history can be reviewed.

The clinic's adjacent pharmacy interfaces directly with the electronic health record. Consultations with the pharmacist can occur via the patient portal on the Internet, by phone, or in person in a private consult room in the pharmacy. Virtually all prescriptions are immediately ready for pick up as the patient leaves the health center.

Patient check out is also quick and easy. Before the patient checks himself out at the wall-mounted kiosk, services have been coded, eligibility has been confirmed with the respective insurance providers, and claims have

been electronically processed. Patient copays are collected at this time and a bill and receipt are printed and presented to the patient. If reports of the visit need to be sent to a nonclinic care provider, they are sent electronically or faxed. The highest level of security was designed into the system to separate the file server from the Cisco server network.

As one might expect given the client, the technology embedded in the clinic goes beyond anything seen in most of today's medical clinics. Inside the care suite, patients (and any accompanying family member) sit in lounge chairs in a living room setting in front of a large flat-panel monitor. The nurse uses diagnostic instruments tucked away in swing-out cabinets under the monitor to record vital signs. As the vitals are taken, the information is automatically recorded in the electronic record, which is displayed on the monitor to enable collaboration between patient and provider. The patient may self-select entertainment, surf the Web, or watch an educational film on a health topic on the large wall monitor.

The interface with the physician occurs initially in the living room of the care suite and then moves to the examination room. Private bathrooms that offer a high level of personal comfort and privacy are located off each exam room. Each has a cabinet in which to hang clothing out of sight, along with a locked space for a briefcase or handbag.

Cisco LifeConnections Health Center, San Jose, California. Jain Malkin Inc. intended this center to be a template for an employee health clinic that mapped every aspect of the patient experience. *Courtesy Jain Malkin Inc. Photo Steve McClelland.*

Cisco LifeConnections Health Center, San Jose, California. Jain Malkin Inc. and the planning team at the health center put the patient experience at the center of the design for their facility. *Courtesy Jain Malkin Inc. Photo Steve McClelland.*

A unique Cisco product called TelePresence enables high-definition video conferencing. This allows companies like Cisco with offices worldwide to conference with colleagues. The TelePresence screen is very large and a specially designed oval table has its mirror image at the other destination, giving the illusion of a large complete conference table with life-size individuals seated at it. Elsewhere, a conference room with multiple large monitors and Cisco's Digital Media Manager displays presentation and healthy living video materials.

A specialized version of TelePresence, called HealthPresence, allows a patient, perhaps in a rural area, to undergo a virtual physical examination and diagnosis by a remotely located care provider. It also enables a physician to consult with specialist colleagues on a difficult case through a large video screen enabled with software that can transmit a patient's vital signs and medical health record, and the patient can actually be interviewed in real time via a Webcam. The product is another example of Cisco's dedication to enabling what it calls the "human network."

Enhanced productivity and elimination of waste are hallmarks of lean design principles. In this case, doing everything the patient needs at one time without the provider flitting back and forth among several patients actually increases productivity, reduces medical error, and produces a higher level of patient satisfaction.

A custom-designed acrylic sculpture wall is featured in the reception area. Light is carried through each horizontal element as if the edges were illuminated.

Optimal medical clinic design layout mandates same-handed examination rooms as opposed to left-handed and right-handed rooms. (Physicians always work on the patient's right side; therefore left-handed rooms involve a compromise.) In exam rooms the sharps container, diagnostic instruments, and supplies are stored in cabinets handy to exam tables but out-of-sight to patients.

Maple is used throughout in custom door jambs and in corner guards that continue to the ceiling. Entries to each care suite consist of five horizontal bands of frosted glazing framed by solid maple mullions and door.

"Zen" tranquility was one aim of design, and it is enhanced by the raked sand carpet pattern, the wood slat ceiling (with HVAC registers invisibly located above the slats), and the corridor lighting consisting of recessed square fixtures creating small pools of light on the carpet. The color palette is warm neutral tones accented by nectarine and pear.

One design feature in particular grew from a concern expressed by the director of facilities. Cisco employees work collaboratively in open work cubicles. For obvious reasons, this is difficult if not impossible for a medical clinic but, to allay concerns about a tight network of rooms with partitions going to the ceiling, circulation spines have a mirror at the top eighteen inches of wall, extending to the ceiling. Combined with the horizontal wood grid ceiling, this makes the ceiling appear to extend to infinity. Also, the main circulation spine is a funnel shape that widens as it gets closer to the exterior, admitting more natural light and leading the eye to the exterior views.

The clinic is on the second floor of the building overlooking treetops, giving the feeling of being in a tree house. Two sides of the clinic preserve a staff corridor and relaxation space suffused with natural light and treetop views. Staff workspaces and offices are off stage, out of patient view. Care providers access the care suites from a dedicated corridor allowing privacy for conversations.

The project achieved LEED gold certification, and compliance with LEED in the use of sustainable materials and healthy indoor air quality is consistent with the wellness philosophy of the clinic.

ATLANTICARE HEALTH SYSTEM - ATLANTICARE ONCOLOGY CENTER

Egg Harbor Township, New Jersey

Using a host of sustainable design strategies, EwingCole created a LEED-gold-certified facility near Atlantic City that proves green design and healthcare can go hand-in-hand. Conscious that hospital settings cause trepidation in patients and that cancer centers in particular can elevate stress levels, EwingCole made a commitment to creating a "healthy" building, one that would benefit the patients and create a tranquil, comforting environment.

Beyond taking special care when selecting colors, textures, and materials, the designers considered the specific functional requirements of those undergoing chemotherapy or radiation, and how to deliver such care in the

AtlantiCare Health System – AtlantiCare Oncology Center, Egg Harbor Township, New Jersey. EwingCole designed this LEED-gold-certified family waiting area at the oncology center. *Courtesy Ewing-Cole. Photo Barry Halkin, Halkin Photography LLC.*

most appropriate environment. The design team also seized the opportunity of working on a site in the New Jersey Pine Barrens, and allowed the natural surroundings to inform the interior design.

To take full advantage of the New Jersey Pine Barrens backdrop, to bring nature into the design, and to keep the building from imposing on its surroundings, EwingCole used copious amounts of glass. This transparency allowed the building to offer views that blurred the line between interior and exterior and permitted sunlight to penetrate its walls. Brick, stone, and Trespa—a building material resembling wood—on the exterior of the 40,000-sq.-ft. structure complemented an interior palette of bright, neutral, natural materials.

The entry atrium, with its abundant glazing, promotes daylighting, and the skylight of the lobby nourishes the growth of trees indoors. The designers also employed energy-efficient measures that included insulation and a high-efficiency cooling and pumping system; use of low-VOC, low-off gassing, and recycled materials; and reuse of as much material from existing walls, floors, and roof as possible. The green roofing system set outside the window of the chemotherapy bays aids the sustainable initiative and also gives patients a literal tie to their natural environment.

Seeking a psychologically uplifting environment, the designers tried to keep the patients' state of mind at the top of their minds throughout the design

process. They created a floor plan that distinguished the entrance for chemotherapy from radiation treatment. Radiation therapy and imaging patients are on the first floor, while medical oncology patients are on the second, which also has shelled space for future expansion and physician time-share space.

Since chemotherapy patients are hooked up to machines for hours with room-temperature treatment running through their bodies, the designers thought it crucial to keep patients warm, yet keep staff comfortable. So they placed radiant heat panels in the ceiling that targeted the patient in the treatment chair but do not make the surrounding space too hot for staff. The chemo bays are decorated with a beach motif, and dune grass is pressed between the panels that separate each patient station. While radiation therapy takes less time and is not associated with pain, the technical machinery can cause some anxiety. To help alleviate this tension, designers included a skylight that floods the areas immediately outside the radiation rooms with natural light.

Its environmentally sustainable strategies ultimately earned the project a LEED-gold rating, although achieving LEED certification had not been an initial goal of the project. "It quickly became apparent how important it is," Lauren Ochs, director of oncology services said, according to EwingCole, "to contribute to 'the greening of AtlantiCare,' and create a true healing/healthy environment for our patients."

AtlantiCare Health System – AtlantiCare Oncology Center, Egg Harbor Township, New Jersey. The oncology center's infusion bay. Courtesy EwingCole. Photo Barry Halkin, Halkin Photography LLC.

CHAPTER 4

Making Yesterday's Hospitals Work Today

Many older hospitals were built when the main purpose of a hospital was to house and treat inpatients. As a result, for decades in the late twentieth century a shockingly high number of hospital beds in the United States went empty. By 1995, the portion of empty beds had reached one-third of all beds, or some 300,000 every night. And though the number stabilized before the beginning of the twenty-first century and has now begun to decline, the initial change itself, and the reason for it, make a good lesson.

The decline in the number of occupied beds was not exclusively the result of new science and new healthcare policies, and therefore it was not reversed by changes in science or policy. Instead, it was in large part a function of architecture, of old-paradigm buildings struggling to survive in a world swept by new paradigms, and it has begun to be reversed in significant measure mostly by architecture. Still today either existing buildings must be reconfigured to serve new healthcare markets and new medical realities, or new construction, along the lines laid out in this work, must be planned. No third choice exists.

The problem is, the choice between the two alternatives can be, in and of itself, difficult to make. Under what conditions does it make sense to renovate an existing facility as opposed to building a new one? Is it even possible—or, at least, economically feasible—to bring an old-paradigm hospital to the level of value and cost-effectiveness required to survive, let alone thrive, in the current financial environment for healthcare?

Of course, this decision has to be made on a case-by-case basis, and we provide some guidelines. However, it is our opinion that, as a general principle,

hospitals built before 1960 should be replaced. In terms of cost-effectiveness, of achieving efficiency for people and for energy, pre-1960 hospitals usually cannot be made to deliver adequate value.

Some hospitals are virtually impossible to renovate. Since old-paradigm facilities have most of their now-vacant space in areas designed for acute care, it is difficult to expand these areas logically as outpatient facilities. Many existing hospitals do not sit on a sufficient amount of land, so expansion is impossible, difficult, haphazard, or clumsy. Few older hospitals were built with vertical expansion in mind. Many also have structural limitations, such as load-bearing walls, low floor-to-ceiling heights, intrusive support columns, and so on, that obstruct major renovation.

Attempting to patch up and remodel buildings like these is old-paradigm thinking. What is needed is the boldness and resolve to break out of inefficient, inadequate policies that are not cost-effective. The hard fact is that realizing new ideas, building according to new paradigms, new conditions and needs, requires new designs and new buildings. Still, some older hospitals, except those built before 1960, may be deemed obsolescent but can quite possibly be renovated satisfactorily.

This may mean demolishing old hospitals and building anew, or it may mean finding alternative uses for "hopeless" facilities and building new ones elsewhere. Such uses may be medical, as they were, say, in the late-twentieth-century renovation of a part of St. Leonard's Hospital, an 1862 facility in the East End of London. The aged building was transformed into a primary healthcare facility for the GP (general practice) unit.

Western Maryland Regional Medical Center, Cumberland, Maryland. Hord Coplan Macht led a multidisciplinary team to design this $268 million replacement hospital. *Courtesy Hord Coplan Macht. Photo Patrick Ross.*

Western Maryland Regional Medical Center, Cumberland, Maryland. Main lobby. *Courtesy Hord Coplan Macht. Photo Patrick Ross.*

It may also be possible to adapt outmoded hospitals to nursing home use, to psychiatric use, and to such nonmedical purposes as prime or secondary office space.

To Build or to Renovate?

If pre-1960 hospital facilities are likely candidates for demolition or alternative use, what about later facilities or more questionable cases? What factors enter into the decision to build new or to renovate?

Begin with the most basic question: Is renovation or new construction cheaper? The answer can be surprising. If markedly new services are to be offered—say, significantly expanded ambulatory services or a long-term-care facility to accommodate an aging community—it may well be more costly to renovate and expand present facilities than it is to build new structures. Other pressures that argue for new construction include the enhancing of professional prestige and employee appeal. A new, state-of-the-art, aesthetically pleasing facility may go a long way toward attracting the best physicians and excellent support staff, which these days are in critically short supply in many areas. Hospitals have learned that they must compete for doctors, but even more so for nurses and technicians in the United States' chronically crisis-ridden support-staff market. Moreover, new facilities featuring patient-centered amenities attract savvy healthcare consumers.

To determine, in a general sense, whether renovation or new construction will be more cost-effective, you should address the following issues:

1. Determine whether the renovation is cosmetic or functional. Cosmetic upgrades rarely require anything more than simple renovation and can improve a hospital's image. Functional renovation is, of course, more extensive and more expensive. First, determine whether the functional renovation can be accomplished without major alteration to the building's core and shell: foundations, structural elements, and exterior walls. On average, if most of the core and shell remain untouched, renovation realizes an 80 percent savings—in core and shell costs only—over new construction. However, functional renovation projects save little if anything over new construction costs in other parts of the building.

2. Consider how old the facility is. This may seem obvious, but it is useful to view the age of the facility in relation to three landmark years: 1947, 1967, and 1972.

The Hill-Burton Act of 1947—officially called the Hospital Survey and Construction Act—was designed to provide federal grants to modernize hospitals that had become obsolete due to lack of capital investment throughout the period of the Great Depression and World War II. Hill-Burton was updated in 1975 by an amendment to the Hill-Burton Program, Title XVI of the Public Health Service Act, which established federal grants, loan

Shriners Hospitals for Children/ Shriners Burns Hospital, Boston, Massachusetts. In some instances, renovations must be squeezed into a very tight site. *Courtesy Odell Associates. Photos Odell Associates.*

guarantees, and interest subsidies for health facilities. Renovations undertaken with Hill-Burton funds carry certain obligations and must comply with certain standards enforced by the federal government, and these can have an impact on renovation projects.

The National Electrical Code was updated in 1967. Renovation of pre-1967 hospitals may well require major upgrading of electrical systems, including the establishment of three separate emergency-power branches: critical, life-safety, and emergency.

Not until 1972 was asbestos identified as a major environmental hazard and prohibited as a building material. Prior to that year, of course, the material was very widely used. The presence of asbestos is not an insurmountable problem, but the cost of asbestos abatement is very high, and the process is time consuming. Abatement also takes precedence over the work of other trades, so it is often necessary to cease work until asbestos has been cleared.

Note that unanticipated inadequacies of infrastructure add substantially to the cost of a renovation project. Experienced consultants in facilities management will tell you there are few if any older hospitals that don't have problems with their infrastructure.

Finally, it is vitally important that all renovation projects, especially those done in-house, be documented carefully. This will avoid nasty—and costly—surprises that emerge during demolition.

3. Evaluate the different levels of use that affect the choice to renovate versus to commission new construction. It is useful to make distinctions among low-, mid-, and high-tech space. Renovating existing facilities to create low-tech space—offices, storage, and the like—requires little in the way of sophisticated mechanical and electrical (M/E) engineering and is relatively unconstrained by code requirements. Renovation of such areas can prove much cheaper than new construction costs.

Mid-tech renovation introduces more constraints and expense, especially in the area of air-exchange systems. Renovation costs of such areas increase, though they can still offer some savings in relation to new construction of such spaces.

High-tech areas that include such spaces as operating suites, ICUs, radiology, imaging facilities, and the like are expensive to design and build anew, but even when renovation is technically feasible, it may be more cost-effective to start over.

4. Determine what impact a renovation project will have on the building's code status. In some jurisdictions, renovating a certain percentage of the square footage of a building requires that the entire building be brought up to code. This might raise costs substantially enough to make renovation less cost-effective than new construction.

5. Consider how the renovation projects will disrupt day-to-day operations, ranging from annoying interruptions to periodic utility disruption to forced temporary departmental relocations. The concessions that staff must make to construction intrusions may raise costs by reducing productivity, while the concessions that construction workers must make to minimize disruption—and to follow infection control risk assessment (ICRA) require-

Women's Center, North Florida Regional Medical Center, Gainesville, Florida. To complement the addition of the Women's Center, the most visible parts of the existing facility were reclad. Clients enter the Women's Center through a designated main entrance. *Photo KD Lawson.*

ments—will likely raise construction costs. Dirt, noise, and the perception of chaos wear on staff members and may have a negative impact on patients, discouraging some from using the facility while it is under construction. Such potentially substantial costs are difficult to calculate. The demolition phase is often the most disruptive, disquieting, and least adequately appreciated by planners.

Hospitals routinely opt for renovation over new construction, even though wholesale gutting of a facility brings renovation costs to as much as 85 percent of new construction costs and, when you factor in the hidden costs of disruption of services and reduced productivity, renovation may even be more costly than new construction. Moreover, it takes 10 to 15 percent more space to put the same amount of function into renovated space because of the necessity of building around existing column supports and other immovable obstacles. This significant loss in available space can easily cut into the savings renovation seems to offer over new construction.

Furthermore, renovation is all too often a departmental project rather than a systemwide project. Old-paradigm thinking is, by its nature, departmental and piecemeal, whereas new-paradigm thinking looks at the entire system and the potential for future expansion and change. Renovation of even a single department should not be undertaken without considering its impact on the institution as a whole and the department's role within the institution.

Finally, renovation, no matter how reasonable the initial construction costs, should not be undertaken at the expense of existing efficient and successful operations, and it should not cannibalize existing facilities in such a way as to inhibit continued development.

The Renovation Process

If, after careful evaluation of facility needs and goals—and this should be carried out with the assistance and advice of experienced architects and engineers—it is determined that a renovation project is more appropriate than new construction, the project must be planned carefully and strategically.

Funding

Depending on the age of the facility and the available construction documentation, major renovation projects are subject to more unpleasant surprises than new construction. Blueprints and engineering diagrams may tell planners, architects, and engineers what is supposed to be in a wall, but, unfortunately, only when the wall is demolished or dismantled does the whole truth emerge. If some part of that truth consists of immovable obstacles or unanticipated electrical and mechanical components, plans may have to be altered accordingly. The master renovation proposal must allow for such contingencies, and funds must be available to cover unanticipated overruns, to keep a project from stalling with disastrous results.

While construction costs are almost certainly the largest item on the renovation shopping list, funding must also cover the costs of the following considerations:

- The financing itself
- Specialized studies
- Medical and nonmedical equipment that may be required temporarily while permanent equipment is unavailable due to renovation
- Temporary facilities
- Additional staff time, including reduced productivity
- Moving and occupancy start-up costs
- Possible loss of revenue
- Cost of soils and materials testing, surveys, legal advice, and of securing the Certificate of Need (CON)

As with any construction project, there may be significant cost overruns, especially in inflationary times, should the work fall behind planned schedule, for example, because of unanticipated structural obstacles.

Consultants

Except for very large corporate or federal institutions, hospitals and healthcare facilities generally cannot support full-time architectural staff, although many development-minded institutions now keep an architectural consultant on call through some form of retainer. For renovation, administra-

OPPOSITE **Griffin Hospital, Derby, Connecticut. These photographs show how a new building skin united the disparate styles of successive additions to the original facility.** *Courtesy The S/L/A/M Collaborative. Top (before) Photo Peter Brown; bottom (after) Photo Nick Wheeler, Wheeler Photographics.*

tors should seek professional consultants with wide experience specifically in medical renovation.

The following is a list of such consultants:
- Marketing specialists
- Business strategy experts
- Financial consultants
- Workflow and organizational experts
- Medical programming/planning consultants
- Cost-estimating consultants
- Architects and engineers

Depending on the preliminary assessment performed by these experts, it may be necessary or desirable also to consult the following specialists:
- Soils engineers (in sites subject to instability or seismic activity)
- Civil engineers
- Waterproofing specialists
- Certified industrial hygienists (CIHs)—especially where the presence of asbestos or other environmental hazards is a possibility
- Medical equipment consultants
- Communications consultants
- Laboratory/pharmacy design specialists
- Interior designers
- Graphics consultants (for signage)
- Food service specialists
- Lighting consultants

Planning

Planning begins with a detailed survey of the following existing conditions:
- Structural frame
- Accessibility for the disabled (A.D.A. and other code compliance issues)
- Utilities (including underground utilities)
- Roof
- Elevators
- Fire exits and other life-safety considerations
- Floor-to-floor heights
- Ventilation
- Electrical capacity
- Existing and usable space
- Wayfinding

If the project involves site modifications, including additional access, new entrances, and parking, site studies are called for.

Of course, the renovation plan must include an assessment of just what services and activities will suffer disruption and how this may be minimized through the identification of swing space for temporary relocation. It may be necessary to rent space off-site or to bring in portable spaces, including prefab units and trailers. It may also be necessary to plan construction in smaller phases to minimize the scope and duration of disruptions. Such decisions require careful analysis of the cost of disruption versus the added costs (and delays) incurred by multiple small construction phases. In consultation with key staff involved in the renovation, a needs assessment should be carried out simultaneously with the facility survey. It may be desirable to encourage the creation of a comprehensive "needs list," which can be prioritized and refined to establish the project's scope.

In consultation with architects and other consultants, and following analysis of the facility survey and needs assessment, a master plan should be developed. Obviously, the plan cannot be established without a full awareness of regulatory requirements; however, the impact of some of these cannot be assessed until the master plan has been completed.

Hazards and Safety Considerations

Administrators and the renovation team must anticipate the following hazards and contingencies:

- Asbestos and its abatement
- Presence of PCBs
- Adverse effects of construction activity on patients and staff
- Heightened risk of infection and contamination of wounds due to airborne dust
- Coordination of construction and occupancy-phasing
- Disruption of critical medical activities
- Disruption of utilities services
- Seismic safety
- Security of construction areas as well as the institution as a whole during renovation exposure, including narcotics and biological hazard areas
- Maintenance of all fire exits, fire-rated occupancy separations, and fire alarm and sprinkler systems
- Unanticipated structural defects or obstacles

Depending on the nature, extent, and site of the renovation, the prevention of infections from environmental contamination may well become

Mercy Medical Center Merced Replacement Hospital, Merced, California. RBB Architects Inc designed this replacement hospital, consolidating two existing hospitals and offering reduced operating costs while more than doubling the patient capacity. **Courtesy RBB Architects Inc. Photo John Linden Photography.**

a significant consideration. A good contamination prevention program details, for example, how construction traffic will be controlled, how construction areas will be sealed off from areas in use, how housekeeping will be maintained at a fastidious level, and how an environmental culturing program will be maintained. At one exemplary renovation, for example, construction workers were assigned exclusive use of an elevator; the construction area was sealed off from the operating room area using half-inch drywall nailed to 2 × 4 framing, with all butt joints taped using air-conditioning tape; and ventilation systems into the operating area were rerouted to avoid construction areas.

The impact of renovation on patient relations also cannot be ignored. Good public relations, based on communicating the extent and purpose of the renovations, address patient worries, head off patient complaints, and keep patients from turning elsewhere for services. A good patient relations program might include a well-designed brochure that briefly describes the hospital's history, its present goals, and its future plans, including the purpose of the renovation construction. Every patient admitted to the hospital should receive a copy. A poster program might also be introduced, and, as an additional gracious touch, a fresh flower included on patient breakfast trays with a cheerful card. Pediatric patients might receive plastic hard hats with the name of the project and a special title such as "Junior Foreman" stenciled across the front. In short, use anything that can shift the focus from the annoyance of the renovation to its purpose.

"Fast-Tracking" Renovations

Back during the days when corporate America still resented Japan for the miracles of its long economic boom and the high quality and high value of its technology and consumer products, Tom Peters and Robert Waterman published a highly influential best seller called *In Search of Excellence*. It was a survey and analysis of successful strategies of entrepreneurship, inventiveness, and management, and one of the concepts it touted that became standard practice in the corporate world was "fast-tracking," a process that works across established bureaucratic barriers and departmental partitions to accomplish a common institution-wide goal quickly, efficiently, and with high-quality, high-value results.

From this concept the construction industry developed today's Integrated Project Delivery (IDP), which is a project delivery method that integrates people, systems, business structures, and practices to garner the talents and insights of all involved, to reduce waste and maximize efficiency. So with IDP at least the fast-tracking concept remains an inviting and seductive one, alluring in the same way as the story of Alexander the Great's using the blade of his sword to resolve the puzzle of the Gordian Knot. Many consultants, architects, and other planning and design professionals believe, however, that major renovation projects do not lend themselves well to fast-tracking. Too many individuals and individual needs and agendas must be meshed with long-range institutional needs and goals and too many pitfalls (as outlined above) exist to make the fast-tracking process a comfortable alternative.

That said, there is a famous historical instance of fast-tracking in a renovation project that bears mention. Back in the late 1980s the outlook for Stanford University Hospital's proposed same-day surgery unit was bleak indeed. It had been stalled for two years after planning had been authorized. Everybody recognized the need for the renovation, since the surgeries performed in the old four-bed ambulatory care unit had increased from 12 percent of the hospital's operations to 25 percent in less than three years. Clearly the facility was overburdened. To make matters worse, it was located adjacent to the hospital's morgue. Despite these incentives, motives, and pressures to get the project underway, it floundered in hospital bureaucracy.

Inspired by the fast-tracking concept, management appointed an individual to serve as what Peters and Waterman called an "executive champion . . . cloaked with clear authority by the CEO and chief operating officer."

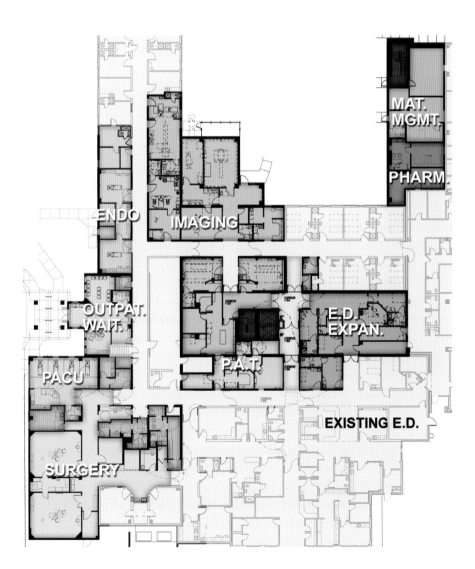

Floor plan for a renovation project.

Armed with concept approval, the "champion" was freed from having to seek approval of each step and became a fully empowered project leader. Her first step was to recruit a representative cross-section of staff from the surgical department, admitting, clinical laboratories, facilities, and medical staff. This relatively small group became what Peters and Waterman famously called a "skunk works"—a "band of eight or ten zealots off in a corner [who] often outproduce product development groups that number in the hundreds."

The Stanford skunk works reexamined all previous proposals and set as its goal the short-term objective of producing an interim solution to the need for expanded ambulatory surgery facilities. Long-term goals would be left to a later, larger hospital modernization project. The team agreed that the short-term focus was necessary, because revamping ambulatory facilities had become critical to the financial viability of the hospital. It was perceived less as a matter of improvement of services than as an issue of survival.

Contrary to traditional planning methods, the skunk works functioned in small clusters coordinated by the leader. In this way, there was no need to coordinate the various, constantly changing schedules of a large number of hospital staff. Tasks were "chunked," broken into mini action plans, each of which was designed to meet some set of needs of a particular constituency. The leadership approach was deliberately "loose-tight," meaning that the leader encouraged individual autonomy and "intrapreneuring" while also maintaining goal-directed overall focus.

The soul of fast-tracking is a champion who works one on one, up close and personal with the various teams and individuals involved in the project. For example, rather than rely on questionnaires, formal studies, and policy statements, the project leader personally walked the director of anesthesiology through a draft of the plan. The anesthesiologist pointed out that a repositioning of recovery beds would avert what could have been a critical and costly traffic-flow problem. This was something no one else had seen before, and, in a more rigid planning environment, the input of this professional might not have been solicited, might have been shunted aside, or might have been delayed in implementation, requiring more expensive and complicated revision.

In this particular project, fast-tracking techniques resulted in a six-month turnaround time, from the beginning of the skunk works meetings to the start-up of the facility. Clearly, the Stanford University Hospital renovation was a success story, and, whenever possible, renovation should be planned in the context of long-term institutional goals in such a way that provides sufficient flexibility for further, as yet unplanned, expansion and modification. We are not in favor of bureaucratic red tape, but we have reason to be concerned about the ability of any project leader, using such techniques as mini-meetings and "chunking," to appreciate all aspects and details of the big picture, a picture whose dimensions are defined not only by space but by human action and interaction, as well as by time itself. Yet, in this very real world, human needs and financial pressures do not always afford the luxury of long planning schedules. In the years since, fast-tracking has increasingly been relied upon as a means of making building projects more flexible and rapidly responsive to changing needs.

Integrated Strategic and Master Planning

Whether you are renovating an older hospital, designing a replacement-in-place hospital, or building an entirely new facility, there is no substitute for a master plan that integrates strategic goals and facility design. Given our emphasis on Synergenial design it should by now come as no surprise that we think the success of such a process depends on the strength of the team that creates it, a team that includes owners, designers, the hospital administrators, and steady input from its end users—medical staff and patients and their families. As much as anything, successful master planning—especially for healthcare facilities—depends on the good listening skills of the architects and designers.

The master planning begins with an early understanding of the goals of the hospital owner and the hospital's administrators—their expectations, the scope of their project, their budget, and the schedule they are operating under. These criteria usually quickly become the primary goals and objectives around which planning and design activities focus. A growing number of architects are collaborating with clients to incorporate the most recent research information and evidence-based design concepts to inform planning and design.

It is important from the start to develop a good working relationship among all members of the key planning team to facilitate a totally interactive team approach, and this often means getting clear from the start the hierarchy of decision making and identifying project champions and user groups. As soon as possible a detailed schedule should be developed to encompass all planning activities.

The integrated master facility planning approach involves developing a strategic plan that includes both functional and operational planning and site and facility planning. It begins with interviews and data gathering to assess

Chart showing Integrated Strategic Planning/Facility Planning/Design Processes.

Integrated Strategic Planning / Facility Planning / Design Processes

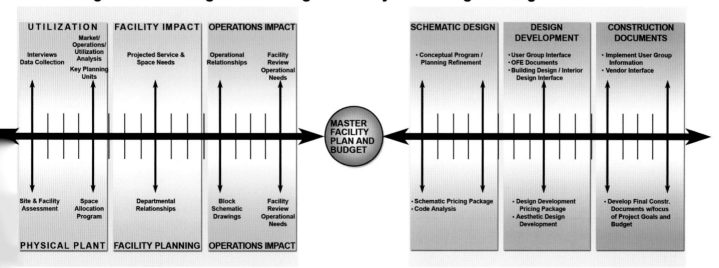

the site and facility and with conducting market, operations, and utilization analyses to assess growth potential. All this involves such activities as:

- evaluating existing project data,
- reviewing existing hospital and campus plans,
- reviewing zoning and city requirement,
- interviewing key staff members,
- creating conceptual master planning options,
- developing a master plan package.

In doing so you are moving from data gathering and assessment to considering the impact of the facility—its projected services and space needs and its key planning units—and weighing facility planning options, creating a space allocation program and laying out department relationships. Then comes, on the functional side of the equation, planning for the operations impact and establishing operational relationships, while on the site and facility side it is time to develop blocking/stack diagrams. The goal is a master facility plan that offers real options, prioritizes projects, establishes the phasing of the projects, creates a budget, and schedules the project's implementation.

A Range of Renovation Projects

BAPTIST MEMORIAL HOSPITAL–DESOTO
Southaven, Mississippi

Designed by ESa, the new patient tower at Baptist Memorial Hospital–Desoto constitutes an expansion and renovation that more than doubles the size of the original hospital and combines classical and contemporary influences to create an environment its architects dubbed "traditional with a twist." Replacing many key areas of the old hospital (see Chapter 7), the renovation enlarged the hospital to meet growing community healthcare needs and enabled its owners to modernize the facility throughout.

During construction ESa met the challenge of maintaining normal operations with several strategies to manage parking and building access for patients, visitors, and staff. At the start, all the hospital's access points—to the emergency room, to the main lobby, to the main admissions level—had to be moved to different locations because the tower was placed at the old front door to the hospital. So before the tower project even began, an additional access road was built on the site and a secondary hospital entrance was temporarily promoted to main entrance.

During the project, a temporary parking lot was built for construction crews, and was later converted to green space. An additional parking lot was created for employees to allow patients and visitors priority space close to the building. Toward the end of the project, parking became a problem near the emergency room door. When it had to be restricted, valet parking was provided.

The construction team communicated and coordinated with the three ambulance services that serve the hospital to ensure that ambulance drivers were aware of the changes to the site three or four weeks in advance. To keep the public informed, the project team updated signage and printed campus maps in the local newspaper. The maps were also available in doctors' offices, so patients could review them before their visits.

The concrete frame of the tower is constructed of conventionally reinforced columns and beams with one-way slabs. Large structural steel joists compose the roof structure; the canopies and a portion of the lobby are also structural steel. Several major components of the hospital were replaced during the tower project, which also included 62,000 sq. ft. of renovation in the existing building, much of which was converted to nonclinical space.

The hospital's power plant was expanded horizontally to make room for two new chillers and a new boiler. One of the hospital's existing boilers was also replaced in the project. Not wanting a separate power plant for the tower,

Baptist Memorial Hospital-DeSoto, Southaven, Mississippi. The new tower's brick and stone complement the existing facility. *Photo © Kieran Reynolds Photography.*

Williamson Medical Center, Franklin, Tennessee. ESa's substantial renovation greatly expanded the existing 1982 facility shown here. *Photo Earl Swensson Associates.*

OPPOSITE TOP Williamson Medical Center, Franklin, Tennessee. In the end, the old hospital got an image makeover into a six-story regional medical center with a seven-story integrated MOB and a new ground-level main entry. *Photo © Kieran Reynolds Photography.*

OPPOSITE BOTTOM Williamson Medical Center, Franklin, Tennessee. Changes to the medical center during renovation included a new main entry. *Photo © Kieran Reynolds Photography.*

the hospital expanded its existing plant, and all valving and piping were integrated so that the new chillers and boilers and cooling towers worked in conjunction with the existing equipment. The project also included the construction of an underground tunnel to connect services to the new tower.

WILLIAMSON MEDICAL CENTER

Franklin, Tennessee

Designed by ESa, this substantial renovation, which encompasses three sides of the facility, expands the existing facility, and reworks every department internally except surgery and recovery, took place while the hospital remained in operation. ESa accomplished the feat by closely partnering with the contractor to carry out the renovation in appropriate and adequate stages. The hospital agreed to aggressive relocations of several departments to streamline the process. Administration, medical records, and physical therapy, for example, were relocated to modular buildings while construction was underway on the emergency department, whose existing space was to be renovated in the first phase of the project.

In the end, the old 1982 140-bed four-story hospital got an image makeover, and its high mix of semiprivate rooms became a six-story

regional medical center with 180 private rooms. The center now includes a seven-story integrated medical office building for an additional 170,000 sq. ft., a 94,000-sq.-ft. hospital addition, and 116,000 sq. ft. of renovations. The changes include a new ground-level main entry; a new emergency department; and new spaces for central registration, food service, lab, obstetrics, physical therapy, imaging, and various other support services. A new 22,000-sq.-ft. outpatient surgery department (see Chapter 7) anchors the first floor of the medical office building with convenient services supported by the hospital. There are also seven level II NICU beds. The new medical office building is connected to the bed tower at all levels for easy patient and physician access, and the new NICU program allows for the full spectrum of obstetric and delivery care.

VIVIAN AND SEYMOUR MILSTEIN FAMILY HEART CENTER
NEW YORK–PRESBYTERIAN HOSPITAL/COLUMBIA UNIVERSITY
MEDICAL CENTER

New York, New York

The new Heart Center at New York–Presbyterian Hospital, with its
165,000 sq. ft. (40,000 sq. ft. of which is renovated space), was an "intervention" designed by Pei Cobb Freed & Partners Architects in the existing hospital complex, aimed at expanding the hospital's cardiology department. "The
most prominent architectural feature of the new building— a multilayered, curved glass wall—not only acts as a counterpoint to the existing masonry buildings but also serves," says Pei Cobb Freed, "to express the vitality and dynamism of the rapidly changing medical community."

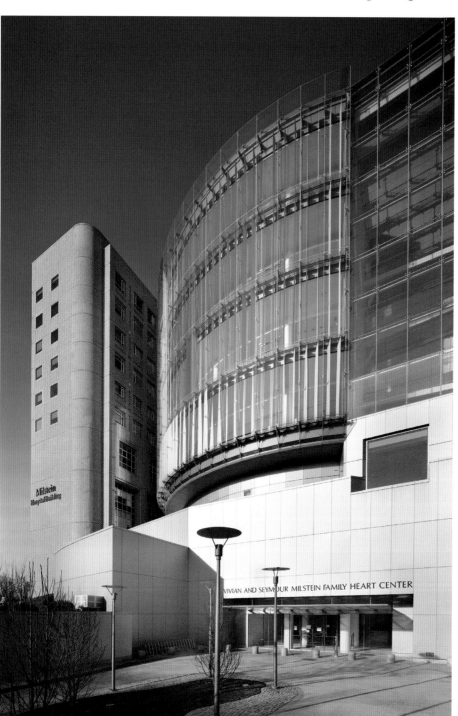

The architects inserted the new six-level facility between the hospital's two existing buildings, both of them substantial structures in their own right. The new hospital is connected to the existing buildings on multiple levels, facilitating continuity of medical departments and functional synergies.

The seating areas behind the glass wall offer spectacular views of the Henry Hudson River and New Jersey Palisades. The double-glass construction allows for energy efficiency and visual transparency. Electronically controlled vertical shades track the movement of the sun, maintain a comfortable interior temperature, and provide a constantly changing façade to the exterior. At night, interior lighting refracts through the glass envelope, which is suspended from the uppermost floor by stainless steel cables.

The vertical organization of the facility shows clearly

through a four-story atrium, which allows natural light inside and helps emphasize what the architect dubs the "spatial generosity" of the building. The entrance and vehicular drop-off lies on 165th Street, where a landscaped arrival court under a sheltering glass canopy welcomes patients and visitors.

The facility provides a full range of medical services, including diagnostics, ambulatory surgery, cardiac catheterization and electrophysiology, vascular ultrasound, medical practice suites, critical-care units, and an education and conference center.

Vivian and Seymour Milstein Family Heart Center, New York–Presbyterian Hospital/Columbia University Medical Center, New York, New York. The heart center's spectacular atrium comes courtesy of its multilayered, curved glass wall, which serves as a counterpoint to the existing masonry buildings of the hospital and helps make the design open and dynamic. *Courtesy Pei Cobb Freed & Partners Architects LLP. Photo Paul Warchol Photography, Inc.*

El Camino Hospital, Mountain View, California. KMD Architects designed a wing of the hospital to retrofit or replace an older facility to meet higher seismic standards by 2013. Otherwise the facility would, by law, have lost its acute-care status. *Courtesy KMD Architects. Photo © 2010 Michael O'Callahan.*

EL CAMINO HOSPITAL
Mountain View, California

Driven by U.S. Senate Bill 1953, the 1994 amendment to the Seismic Safety Act, El Camino Hospital in Mountain View—some forty miles north of San Francisco—developed with architect KMD a comprehensive plan for a structure that not only surpassed the new requirements but also provided state-of-the-art care. The language of the law, now also included in the California Health and Safety Code, requires that buildings considered hazardous or at risk of collapse or significant loss of life in the event of an earthquake be replaced or retrofitted to higher seismic standards by 2013 or lose their acute-care services. So, in response, El Camino renovated some 105,000 sq. ft. of the original structure and added a new, 460,000-sq.-ft. general acute-care hospital.

The new facility's key components include a sixteen-room integrated surgical and intervention platform, a multitrack emergency department, and flexible nursing modules that offer 28 critical care and 180 acuity adaptable beds. A large (22,000 sq. ft.) public mall marries the new hospital with existing buildings and helps clarify wayfinding. The mall—designed with idealized patients and staff in mind—houses retail shops and convenience services.

To help cut costs, the renovated space, now called the North Addition, consolidates outpatient services, expands the energy center of the old hospital and relocates the service docks. Overall, designers

organized the new hospital site to emphasize its front door, which simplifies access to the hospital's services and improves crowd circulation
throughout the building. The new entrance mall also allows for future
development of medical offices, staff and patient family housing, and additional structured parking.

Importantly, the planning effort itself included a community relations
track and allowed for working closely with state and local authorities, a key
to facilitating the approval process under the updated seismic compliance
regulations.

*El Camino Hospital, Mountain View,
California. The light-filled, spacious
renovation and replacement design
aimed at meeting new seismic requirements, simplified access to services,
and improved crowd circulation.
Courtesy KMD Architects. Photo
© 2010 Michael O'Callahan.*

PIEDMONT FAYETTE HOSPITAL

Fayetteville, Georgia

Early master planning for future expansion during ESa's design of the initial hospital allowed the expansion of Piedmont Fayette Hospital over eight years later (which—at 153,000 sq. ft.—more than doubled the existing space) to occur with minimal disruption to operational services.

The expansion's design needed to accommodate growth and to separate the inpatient and outpatient entries, yet still to maintain a connection between the two. ESa accomplished this with an extension of the existing pedestrian mall leading from the original entry (now used for inpatients) to connect seamlessly to the new outpatient entry. The expansion includes a new outpatient entry and lobby; spaces for a new women's obstetrics program; the relocation and creation of new and enlarged dietary and dining spaces to allow imaging, diagnostics, and

Piedmont Fayette Hospital, Fayetteville, Georgia. This expansion included a new women's health center of excellence on the third floor. *Photo © Rion Rizzo/Creative Sources.*

pre-admission testing to expand into the former dietary areas; and the relocation of the intensive care unit with the emergency department expanding into the former ICU space.

With the expansion also came the establishment of two new centers of excellence with all related services aligned and on one floor: coronary care on the second floor and women's health on the third. In an additional phase, more floors were added to allow for increasing the number of private patient rooms.

Piedmont Fayette Hospital, Fayetteville, Georgia. Brick on the dining walls establishes a seamless transition to the brick exterior in the two-story atrium. *Photo © Rion Rizzo/Creative Sources.*

WING MEMORIAL HOSPITAL AND MEDICAL CENTERS
SURGICAL CENTER AND BED TOWER
Palmer, Massachusetts

Built in the late 1940s, the aging Wing Memorial Hospital, near Springfield, Massachusetts, badly needed updating, but the old building—with its constricted interior heights and narrow floor plates—made major mechanical and electrical retrofits difficult and costly, hampered the crucially needed changes, and precluded the hospital's ability to deliver state-of-the-art healthcare.

Wing Memorial Hospital and Medical Centers, Surgical Center and Bed Tower, Palmer, Massachusetts. Designer Payette's commitment to natural light and exterior views for the renovation is evident in the new entrance lobby. *Courtesy Payette. Photo © Warren Jagger Photography.*

To address the problem, Wing Memorial came up with a master plan that called for constructing a new addition to house several major clinical programs relocated from the existing hospital. Architects at Payette saw this as the necessary first step of the eventual outward migration of all the key clinical programs from the old hospital to a new facility. Meanwhile, the existing infrastructure would be confined to primary care clinics and support services for the building.

The first floor of the 60,000-sq.-ft. addition includes a surgical suite comprising three operating rooms, ancillary support, two endoscopy and minor procedure rooms, and a sixteen-bay preoperative unit. The second floor houses forty medical or surgical beds and six critical unit beds. Although budgetary constraints limited the facility to eighteen private and eleven semi-private rooms, the arrangement actually proves well suited to the facility's elderly patient population. The desire to provide natural light and exterior views in large part dictated the arrangement of the inpatient rooms.

Wing Memorial also felt it important for the renovation to maintain a clear connection to the hospital's existing central corridor because it was key to the circulation scheme of the entire building. When the new design introduced a significant grade change between the hospital and the access road, designers found it necessary to create the new entry level 14 ft. below the first floor of the existing hospital. This entry accommodates vehicle drop-offs outside the new lobby and registration area. Designers then added a secondary entrance on the hospital's first floor, adjacent to an enlarged parking lot on the same grade.

The new addition also made it necessary for the hospital to relocate its helipad, which allows for a more convenient placement on a direct path to the existing hospital's emergency department.

Wing Memorial Hospital and Medical Centers, Surgical Center and Bed Tower, Palmer, Massachusetts. Designer Payette's plan called for constructing a new addition to house several major clinical programs relocated from the existing hospital. *Courtesy Payette. Photo © Warren Jagger Photography.*

Kettering Medical Center-Sycamore Hospital Addition and Physician Office Building, Miamisburg, Ohio. LWC Incorporated's redesign of the addition offers a more welcoming entrance to the hospital. *Courtesy LWC Incorporated. Photo Ken Schory, Springboro, Ohio.*

In general, the architects wanted to make sure the building's geometry and form reflected the network of pedestrian paths that surrounded the building and that the landscaping reinforced a connection between the building's interior program and existing site features. In short, they sought what they called "a dialog of materiality" between the look of the building and its surroundings.

KETTERING MEDICAL CENTER–SYCAMORE HOSPITAL ADDITION AND PHYSICIAN OFFICE BUILDING
Miamisburg, Ohio

This forty-year-old hospital had begun to have image problems associated with the institutional aesthetic of a by-gone era in hospital design. For the architects, the renovation offered two challenges. One was to establish a new image for the place, what nowadays marketing specialists call rebranding. The other was to create a facility that better served patients. Both would make the hospital more appealing to potential patients and to the surrounding community.

The design that LWC Incorporated created offers a more welcoming entrance to the hospital and a new physician office building. These renovations provide a better customer service experience for patients and their families, and they establish a new brand for the hospital within its service area. The facility's patient-focused design highlights include an open and

inviting lobby area, a one-stop center for preadmission testing and registra- tion, a blood-drawing area, a gift shop, a pharmacy and food service, physician office space, and an entrance and parking sited specifically for convenience.

These updates and makeovers were enhanced by new landscaping and an entry canopy that invites natural light and a breath of the outside into the hospi- tal, making the lobby not only a calm and serene area but also an aide to uncom- plicated wayfinding. The 70,000 sq. ft. of the new lobby, and the 80,000 sq. ft. of the new office building add not only space, but an appealing architectural state- ment to the hospital that help negate its tired, out-of-date look.

Kettering Medical Center-Sycamore Hospital Addition and Physician Office Building, Miamisburg, Ohio. This open and inviting lobby is one of the highlights of the LWC Incorporated patient-focused design of the addition. *Courtesy LWC Incorporated. Photo Ken Schory, Springboro, Ohio.*

FRANCES WILLIAMS PRESTON BUILDING
VANDERBILT–INGRAM CANCER CENTER
Nashville, Tennessee

Named for the former CEO and president of Broadcast Music Inc., this six-story addition creates a new front door for the Vanderbilt–Ingram Cancer Center and Vanderbilt's Medical Research Building II. The striking curved glass façade brings natural light into the new wraparound expansion at the front of the original building.

Noteworthy here, because the project was driven by the program need for a prominent entrance and by the existing buildings and materials, the new facility introduces an updated, contemporary design compatible with that space. To maintain consistency with the exterior colors and building

Frances Williams Preston Building, Vanderbilt-Ingram Cancer Center, Nashville, Tennessee. The lobby of the new six-story addition to the center, which was named for the former CEO of BMI (Broadcast Music, Inc.), Frances Williams Preston. *Photo Scott McDonald © Hedrich Blessing.*

materials of the existing building (and with the rest of the structures on the Vanderbilt University campus), ESa carefully matched the red brick, glass, and precast elements.

In scope, the expansion includes a two-story lobby level, a second-floor core connection to the existing plaza, new office space on floors three through seven, and primarily conference space on the eighth floor, for a total of 52,000 sq. ft.

The extant brick-covered, concrete columns on the building's exterior, which are massive in size, became interior elements covered in a cherry wood veneer after the brick was removed.

KAISER PERMANENTE TEMPLATE HOSPITALS
Antioch, California
Modesto, California
Irvine, California

A few years back, Kaiser Permanente faced a situation familiar to many a healthcare provider and hospital administrator in the United States. Growing demands from patients, an increasingly complex regulatory environment, and escalating construction costs combined to complicate the organization's plans to develop twenty new or replacement hospitals in the ten years Kaiser had given itself to satisfy its rapidly growing membership. Faced with this daunting challenge, the architect SmithGroup and the Canadian project management firm Stantec joined Kaiser strategists, California state regulators, and local contractors to devise the Kaiser Template Hospital, a pioneering design for multiple hospitals identical in planning yet fully adaptable to different locations.

Kaiser Permanente used the template hospital design to collect expert advice from professionals both inside and outside the organization, and thus the process took on a collaborative, thinktank atmosphere as Kaiser included not only architects, engineers, and contractors, but also all hospital constituents—physicians, clinical staff, and administration—from the very beginning. For decades, ESa has called this kind of approach Synergenial. As Kaiser employed

Kaiser Permanente Template Hospitals, Antioch, Modesto, and Irvine, California. Designed by SmithGroup, this entrance to the Antioch facility reflects the pioneering effort to design for multiple hospitals identical in planning yet fully adapted to their locations. *Courtesy SmithGroup. Photo Robert Canfield Photography.*

Kaiser Permanente Template Hospitals, Antioch, Modesto, and Irvine, California. This side view of the Irvine facility shows just how flexible SmithGroup's template design could be when compared to the exterior of, say, the Antioch facility. *Courtesy SmithGroup. Photo Robert Canfield Photography.*

this special kind of team effort, it helped define the best operational practices and departmental relationships within the hospital. Based on these practices and relationships, the template was designed to outline common structural and building systems, planning concepts, floor plans, equipment and furnishings, and construction techniques, all adaptable to a range of different sites.

Designed to accommodate from 174 to 270 beds in structures ranging in size from 340,000 to 430,000 sq. ft., template hospitals include attached ambulatory surgery centers and medical office buildings. Given their high level of built-in flexibility, these facilities easily accommodate future expansions and unforeseen but needed changes. Their uniform design is critical to managing and adapting to changing technology and developments in the best practices of care throughout the Kaiser organization, all aimed ultimately at improving patient care and reducing medical errors.

Kaiser's chief concern was to create a comfortable, convenient environment for patients. The wayfinding of template hospitals is organized around their central spines, which are filled with natural light. Daylight enters all the buildings, regardless of any one building's orientation, through windows, glass-walled walkways, and interior courtyards with landscaped foliage, gardens, and dining terraces. Their nursing towers are configured in a triangle, with a single entrance to the units and decentralized nurses' stations wrapping the cores. Patient rooms are arranged around centralized work spaces. These configurations, with vertical service connections to other floors, allow for simple staff connections among the units and offer nurses quick and easy access to patients, records, and supplies. Patient rooms include areas for family and visitors, as well as convertible furniture for overnight guests.

Of the three template hospitals showcased here, Kaiser's Antioch Hospital, near San Francisco, was the baseline four-story template. It was designed with one-half of a nursing floor as shell space for future growth of beds. The Sand Canyon Hospital in Irvine, California, has a six-story nursing tower configuration with the upper two and one-half floors of the nursing tower developed as shell space for future growth of beds and other functions. The Modesto hospital has a five-story nursing configuration with the upper one and one-half floors of the nursing tower left as shell space for future bed growth.

Kaiser's template approach to hospital development offers a tactical response to the challenges of delivering healthcare today. The template significantly reduces the cost and time to design and construct individual facilities while ensuring a universal standard of care throughout the hospitals, improving patient safety and helping to ensure a healing environment.

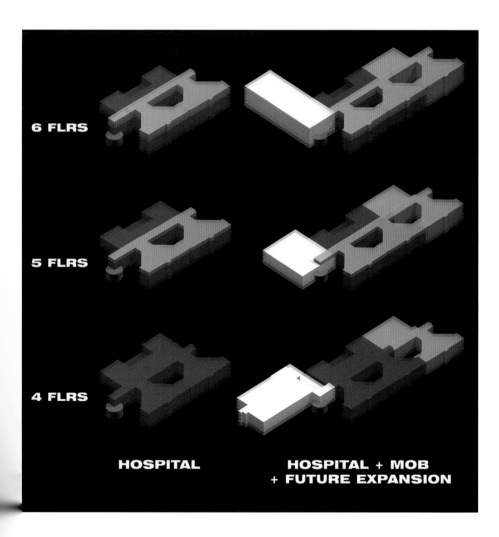

6 FLRS

5 FLRS

4 FLRS

HOSPITAL

HOSPITAL + MOB
+ FUTURE EXPANSION

Kaiser Permanente Template Hospitals, Antioch, Modesto, and Irvine, California. Diagram. *Courtesy SmithGroup. Photo Robert Canfield Photography.*

CHAPTER 5

The Emergency Unit

ccording to recent reports from the Institute of Medicine, the nation's emergency care system remains at the breaking point. As early as 1989, an informal poll of the American College of Emergency Physicians and another by the Emergency Nurses Association had found overcrowding in hospital emergency departments to be a problem in every state in the nation. And the problem continued to grow. In a random survey of 836 emergency department (ED) directors published in the February 2001 issue of *Academic Emergency Medicine*, 91 percent of those responding from all fifty states reported overcrowding in every kind of hospital—public, private, academic, rural, urban—as a problem that occurred in 53 percent of the cases several times a week. Moreover, some 31 percent reported daily overcrowding. Indeed, McCraign and Burt reported in 2004 that not only did the number of patients visiting EDs increase by 23 percent between 1992 to 2002 but the number of hospital EDs declined during those same years by 15 percent.

To the casual observer, the emergency care crisis that began developing in the late 1980s and early 1990s was most obviously linked to violent crime, especially drug-related crime, in cities and suburbs (and even some rural areas). No doubt, the crack epidemic of the late twentieth century seriously strained EDs. But burgeoning violence and victims who could not pay for care were just part of the problem. For one, crime rates and drug use steadily declined after the mid-1990s with no concomitant drop in emergency room (ER) usage.

Instead, the hospital emergency department became a care provider of last resort—really, of only resort—for a large segment of the American population, which, uninsured or underinsured, could not afford to pay for the

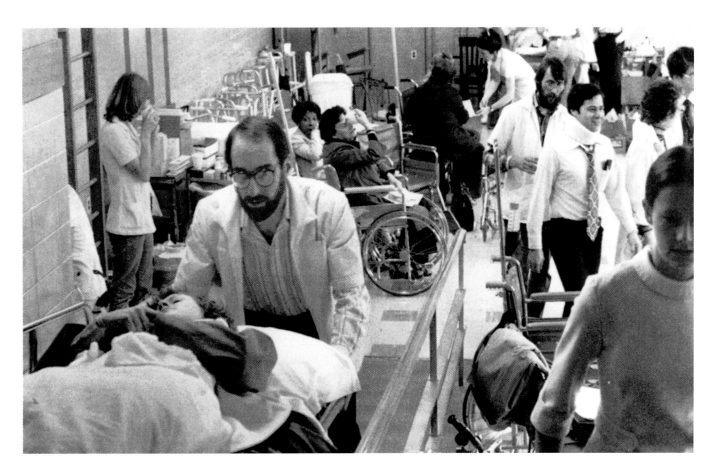

services of a family physician or alternative primary care providers such as ambulatory care centers. Although the overhaul of the U.S. healthcare insurance system will ultimately address the problem, EDs will remain on the frontline for some time.

In the early 1990s, many healthcare experts were struck by the evidence that overcrowding was primarily limited to teaching hospitals and inner-city facilities. That, too, has changed. Clearly, the overburdening of the emergency department has not been exclusively an urban crisis.

In fact, the Institute of Medicine identified five principal problems creating the crisis in the country's EDs: (1) the overcrowding due to a lack of medical insurance that sends too many people to the ED seeking primary care or after an untreated medical condition has become urgent; (2) the variation and fragmentation in service that results in many cities from poor coordination among emergency medical services agencies and EDs; (3) the shortage of on-call specialists resulting from the difficulty many hospitals experience in getting paid for ED services, added to the high risks and liability that many physicians and nurses assume when working on ED patients they don't know; (4) the lack of disaster preparedness that EDs, usually already operating beyond capacity, are ill-equipped to provide, especially since federal funding (hitherto at least)—even given homeland security—has been stingy; and (5) shortcomings in pediatric emergency care for children who make up 27 percent of all visits to the ED.

Despite the growing need for change, most EDs remain what they were originally designed to be: facilities to treat sudden life—or limb—threatening

The emergency room bustles with activity following a disaster. In addition to meeting the community's emergency-care needs, emergency departments have become overburdened by a large segment of the American population who use emergency rooms in place of family physicians or alternative primary-care facilities. *Courtesy CORBIS.*

117

illness and injury. They are not designed to meet the needs they are being asked to meet, treating nonurgent care and in some cases, serving as de facto clearing houses for hospital admissions.

We address all of these problems in this chapter.

New Directions

Numerous factors increase the risk of committing an error in the ED, and good designs should address such issues. Those recently identified by the Hospitals and Health Networks include overcrowding, which often means that patients leave without being seen; the several different doctors and nurses often involved in the care of a single patient; very ill or badly injured patients; barriers to communication; the use of multiple types of diagnostic and treatment technology; the severe shortage of healthcare workers; the already mentioned lack of an established, long-term relationship between ED providers and ED patients; the rapidly evolving nature of the healthcare field itself; the uncontrollable nature of workflow such as surges in patient visits or frequent distractions and interruptions; and the increasingly poor health—especially the growing number of those with chronic conditions—of the patients who use EDs.

In addressing many of these problems many experts in hospital architecture have lately turned to the lean design process—discussed in Chapter 3—aimed at producing designs to help the work done in a facility to flow better by studying the movements of patients and staff through such facilities, identifying essential tasks and eliminating unnecessary ones, reducing variations in the way work is conducted, and identifying and removing anything that hinders such work.

Typically patients entering the ED check in at a reception desk and, from there, they are called to a private nurse triage room. The goal is to get the patient into a treatment room as quickly as possible. The most serious cases arrive by ambulance, and ambulatory patients complaining of chest pain get an immediate electrocardiogram (EKG) and blood tests to determine their status. The architect or medical facilities planner looking at this situation readily arrives at design as a solution—the effective use of space aimed at facilitating triage and distinguishing between those patients who require emergency care and those who fall into the urgent and nonurgent categories. The ED crisis cannot be resolved by design measures alone, but lean operations and design efficiencies certainly can help.

Emergency departments are expensive to run, and realize little, if any, revenue, though a high percentage of admissions to a hospital in general, where treatment is more profitable, often comes through the emergency room. The community mission of the ED, as well as its revenue problems, can be improved by providing facilities that segregate emergency from nonemergency cases. The situation can be further improved by community-oriented hospital programs and facilities that emphasize prevention of disease and, especially, prevention of injury. Ultimately, healthcare reform that provides primary care for the millions who have been using EDs basically as a family doctor will, over time, also make a very real difference.

Some hospitals—faced with funding emergency departments that for now remain centers of deficit—may opt to do without trauma-oriented, dedicated emergency care facilities altogether. And those who are renovating existing structures may well convert the ED to some other use, such as ambulatory or primary care. But new hospitals may ask architects to design ambulatory care centers and primary care centers to compete with the free-standing ambulatory ("immediate") care centers currently popular in many parts of the country.

Historical Legacy of Managed Care

By the end of the twentieth century, it was clear that comprehensive health-care reform, which had seemed inevitable in the mid-1990s, was not going to become a reality any time soon. Thus, instead of some form of universal care as part of a total federal health reform package, which would probably have designated certain EDs as primary care providers for their communities and thus given emergency care official sanction, hospitals were faced with the cost-conscious minions of managed-care programs who wanted nothing so much as to drastically reduce expensive trips to the emergency room and discourage use of the ED as a primary care provider. But despite every roadblock the HMOs could erect, including gatekeepers ever mindful of patient "abuse" of the ED, emergency rooms continued to overflow with patients suffering from less-than-life-threatening traumas.

Part of the problem was that the shortage of primary healthcare providers in many communities continued to prevent EDs from totally segregating emergency and primary care functions. Part of it was that their very efforts at cost containment prompted many providers to negotiate with EDs to provide after-hours care. And part of the problem, as we have already discussed, was that millions remained outsiders to the health-insurance system; the poor, without insurance and without other means, really had nowhere else to go. They not only continued to use the emergency room as their doctor's office but increased their visits. Particularly in heavily populated urban areas, all these considerations lead to volume expansion in nonemergency care. Certainly in the current economic crisis, as states and localities continue to cut funding for social services, ED volume will increase in such areas as acute infection, psychiatric disorders, and conditions related to social distress (chiefly homelessness).

For hospitals providing emergency services, it is and will continue to be essential to adequately fund forward-looking design and building of the ED to promote quality, productivity, flexibility, and safety, to make sure—as the lean process holds—unnecessary work is avoided, more work can be done in less time, and better work accomplished with less effort. The design strategies we outline next are intended to suggest ways in which ED operations can be made more cost-efficient and can even be made to generate revenue, particularly from nonemergency care.

When designing EDs, the following issues must be considered:
- Helicopter access
- Triage
- Waiting area
- Treatment spaces
- Staff and support spaces
- Accommodation of data and diagnostic technologies
- Flexible design for flexible response
- Specialty emergency treatment provisions (epidemics, floods, terrorist attacks, etc.)
- Security
- Convenient parking
- Prominent signage and entryways

Helicopter Access

Virtually all hospitals with emergency facilities should plan for helicopter access. In the case of EDs that handle significant volumes of helicopter-ambulance traffic, the landing facility should be located to provide direct access to the ED. In large hospitals that customarily receive patients by helicopter, the landing area may be positioned to share access among the ED and other departments (such as pediatrics, a burn unit, and so on). Urban campuses, likely to be surrounded by tall structures, make for tricky flight conditions and—like all helicopter landing facilities—must coordinate with the Federal Aviation Authority to determine the safest flight path into the heliport. EDs in smaller hospitals also benefit from a strategically placed helicopter landing pad for rapid transfer of patients whose condition requires the advanced facilities of a larger medical center. The complexity of the landing pad design depends on the amount of anticipated usage. In remote areas, an airstrip for fixed-wing aircraft may be part of the ED's system of access.

Triage

One of the realities hospitals must face is that, for many patients, the emergency room is the "front door" to the facility. Unfortunately, in traditional EDs, the triage is rudimentary, and ad hoc. Careful planning of this area allows for quicker assessment and treatment of dire emergencies.

Additional Access Considerations

Because it is essential to make entry crystal-clear, design should include prominent highway or street signage and bold, lighted departmental entry signage. The walk-in and ambulance entrances should be covered, and, for large facilities, a garage-type ambulance entrance should be considered.

Special parking facilities are essential to access and to promoting the ambulatory and primary care functions of the department. Traffic patterns must not conflict with driveways for emergency vehicles; and parking spaces for patients, ED staff, and law enforcement officers should be very clearly designated. It is important that there be no confusion concerning the location of the ED parking area.

The same clarity should carry over seamlessly into the entrance and reception area, with a clearly marked and strategically positioned reception desk and a triage area adjacent to it. It is advisable to position the security office so that security personnel can readily monitor the reception area. (Security is discussed in greater detail below.)

The ambulance entrance must also be clearly and unmistakably marked, and a nurses' station should be included at the entrance, with an ample alcove for stretchers, gurneys, and wheelchairs, so that these may be kept clear of the entrance. It is essential to equip the ambulance entry area with automatic sliding doors, as opposed to manually operated swinging doors. Care should be taken to prevent walk-ins from using the ambulance or trauma entry in lieu of the walk-in entry. This can be achieved architecturally by plantings, by the use of berms, and by other measures. Clear designation of parking areas also helps separate trauma from walk-in entry.

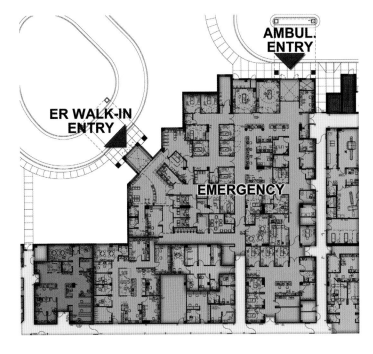

An emergency department floor plan created by Earl Swensson Associates.

Waiting Area

One measure of the success of an ED is how little the waiting area is used. The object is to make an ambulatory patient's stay in this area as brief as possible. Still, even in the most efficient emergency facility, the waiting area is a very important element that, traditionally, has been slighted or treated as an afterthought.

The waiting area communicates very powerful nonverbal messages. If the ED is a hospital's alternative entrance, the ED waiting area is, in large measure, the place where patients form their first impressions about the hospital as a whole. Old-paradigm design treated the waiting area as a space-consuming necessary evil. New-paradigm, patient-centered design regards it as an opportunity to express concern for the patient's comfort. It is important to ensure that an adequate amount of seating is provided. Calculations of the necessary seating should assume that each patient is accompanied by a friend or relative. Colors should be cheerful, with an emphasis on timeless rather than trendy hues. Furniture should, of course, be comfortable. Modular seating groups are available that approximate a soft, residential appearance, yet provide durability, including changeable upholstery covers. The anti-institutional, patient-oriented image of the facility can be further enhanced by individual chairs arranged in attractive groups rather than in bus station–style rows. If possible, a certain number of high-backed chairs should be reserved for geriatric patients, who may have difficulty sitting and rising, and bariatric accommodations should be provided.

Next to adequate and comfortable seating, the right lighting is critical. If possible, a combination of overhead, recessed, and indirect lighting is desirable to enliven and humanize what might otherwise be a threatening institutional space. Table lamps secured on coffee tables or side tables add a residential feeling. The coffee tables should not have decorative reveals, which could act as containment areas for spilled liquids and blood. If possible, natural light—especially from windows with a pleasant view—should be fully exploited. If artwork is used to decorate walls, track-lighting spotlights can highlight it. Such lighting might also be used to illuminate wall-mounted magazine racks.

Just as natural lighting has a soothing effect by allowing the patient to make contact with the outdoors, so well-kept and attractive plants help to maintain a sense of the presence of the familiar, pleasurable natural world. Televisions should be placed in a corner or alcove where they will not disturb patients who desire quiet but can—along with other sources of positive distraction—assist patients and families in coping with stress.

Carpeting is a very controversial feature in some new ED waiting areas. It has the advantages of lending a feeling of warmth to the area, greatly reducing noise, and reducing the chance of accidental slipping and falling. Products should be durable, and antimicrobial treatments of them inhibit growth of microorganisms, including those that cause infection, create odors, or provoke allergic reactions. A level loop pile is most appropriate in a heavily trafficked waiting area and will not pose an obstacle to wheelchair maneuvering. It is this latter consideration that must be most carefully thought out before installing carpet. The higher-pile carpets should be avoided, because they can make maneuvering wheelchairs difficult. Alternatives to carpeting include attractively patterned vinyl tile and tile with border designs.

The waiting area should have ample trash receptacles and vending machines; it is preferable that the latter be assigned to a dedicated space or alcove to be to sensitive patients who cannot eat or drink or who experience nausea. Waiting-area amenities include access to an adequate number of public telephones and restrooms and a coat-hanging area. In situations where theft may be a problem, small lockers can be provided. The waiting area should be in full view of the reception desk, and in the children's waiting area, a play area should be designated. If a play area is included, provision should be made for adult supervision, either by hospital volunteers or family members.

Treatment Spaces

Treatment spaces can be trauma rooms, general examination rooms, and specialized rooms. The trend these days, however, is toward "universal" rooms in EDs, with perhaps a few specialized rooms.

The following treatment spaces should be available in all EDs, if possible. However, smaller EDs may not include all these spaces (refer to the Facility Guidelines Institute's latest *Guidelines for Design and Construction of Health Care Facilities* for specific requirements):
- Triage area
- Trauma/resuscitation room(s)

- Bariatric treatment room(s)
- Urgent and nonurgent examination/treatment room(s)
- Suture/minor treatment room(s)
- Quiet room(s)
- Secure holding room(s) for psychiatric emergencies
- Pediatric examination/treatment room(s)
- OB/GYN room(s)
- Eye examination room(s)
- Cast/orthopedic room(s)
- Decontamination room(s)
- Observation room(s)
- Chest-pain observation room(s)
- Fast-track room(s) (for primary care: sore throats, minor injuries, etc.)
- Emergency dental treatment room(s)
- Airborne infection isolation room(s)

Of the treatment spaces listed, observation rooms are the most controversial. Some authorities believe that these rooms are not only a waste of space but also promote the holding of patients unnecessarily, while others believe observation rooms are a valuable component of any ED.

Special design consideration must be given to decontamination rooms, whose drainage systems and sewer connections must be designed specifically to handle hazardous material. Usually a holding tank system must be included in the design to collect hazardous waste for safe disposal later. Provisions should be made for handling biological and radioactive hazards, and the decontamination room should also have an independent, filtered ventilation and exhaust system.

Depending on the size of the hospital and the ED, diagnostic, laboratory, and medication facilities may be fully shared with other departments or may, in varying degrees, be available within the ED. The trend is to include at least diagnostic imaging facilities adjacent to the department and perhaps a stat laboratory as well as a modest pharmacy. In the absence of a departmental laboratory or pharmacy, a fast, efficient transport (pneumatic tube system) and data communication system must be in place (we discuss this in detail shortly), along with design provisions to accommodate major diagnostic and other equipment. However, even in emergency departments where the inclusion of major diagnostic hardware is not anticipated, adequate space, electrical, and data transmission provisions need to be made for the bedside telemetry and diagnostic equipment presently available and for emerging remote telemetry technologies. All treatment rooms should be designed with sufficient space to accommodate computers.

Additional examination rooms may be required in emergency departments that are offering fast-track care: quick service for uncomplicated, nonurgent cases. Some emergency departments also dedicate a portion of their facility to industrial medicine, perhaps serving a local employer. In addition to the treatment spaces, provision must be made for nurses' stations and workstations.

Staff and Support Spaces

The basic staff and support areas required for virtually any ED include the following:

- Registration/admissions
- Grief counselors/bereavement room
- Physicians' offices
- Nurse manager's office
- Security station/office
- On-call room (with toilet and shower adjacent)
- Patient restrooms
- Staff restrooms/lockers/showers
- Staff lounge
- Physician/family consultation room
- Staff conference room
- Communications/disaster coordination room
- Physician dictation/computer workstation
- Chart/record room
- Patient tub/shower
- Soiled workroom or soiled holding room
- Stretcher/wheelchair storage
- Clean workroom or clean supply room
- EMS communications center
- Equipment and supply storage
- Pharmacy/medication area
- Biohazard waste-holding (red bags)
- Environmental services (housekeeping) room
- Communications/electrical equipment rooms

In planning EDs flexible enough to accommodate the current state-of-the-art and evolving technologies, support areas should be designed with telecommunication and data processing transfer requirements in mind. It is also important to approach such staff areas as lounges and conference rooms with the same humanity that is devoted to creating pleasant patient waiting areas. A quiet, restful oasis is crucial to maintaining staff morale and contributes greatly to staff performance and retention. Note that the staff conference room can be designed with sufficient flexibility to double as a disaster services coordination area.

Accommodation of Data and Diagnostic Technologies

Many EDs include imaging equipment within the department. Proper shielding and reinforcement must be integrated into the design to accommodate this equipment. In smaller facilities, the ED may share imaging equipment with another department, in which case it is very desirable to locate the ED adjacent to Imaging.

Over the last half century, as new imaging technologies superseded X-rays as diagnostic tools, some—because of their size—are currently inappropriate for most ED situations, but even CT scanners and MRIs can be incorporated in some settings where diagnostic services are offered on an outpatient basis. In all such cases, usage should be weighed against the cost of duplicating the equipment and staff of other departments.

Ultra-Fast CT, for example, is easily installed and well suited to the outpatient setting, and therefore to the ED. Likewise, ultrasound technology has many emergency applications, and the equipment is sufficiently portable as to require little in the way of special design considerations.

The Picture Archiving and Communication System (PACS)

St. Vincent's South Tower, Birmingham, Alabama. A healing, embracing environment becomes evident upon entering the emergency department. *Photo © Kieran Reynolds Photography.*

digitizes, archives, and transmits medical imaging data. It plays a large role not only in the ED but throughout the hospital. These days imaging equipment uses directly digitized images rather than photographic film, and such images can be instantly transmitted electronically to specialists elsewhere in the hospital or at another institution for instant consultation.

It is difficult to predict whether emerging technologies will make obsolete the design demands of large imaging, CT scanning, and MRI installations. While whole-body, real-time imaging devices may become very large, it is more likely that equipment suitable to an emergency setting will become smaller and more portable. In ED design, then, it is best to provide mechanical and electrical flexibility and to provide space, with the appropriate data and electrical connections, for computers and other equipment, preferably in each treatment room. Today and for the immediate future, the standard bedside requirements for ED treatment rooms include the following:

- Oxygen
- Compressed air
- Vacuum system
- Nurse call system
- Emergency call system
- Direct (work) and indirect lighting fixtures
- Storage space for airway and suction equipment
- Bedside work space and countertop
- Computer space with electrical and network/data transmission connections
- Monitoring equipment space with electrical and data transmission connections
- Portable monitoring

- Electrical outlets, including those required for computer access, plu[s] 220-volt access
- Emergency generator access
- Closed storage space
- Trash and sharps containers
- Oto/ophthalmoscope (mounted or portable)
- Ceiling track IV (larger treatment room)
- Hand-washing station
- Exam light

Flexible Design for Flexible Response

A design may be flexible in two ways: it may either allow for ease o[f] expansion, alteration, and renovation; or it may allow for varied use as condi[-]tions demand. In the design examples discussed in this chapter we have see[n] some instances of both types of flexibility. Flexibility has become of increas[-]ing importance in ED design.

Designers will be asked to create EDs in which the proportion of emer[-]gency versus urgent versus nonurgent patient care can be readily and easil[y] varied. In some settings, the ED may be designed chiefly as an ambulator[y] primary care center with a relatively small emergency area located near area[s] that can be readily transformed into additional emergency areas in times o[f] high demand, mass accident, natural disaster, or terrorist attack. Added flex[-]ibility can be achieved by designs that provide for "special care" beds adjacen[t] to the ED to expedite patient flow. These beds may also serve as a recover[y] area when the ED is adjacent to ambulatory surgery.

Strategies for reducing patient transportation are among the leadin[g] motifs of advanced hospital design. Thus, where possible, imaging equipmen[t] should be available in the ED itself. It is preferable not to have to transpor[t] the patient to radiology. Future EDs may feature large critical-care rooms tha[t] transform into an imaging suite without having to move the patient at all[.] Portable walls could open up to accommodate a crash team, and the roo[m] could also serve as a limited operating theater by means of a mechanical sys[-]tem that provides for the correct air exchange and sterile conditions.

Such strategies take the emergency-department-as-front-door concep[t] to the extreme of becoming a "front door" that does not so much admit th[e] patient into the hospital as admit the hospital to the patient.

Specialty Emergency Treatment Areas

Old-paradigm hospital administrators had to decide how extensive a[n] emergency department to design. New-paradigm hospital administrator[s] make the decision in relation to provisions for ambulatory primary care[,] which, for the vast majority of hospitals, is becoming an important mean[s] of generating revenue. One issue that designers must resolve is the degre[e] of specialization the ED, as opposed to a separate ambulatory care facility[,] requires. This issue aside, the trend in larger EDs is toward incorporatin[g] specialized treatment rooms into the facility's design or even providing indi[-]vidual, specialized emergency facilities.

The pediatric ED is the most common specialized ED. Its treatment areas have many of the same characteristics of adult EDs practicing family-centered care, but equipment is specific to pediatric applications. Pediatric EDs present opportunities for imaginative design, decoration, and positive distractions. Individual seating is not necessary in waiting areas, and continuous seating (common seat and back) for parents saves room to create a play area for children. Carpeting is an excellent floor covering choice for the children's waiting area. Toys and television may be provided; it is also a good idea to decorate an area with children's artwork. This establishes an emotionally reassuring bond between present visitors to the pediatric ED and other children who have been there before. With pediatric EDs, it is especially important to pay attention to the trend toward family-centered care addressed specifically in Chapters 8, 9, and 13.

Other specialty services within general EDs include cardiac, ophthalmic, ear-nose-throat (ENT), OB/GYN, and psychiatric rooms. Ophthalmic and ENT rooms require special chairs, lights, and other equipment. OB/GYN facilities should communicate directly with the hospital's inpatient OB/GYN department. Psychiatric emergency facilities require special security rooms, as well as rooms that are quiet and relatively isolated from other patients—particularly critically ill or injured patients, whose presence may aggravate emotional distress.

Security

Security is an issue of sharply increasing concern in EDs. Psychiatric emergencies have always presented special security problems; violent patients must be prevented from hurting themselves and others. However, EDs are also vulnerable to criminal violence from two main sources: substance abusers in search of narcotics and gang members seeking revenge on rivals who are being treated. Today, of course, there is the added worry of a terrorist attack.

Ideally, the ED—as a hospital's alternative "front door"—should be a place of welcome, offering the promise of care, comfort, aid, and solace. The reality is that contemporary ED design must provide for adequate security. A security office should be located adjacent to the reception desk and should command an overall view of the principal ambulatory entrance and nearby parking areas. More remote areas of the ED, including the ambulance entrance area, should be monitored in the security office by strategically positioned closed-circuit television cameras. The pharmacy or medication room, which should be equipped with appropriate locks, should be alarmed and monitored by closed-circuit television. The secure pharmacy area might be accessed by electronic combination or magnetic-stripe card locks, and each entry should be recorded by computer, along with the name or code of the person accessing the room.

If security facilities are designed as integral elements of the ED, they will do little to defeat the user-friendly image of the department. Indeed, they may add to the patients' sense of well-being, of having placed themselves in the capable hands of those concerned for their welfare and safety. Given an ED's necessarily exposed location, the security presence—as part of a deliberate design strategy—also improves staff morale and promotes retention of skilled personnel.

MEADOWS REGIONAL MEDICAL CENTER
Vidalia, Georgia

Meadows Regional Medical Center (MRMC) is a new sixty-five-bed acute-care replacement hospital that includes thirty-two medical/surgical beds, eight ICU/CCU rooms, twelve progressive care rooms, seven labor-delivery-recovery rooms, six antepartum/postpartum rooms, a nursery, six operating rooms, six postanesthesia care units, two endoscopy/minor procedure rooms, a central registration area, diagnostic imaging facilities, cardiac catheterization labs, a laboratory, an outpatient infusion center, expanded cardiopulmonary testing and treatment areas, and an ED with twenty treatment rooms.

Designed by ESa, MRMC incorporated lean principles into its existing ED. With the help of Georgia Tech's Enterprise Innovation Institute, the hospital reduced the times needed for admitting and treating patients and for discharging noncritical ED patients. These changes include standardizing mobile supply stations; labeling racks, trays, and drawers; installing a colored-flag system outside patient rooms; issuing patients red allergy armbands to alert medical staff; and adding patient holding areas for those who need to see a doctor but don't require a room. Already a part of MRMC's existing ED, these lean concepts molded the design for the ED at the new facility.

In all, the designers were careful to minimize any barriers to the facility's ability to provide convenient and efficient patient care.

TOP LEFT Meadows Regional Medical Center, Vidalia, Georgia. The exterior of the acute-care replacement hospital, designed by Earl Swensson Associates. *Photo © Kyle Dreier Photography.*

BOTTOM LEFT Meadows Regional Medical Center, Vidalia, Georgia. The dining area. *Photo © Kyle Dreier Photography.*

LEFT New Pavilion at Paoli Hospital, Emergency Unit, Paoli, Pennsylvania. The new emergency department, with its private rooms and four evaluation stations, can handle 45,000 patients annually. *Courtesy EwingCole. Photo Matt Wargo.*

BELOW New Pavilion at Paoli Hospital, Emergency Unit, Paoli, Pennsylvania. The new emergency department, almost double the size of the old one, is located on the ground floor of an expansion of the hospital. *Courtesy EwingCole. Photo Matt Wargo.*

NEW PAVILION AT PAOLI HOSPITAL EMERGENCY UNIT

Paoli, Pennsylvania

When rapid growth in the Philadelphia-area communities surrounding Paoli Hospital led administrators to almost double the size of facility to half a million sq. ft., it was the largest expansion in the hospital's history. Architect Ewing Cole used the opportunity to design an ED for the new pavilion that is four times the size of the hospital's original emergency unit and built according to the tenets of evidence-based design to foster the best possible emergency care in a convenient, supportive environment.

Located on the ground floor, the new ED, with its private treatment rooms, is ready to handle 45,000 patients annually. Managing this high-volume traffic is critical, so the new ED houses four evaluation stations to enable more rapid patient assessment and includes a fast-track system to permit quicker treatment for patients with less serious conditions.

Advanced imaging equipment, including CT and MRI, are strategically located adjacent to the ED, and so is the hospital's new pharmacy, allowing patients to receive medications immediately. Comfortable seating options accommodate all guests, including bariatric patients and visitors. The new ED offers a separate play area for children and a lounge for emergency medical services personnel. The new ED's floor patterns assist in wayfinding, and the fabrics used in its furnishings contain biostats and moisture barriers to discourage bacterial growth.

METHODIST CHILDREN'S HOSPITAL OF SOUTH TEXAS

San Antonio, Texas

ESa designed an emergency department expansion—to 35,670 sq. ft.—to increase the capacity of the ED of the Methodist Children's Hospital from fifteen exam rooms to a total of thirty-two. The additional seventeen rooms include two new trauma rooms, pediatric psychiatric exam rooms, standard exam rooms, and triage positions.

One of the expansion's primary goals was to improve the functionality and visibility for the nursing staff. A new central nurses' station allows easy access to the exam rooms and provides much-needed support space. The project's scope also encompassed the creation of a new Children's Hospital entry. The site and topography made it necessary for the hospital and its emergency department to share the same drop-off point and two-story lobby. A low dividing wall separates the emergency function from the main Children's Hospital lobby, even as the design still allows natural light from the full-height curtain wall to flood in. The "Kid's Express," a pre-admittance function for the hospital, can be accessed from both sides of the wall. Parking is connected to the main entry by a monumental exterior staircase, highlighted with color-changing LED lighting to make wayfinding easier.

Another goal of the project's expansion/renovation design was to create ease for the ultimate build-out of approximately forty-two exam positions. The structure is designed to accommodate nine future floors that will connect to the Children's Hospital for additional pediatric beds and hospital services.

TENNITY EMERGENCY DEPARTMENT AT
EISENHOWER MEDICAL CENTER
Rancho Mirage, California

Hoping to change the way traditional hospitals sometimes added to the stress of those who, frantic and in pain, stumbled onto their emergency rooms seeking relief, Moon Mayoras Architects worked with interior design architects and art consultants at Jain Malkin Inc. and Syska Hennessy Group Inc. to create a cutting edge 40,000-sq.-ft. ED at the Eisenhower Medical Center in Southern California.

Entering the facility through a translucent glass vestibule, patients encounter a serene garden with flowing water, boulders, and a large, slowly rotating granite ball fountain. The designers placed seating in the ED in groupings, offering a range of choice and privacy. Instead of the typically blaring television, they included a large monitor that played a DVD of a coral

Tennity Emergency Department at Eisenhower Medical Center, Rancho Mirage, California. The designers placed the seating in groupings that offered a range of choice and privacy. *Courtesy Jain Malkin Inc. Photo Steve McClelland.*

reef. They located quiet areas adjacent to magazines and bookcases and provided lighting for reading. They created changing ceiling heights and varying soffits and light fixtures to offer variety in lighting levels and contribute to the overall mood and comfort of the space. The hand-blown glass art pieces, which they had glued into position within wall niches, became a part of the interior design.

The designers created nurses' stations that have a sculptural quality, which carries the design features of the lobby into the patient care areas. They employed the vibrant color palette and sweeping floor patterns and ceiling soffits along with artwork to establish clinical areas that are as interesting as the main lobby. The large backlit film images of nature they incorporated into the ceilings in treatment rooms are meant to reduce stress for both patients and family members. The finishes the designers used—such as patterned metal on the columns and wood-toned handrails—provide protection in a busy, fast-paced environment, as does the slate on floors and specific walls of the waiting area and triage. Used to great aesthetic effect, the metal and slate are also durable and easy to maintain.

The goal throughout was to ensure that the Tennity ED incorporated into its very interior design a healing environment that caught the eye, relaxed the soul, and comforted its users during what was bound to be an especially trying and stressful time.

Tennity Emergency Department at Eisenhower Medical Center, Rancho Mirage, California. The goal throughout the design was to incorporate into its interior design a healing environment that caught the eye of and relaxed and comforted its users. Courtesy Jain Malkin Inc. Photo Steve McClelland.

Tennity Emergency Department at Eisenhower Medical Center, Rancho Mirage, California. Upon entering, patients and their families encounter a serene garden with flowing water, boulders, and a large, slowly rotating granite ball fountain. Courtesy Jain Malkin Inc. Photo Steve McClelland.

RIVERSIDE REGIONAL MEDICAL CENTER

Newport News, Virginia

Built in 1963, the old Riverside Regional Medical Center, a 576-bed hospital, was badly in need of an image makeover. Its forty-year-old bed tower was to remain in place, but its aluminum curtain wall called for a major upgrade, not just because of its dated institutional appearance, but also because it was insufficiently insulated and not much of a barrier to moisture. Beyond saving and modernizing the tower, the hospital itself was to be expanded and a new exterior look created that would serve the facility for at least the next fifty years. The new skin, then, needed to be energy efficient, to prevent water intrusion, and to improve the tower's acoustical performance, which led to the use of metal panels because they were lightweight and offered a range of design and color options.

It was also important that the first phase of the ESa-designed expansion happen quickly, to minimize the shutdown time of patient rooms and clinical spaces on exterior walls. And the new system had to be modulated to work within the grid of the existing curtain wall/spandrel panel design. This phase involved some 23,000 sq. ft. and the renovation another 7,000.

Central to the design is an Emergency/Trauma Center, which doubles the space of the existing emergency department. (Given the limited site availability, this expansion was planned to serve as the base for the future "replace-

Riverside Regional Medical Center, Newport News, Virginia. Central to the expansion and image makeover, designed by ESa, was a new look, evident in the crisp new exterior, and a new emergency/trauma center. *Photos © Ferrell Photographics.*

Riverside Regional Medical Center, Newport News, Virginia. The dramatic new look and new use of space was also central to its expansion and image makeover. *Photos © Ferrell Photographics.*

in-place" bed tower.) The new ED consists of forty-two individual treatment rooms, eleven of them designated "fast track and intermediate" for minor emergencies and faster discharges. The new design created treatment quads of four rooms each, focusing on patient care and increasing nursing efficiencies. MRI, PET, CT, and the catheterization lab are now strategically located in close proximity to the ED. Separate ambulance and walk-in entrances are also provided. An MRI addition; a 16,300-sq.-ft. freestanding ambulatory surgery center with four operating rooms, six recovery rooms, and four step-down recovery rooms; and a new spacious main lobby also became part of this phase.

The next phase of the project includes the addition of a new tower for surgery, a gastrointestinal lab, pre- and postprocedural care, ICU and step-down beds, a new lobby, and registration services for surgery and invasive services. The three-story addition completes the ancillary base for future replacement beds in two floors. To the existing 68 beds on the second floor will be added 144 future beds on the fourth and fifth floors. The third floor houses mechanical and electrical services to supply this addition and serve future floors as added. In the current project, a new transitional elevator bank was designed to manage traffic between the low, existing tower and the new tower via double-ended elevators. Finally, a new pharmacy and new central sterile processing are located on the ground floor, which has vertical access to both towers.

JOHN MUIR MEDICAL CENTER, WALNUT CREEK CAMPUS
Walnut Creek, California

Located in the San Francisco Bay area, the John Muir Medical Center, which was undergoing a 450,000-sq.-ft. expansion and remodeling at its Walnut Creek Campus, needed a new emergency department that could handle 65,000 patient visits each year. Architects at Ratcliff not only expanded the ED to 30,000 sq. ft. but also relocated it to a more prominent position in the facility, doubling (and ultimately tripling) the number of treatment stations for the hospital. The new ED was designated as the trauma center for Contra Costa County and part of Solano County.

The ED spaces are arranged in several treatment zones with separate clinician stations to improve organizational clarity and streamline the care given. These treatment zones include a fast-track unit, an observation unit, two acute-care units, and a critical care area for cardiac resuscitation and trauma.

The newly renovated facility increases waiting area spaces with a main lobby and three satellite waiting rooms to accommodate patients' family and loved ones, and, in all, this first phase of the renovation comprises thirty-one universal treatment rooms, four major trauma rooms, a dedicated CT scanner and two radiology rooms, quiet treatment areas, a negative pressure area, two full-isolation treatment rooms complete with anterooms and toilets, security

John Muir Medical Center, Walnut Creek Campus, Walnut Creek, California. The entrance to the new and expanded emergency department was relocated to assume a more prominent position in the facility. *Courtesy Ratcliff. Photo © 2009 Tim Maloney, Technical Imagery Studios.*

at walk-in and ambulance entries, and a dedicated work area for paramedics and emergency workers.

The ED is situated one floor below the new surgery department, which provides for a direct connection between the two departments—and for a direct connection to the new rooftop helistop via two high-speed elevators that also allow for rapid arrival of trauma cases.

ST. MARY-CORWIN MEDICAL CENTER
Pueblo, Colorado

Most of the century-old hospital was originally built—and renovated—in the 1950s, with later additions in the 1980s. The new expansion and renovation, designed by John Holsher of RTA Architects in consultation with ESa, updates the facility to enable it to better provide the level of patient care necessary in today's competitive medical environment. The first phase of a replacement-in-place process, the project focused on eliminating inefficiencies and duplications by reassembling the core outpatient services of the hospital around a more compact, easily navigated facility. At the heart of the 244,000-sq.-ft. facility is a new outpatient entry lobby with centralized registration and direct access to major outpatient services, including diagnostics and same-day surgery.

Above the ancillary services is a new expandable and flexible patient tower, providing a twenty-bed ICU, twenty-four-bed advanced telemetry unit and thirty-six-bed medical/surgical unit. The final part of the project is a new 46,000-sq.-ft. comprehensive cancer center, which offers support and treatment services for much of Southern Colorado and includes three linear accelerators and twenty-one infusion stations.

A showpiece of the expansion is the new emergency department, which has been situated to share a main entrance canopy with the outpatient lobby. The old ED had seventeen rooms; the new ED twenty-six—and it provides direct access to the new diagnostic imaging department. The expansion also includes a new same-day surgery department with greatly improved staging and waiting areas.

John Muir Medical Center, Walnut Creek Campus, Walnut Creek, California. The newly renovated center included increased waiting area spaces with a main lobby and three satellite waiting rooms to accommodate family and loved ones. *Courtesy Ratcliff. Photo © 2008 Doug Salin.*

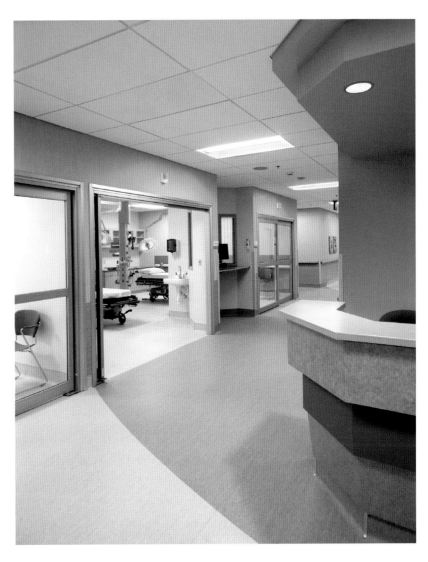

St. Mary-Corwin Medical Center, Pueblo, Colorado. The emergency/ trauma center doubled the space of the existing emergency department. *Courtesy Earl Swensson Associates and RTA Architects. Photo © Ed LaCasse Photography.*

St. Mary-Corwin Medical Center, Pueblo, Colorado. At the heart of the center is an outpatient entry lobby with centralized registration. *Courtesy Earl Swensson Associates and RTA Architects. Photo © Ed LaCasse Photography.*

MERCY MEDICAL CENTER
EMERGENCY DEPARTMENT
Des Moines, Iowa

At Mercy Medical Center, doctors and nurses were struggling to care for emergency patients in an ED designed and constructed thirty years ago, and they were hard-pressed to keep up with the increased traffic and the changing demands of today's patients. Taking a hard look at the hospital's current operational model, RDG Planning & Design developed a plan that would allow the ED to grow, become more efficient, and improve its delivery of care.

The plans resulted in a 25,000-sq.-ft. addition and 18,000 sq. ft. of remodeled space. The first floor of the addition houses a new trauma bay, an improved chest pain unit, and a new ambulance garage with plenty of overflow ambulance parking nearby. The second-story of the addition accommodates all of the department's support functions and offices. Above the addition, accessed by a dedicated elevator, a new rooftop helipad (with a snow-melting system) allows for safer and more direct access for emergency medical helicopters to and from the hospital. This greatly increases the landing and take-off options for helicopter pilots and provides a much needed space separating vehicular and pedestrian traffic.

Mercy Medical Center, Emergency Department, Des Moines, Iowa. A nurses' station in the new emergency department. *Courtesy RDG Planning & Design. Photo Kun Zhang.*

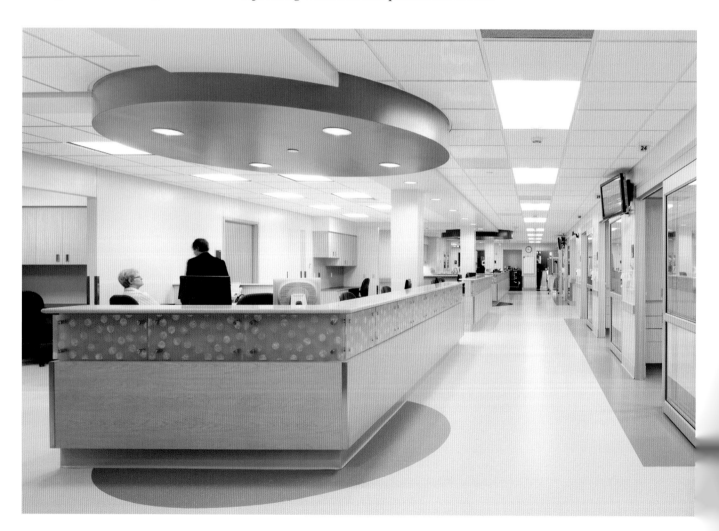

In addition to the features already mentioned, the new ED features a new atrium lobby, an enhanced triage area, forty new treatment rooms, decentralized nurses' stations, a dedicated decontamination area, an isolation room, a new emergency dispatch center, and new emergency services office space. The remodeling took place in three phases so the ED could maintain its patient volumes and simplify work and patient flows while its new "universal" treatment rooms and readily accessible nurse stations were being designed and installed.

Mercy Medical Center, Emergency Department, Des Moines, Iowa. The new lobby of the remodeled emergency department, designed by RDG Planning & Design. *Courtesy RDG Planning & Design. Photo Kun Zhang.*

LeConte Medical Center, Sevierville, Tennessee. Clear visibility of such destinations as waiting, reception, and the public elevators enhance wayfinding immediately upon entry into the lobby. *Courtesy Earl Swensson Associates and BarberMcMurry architects. Photo © Kyle Dreier Photography.*

LECONTE MEDICAL CENTER

Sevierville, Tennessee

Planned more in keeping with a 200- to 300–bed hospital, the replacement ED can now accommodate its sizable tourist traffic resulting from the hospital's location in the foothills of the Great Smoky Mountains in a town that serves as an entry station into Pigeon Forge and the national park beyond.

The seventy-nine-bed hospital itself is some 200,000 sq. ft.; the medical office building associated with it, 30,000 square feet. There is also a 30,000-sq.-ft. women's center and a 16,000-sq.-ft. cancer center on the medical campus.

ESa made sure the campus was aesthetically compatible with the architecture of historic Sevierville. Designers incorporated simplified wayfinding into the design: the main entry serves three easily recognizable destinations—the hospital, medical office building, and women's center. Healing is enhanced by the ample use of curtain walls and windows, which allow natural light into the spaces, and all patient rooms have windows that look onto the picturesque East Tennessee foothills.

LeConte Medical Center, Sevierville, Tennessee. The emergency department is key to this new replacement facility. *Courtesy Earl Swensson Associates and BarberMcMurry architects. Photo © Kyle Dreier Photography.*

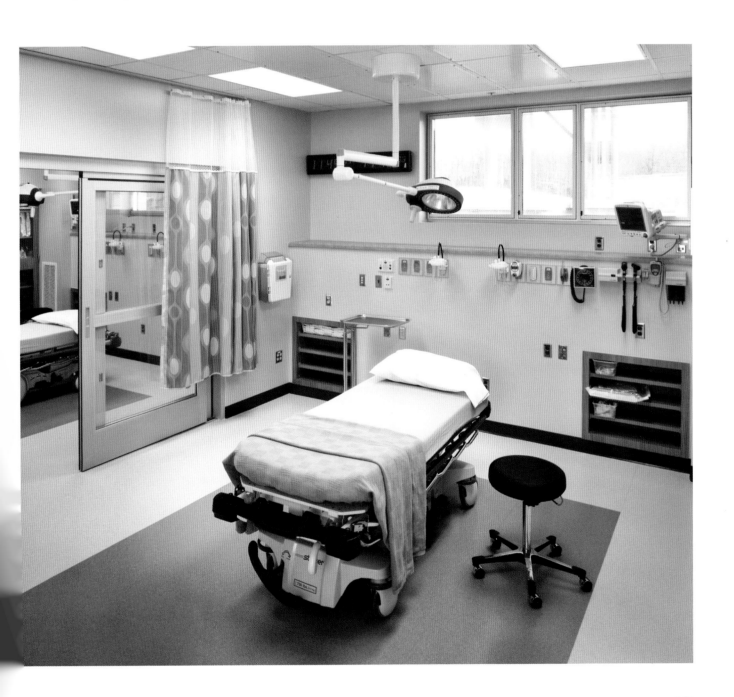

CHAPTER 6

Diagnostics

Effective diagnostics are essential for contemporary healthcare facilities, and at the same time they frequently suffer the impact of swift-changing technology and advances in medical practice. Architects and designers need to keep abreast of new developments and directions in diagnostics to ensure that their designs don't stand in the way of the changes in equipment and practice that, say, such relatively recent developments as the growth of women's diagnostics require in today's hospitals. Not only do such changes have a direct impact on the space needs of modern facilities, but they also decidedly affect the cost of contemporary healthcare and healthcare design.

Diagnostic Imaging

Diagnostics areas are among the most expensive hospital and healthcare facility spaces to design and to equip. Not only are the initial capital outlays high, but technology also tends to evolve so rapidly that upgrading, retrofitting, and redesigning are inevitable and must be expected. On the positive side are the extraordinary diagnostic—indeed, life-saving—benefits of state-of-the-art imaging technology and the potential for generation of revenue (imaging has always been a key profit area for hospitals and will probably remain so).

The field of contemporary diagnostic imaging technology has evolved into a welter of modalities identified by an alphabet soup of acronyms:

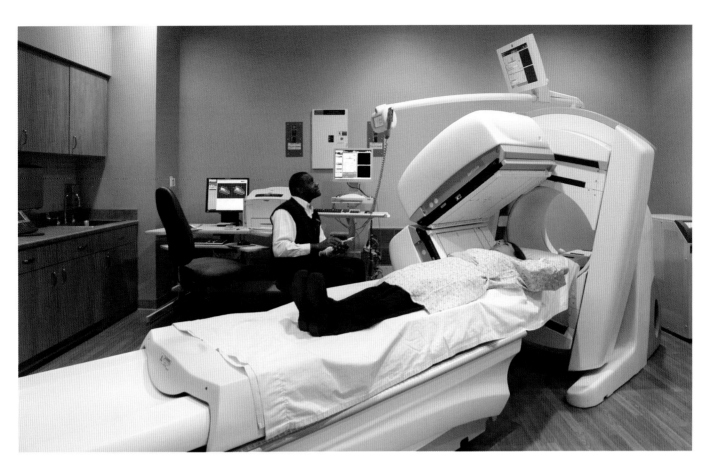

One Nineteen Health and Wellness, Hoover, Alabama. A spa-like color and finishes palette continues into diagnostics spaces. *Photo Vince Wallace/ Silver Hill Images.*

- CT (Computed Tomography—"CAT scanner")
- MRI (Magnetic Resonance Imaging)
- US (Ultrasonography)
- DSA (Digital Subtraction Angiography)
- PET (Positron Emission Tomography)
- SPECT (Single-Photon Emission Computed Tomography)
- PACS (Picture Archiving Systems)
- IR (Interventional Radiology)
- SPECT/CT (SPECT camera in combination with CT scanner)
- PET/CT (PET scanner in combination with CT scanner)
- MRI/PET (MRI scanner in combination with PET scanner)

These are just the most prominent contemporary technologies. They do not include the X-ray, the "conventional weapon" in the arsenal of diagnostic imaging, which has undergone a technological transformation with the advent of Digital Radiology (DR) and Computed Radiology (CR). Ionizing radiation is still used to produce images with conventional analog equipment, DR, and CR. The difference now lies in how the images are captured. With analog imaging (conventional film screen imaging), the images are captured on X-ray film, processed, and stored permanently on such film. With CR, the film is replaced with a reusable imaging plate. The image is stored on the plate, inserted into the cassette reader (still analog at this point) and then "read" and translated into a digital image. With DR, the imaging detector is permanently placed inside the imaging device, so there is no cassette involved and patient throughput increases. Permanent storage of both the CR and DR images is achieved through Picture Archiving Systems (PACS). So conventional X-ray imaging with a detector of some type, be it CR or DR, will continue to be an important part of patient diagnostics.

CT technology has become more specialized, particularly with the development of multislice CTs, which allow for improved speed and increased resolution, lower costs, and broadened clinical applications. Hospitals use different machines from those in imaging centers and doctors' offices. Most hospitals use a 1.0T (to) or 3.0T machine to do all of their scans. The difference lies with the field strength and the ability to detect chemical changes within the body earlier. Lower field-strength magnets are typically found in the outpatient imaging centers and physician's offices, while more costly, higher field-strength magnets are used in larger, hospital settings. Lay persons, architects, and even planners and physicians themselves are hard-pressed to assess precisely all the applications and benefits of each modality.

In the last three decades, requests for routine radiographic and fluoroscopic procedures have decreased while nuclear medicine, ultrasound, CT, and MRI procedures have sharply increased. Not only are patients themselves demanding more tests, but, because the recently improved versions of MRIs and CT scans can take minutes rather than hours to produce clearer images, doctors are also using them more often to diagnose a wider range of illnesses, including many common ailments such as appendicitis and lower back pain, which helps cut down the amount of exploratory surgery needed and provides a diagnosis within a short amount of time—critical for treatment of an acutely ill patient.

The new ultrafast machines proved so popular that by the turn of the twenty-first century, HMOs and others were complaining about imaging costs growing faster than pharmaceutical costs. These trends have a profound impact on design because MRI and CT equipment take up a lot of space compared to traditional radiology.

As the new technologies have produced clearer diagnostic images, the boundaries between the various modalities and their appropriate applications have tended to blur. More and more, CT, MRI, and ultrasound are crossing over into what had once been designated the exclusive domain of one or the other. In the early 1980s, for example, CT was judged the ideal modality for studying the central nervous system. Then the more expensive space- and design-intensive MRI took the lead in that role. CT was used extensively in studies of the abdomen and joints, but continued improvements in MRI—shorter scanning time and enhanced image contrast—prompted many physicians to order MRI work for cardiovascular, abdominal, and orthopedic studies. Through much of the 1980s and 1990s, one of the two modalities would capture center stage with an exciting advantage, only to lose it when the rival technology responded. Since the end of the twentieth century, however, both technologies have been hotbeds of development and neither shows signs of cooling off.

From 1997 to 2000, CT technology moved from "step and shoot" imaging to multislice computed tomography (MSCT), and with this change, single-slice scanning became passé. Faster and clearer, MSCT allows doctors to perform diagnostics more readily on uncooperative or critically ill patients and trauma victims; it catches structures—such as lesions—previously unidentifiable by CTs; and it creates the potential for new applications such as CT angiography, virtual colonoscopy, and pulmonary embolus evaluation that may greatly reduce the need for more invasive procedures. While MSCTs can cover an anatomic region four to six times faster than older CT technology, their drawbacks include increased doses of radiation, which has become a growing concern. Efforts to find a way to reduce such radiation will have a major impact on the continuing evolution of CT.

The most recent developments in MRI technology have been directed toward making scanners faster, more open, less expensive, and with higher field strength. Special systems have been designed for limited imaging of the head, breast, and extremities, while "open" systems—which cut down some of the claustrophobic discomfort of MRIs—are being developed with higher field strengths to overcome the resolution problems inherent in their lower-strength magnets.

The interest in cardiac MRIs has grown tremendously. Indeed, cardiac MRI units have become an important clinical tool for cardiologists, a specialty that well illustrates the impact of modern diagnostics. Great advances have been made in noninvasive cardiology—cardiovascular MRIs, X-ray computed tomography in ischemic heart disease, and nuclear cardiology use in heart failure—that not only provide better diagnostic information but increasingly guide therapies (along, of course, with information derived from clinical histories and examinations). The point is, all this has drastically reduced the need for exploratory invasive procedures and for the time, space, and personnel they require. The inclusion of interventional MRI (IMRIs) in the surgical suite opens up new horizons in neurological imaging during a surgical procedure.

Physicians, administrators, planners, and architects worry about which big-ticket systems to specify and design for, especially given the rapid pace of development in the field of medical technology. Ultrasound, for example, which was once a competitor with CT and MRI for some of the same diagnostic territory (being wholly noninvasive except for the emerging field of intravascular ultrasound, far less expensive, and far less design-intensive than either CT or MRI) has become instead a starting point. Today, ultrasound equipment is owned by almost all U.S. hospitals, and the vast majority of them offer full ultrasound diagnostic services. CTs and MRIs are considered complements, not competitors, to ultrasound and are as essential.

Single-Photon Emission Computed Tomography (SPECT) provides three-dimensional radionuclide imaging information, estimates regional blood flow, measures organ volumes, and provides continuous data sampling of the heart in action. And compared, say, to Positron Emission Tomography (PET), SPECT is relatively inexpensive, costing in the hundreds of thousands rather than millions of dollars. Although multihead systems, which are more accurate, cost a bit more, single-head gamma cameras are very rare if not nonexistent these days. Almost all facilities purchase a variable angle dual-head gamma camera for throughput and flexibility. Many facilities have also adopted SPECT/CT, a combination SPECT and CT scanner.

PET, however, remains the *sine qua non* of imaging, providing information that other technologies cannot provide, including the detection of metabolic activity in heart muscles that otherwise appear dead and the detection of brain abnormalities that elude other diagnostic methods; it can provide precise information on whether a tumor responds to treatment. Its major drawback is still price. A cyclotron makes the radioactive isotopes used as tracers but it costs millions of dollars for equipment and installation. Most facilities have their PET pharmaceuticals delivered just as they do for Nuclear Medicine and thus do not have the expense associated with a cyclotron. Generally, those with cyclotrons are research facilities. Today, nearly all nuclear cameras sold are PET-capable. In addition, diagnosticians have discovered that PET imaging combined with CT scanning greatly enhances the results of both, so combined PET/CT systems have become standard. And as PET/MRI technology becomes available, it may replace PET/CT.

While the value of such technology (especially versus its cost) is sometimes debated, most hospitals invest in equipment to remain up-to-date and competitive, to improve the quality of care they offer, to meet the growing demand in the community for such technology, to create new revenue sources, to provide more cost-efficient service, and to improve financial viability. Some argue that digital imaging gained a foothold in the imaging department because it offers value-added services. It moves the hospital toward electronic medical records (EMR), freeing up valuable real estate once dedicated to film file storage. Images can be shared instantaneously throughout the healthcare facility, which promotes faster diagnosis and reaction time for the patient to be treated properly. And there is a significant reduction in lost films. The move to CR/DR imaging has also been driven by Environmental Protection Agency (EPA) issues that revolve around the use of chemicals to process film and the disposal involved in that process.

Such technology can have an impact on staffing. As imaging department administrators saw their volume greatly increase year after year in the mid 2000s, the number of graduates in radiology residency declined. And while that may be improving, hospital diagnostic imaging departments still have to take into account freestanding diagnostic imaging centers. Individual hospitals, whether expanding, renovating, or building anew, have to decide whether to compete with these facilities for staff and patients or to cooperate with them.

PACS has played a role in determining the number of hospitals that invest in full on-site imaging facilities or outsource some of the work to freestanding diagnostic imaging centers or other providers. PACS stores as well as transmits digitized diagnostic images. At the very least, PACS facilitates medical consultation, allowing, for example, physicians in Chicago to discuss, in unprecedented detail and with real-time immediacy, a case in a hospital in Little Rock. Smaller hospitals can own and maintain scaled-down versions of certain diagnostic equipment, perform diagnostic procedures on-site, and transmit the data to a larger regional facility for processing and consultation—or send it out of the country 24/7 for the image reading coverage now available when staff radiologists are not. PACS has opened up possibilities for technology sharing among hospitals, among freestanding facilities, and among freestanding and hospital facilities.

Hospitals will continue to invest heavily in diagnostic equipment and the building design that goes with the equipment. It is also likely that freestanding diagnostic facilities will continue to proliferate, which means that both hospitals and freestanding centers will have to realize the importance of not only providing a design that meets the technical and logistical demands of the diagnostic hardware but also of a design that promotes diagnostic services through a patient-centered orientation. As in the hospital as a whole, patients want to feel that they are benefiting from the best technology available, but they do not want to feel as if they are depending solely upon machines.

Atrium Medical Center, Middletown, Ohio. Designed by ESa, the center marks a new era of family-centered care and state-of-the-art technology for Middletown and the surrounding area. *Photo Scott McDonald © Hedrich Blessing.*

In general, while designing for such technologies, administrators and architects should keep in mind the increasing number and varying types of modalities and the way they rapidly evolve. Location becomes especially important, not only because of the size and special requirements of some imaging technologies but also because of the need to remain especially flexible for the future development of new modalities and for new applications of existing modalities. For example, image-guided surgery is revolutionizing traditional surgical techniques, and because it relies on diagnostic testing technology such as CT scans and MRIs to create the three-dimensional images it streams in real time to the surgeon as he or she operates, it has many implications for the future location and equipping of diagnostics and diagnostic centers. General imaging departments, and their designers, need to be aware of this new, more dynamic use of what was once a strictly diagnostic function when designing their space within healthcare facilities. The high resolution that interventional MRI imaging may require can produce significant structural and siting issues, particularly as these systems are often placed above grade.

Special attention should also be paid to patient privacy and to making the spaces for given modalities used by several different specialties, such as cardiologists, neuroradiologists, radiologists, and those practicing both invasive and noninvasive procedures. Here, too, cross-training of staff and cross-utilization by physicians are especially important. In this rapidly changing area of medical practice, flexibility of design is especially important.

Designing space for diagnostic equipment requires specialized knowledge of the technical requirements of the equipment and effective, ongoing communication with technical representatives of the equipment manufacturers. Many architectural firms subcontract equipment consultants. In some cases, the hospital or healthcare facility contracts these experts directly. A few architectural firms command the in-house expertise to specify equipment as part of the total design package. The discussion that follows is intended to outline new directions in the design of these facilities and deliberately avoids extensive technical detail.

Design for conventional radiography is relatively straightforward because the space required is self-contained. To be sure, the planner and architect must ensure that the facilities meet state and federal codes for radiation protection, and a certified physicist should be consulted regarding the type, location, and amount of protection required. But conventional radiography does not require the scope of support facilities—control rooms, equipment rooms, computer rooms, and patient-holding areas— that more advanced imaging technologies like CT and MRI demand. CT and, even more, MRI equipment also require more space than conventional radiography just to accommodate the apparatus. While designers must cope with radiation protection in the case of conventional radiography equipment, they must design safely for high-energy magnetic fields in the case of MRI, the dangers of which are not as clearly understood; minor effects—such as interference with computer monitors on floors above the MRI or in other locations relatively remote from it—are likewise hard to predict.

Even for a conventional radiography facility, designers should create a patient-friendly environment. Although conventional X-ray and fluoroscopy equipment may seem inherently less psychologically threatening to patients than formidable CT machinery or claustrophobic MRI equipment (today's open systems have helped soften that perception), designers should still devote thought and resources to ensuring patient comfort.

Another general design rule is to specify as much additional space in the technical areas of the "imaging suite" (the term architects now generally use to refer to the radiography facilities they design) as practical to allow for cost-effective upgrading of equipment over time. While it is true that, in general, electronic devices are getting smaller, advances in diagnostic imaging have resulted in larger, more complex equipment, particularly in the case of equipment for whole-body imaging.

Particularly careful thought must be devoted to integrating the diagnostic suite within the overall plan of the hospital and making it easily expandable. The suite should be readily accessible to outpatients—for example, it may require careful attention to parking—as well as to patients in various hospital departments, including emergency. All other things being equal, the most practical location for the imaging suite is on the ground floor. Here, it is most readily accessible to outpatients, floor load-bearing and shielding are easier and less expensive to manage, and ceiling height requirements are usually easier to meet. In addition to engineering floors for the heavy loads of MRI and other imaging equipment and shielding, ceilings must be engineered with the appropriate supports and shielding for ceiling-mounted equipment. Ample raceways or interstitial floor space need to be provided for ducts and wiring.

The imaging suite may accommodate at least the following imaging modalities:
- Angiography
- CT
- Diagnostic radiography
- Fluoroscopy
- MRI
- Ultrasound
- Nuclear medicine

More and more hospitals are also including the following modalities:
- PET
- SPECT
- Fusion imaging (SPECT/CT, PET/CT, PET/MRI)

Support Spaces

As mentioned above, advanced imaging technology requires an array of support spaces in addition to the rooms that actually house the diagnostic apparatus. We discuss the special support facilities required for each diagnostic modality as we discuss the individual modalities. Certain support areas, however, are common to the entire imaging suite. These include:
- Waiting and reception areas
- Holding area
- Toilet rooms
- Dressing areas
- Staff facilities
- Office(s) for radiologist(s) and assistant(s)
- Clerical area
- Consultation area
- Contrast media preparation area
- Quality control area
- Clean utility room(s)
- Soiled utility room(s)
- Secure storage area for drugs and medication

Some of the above areas require discussion.

The machinery of diagnostic imaging is truly among the wonders of modern medicine, and most patients realize this and are grateful for the existence of such equipment. That said, no other medical procedure except surgery creates more apprehension, fear of the unknown, and expectation of pain and discomfort than major diagnostic procedures. Even when these procedures don't cause actual physical pain, they do often involve prodding, poking, and probing by strangers, the forced ingestion of large quantities of fluids (as in barium studies), full-bladder discomfort (as in certain ultrasound studies), and similar emotional "insults" (such as the potentially claustrophobic masks and wiring of a sleep study). Add to this the overshadowing presence of heavy machinery made of cold stainless steel that is capable of generating high dosages of radiation, and you have the makings of a very intimidating, stressful experience.

Thoughtful design of waiting areas can help to alleviate some of this stress. Carpeting, upholstered residential-style seating (grouped rather than arranged bench-style), pleasant wall coverings, and artwork all contribute to a feeling of well-being. If possible, windows and skylights should figure into the design to provide natural light and contact with the outdoors.

It is important to keep the ambulatory waiting room entirely separate from the patient-holding area, which is for inpatients who will mostly be attired in hospital gowns and lying prone on stretchers or sitting in wheelchairs. However, to the degree that it is possible and practical to do so, carry through as many of the residential design features of the waiting room into the dressing area and even into the actual procedure rooms. Avoid sharp transitions from the "outside" world to the "clinical" world.

Holding Area

This area, strictly separated from the ambulatory waiting room, is designed as a waiting area for inpatients undergoing diagnostic procedures. It should include chairs and plenty of space for stretchers and wheelchairs. The name "holding area" unfortunately suggests an impersonal, even rather inhumane, space—so much so that some architects, planners, and caregivers prefer to call the area "subwaiting." The same degree of sensitivity to feeling that goes into the design of the ambulatory waiting area should be applied here as well. If natural light is available, exploit it. Wall coverings and artwork should be cheerful and nonclinical. Since many patients here will be lying on their backs, consider a ceiling mural. If the building is a ground-floor facility, consider a skylight. At the very least, the holding area should be designed to minimize the disquieting effect of bustling activity. Patients on stretchers should always have direct access to staff, either through a call button or by being within view of a control area.

Like the holding area, the dressing area should be entirely segregated from the ambulatory waiting area. Each dressing area should be equipped with comfortable seating and a secure place to hang or store clothing. Carpeting is desirable, and a mirror is a must. A magazine rack and, perhaps, a small-scale print or other artwork can lend welcome touches of humanity and make additional waiting time more enjoyable. Once the patient is in a gown, it is highly desirable to allow him or her to wait in the privacy of the dressing area.

Staff Facilities/Office(s) for Radiologist(s) and Assistant(s)/Consultation Area

These important support areas of the imaging suite should not be afterthoughts. As patient-centered design has become a key issue, so has staff-centered design. A pleasant and humane working environment is not only vital for efficiency and cost-effective operation on a day-to-day basis, but it also improves staff morale and serves to attract and retain top-quality staff.

The work of the imaging department is intensive and exacting. It is important to provide facilities for personnel to take work breaks. Staff facilities include restrooms and a lounge with lockers. Since nurses and technologists often find precious little time to leave the facility for meals, include a dining area within the lounge to accommodate them. It is also important to provide an area specifically designed for consultation with referring physicians and others. This room should be located away from direct patient activity areas and should be private so that conversations will not be overheard. Also, it should have equipment for viewing the results of diagnostic imaging and for studying the results of other diagnostic tests.

General Considerations for Procedure Rooms

Different imaging modalities require differing mechanical/electrical (M/E) and structural support; however, two principles generally apply to all of these areas. The first is to plan for more space in each procedure room than may be thought absolutely necessary. The general trend is toward subminiaturization in high technology, but, as we have observed, it is impossible to declare with certainty that diagnostic hardware will likewise shrink. It may, in fact, continue to make greater demands on building space. Since hospitals can get swept up in the urge to provide the latest technology, it is essential to remember that all these units are designed to serve patients and that, in meeting the needs of the technologies, patients do not suffer inconveniences or even needless risks.

The second general principle is that the necessarily high-tech clinical areas of the imaging suite do not have to look uncompromisingly clinical.

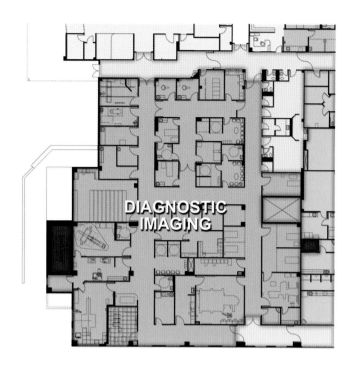

DIAGNOSTIC
IMAGING

A diagnostic imaging floor plan created by Earl Swensson Associates.

Some architects and designers bred on the form-follows-function dictum have expressed backlash sentiments about the trend toward introducing ideas from mall, hospitality, and even residential design into the hospital environment, protesting that these elements are merely feeble attempts to disguise the hospital's true function. Poorly done, such design gestures are, in fact, feeble.

But thoughtfully and imaginatively designed and executed architectural elements that humanize the hospital environment do have a positive impact on healthcare, including patient well-being, staff morale and retention, and the facility's financial viability. Indeed, successful attempts to humanize these clinical settings can be an asset in recruiting talented clinicians. The introduction of these elements does not violate the concept of form following function if architects, planners, and administrators agree that the ultimate function of the hospital is to maintain or restore the health of the patients who use it. Architectural environments that separate mind and emotion from the physical body partake of the outmoded paradigm that also regards patients as sets of organs or physical disorders rather than whole human beings. It is not that one view is wrong and the other right, but that the former paradigm has shifted toward the latter. It is not a question of wrong or right, but of the reality in which architecture and health care currently exist or are moving toward.

Therefore, even at the business end of the imaging suite, design should be humane. Waiting-room amenities like carpeting and plush seats are impractical in the imaging rooms themselves, but variable lighting, comfortable seating, cheerful but dignified wall coverings, and even artwork are not only feasible but also desirable. Since some imaging modalities require complex shielding systems for radiation or radio-frequency interference—thick concrete walls are typical in cancer treatment areas—windows in these spaces are usually impossibilities. However, serene artificially backlit stained-glass transparencies have been used to introduce an element of color, light, and interest into imaging rooms. Used in ceilings, such dramatic decorative elements provide a welcome focus for patients who must remain motionless on their backs while undergoing CT scans or MRI work. Using backlit photo murals and bringing natural light into imaging rooms are other ways of introducing an element of the outdoors into these necessarily isolated spaces.

As a practical and humane consideration, patient toilet facilities should be clearly marked and available immediately adjacent to the imaging room. To promote efficient traffic flow, the toilet should have an exit to the area outside the imaging room. Ready availability of a toilet is especially important—and reassuring—to patients undergoing barium studies of the colon, ultrasound studies of the abdomen, or other diagnostic procedures involving bowel or bladder discomfort.

Angiography Rooms

Digital angiography requires about twice the space usually allocated to the conventional radiographic/fluoroscopic room. According to the Facility Guidelines Institute's 2010 *Guidelines for Design and Construction of Health Care Facilities*, the minimum area of the procedure room should be 400 sq. ft., with an adjacent control room, for single-plane rooms. Biplane rooms should be 600 sq. ft. minimum. Rooms used for OR applications should be 800 sq. ft. Ceilings need to be high enough to accommodate suspension of tubes and monitors, and are driven by specific vendor requirements, surgical lights, and equipment booms. Adequate provisions must be made for the extensive cabling required. The procedure room should include ample ready storage space and a surgical scrub sink located near the staff entry but not in the room itself.

Adjacent support areas to the procedure room are the control area, equipment room, and a soiled utility room. The control area and equipment room house diagnostic imaging generators, recording equipment, and other electronic gear, generally rack-mounted as modules. A supplementary air-conditioning system may also be provided for the equipment room, designed specifically for the anticipated heat gain in the room and to meet the cooling needs of the computers and diagnostic equipment.

Hybrid Angiography/Surgery Rooms

Recent years have seen an evolution toward the merging of imaging and surgery to create a category of rooms called "hybrid ORs." In general these rooms are angiography labs that are also fully equipped for general or specialty surgery. The concept is that if a patient undergoing angiography experiences difficulty, the imaging equipment can be moved out of the field, surgical equipment moved in, and surgery performed immediately without transporting the patient to another properly equipped OR. Planning and design of the hybrid OR can vary widely depending on the procedures to be performed. Space required for a hybrid OR, including the procedure, control, and equipment rooms, is approximately 1200 sq. ft.

As with other surgery rooms, the hybrid OR will require multiple information displays including both arm-supported and wall-mounted locations—and integrated surgical video control for capturing, recording, communicating, and displaying images. Additionally a hybrid OR intended for electrophysiology (EP) will require additional displays for equipment. Ceilings must be coordinated to accommodate the location and movement of the angiography C-arm rails, surgical lights, equipment and anesthesia booms, video displays, and the EP cockpit—as well as the typical HVAC supply and return ducts, room lighting, and so on. Complexity has led some designers to employ a roomwide above-ceiling grid structure.

Care should be taken to locate and position a charting station housing the video equipment where the circulating nurse can chart, pull up PACS images for display during the procedure, set up and control the video system and still maintain eye contact with the surgeon.

Control room design requires attention to the multiple computers, keyboards, and displays required for support and operation of the multiple systems and modalities within the suite. Room UPS is required to continuously support procedures during power disruptions—as well as adequate HVAC to maintain acceptable room temperature for both the procedure and support equipment.

Supporting spaces for pre- and postoperative care and postanesthesia recovery, nurse control, etc. are typical of similar special procedure and surgery departments.

Cardiac Catheterization Room

Most of the design principles enumerated above for digital angiography apply as well to cardiac catheterization. Formerly, long-term storage of cine-film was a major consideration in designing the cardiac catheterization room. But with digital imaging playing a predominant role in cardiac catheterization and angiographic procedures, storage space has become less critical. However, space for a dedicated computer workstation might be provided for onsite viewing, study, and enhancement of imaging data.

Both the digital angiography room and the cardiac catheterization room may have separate holding areas. Depending on the size of the imaging suites, these facilities might also warrant separate waiting rooms. Because of the invasive nature of the angiographic and catheterization procedures, segregation of inpatients and outpatients is essential. Sometimes cardiac catheterization patients need emergency surgical procedures. Maintenance of sterile isolation is, therefore, of great importance. Sometimes patients are staged through the outpatient same-day surgery area. In some settings, this may be a mobile facility.

CT Suite

The imaging room should be large enough to accommodate the formidable gantry and table assembly to allow ample room for personnel to maneuver around the table. As discussed above, the designer can include many patient-centered elements to humanize the clinical nature of the space. Lighting should be variable, with bright fluorescent illumination available for setup and soft, rheostat-variable, background-level incandescent lighting for patient comfort during the actual imaging procedure. The path to the CT table should be clear and straight. Casework should be located on the opposite side of the CT table (away from the door) and the ceiling-mounted injector should be located on this side of the table as well to provide a clear pathway for staff to transfer critically ill patients onto the CT table.

Adjacent to the procedure room is a control area, which houses the operator's console, the imaging technologist's viewing desk. Until a few years ago, a separate equipment room was required to house the computer transformer, and other necessary electronic components. Newer units incorporate the computer in the control or operations console and do not require a separate room. CT and other high-volume utility spaces require special detailing to hide cabling and computer wiring, which is not only an eyesore but is also a trip hazard. Many CT scanners will dissipate heat to the room although water-cooled systems are still available.

The CT suite should have its own holding area that is large enough to accommodate at least one waiting patient for each procedure room. Depending on the size of the imaging facility, the CT suite may also have its own dedicated waiting room.

Diagnostic Imaging Rooms

Conventional imaging requires a large room. ESa's clients frequently look for 350 sq. ft. including the control area. Some special situations require additional design consideration. Mammography, for example, which might be available as part of diagnostic imaging or separately in the OB/GYN department, ambulatory service, specialized women's ambulatory unit, or a freestanding facility, presents opportunities for market-driven design. Although physicians disagree about the scope of mammography as a routine screening procedure, it is likely to continue routinely to serve a significant number of women. The mammography unit should, therefore, be designed to appeal to women, and the emphasis should be on creating a patient-friendly and convenient environment. Space must be larger if biopsies are also performed there. If windows are added they must be covered with blinds for privacy. Alternatively, windows may be omitted entirely and attractive wall coverings and artwork used to brighten the walls.

Since mammography appeals to a particular and well-defined segment of the diagnostic marketplace, it is advisable to provide a dedicated waiting area for this service, including a gowning room adjacent to the mammography room—even when the mammography suite is part of a larger imaging department or freestanding facility. A separate room should also be included for educational purposes, with such tools as reference books and discs. Again, the waiting area should be designed with women in mind and should suggest personal care values rather than a clinical aura.

Depending on the size of the facility, mammography can often be adjacent to ultrasound for a consolidation of women's imaging services. A typical women's suite would accommodate mammography, ultrasound, bone-density imaging (densitometry), and biopsies.

Ultrasound Rooms

Ultrasound is less costly than many other imaging systems. It does not require lead-lined walls, and its units are portable. Many physicians own and operate such equipment in their offices, and ultrasound diagnostic services are offered in many freestanding facilities. Various hospital departments, including OB/GYN, emergency, and cardiovascular, are likely to have their own units. Unlike CT and MRI, ultrasound technology can be easily accommodated in a wide variety of settings.

Procedure rooms for ultrasound examination, then, can be relatively small, preferably 140 to 160 sq. ft. No special control or storage rooms are required. While many self-contained systems can print out an instant image of the ultrasound test, ultrasound images are completely digital so the majority of fully digital hospitals do not print out images; they send them directly to PACS. For those facilities who do require hard-copy documentation, either for the referring physician or the radiologist, they usually use a tabletop dry laser imager or a thermal paper printer.

A cost-effective, noninvasive, and highly convenient modality, ultrasound has made inroads into the diagnostic territory of CT and MRI. Ultrasound can be used to study virtually any part of the body, except lungs, intestines, and skeleton, and its applications are limited only by the creativity of clinicians using it. In most settings, then, designers will be asked to create facilities to accommodate a fairly high volume of patients, which means careful attention to the waiting area and to making each patient bay or procedure room pleasant, nonclinical, and unthreatening. Design and material resources are well devoted to patient amenities in this highly competitive area of diagnostic imaging.

MRI Suite

Magnetic resonance imaging generates powerful magnetic fields, forceful radio-frequency transmissions, repetitive noise, and pulsating vibrations. All of these make very significant structural demands and impose rigorous architectural constraints. Various technical publications, including, first and foremost, those issued by the equipment manufacturers themselves, specify safety and other operating requirements. These vary depending on the type of MRI equipment installed, and researchers and manufacturers are continually evaluating optimal magnetic field strengths for various imaging applications. It is, therefore, impossible to promulgate any single standard to ensure safety as well as freedom from data artifacts, especially since the future will likely bring new equipment with new requirements. However, in general, planners, architects, and engineers must determine effects of the following:

- Metallic structures, vehicles, and electrical equipment on the MRI system, which can result in imaging errors
- The magnetic field of the MRI equipment on personnel and equipment
- Vibration and sound of the MRI equipment on personnel and equipment

Once these issues are addressed, planners, architects, and engineers must determine whether the MRI system can be retrofitted into an existing structure or whether a new facility must be built. An interim solution may to lease mobile and/or modular MRI units. Operation of such mobile units may help a hospital establish a need for a built-in accommodation of technology.

If possible, the MRI suite should occupy a ground floor with no occupied space below, thereby eliminating one dimension of the magnetic field's effect and the effect of structural, electrical, and radio-frequency (RF) interference sources on the magnetic field. The magnet and, especially, its necessary shielding, exercise tremendous load demands, making a ground-floor location more cost-effective. Ground-floor locations also make it less costly to achieve the above-average floor-to-floor height MRI equipment generally requires.

Engineering studies must assess the effect of the magnetic field on personnel, operations, and structural members elsewhere in the building and in the vicinity of the building. A faulty installation can, of course, prove extremely costly as well as hazardous. RF studies must also be conducted to determine the extent and nature of existing RF fields that can interfere with and distort imaging.

If the MRI facility is being installed in an existing building, wall openings and corridors must be wide enough to allow safe movement of the magnet during installation. The facility must also allow for total accessibility to the MRI equipment for maintenance and upgrading. Even if the facility is new, the design must account for pathways and access doors or removable walls for replacing a unit or upgrading it. If the magnet is of the superconductive type, it is important that its cryogen—either liquid nitrogen or liquid helium (some use both)—can be replenished conveniently and expeditiously. Another important utility consideration is a dedicated cooling system capable of keeping the temperature sufficiently low to dissipate the huge number of BTUs per hour produced by such equipment.

Although MRI equipment may get smaller (and this trend is being reversed in some cases by new, large-bore systems designed to better accommodate large and claustrophobic patients), it remains very high technology, and, as such, subject to upgrading. The recent trend toward more powerful equipment will demand more space. Renovation of highly shielded areas is extremely costly. It is advisable to build these areas with an eye toward future expandability and upgrading to a more powerful magnet, in other words, design to expand outward or to absorb adjacent soft spaces should the need occur.

Support areas in an MRI suite include control rooms, equipment rooms (including separate storage for liquid nitrogen and helium, though typically, storage for these are no longer required in current production methods and single cryogen systems are the norm), and a computer room. The powerful magnetic field generated by the MRI device means that most of these rooms should be located at least 23 ft. from the center of the magnet. A control room for housing imaging recording devices must be designed to be a specified minimum distance from the magnet's center.

Given the degree of clinical crossover between CT and MRI modalities, these modalities may share such facilities as patient holding and physician reading areas. However, entry into the fringe area of the magnetic field generated by an MRI device must be strictly regulated and protected by a metal detector. No ferrous metal objects can be allowed near the magnet, since these might easily become deadly missiles. Patients with pacemakers or electronic dose-administering devices must remain far away from the fringe area. If any facilities are shared, the design must ensure that no unauthorized or unchecked staff members, patients, or others wander into the area of the magnetic field. Designs now plan for multiple safety zones—the *Guidelines for Design and Construction of Health Care Facilities* calls for four—to buffer the MRI's operation and protect patient and staff from harm.

The single biggest complaint patients make about MRI examinations is that they feel claustrophobic and isolated. MRI is a physically painless procedure, but it can be psychologically trying. At minimum, the design must allow for adequate air-conditioning, noise reduction, and ventilation, particularly of the cryogen that cools the magnet. A cryogen vent system is a standard required component of all superconductive MRI systems.

As in other necessarily windowless environments, backlit photomurals or artificially illuminated stained-glass artwork can help relieve any sense of claustrophobia. While circulation patterns should separate patients from technologists, patients should be able to see the technologists so that they do not feel that they have been shut in or abandoned. Another aspect of circulation is the inclusion of a quick, direct route out of the magnetic field fringe area. In the event of a medical or surgical emergency during or immediately after the MRI examination, the patient must be moved quickly to an area where the magnetic field will not adversely affect such monitoring equipment as an EKG. (Newer monitoring and anesthesia equipment as well as infusion pumps are being designed with nonferrous materials, which are not affected by the MRI magnetic field.) Anesthesia machines, patient monitors, and infusion pumps are available for MRI suites and are quite common. Even MRI facilities that are part of a hospital campus are sometimes housed in a separate building.

PET Suites

Like MRI, Positron Emission Tomography (PET) presents unique design requirements. The first step in planning is to select the equipment vendor, since PET equipment differs greatly in size and configuration, and most facilities that have or will adopt PET purchase PET/CT scanners. Planners and architects should also work with the chosen vendor from the start to plan the facility. Areas must be allocated for the procedure room, heat-exchange rooms, laboratory facilities, patient preparation rooms, a viewing area, and support facilities, such as a waiting room, offices, and a conference room. If isotopes are to be created on site, a cyclotron must be included. (Most facilities do not have a cyclotron; instead, their radiopharmaceuticals are delivered from an outsourced pharmacy.)

In the event that the facility will house a dedicated cyclotron, load-bearing concerns are critical. Cyclotrons are heavy and require shielding just as heavy. Moreover, the floor plan must closely integrate the cyclotron with a hot lab and, in turn, the scanner, since many radio-isotopes have extremely brief useful lives—a matter of minutes, in some cases—and transfer from the cyclotron to the hot lab to the scanner must be accomplished quickly and efficiently.

Aside from the design considerations to accommodate the technology, it must be recognized that a high percentage of any PET installation's patients will be outpatients. As with other sophisticated, high-ticket imaging services, patient-friendly waiting and reception facilities are essential. If the facility is freestanding—as part of a hospital campus or run as an independent service—provision should also be made for receiving nonambulatory patients by ambulance. Given the expense of PET, it is likely that regional facilities will receive critically ill transfer patients from various hospitals.

Nuclear Medicine

PET and some other, usually invasive, diagnostic imaging procedures may fall under the heading of nuclear medicine rather than diagnostics and could be housed in a nuclear medicine department rather than within an imaging suite. Design for nuclear medicine is addressed in Chapter 10, but more generally since both diagnostic imaging and cardiac diagnostics share a need for this technology, facilities design must either duplicate it, which is wasteful and inelegant, or place it in a mutually convenient zone so that it can be shared. PET usually requires a dedicated area of the nuclear medicine department to address unique shielding and dosing (hot lab) requirements.

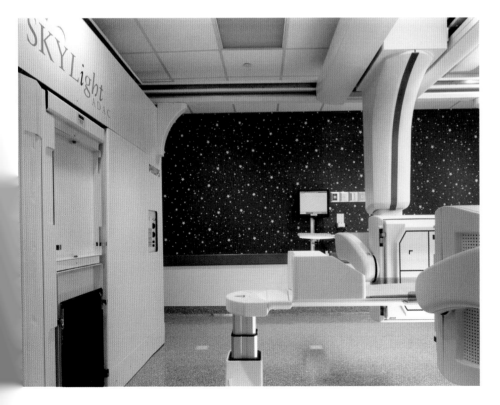

Monroe Carell Jr. Children's Hospital at Vanderbilt, Nashville, Tennessee. Glow-in-the-dark stars on wall covering help to create a friendlier environment in a nuclear medicine suite. *Photo Scott McDonald © Hedrich Blessing.*

Digital imaging has become the norm in healthcare. Providing space and infrastructure for capturing and storing digital images—and providing space for access and viewing—is an integral part of imaging department design.

Imaging studies represent the largest data files transported via networks. Designing network equipment rooms that are properly sized, located, powered, and cooled is a necessity. Ideally all imaging modalities should be served from a single network equipment room. Data cabling specifications severely limit cable distances—thus, a network equipment room can typically serve spaces within a 150-ft. radius of the room. Network equipment rooms should be sized to accommodate all the equipment required, and, in ORs with integrated surgical video, the minimum network equipment room size should be increased to accommodate the additions. Power requirements include a mixture of 120-volt and 208-volt circuits with total power capacity exceeding 15,000 watts. Unlike electrical equipment rooms that merely transform and switch power that is used elsewhere, virtually all power consumed in network equipment rooms is converted to heat and must be evacuated by the HVAC system.

Although the computer CPUs that support PACS workstations are continuing to decrease in size, and displays are high-definition flat panels, overall workstation size remains governed by the quantity and size of displays. Counter space should be designed accordingly with an adjacent workstation to accommodate EMR entry, a telephone, and dictation (which may be integral to the telephone). PACS reading rooms should be equipped with dimmable, indirect lighting, and when windows are present light-blocking shades are required. Care should be taken in planning door swings to avoid even momentary introduction of bright light.

Bedside Diagnostics

Before we review examples of humane design for diagnostic facilities, we should take note of an aspect of the patient-centered approach that may have a significant design impact. Patient-centered treatment goes beyond providing a pleasant architectural environment for medical consumers. It is also a treatment philosophy based on the decentralization of caregiving. A prime tenet of this approach is that, whenever possible, service delivery should occur as close to the patient's location as possible and should be administered by a small cadre of caregivers who, because they follow through with a particular patient throughout the course of treatment, provide the patient with great continuity of care.

The patient-centered approach applies to diagnostic imaging. Obviously, CT and MRI equipment cannot be trundled to the bedside, though portable CT for head imaging is now available and often used in ICU environments in university and high-end neuro hospitals. Even portable whole-body CTs are now available, but their clinical utility has yet to be established. Certainly some ultrasound equipment can be used bedside, and chest radiography—the single most frequently performed radiological examination—is also portable. This has been made highly practical and efficient through the digital storage of chest images, coupled with a PACS and teleradiology capability. The digital storage of images and the ability to transmit those images virtually anywhere electronically is a trend of very great importance. Digital imaging makes it unnecessary to expose films, transport them to a central facility for processing, and then transport them to the radiologist's desk for examination.

True, bedside radiography is typically only used when the patient is critically ill and cannot make the trip to the imaging department, and the quality of the radiographic imaging exam performed bedside is usually not of the same level as those performed on a fixed imaging system. But even if mobile bedside radiography has not replaced the need for fixed imaging equipment within the imaging department, the fact that it can be performed at the bedside points to a future when the nature and design of the diagnostic imaging facility required will be affected, when space ordinarily devoted to routine conventional radiographic examination may be freed up for use with more advanced and space-hungry modalities.

ATRIUM MEDICAL CENTER

Middletown, Ohio

ESa designed a new medical center to replace the ninety-year-old Middletown Regional Hospital, which was landlocked on a 26-acre campus in the middle of a residential neighborhood and cut off from much of the community. The old hospital would have cost substantially more to upgrade effectively, so the new Atrium Medical Center was conceived.

At Atrium Medical Center, family-centered care and state-of-the-art technology support a full range of expanded services, including cardiology, emergency services, oncology, and surgery. As the centerpiece of a nearly 200-acre campus, the medical center marks a new era of healthcare delivery for Middletown and the surrounding area with 250 all-private patient rooms, an attached five-story professional building, a two-story, 44,000-sq.-ft. cancer center, and a one-story, 27,000-sq.-ft. behavioral health pavilion. The designers took extreme care to allow for flexibility and expandability of the center, placing all key departments on outer walls.

The new emergency department has sixty-one treatment rooms, serving 80,000 patients annually. Locating imaging services convenient to

Atrium Medical Center, Middletown, Ohio. The window and flooring help create a soothing ambiance in the diagnostic suite. *Photo Scott McDonald © Hedrich Blessing.*

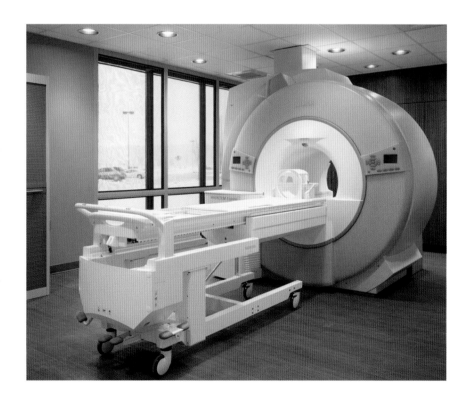

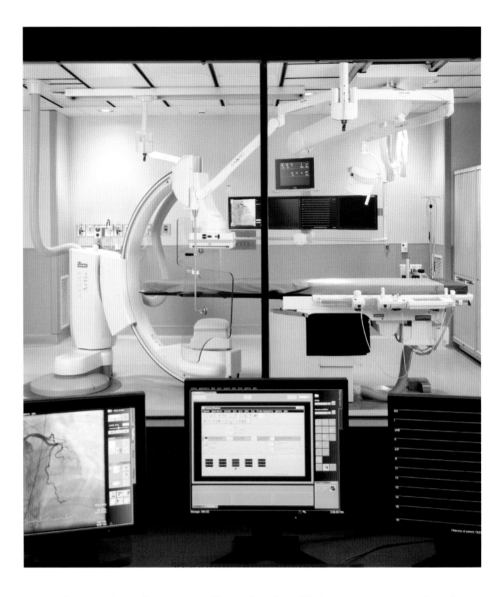

Atrium Medical Center, Middletown, Ohio. Cardiology services have expanded from noninvasive services at the old facility to open-heart surgery and interventional cardiology. *Photo Jeff Millies © Hedrich Blessing.*

ED and outpatient diagnostic allows for the efficient movement of patients through the facility.

The heart of the new facility, its four-story North Tower and five-story South Tower, make up the hospital's diagnostic and treatment areas. These towers are adjoined on floors two through four. Each tower has forty-eight rooms that are clustered in three pods of sixteen rooms each. A central core in the middle of each pod provides convenient supply, medication storage, and nourishment, as well as clean and soiled utility rooms, with pneumatic tubes servicing each area. Each floor of the North Tower is also directly linked to the medical office building. The pharmacy is located for ease of access to patient beds.

Open-heart surgery, catheterizations and angiography are performed in the hospital's surgical services department on the second floor of the North Tower. The cardiovascular surgery intensive care unit is located on the second floor of the South Tower, as are the other cardiac care units. These hospital services are aligned with the cardiac care center in the medical office building, which includes a heart failure center and areas for outpatient cardiology, nuclear cardiology, and cardiac rehabilitation care.

The hospital's medical and surgical patient rooms are on the fourth floor of both the North and South towers. Charting alcoves along the corridors of the patient units give caregivers space to work near patient rooms. In noncritical care units, windows brighten each alcove. A film applied to the glass helps protect patient privacy by obscuring the view of the computer screen. Computers are also located on the headwall of each medical/surgical patient room.

The fifth floor of the South Tower houses a rehabilitation department that includes two independent living apartments designed to reacclimate patients with daily living routines. Each apartment is a certified patient room with a private bedroom and bathroom arranged in a suite formation—a living room, a kitchen, a dining, and a laundry area. With the current healthcare facility taking up only 70 acres of the 200-acre site, the entire medical center, including diagnostic imaging, was designed to grow as future needs change.

UCSD HILLCREST MEDICAL CENTER
INPATIENT MAGNETIC RESONANCE IMAGING (MRI) SUITE
San Diego, California

Architect Childs Mascari Warner remodeled part of the University of California's Hillcrest Medical Center in San Diego to create a new, 5,600-sq. ft., state-of-the-art MRI suite that offered powerful 3-Tesla MRIs, incorporated the safety zones outlined by the American College of Radiology (ACR), and allowed for future developments in magnetic or CT imaging.

UCSD Hillcrest Medical Center, Inpatient Magnetic Resonance Imaging (MRI) Suite, San Diego, California. The MRI suite creates a more relaxed experience by using principles garnered from the natural phenomenon of slot canyons. *Courtesy Childs Mascari Warner Architects. Photo Vance Fox Photography.*

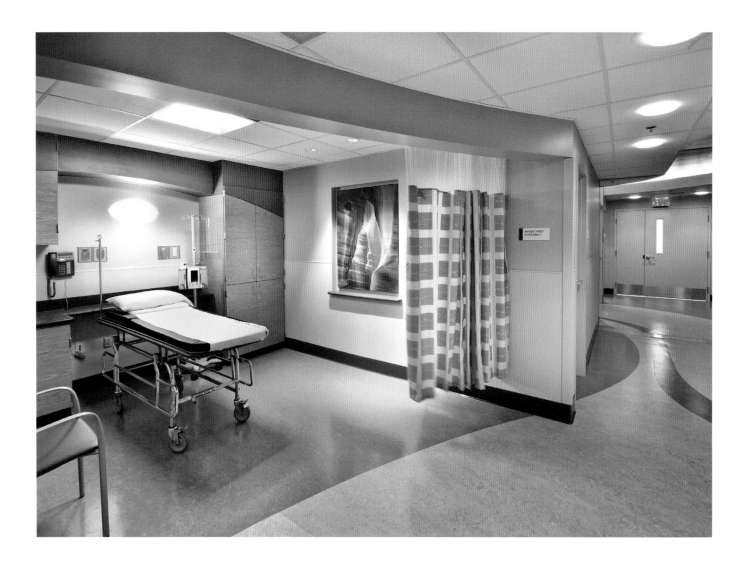

UCSD Hillcrest Medical Center, Inpatient Magnetic Resonance Imaging (MRI) Suite, San Diego, California. The designers of the MRI suite sought to carry the patient through a succession of warm, intimate spaces. *Courtesy Childs Mascari Warner Architects. Photo Vance Fox Photography.*

The designers sought to address typical patient anxieties about claustrophobia and noise by creating a more relaxed experience. To do so, they abstracted some principles from the natural phenomenon of slot canyons, which though narrow are both intriguing and beautiful.

They designed the suite to carry the patient through a succession of warm, intimate spaces that culminate in the scan room. They sought to make the scan room itself, as they described it, "a quiet place of wonder." They used a curved, wood veneer ceiling, backlit alabaster panels that extended the limits of the walls, and an opened-up horizontal space, to engage the patient's attention and allay his or her feeling of confinement during the scan. And they deployed sound-absorbing material in the ceiling system and walls to mitigate the noise produced by the magnet.

The hospital, too, saw the cutting-edge facility, with its user-focused design's beauty and sound qualities, as an aide in both attracting and retaining quality staff.

PARRISH MEDICAL CENTER
Titusville, Florida

As mentioned in Chapter 4, older facilities often no longer work because medicine these days increasingly requires more space, especially to keep abreast of the latest in medical technology. And nowhere is the latest technology more critical than in diagnostics. Parrish Medical Center, located some 50 miles east of Orlando, Florida, was designed by ESa as a replacement facility to serve primarily outpatients and accommodates the latest in technology, while providing an environment that encourages wellness and promotes healing.

Providing the same number of beds as the hospital it replaces, the 210-bed facility has 70 more private rooms than the old hospital. Nearly half of

Parrish Medical Center, Titusville, Florida. The MRI suite primarily serves outpatients. *Photo Scott McDonald © Hedrich Blessing.*

the patient rooms look out on a four-story atrium designed to put patients and visitors at ease with its warm textures and cheerful finishes, which suggest a hotel. Colonnades form the "Circle of Life," which acts as both the hospital's architectural signature and a wayfinding hub where, staff, dressed in blazers, greet patients and families, acting something like concierges. Designed to meet the criteria of the Florida environment, the hospital has welcoming, contemporary features. But patients know, too, they are getting the latest in technology. Indeed, the hospital held off purchasing advanced medical equipment as long as possible to ensure it had the latest in diagnostics and other medical areas, suspending work in some areas to allow more time to incorporate these new technologies.

The 371,000-sq.-ft. not-for-profit hospital blends aesthetics, convenient service adjacencies, and cost-efficiency within a softly curving skin. In the first Parrish Medical Center, built in the 1950s, patients had to walk the entire length of the hospital to get to registration, proving especially difficult for wheelchair-bound patients or those unsteady on their feet. In the new facility, the south entrance is solely for surgical patients, and registration is right at the door to the elevator. Improving service adjacencies was a priority. The new cardiac catheterization lab was placed next to the ICU and on the other side of the OR, so anesthesia support and ICU support fell within a few feet (in the old facility, the cath lab was on the first floor, ICU on the second floor, and the OR across the building). Most pertinently, Parrish Medical Center now also offers diagnostic and other outpatient services that previously were not offered in the original facility, responding to Florida's nearly 10-percent increase in patient volume since the new center opened in late 2002. In addition, special women's health services are now available with separate diagnostic areas and a full-service birthing center. Saving steps in the process of caring for patients is central to the center's key practices, as demonstrated by the integration of several key physicians into the facility.

As one of the first participants of the Pebble Project, the facility collects data for the Center for Healthcare Design. This data helps determine the effects of the environment upon patient satisfaction and staff retention.

MOUNT SINAI MEDICAL CENTER
New York, New York

Architect Norman Rosenfeld, consulting principal at Stonehill & Taylor, completely redesigned and expanded Mount Sinai Hospital's imaging facilities and renovated the space for its inpatient radiology department.

The new imaging services—providing separate accommodation for its inpatient and outpatient populations—added 25,000 sq. ft. A complex project, the new imaging facility was constructed over several years in four phases to assure continuous operation and minimal disruption to its operation.

Dividing the project into phases made it possible for Mount Sinai to incorporate evolving diagnostic technology and advances in imaging. To help keep the radiology staff abreast of the state-of-the-art technology—and pre-

pare for future developments—the architects created an education and training center consisting of seventy-five seats, an integral component of the expansion program.

The renovation of inpatient radiology included eight radio fluoroscopy, five angiography, two spiral CT, and five ultrasound suites. The multiphase, 45,000-sq.-ft. project increased the hospital's capabilities to better diagnose and treat patients, effectively bringing it into the twenty-first century. Though all the work took place in the area of the original department, the hospital was able to operate its inpatient radiology services continuously throughout the 30-month construction period.

The renovation schedule was fast-tracked to bring new technology on-line as rapidly as possible, and the renovation and expansion together brought the total space devoted to imaging to a total of 70,000 sq. ft.

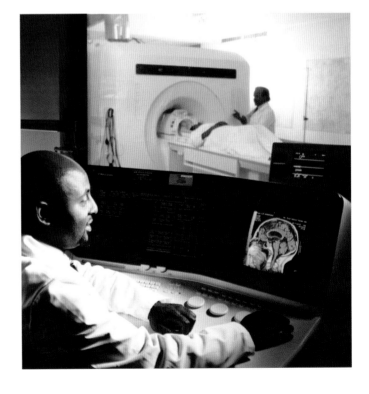

Baptist Diagnostic/Oncology Center-North Mississippi, Oxford, Mississippi. Diagnostics constitute one of the three distinct zones for this state-of-the-art new outpatient facility. *Photo © Robt. Ames Cook.*

BAPTIST DIAGNOSTIC/ONCOLOGY CENTER-NORTH MISSISSIPPI
Oxford, Mississippi

Diagnostics constitute one of the three distinct zones for this state-of-the-art new outpatient facility designed by ESa. In addition to diagnostic imaging, the other two zones dominating the 42,485 sq. ft. facility are an oncology treatment center with a linear vault and an oncology clinic. Diagnostic and cancer treatment areas each have a dedicated lobby. Equipped with the latest technology, the center provides chemotherapy, radiation therapy, and such diagnostic procedures as mammograms and ultrasound.

In addition to the latest technology, the facility boasts lobbies and clinical areas designed to have a soothing, calming effect on patients and families during what is naturally a frightening time in their lives. To that end, natural light streams in through the wealth of windows in the two-story entries, and decorative acoustical panels minimize unnecessary noise. The building's design incorporates various light levels: task, ambient and natural.

MERCY MEDICAL CENTER
IMAGING SUITE
Des Moines, Iowa

For Mercy Medical Center—a recently constructed and owner-occupied hospital tower in central Iowa—RDG Planning & Design created one of the premier 3-Tesla MRI suites in the state. From the outset RDG's design team and Mercy administrators and professionals collaborated to develop a plan that allowed for expansion of the suite as demand increases—rooms had to be

Mercy Medical Center, Imaging Suite, Des Moines, Iowa. Patient comfort and privacy took priority, beginning with the reception area. *Courtesy RDG Planning & Design. Photo Kun Zhang.*

Mercy Medical Center, Imaging Suite, Des Moines, Iowa. Finished in soothing wood tones, the MRI suite uses natural light to help create a tranquil setting of what design firm RDG Planning & Design calls a "simple elegance" aimed at alleviating the stress associated with receiving an MRI scan. *Courtesy RDG Planning & Design. Photo Kun Zhang.*

designed within an already occupied facility without disrupting hospital operations. The project called, then, not only for special acoustics and shielding but also for the precise coordination of construction and the transport of the MRI unit. Seeking to make sure its patients remained safe throughout the process, the hospital and its designers adhered strictly to the most recent MRI safety guidelines, separating spaces into zones for operation and construction.

Patient comfort and privacy took priority, beginning with the waiting room and continuing through to the MRI scan room. In the waiting area, the design provided private registration bays. Once registration is completed, patients are directed to separate women's and men's subwaiting and changing areas, located within a few footsteps of the MRI scan room. From there, they can move on to the private, staff-monitored prep areas outside the control room for both outpatient and inpatient care.

The suite was finished in soothing wood tones, and natural light also helps to create a tranquil setting of what RDG called "simple elegance" that seeks to alleviate the stress associated with receiving an MRI scan. Even as it enhanced workflow, the design aimed to provide, above all, a positive patient experience.

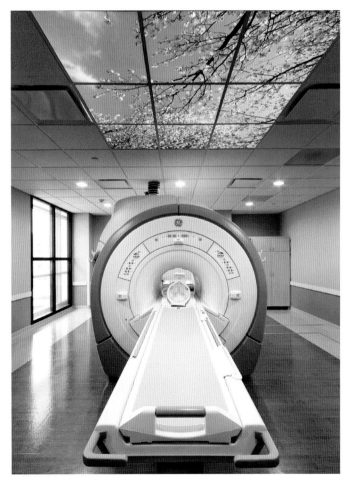

CHAPTER 7

Surgery Facilities

Acute-care centers almost always perform four general classes of surgery: major invasive procedures, universally invasive rigid endoscopy, surgical intervention that treats patients without extensive invasion (balloon angioplasty, lithotripsy, laser procedures, and so on), and ambulatory, outpatient procedures. Too often, the design of traditional hospitals fails to differentiate these classes adequately and efficiently. This chapter considers design strategies for accommodating all four classes of surgery, as well as an additional, intermediate class—short-stay surgery.

It is essential that hospital planners assess surgery needs before design—of new construction or renovation—begins. Today, in many hospitals, outpatient surgery makes up 75 to 80 percent of the surgery load. This means that designers must devote careful consideration to outpatient waiting and reception areas, staging and holding areas, and recovery needs. Waiting and recovery areas should also accommodate companions and family members. In addition, even for surgical inpatients, it is desirable to provide separate staging and recovery areas for trauma versus nontrauma cases. Hospitals must also determine where such procedures as balloon angioplasty, certain types of laser surgery, and lithotripsy will be performed. Many of these kinds of procedures can be done in ambulatory facilities entirely separate from the surgical department, including in the physician's office.

Planning the number and type of surgical facilities depends on at least the following eleven factors:

1. Number of surgical procedures performed (based on a total of all patient beds and a study of the preceding five years in an existing facility, or

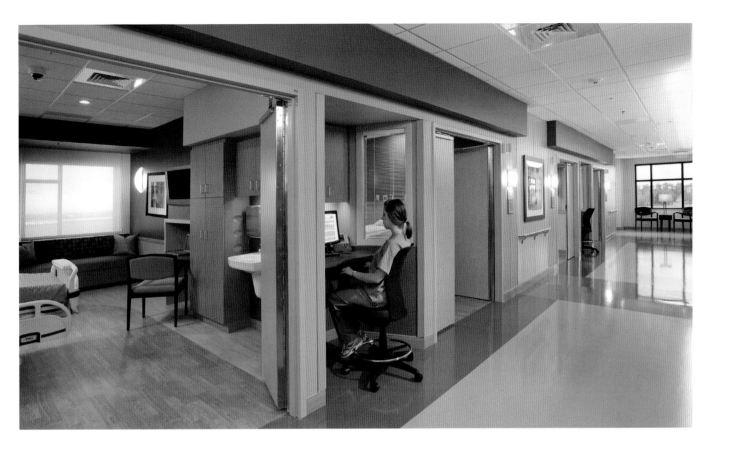

St. Anthony Hospital, Lakewood, Colorado. Medical/Surgical acute-care corridor. *Photo © Michael Peck.*

for new facility construction, based on projections extrapolated from comparable existing facilities).

2. Type of surgery performed (based on the above studies/projections).

3. Average length of surgical procedures (based on the above studies/projections).

4. Number of inpatient versus outpatient surgeries (based on the above studies/projections).

5. Number of emergency surgeries performed (based on the above studies/projections).

6. Planned hours of availability of surgical facilities for scheduled procedures.

7. Number of critical-care beds available for surgical patients. (Note that fewer than 20 percent require such beds.)

8. Surgical needs of the community.

9. Use rate of existing operating rooms (based on the above studies/projections).

10. Physician population (for example, is it high in orthopedic surgery, urology, etc.).

11. Effect of emerging technologies on surgery. (Laser and other minimally invasive surgery [MIS] techniques have already had a great impact and change the design requirements of the "operating room.")

Throughout this book, we reiterate the prevailing trend toward the removal of barriers that have traditionally set the hospital environment apart. Indeed, the trend toward ambulatory and short-stay surgery is part of the movement toward integrating the hospital and healthcare facility with the surrounding community and environment. However, even in the most progressive hospitals, the general-purpose surgical suite is one function area that still requires something like the traditional barriers. The surgical suite must provide a safe environment for the patient undergoing surgical intervention. Toward this end, four conditions must be achieved:

1. The surgical suite must be relatively isolated within the hospital to exclude unauthorized persons.

2. The surgical suite and, in particular, the operating rooms themselves must be bacteriologically isolated from the rest of the hospital.

3. The surgical suite must provide direct access to all of the equipment, supplies, and instruments required for procedures without the necessity of leaving the protected area.

4. The surgical suite serves to centralize requisite staff, a condition that has become more vital than ever as the surgical staff has evolved into a coordinated team of highly trained specialists.

The surgical suite consists of operating or procedure rooms, sterile and nonsterile storage areas, sterile and nonsterile corridors (to facilitate traffic flow), and support areas. These support areas include preoperative holding areas (increasingly important as more facilities offer ambulatory and short-stay surgery, in which the patient is not admitted to an overnight bed), a recovery room (again, increasingly important to designers, since ambulatory patients are released directly from this area), and satellite pathology laboratory facilities. There are four generally accepted surgical suite layouts, each designed to maintain a "three-zone concept," which consists of an unrestricted area, a semirestricted area, and a restricted area.

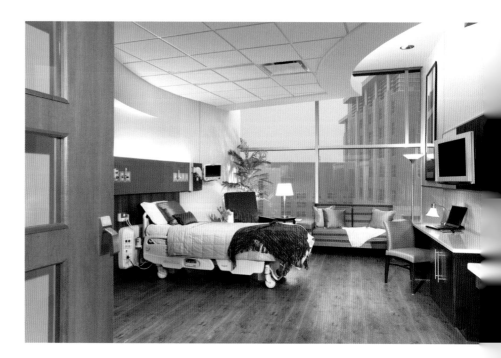

The Heart Hospital Baylor Plano, Plano, Texas. RTKL Associates Inc. designed the patient rooms to include family zones with wireless connections, work spaces, and comfortable furniture. *Courtesy RTKL Associates Inc. Photo © Charles Davis Smith.*

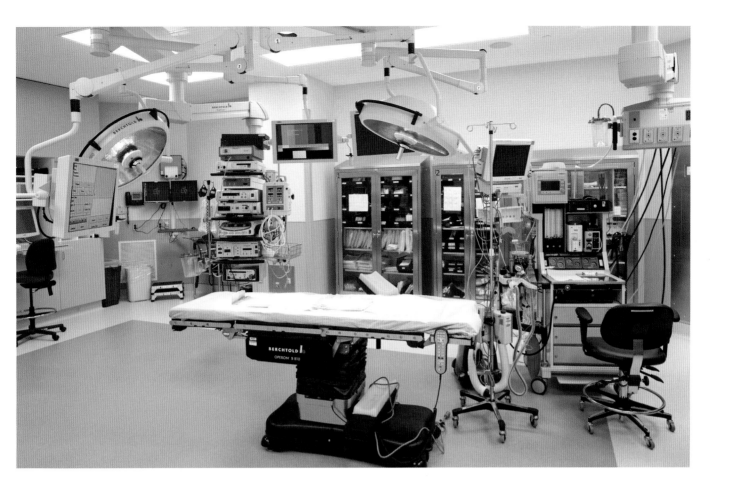

The unrestricted area is the entrance and exit from the suite and often includes the holding or preoperative area, the postoperative area or recovery room, and dressing rooms, lounges, offices, and receiving or storage areas. The semirestricted area contains storage areas for clean and sterile supplies, sterilization, processing, and distribution area for instruments and equipment. The restricted area consists of the operating room itself as well as adjacent substerile areas, where scrub sinks and autoclaves are located. Storage areas for supplies that may be needed during procedures are also located here.

The four basic surgical suite layouts include the central (single) corridor plan; double corridor plan; peripheral corridor plan with sterile core; and cluster, pod, or modular plan. The central corridor plan is the simplest of the four but also the least flexible and least isolating. It is practical only for small surgical suites of two to four procedure rooms. All facilities are accessed from a single, central corridor.

The double corridor plan is usually a U- or I-shaped configuration suitable for five to fifteen procedure rooms along the periphery of the corridors, with the central area between the corridors providing rooms for sterile supply, instrument sterilization, processing, distribution, and other ancillary functions. This configuration furnishes greater isolation than the central corridor design, and it is an economical means of sharing support facilities among a number of procedure rooms. However, it does not offer flexibility for later expansion, and it does not facilitate ease of communication (for supply and

St. Vincent's OrthoSport Center & Medical Tower, Birmingham, Alabama. Surgery facility, designed by Earl Swensson Associates. *Photo © Viscom Photographics.*

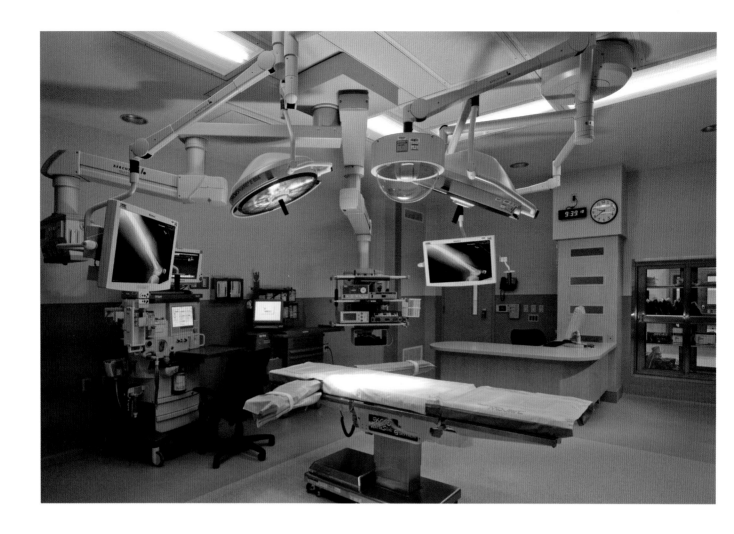

OrthoColorado Hospital at St. Anthony Medical Campus, Lakewood, Colorado. Green lighting enables the surgeon's eyes to better distinguish small details and proves particularly helpful in reducing glare from video monitors. *Photo © Michael Peck.*

transport of patients) with other hospital areas. It also does little to minimize the risks of cross-contamination from one procedure room to another.

The plan that provides the most stringent isolation of procedure rooms from the rest of the hospital and from one another is the peripheral corridor design. This design divides the surgical suite into a nonsterile outer core and a sterile inner core. The outer-core corridor rings the procedure rooms, which, in turn, surround an inner-core corridor that provides communication between the procedure rooms and a central sterile storage area. While this plan ensures a high degree of sterile isolation, it is very space-consuming and demands strict regulation of a somewhat complex traffic-flow pattern, thereby tending to increase the shunting of patients.

What is perhaps the most practical and flexible layout is also the newest. The cluster, pod, or modular design consists of a small number of procedure rooms clustered around a central core area, which allows for sterile distribution of supplies among the four procedure rooms via pass-through doors or windows. Each surgical suite might contain three, four, or five pods, and the suite is accessed by a peripheral corridor surrounding the entire suite. Not only does this design provide for excellent isolation, it is also highly flexible, offering maximum potential for future expansion. The pod or cluster plan is inherently elegant and economical and lends itself to a virtually infinite variety of floor plan configurations and overall building footprints.

The Procedure Room

General Considerations

Many shapes have been tried for the procedure room itself, but there is little practical reason to vary from the basic rectangle or square.

The 2010 *Guidelines for Design and Construction of Health Care Facilities* suggests that each general OR should have a minimum clear area of 400 sq. ft., exclusive of fixed or wall-mounted cabinets and built-in shelves. They call for a minimum 20-ft. clear dimension between such fixed cabinets and built-in shelves. This would probably prove suitable for general procedures, although the trend is toward larger spaces of 600 sq. ft. minimum, and in trauma ORs you might see 650 to 750 sq. ft. Minor surgery, cystoscopy, endoscopy, and most outpatient surgery requires less space—the *Guidelines* call for a minimum of 350 sq. ft. for surgical cystoscopic and other procedures. Technology- and equipment-intensive surgical procedures such as cardiac, orthopedic and neurosurgery require 600 sq. ft. of floor space (plus a minimum clear dimension of 20 sq. ft.), according to the *Guidelines*, to allow for additional personnel and/or large equipment. The trend toward performing more rigid endoscopic procedures requires large procedure rooms to accommodate equipment. Some of the new hybrid operating rooms—discussed below—need to be much larger, in the 800-sq.-ft. range, since they must be flexible enough to accommodate several kinds of procedures and surgery teams and complex ceiling-mounted equipment. After careful study of the hospital's surgical requirements, procedure rooms of varying space configurations should be planned.

Finishes should be as nonporous as possible, since rough or porous surfaces readily harbor bacteria. Floor and wall materials should be applied as seamlessly as possible. The material must be able to withstand repeated washings with harsh germicidal cleaners. The current favored materials are laminated polyester with an epoxy finish, hard vinyl flooring that can be heat-sealed seamlessly, and ceramic glass panels that can be seamlessly sealed. Floor-wall junctions should be curved to facilitate cleaning. The top surfaces of any casework that is not built-in should be sloped for ease of cleaning. For the same reason corners should be curved or 45-degree angles.

Color

Color in the procedure room is now a topic of discussion. The green that is universally used in surgical gowns, towels, and sheets is often used in a lighter hue as the dominant color in the operating rooms themselves. The green was introduced in 1914 by San Francisco surgeon Harry Sherman, who complained about the glare caused by the traditional white operating-room appointments. He argued that green not only reduced glare and was relaxing—psychologically "cool"—it also contrasted vividly with blood and predominantly pink tissue, helping to keep the surgeon's eyes acute to these vitally important hues.

While many procedure rooms are still designed with green or other cool pastels, many others now feature warmer tones, including beige, pale gold, and

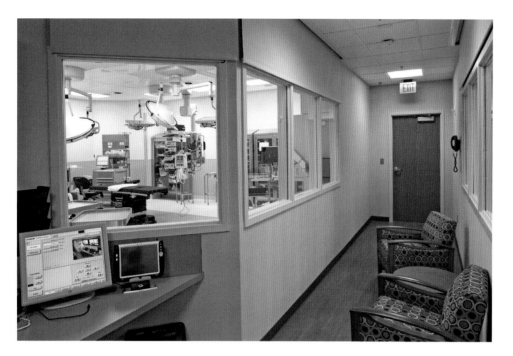

St. Vincent's OrthoSport Center & Medical Tower, Birmingham, Alabama. Surgery facility designed by Earl Swensson Associates. *Photo © Viscom Photographics.*

aqua. Peach and rose tones have also been used, but such colors may inhibit quick detection of gross contamination and are, therefore, not ideal choices. According to numerous recent interior designers, operating-room green is perceived as sickly and depressing. Another trend is the use of more than one dominant color, a design element introduced to relieve the visual fatigue and lapses in concentration that may be caused by exposure to an expanse of a single color.

Color, of course, is a key issue in patient-friendly design. Therefore, the use of color in the procedure room should be considered not only from the point of view of improving staff performance by reducing fatigue and enhancing concentration, but also from the point of view of the patient, whose well-being (and sense of well-being) may be enhanced by alternatives to the sickly OR green.

Ventilation and Clean-Room Technology

The current standards for the operating room environment address air-exchange rate, filtration, temperature, humidity, and the maintenance of positive pressure.

Current generally accepted standards call for a ventilation system that provides for fifteen to twenty-five air changes per hour, to follow the 2009 *Clinical Infrastructure Matrix and Operational Benchmarks* of the Facilities Planning Forum Advisory Board, which are higher than the 2010 *Guidelines* minimum requirements. The U.S. Department of Health and Human Services specifies fifteen changes, of which at least three must consist of fresh outside air. Local codes vary; some require 100 percent outside air, while others allow up to 80 percent filtered, recirculated air. Prevailing standards call for air-filtration systems that achieve 90 percent efficiency in accordance with American Society of Heating, Refrigerating, and Air-conditioning Engineers (ASHRAE) Standard 52-76.

Prevailing standards for temperatures are 68 to 73 degrees Fahrenheit, according to the *Guidelines*, with a relative humidity of 30 to 60 percent. The humidity standard, which was established during an era of flammable anesthetics, is subject to reevaluation in light of the general adoption of nonflammable anesthetics. A lower relative humidity is less conducive to bacterial growth. OR temperature settings should be determined in consultation with the surgeons who will be using those rooms.

Finally, the operating room should have a positive pressure of about

.0005 inches of H_2O relative to the surrounding area. This is to ensure that only filtered air, not ambient air, enters the operating room.

In general, most authorities agree that the current prevailing environmental standards are acceptable for general surgery, producing a clean wound infection rate of less than 1 to 2 percent. However, designers of some recent operating rooms intended for high-risk interventions, including transplantation surgery and other procedures involving the introduction of immunosuppressive drugs and surgery on elderly or infirmed persons highly susceptible to infection, have advocated the use of "clean-room technology," which borrows some of the techniques developed by high-tech industries (for example, manufacturers of microprocessor chips) that require extraordinarily contaminant-free environments.

Clean-room operating-room design has become increasingly common. In addition to more sophisticated filtration and pressurization equipment, these rooms can use laminar airflow clean air systems rather than the conventional plenum air-handling systems. Plenum systems are essentially very efficient and highly filtered air-conditioning and ventilation systems, whereas laminar airflow can involve vertical ceiling-to-floor or horizontal, ceiling-borne, wall-to-wall systems or yet other configurations. Low-return registers—a minimum of two per room, on opposite walls or corners—are also required by most regulatory agencies.

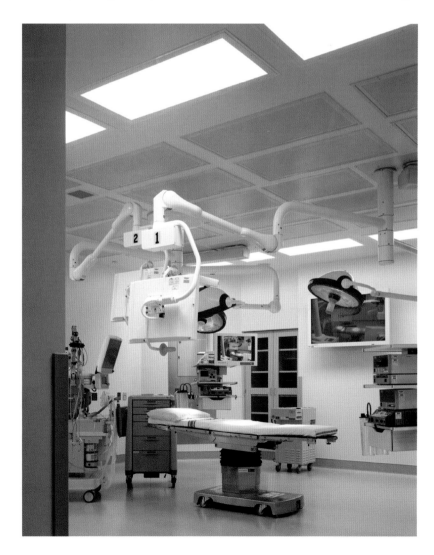

Rockingham Memorial Hospital, Harrisonburg, Virginia. Open-heart surgery room designed by Earl Swensson Associates. *Photo Scott McDonald © Hedrich Blessing.*

Lighting

Lighting in the operating room is obviously critical. Two types of illumination are required: general (ambient) room lighting and task lighting. These two sources must be coordinated to provide maximum visibility of the wound, yet provide a restful field of vision away from the wound, while still providing sufficient, glare-free illumination for other members of the surgical team. Moreover, care must be taken to ensure that the task lighting does not unduly raise the temperature of the surgical field (the area directly around the wound or incision).

Recent innovations in fiber optics continue to influence choices in task lighting, and needs and preferences vary depending on the type of procedure and the individual surgeon. Experts agree that, while the architect or lighting engineer is chiefly responsible for specifying the ambient lighting in the procedure room, the surgeons who will use that room should be consulted on what illumination to make available. And it is key to allow for adjusted light levels—for example, with dimmers.

Finally, the color of the light is a significant consideration, since it is critical for the surgeon to be able to assess the state of tissues accurately and without distortion. In a classic letter to *Plastic and Reconstructive Surgery*, plastic surgeon Dr. Hugh A. Johnson noted that he preferred to examine patients by natural north light—the kind of light long favored by artists for its absolute trueness to color. While it is unlikely that operating rooms will be constructed with northern exposure in mind, ESa and other architectural firms have encouraged the use of windows in operating rooms wherever appropriate and possible. It is often desirable to design operating rooms so that the windowed wall faces an enclosed courtyard. In any event, lighting designers for operating rooms need to be aware of the importance of achieving a color/temperature mix that closely approximates natural light. Recently, lighting has been developed that so closely simulates daylight, it is often used in mock windows. Operating rooms in which eye surgery is performed should not have windows or, if windows are present, internal blinds or LCD blackout technology should be available to block out the light.

The Impact of New Technologies

While such advances as clean-room technology make high-risk and cutting-edge major procedures possible, the principal effect of new technologies has been to decrease the number of traditional inpatient surgical procedures. For a number of decades, hospitals felt the need either to restructure significantly for ambulatory surgical care or give up that growing market to freestanding ambulatory surgery centers (ASCs) and private physicians who perform office surgery, but that trend, at least for major hospitals, has faded. The issues involved in designing freestanding ambulatory surgery facilities as well as hospital-associated ambulatory surgery facilities will be discussed in Chapter 10. However, we briefly review the relevant technologies here for their impact on the market and design of inpatient surgical facilities.

Endoscopic Surgery

Endoscopic surgery is one of the surgical technologies that is now prompting hospitals to reshape their surgical service strategies. It is used in the vast majority of cholecystectomies, prostate cancer stagings, and certain lung procedures; in kidney removals; and in appendectomies, hysterectomies, and hernia repairs. Endoscopic surgery plays a significant role in such procedures as vagotomy and bowel and colon resections. Some endoscopic surgery procedures can be performed on an ambulatory basis, while others—such as hernia repair, which require a much smaller surgical wound and less intensive anesthesia—are conducive to short stays. While most surgeons are enthusiastic about endoscopic surgery, some still caution both patients and practitioners to be wary of uncritical acceptance of the technique in all situ

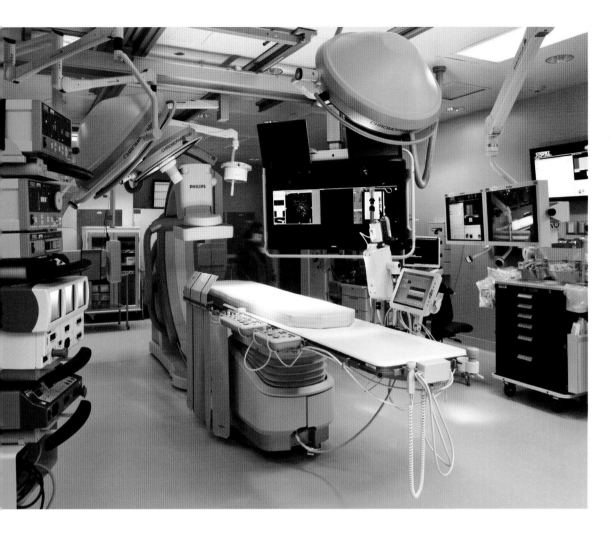

Critical Care Tower, Vanderbilt University Medical Center, Nashville, Tennessee. Notice once again the use of detail-enhancing, glare-reducing green lighting in the surgery room. *Courtesy Earl Swensson Associates and Don Blair & Partners Architects, LLP. Photo © Kyle Dreier Photography.*

tions. However, even the most skeptical surgeons compare the magnitude of the impact of endoscopic surgery to the impact of anesthesia, which was introduced over a century ago.

Gynecologists were among the first to make widespread use of laparoscopes, primarily to perform tubal ligations and to diagnose pelvic pain and fertility problems. As fiber optics and surgical instruments were developed to use in conjunction with the laparoscope, surgical procedures began to take their place beside the diagnostic uses. Coupled with surgical laser technology, endoscopic surgery continues to thrive.

Arthroscopy

Arthroscopy uses a technology similar to the laparoscope to permit small-incision, ambulatory or short-stay surgery on joints. The nature of the surgery is such that it might be offered not only in hospital ambulatory surgery facilities and freestanding facilities but in dedicated sports medicine departments or freestanding sports medicine clinics.

Laser Surgery

Numerous laser procedures can be performed outside of an operating room, in either a physician's office or a special procedure room that is much smaller than a conventional operating room. However, various major inva-

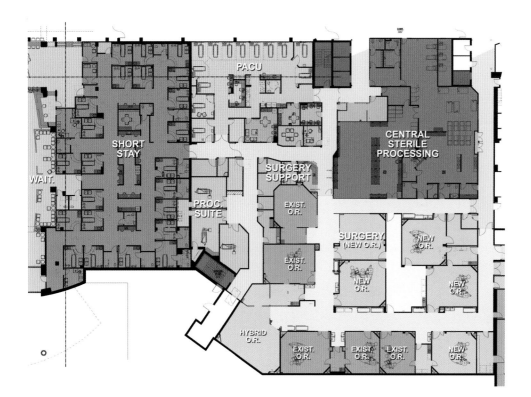

A surgery facilities floor plan created by Earl Swensson Associates.

sive procedures employing lasers do require a conventional operating room that is specially modified for laser use. Certain laser types, such as the endoscopic Nd:YAG laser, have special power requirements, which need to be addressed in the M/E facilities of the procedure room. Most modifications consist of designing or adapting ceilings for mounting microscopes and video monitoring equipment. Operating rooms intended for cystoscopy and other minor procedures can be as small as 350 sq. ft., according to the *Guidelines*, and 400 sq. ft. for the use of CO_2 lasers, which are equipped with a smoke evacuator.

Finally, special consideration must be given to finishes in laser procedure rooms and to minimizing vibration. Walls in laser rooms cannot be reflective; therefore, high-gloss epoxy-base paints must be avoided, and tile or vinyl work should have a buff finish in medium tones rather than light colors. The walls must be free of glass or windows, which could reflect and bounce the laser beam. A laser procedure room, especially when the laser is used in eye surgery, must not be subject to vibration. This is an issue that must be addressed in terms of structural design, materials, and adjacencies.

Noninvasive Radiosurgery

Nuclear medicine departments perform noninvasive radiosurgery procedures primarily on malignancies of the brain. These include gamma knife surgery, in which cobalt radiation is carefully directed at the malignancy, and a newer technology called stereotactic radiosurgery, in which a special skull-positioning headset focuses radiation directly and exclusively on the malignancy. The gamma knife procedure requires a linear accelerator and radioactive cobalt isotope fuel, as well as various support and shielding measures. Some stereotactic devices use microwave-generated energy, which does not require fuel or an accelerator.

Lithotripsy

Lithotripsy is an alternative to surgery for the treatment of kidney stones. In hospitals, this treatment modality is generally assigned to the radiology department. It can even be adapted as a mobile technology; however, a recovery room should be adjacent or nearby.

Image-guided Surgery

Image-guided surgery is the general term used for any surgical procedure where the surgeon uses indirect visualization to operate, by employing imaging instruments in real time, such as fiber-optic guides, an internal video camera, flexible or rigid endoscopes, ultrasonography, MRI, and so on. Most such procedures are minimally invasive. The technology for such surgery was originally developed for treatment of brain tumors, but it has most often been used in surgery of the sinuses, to avoid damage to the brain and the nervous system.

A hand-held surgical probe is an essential component of any image-guided surgery (IGS) system. During the operation, the IGS system tracks the probe position and displays the anatomy beneath it as three orthogonal image slices on a workstation-based, three-dimensional imaging system. Existing IGS systems use different tracking techniques including mechanical, optical, ultrasonic, and MRI. The Medtronic Stealth Station is the most widely used navigation system on the market, and it employs both electromagnetic and optical tracking technology.

The precision provided by IGS technology allows surgeons to create an exact, detailed plan for the surgery, to calculate, for example, where the best spot is to make the incision, the optimal path to the targeted area, and what critical structures must be avoided. The technology for this surgery is not unlike that used by our global positioning satellite systems, but before any such image-guided operation can take place, the patient must undergo diagnostic testing such as a CT scan or MRI (though these are increasingly designed into some ORs). These images are then converted into three-dimensional images showing the patient's organs, muscles, tissue and nerves, and surgeons use this information to plan the operation. Because the view is so precise and so controllable, a surgeon can actually see where healthy tissue ends and a brain tumor begins, or precisely where on the spine to place a pedicle screw to maximize patient mobility.

IGS technology promises in many ways to revolutionize traditional surgical techniques and may have a major impact on imaging department design, as we mentioned in Chapter 6, and on ORs. Image-guided ORs are increasingly considered an asset in trauma centers, for example.

Robotic Surgery

Surgeries that employ robotics, like the Da Vinci system, to conduct minimally invasive procedures have become common. The minimally invasive machines offer surgical precision and results unmatched by the human hand that overcome the limitations of both traditional open surgery and conventional minimally invasive surgery.

The idea of robotics in surgery got its start in the military. The goal was to develop technology a surgeon could use to perform an operation from a remote location on an injured soldier in the battlefield. This concept evolved into robotics to enhance surgical performance with the surgeon usually guiding the robotic arm from a location in or adjacent to the operating room.

The surgeon sits at a station peering at a monitor that shows a magnified view of the surgical field. A computer mimics and enhances his hand movements, making them more precise by dampening even a tiny tremor in the surgeon's hands, which might otherwise be a problem, under high-power microscopic magnification.

Urologic, gynecologic, cardiothoracic, and general surgery are performed today with robots like the da Vinci Surgical System. Fallopian tube repair in women, microsurgery on the fetus, and minimally invasive coronary bypass surgery are examples of procedures now being performed that were extremely difficult if not impossible before this technology.

Robotic surgery of course has an impact on OR design, usually requiring more square footage for larger equipment as mentioned above under general considerations and sometimes separate control areas, which vary depending on the system and the equipment.

Restructuring the Surgical Department for Ambulatory or Short-Stay Procedures

In Chapter 10 we explore design alternatives for hospital-associated dedicated ambulatory surgery facilities and freestanding ambulatory surgery facilities. However, many hospitals are choosing to "mainstream" inpatients and out-patients by adapting their traditional inpatient surgical services to serve both types of patients.

Usually, this entails an enlargement and upgrading of preoperative (holding) and postoperative (recovery) facilities to create a more patient-friendly environment. The chief complaint among outpatients in this arrangement is a perception that the recovery-room nursing staff devotes more time to the inpatients than outpatients.

Mainstreaming can be a workable interim alternative in hospitals that, for various reasons, are unable to create dedicated outpatient surgery facilities. In smaller hospitals and in hospitals located in medically underserved areas, integrating the outpatient and inpatient surgical services may also be an economical means of adapting to the changing nature of surgery. However, in larger hospitals and more highly competitive markets, the establishment of a discrete ambulatory surgery facility is the prevailing trend and, in many cases, is probably crucial to remaining competitive or even financially viable. As "in and out" surgery in one day or less becomes ever more common, patients increasingly value the access, parking, upscale support, and other conveniences associated with the discrete ambulatory facility.

Hybrid Operating Rooms

In response to the changing nature of surgery, both in its technology and in its economics, hybrid operating rooms, which allow for maximum flexibility, especially with cardiovascular patients whose treatment often involves a combination of surgical and interventional procedures, are coming to the fore. Unlike traditional surgery, these interventional procedures involve catheters to get inside blood vessels for diagnostic tests or to repair damaged vessels or other heart structures. That means that cardiovascular specialists have been leaders in hybrid therapies and in the trend of collaborating surgeons who use the new hybrid operating rooms.

The operating rooms are specially designed to allow surgeons and physicians to perform combinations of catheter-based, conventional, and less invasive surgical procedures, and thus to streamline care for patients who need multiple procedures as part of their treatment.

As mentioned earlier, the rooms are large and can include, for example, custom-designed imaging systems on robotic arms that integrate intravascular ultrasound, dynamic CT imaging, angiography, and other imaging technologies. They allow certain patients to have a same-day, one-stop process, such as a cardiac catheterization to check coronary arteries before planned valve surgeries, or they can accommodate, say, a hybrid stent procedure and valve surgery.

Such rooms can allow cardiovascular surgeons and intervention specialists to work side by side, for example, outfitted with fixed fluoroscopy, an imaging device that provides real-time, moving radiology images. Traditionally, only the hospital's cardiac catheter lab featured such devices used by intervention specialists in minimally invasive procedures such as angioplasties. In the long run, this kind of cooperation promises fewer surgeries, safer procedures, shorter hospital stays, faster recoveries, and better outcomes.

The Heart Hospital Baylor Plano, Plano, Texas. RTKL designed the Heart Hospital with an upscale, hotel-like environment, including good views to the outside and eye-catching accents on the walls. *Courtesy RTKL Associates Inc. Photo © Charles Davis Smith.*

The Holding Room

Before the 1980s, it was common to transport patients directly from their rooms—or the ward—to surgery, or to hold them for a time on a gurney out in the department corridor or at best in an alcove near the procedure room. During the 1980s, dedicated preoperative holding rooms began to become accepted practice as a more humane alternative to corridor park-

Centennial Medical Center, Nashville, Tennessee. Exterior. *Photo Norman McGrath.*

ing and as a way of ensuring preoperative continuity of care under members of the preoperative nursing staff. With the increase in ambulatory and short-stay surgery, these holding areas became increasingly important over the next three decades, since many patients were admitted directly to them. In most cases nowadays, a formal staging area makes it unnecessary to admit surgical patients the day before the scheduled procedure.

More recently, the holding room has undergone a transformation into a preoperative testing center or care unit. The change in terminology is significant in and of itself. "Holding" implies a passive form of workflow management, and many patients might well question if there is any real difference between the concept of a holding room and a corral. In contrast, a preoperative testing center or care unit implies active steps toward preparation for surgery, streamlining the process and making for fewer patient stops. Such units, where preoperative evaluation is performed, can do much to address the gap in care that might result when a patient is admitted to surgery on the day of the procedure rather than on the day before.

Recovery Room (Postanesthesia Care Unit)

The patient should leave the operating room and undergo the early stages of recovery in a single-bed cubicle. Light levels should be relatively low, and soothing indirect light is best. Designers need to be careful about specifying fluorescent or direct, downward lighting in recovery areas. It is important that the lighting approximate natural light as much as possible, since caregivers can tell a great deal about the patient's condition from his skin tone. Somber color schemes should be avoided, but designers need to be aware that patients recovering from anesthesia can often suffer headache and nausea (rather like a bad hangover). Irritating lights or bold color patterns can aggravate this unpleasant condition.

An alternative to curtained recovery cubicles are small rooms with wide glass doors. Closed doors provide quiet and privacy, yet they also permit the nursing staff to monitor recovery unobtrusively and efficiently.

After the patient is sufficiently alert and stabilized, he or she is either transported to a room if an inpatient or to a second-stage recovery area, sometimes called the discharge holding area or lounge.

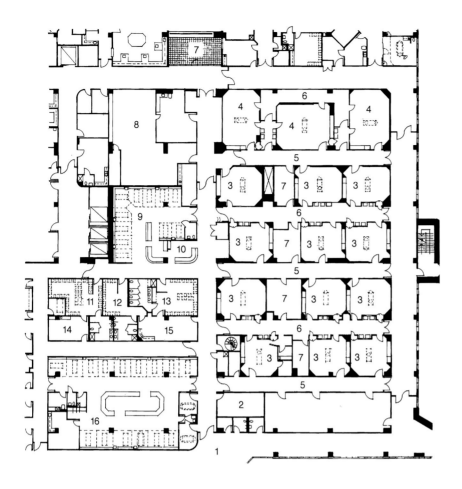

Centennial Medical Center, Nashville, Tennessee. Floor plan of second floor showing surgery/recovery.

1. Family waiting area
2. Pharmacy
3. Operating rooms
4. Heart operating rooms
5. Patient corridors
6. Staff corridor
7. Clean storage areas
8. Work area
9. Patient holding area
10. Nurses' station
11. Men's/physicians' lockers
12. Male staff lockers
13. Female staff lockers
14. Physicians' lounge
15. Staff lounge
16. Recovery room

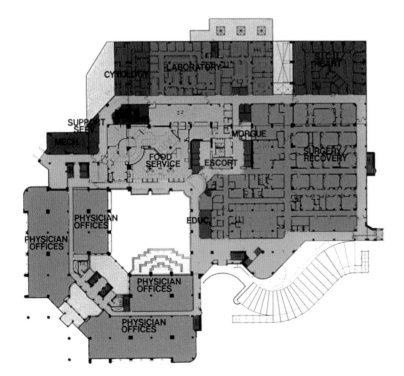

Centennial Medical Center, Nashville, Tennessee. Floor plan, second floor.

Baptist Memorial Hospital-DeSoto, Southaven, Mississippi. Patient floor reception desks have unobstructed views to the elevator lobby for the benefit of security and for helpfulness to visitors. *Photo © Kieran Reynolds Photography.*

Discharge Holding Area/Lounge

Ambulatory surgery patients can generally be discharged directly from the recovery room, but many short-stay surgical patients and even certain same-day surgical patients cannot be safely discharged directly from recovery. Depending on the occupancy rate at the hospital in question, it may be practically or financially infeasible to transfer these patients to a surgical bed. One answer to this dilemma is the discharge holding area or lounge. This is a comfortable area, pleasingly decorated and equipped with such amenities as recliner-style chairs, televisions, and reading materials, as well as provision for meals and the administration of any required medication. Patients are monitored by licensed practical nursing staff and patient-care assistants. The discharge holding area can also serve as the site of postoperative patient education—a relaxed place for a caregiver to review with the patient any necessary postoperative self-care steps. Of course, this area can also be used by ambulatory patients who, for one reason or another, are not quite ready to go home, but have sufficiently recovered to no longer warrant occupying valuable recovery room space and recovery staff resources. Thus, the discharge holding area provides a considerable measure of flexibility in a surgery unit that serves a mix of inpatient, same-day, short-stay, and ambulatory patients.

Recovery/Discharge Trends

A number of hospitals have addressed discharge of patients from same-day and short-stay surgical procedures by either contracting with nearby hotels or entering into joint ventures with hotel developers for patient lodging. The hotel stay is an alternative to an extended hospital stay for patients who require more care and supervision than they can be given at home, but do not require the more intensive care hospital settings provide.

We end this chapter with overviews of contemporary surgical departments. (Design examples for ASCs—surgery facilities in an ambulatory setting—in general appear in Chapter 10.)

BAPTIST MEMORIAL HOSPITAL-DESOTO

Southaven, Mississippi

Surgery facilities are key to Baptist Memorial Hospital-DeSoto's new eleven-story patient tower, designed by ESa. Intended to better position the hospital to serve the high-growth area of northern Mississippi and to accommodate the latest advances in medical practice, the design draws on Mississippi's architectural heritage, while deploying state-of-the-art technology and patient care.

The new surgery department contains eleven surgical suites, with space to add two others in the future. The new surgical suites are almost one-and-a-half times the size of those in the original facility, a size much more in keeping with what today's surgical equipment can require of operating rooms. New surgical support areas include a postanesthesia care unit, a recovery unit, central sterile processing, and staff lounge and lockers. Each suite has an integral holding alcove, allowing patients being transported to and from surgery to be wheeled to a wait station free of hallway traffic and noise.

Nursing efficiencies are designed into the hospital's medical/surgical patient floors, each providing forty-eight private patient rooms arranged in four pods of twelve. In addition to each floor's central workstation, decentralized nursing stations and decentralized supplies in the pods allow each unit to be self-sufficient. The bathrooms of the mirror-image rooms back up to one another for cost-efficiency. A large emergency department boasts fifteen more exam rooms than the previous ED. An adjacent pediatric ED has its own separate waiting room.

Inside the new building, pineapples and damask, traditional Southern motifs, are represented in stylized form in wall coverings, fabrics, and carpets throughout the hospital, and quilt patterns are incorporated into the flooring, drawing visitors down the corridor to the patient rooms. In the main public spaces, darker accent bands in the porcelain tile floors also lead visitors to various areas. Circles off the main rotunda create smaller, more intimate spots within the larger space. A fountain in the entry rotunda serves as a focal point for wayfinding. Indeed, the fountain is also one of many features designed to soothe people who use the building. Garden views, natural light and the building's symmetrical layout all create a relaxing environment. The color palette was taken from the local landscape, with hues meant to invoke the rich soils and silts of the Mississippi River delta. Walnut and maple, both local woods, are used in the building, too.

The existing hospital was a three-story, 199-bed facility often overwhelmed with more patients than available beds, with scattered services, a nondescript exterior and entry, and outdated rooms cramped by new technology. The new tower effectively increases the hospital's role in the community with greater visibility and with the provision of expanded services in a healing environment.

Memorial Hospital of South Bend, South Bend, Indiana. The video integration system in the ORs comes with an EMR system and a state-of-the-art nurse documentation station. Courtesy BSA LifeStructures. Photo Stephen B. Ruemmele (former BSA LifeStructures employee).

MEMORIAL HOSPITAL OF SOUTH BEND
South Bend, Indiana

Expansion proved the right fit for this Midwestern surgery program and healthcare campus. Seeking to keep pace with contemporary surgery departments, which have become a mix of the needs of

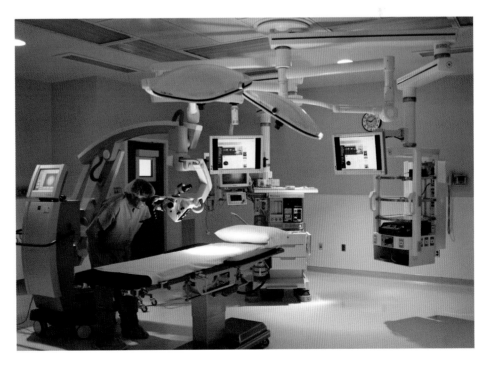

various surgical specialties and the requirements of advancing technology and equipment, this multiphased surgery expansion, designed by BSA Life-structures, added a building with three stories and a basement to the South Bend campus of the Memorial Hospital & Health System, in all 30,000 sq. ft. of renovated space and 156,000 sq. ft. of new space.

Memorial's new surgery area consists of sixteen ORs, including several specialized rooms. The specialized operating rooms provide the latest technology and room layouts. Specialties include trauma, neuro, spine, ortho, cardiovascular, and robotic surgery.

The technology in the new ORs is managed through a video integration system, allowing the display of multiple images. These images may be from a variety of sources, including the patient's own medical record. The video integration system is accompanied by an EMR system and a nurse documentation station. The OR lighting system is a combination of the second-generation LED surgical lights, a set of green lights for minimally invasive procedures, and dimmable general-purpose lighting. These ORs also include an integrated ceiling system for light and boom mounting, sterile air delivery, and the combination lighting system.

The OR sizes range from approximately 530 sq. ft. for general and minimally invasive procedures, to 750 sq. ft. for trauma and spine cases.

WILLIAMSON MEDICAL CENTER
Franklin, Tennessee

Hoping to capture the primary service market of its location outside of Nashville, Tennessee, the Williamson Medical Center saw the need to build an outpatient surgery center to house and promote its strong outpatient program as well as to stem the flow of the county's residents to more competitive outpatient facilities in nearby Nashville. While the hospital already did a significant amount of outpatient surgery, patients undergoing these procedures had to go through the full normal hospital diagnostic and admitting process before having outpatient work done. The separate center now enables the process to be as quick and easy as possible.

At first, the medical center considered building a freestanding outpatient surgery center separate from its hospital, but, in the end, its site proved more

Williamson Medical Center, Franklin, Tennessee. The nurses' workstation in the outpatient surgery center has a direct line of vision to pre- and post-op patients. *Photo © Kieran Reynolds Photography.*

Williamson Medical Center, Franklin, Tennessee. The outpatient surgery center, the anchor tenant of a medical office building, is located immediately off the vestibule of the medical office building's main entrance. *Photo © Kieran Reynolds Photography.*

conducive to building an integrated facility. The independent surgery center, the anchor tenant of a recently completed medical office building, is located immediately off the vestibule of the medical office building's main entrance. The surgery center constitutes part of Williamson Medical Center's $80 million overall expansion and renovation (see Chapter 4). The new 22,162-sq.-ft. outpatient surgery center offers the best of both worlds with its separate storefront convenience as well as attachment to the hospital through a connecting corridor. A separate, discreet discharge exit is provided at the opposite end of the suite.

In designing the medical center's expansion, ESa took advantage of the site's natural 14-ft. drop to maximize outpatient surgery access without compromising access to hospital support and outpatient service at the lower level. Integrating the new center with the hospital allows it to outsource support services—lab, central sterile processing, pharmacy, and environmental services—for operational efficiency.

Multiple outpatient invasive specialty services include cosmetic, eye, and gynecological surgeries. The hospital, which does a sizable number of endoscopies, moved that procedure to the outpatient surgery center as well. Designed to accommodate the various specializations, the center uses all its rooms for the range of surgery options instead of having some dedicated to specialties. This flexibility of OR assignment eliminated underutilization of these costly facilities.

Registration and preprocedural testing is done in the confines of the surgery center. Staging and recovery are adjacent to the postsurgery unit. Private patient bays swing from one purpose to another quickly and easily, maximizing operational efficiency and minimizing duplication of patient beds for pre- and postprocedural care.

This surgery center's direct connection to the hospital allows physicians to save valuable commuting time by scheduling both inpatient and

Renaissance Surgical Arts at Newport Harbor, Costa Mesa, California. With space at a premium, designers Anthony C. Pings and Associates were careful to define the difference between clinical needs and emotional wants for both patients and caregivers and to make them both part of a critical design matrix, seeking the maximum patient privacy possible under the circumstances. *Courtesy Anthony C. Pings and Associates. Photo Wundr Studio, Terrance Williams.*

outpatient surgery in the same shift as well as being convenient for post-op follow-up. If complications arise following outpatient surgery, patients can be transferred to the hospital quickly, without the need for ambulance or helicopter transport. And if the outpatient surgery center needs to expand in ten or twenty years, the facility is designed to do so easily. It could grow from its current four operating rooms to six or even up to eight without compromising adjacent growth of the hospital.

RENAISSANCE SURGICAL ARTS AT NEWPORT HARBOR
Costa Mesa, California

When the surgical needs of this Los Angeles edge-city facility outstripped the space available for them on the first floor of its four-story building, architect Anthony C. Pings and Associates retrofitted this leading-edge ambulatory surgery center.

Although they designed the center around extensive studies of what its potential patients and caregivers wanted, the architects knew from the start that space was at a premium for all locations and that some of the project's 18,680 sq. ft. of space would necessarily be located on the second floor. In addition to the eight operating rooms and two special procedure rooms planned for the space, they included an office shared by surgeons working at the center to serve nonsurgical patients. But the biggest problem created by

the limited space was the need to wrap a single-function floor plate around a building with a vertical service core in its center, which made the retrofit of electrical, mechanical, and fire ratings a monumental challenge. (One result was that the project's sterilization systems expanded the edge of current technology.)

Given all the space restraints, the designers were careful to define the difference between clinical needs and emotional wants for both patients and caregivers and make them both part of a critical design matrix. They sought, for example, to offer the maximum patient privacy possible under the circumstances. They designed the pre-op and step-down units as stalls that separated each patient, yet allowed staff continuous visual access. They made the end panels operable to allow privacy yet immediate access. And they even chambered the waiting room to develop seating zones for dissimilar patient groups and family seating clusters.

The designers also sought to provide a surprising warmth to the facility. While they maintained the same clinical standards as any hospital or ambulatory service facility, they researched extensively different finishes and products that allowed them to come up with a new mix of seemingly unhospital-like surfaces and textures. The operating rooms, for example, have granite wainscoting. As it turned out, the few granites they found that met hospital standards functioned better than wall bumpers—and they added an unexpected elegance.

Renaissance Surgical Arts at Newport Harbor, Costa Mesa, California. The designers also sought to provide a surprising warmth to the facility, extensively researching different finishes and products that allowed them to create and mix surfaces and textures not typical of many hospitals. *Courtesy Anthony C. Pings and Associates. Photo Wundr Studio, Terrance Williams.*

CHAPTER 8

Critical Care

Many people—caregivers, architectural and design professionals, and patients—regard critical-care facilities as the heart of the hospital. The definition of the critical-care unit (developed by the Joint Commission on Accreditation for Hospitals) supported this common perception by calling critical care an appropriately equipped area of the hospital where there is a concentration of nurses, physicians, and others. There a seriously ill patient can expect the maximum of care: the very best the hospital has to offer in terms of personnel and technology.

For this reason, it is particularly alarming to review the literature that suggests the critical-care environment [referred to as CCU] can adversely affect patient health while simultaneously increasing stress and fatigue among the physicians, nurses, and others who work in these areas.

If, for better or worse, the critical-care unit is a powerful distillation of what the hospital has become, it concentrates in particular on the technology of modern medicine, bringing to bear on each patient a panoply of machinery monitors, and invasive, movement-restricting tubes and electrical leads. In some older CCUs, the focus has been not so much on the patient as on the disease or disorder, as if the procedures necessary for sustaining life in the physical sense were somehow incompatible with simultaneously sustaining emotional well-being. A past assumption seems to have been that the CCU patient was either unconscious and unaware of his surroundings or too sick to care about them. The problem is that emotional health cannot be neatly isolated from physical health. What is stressful or depressing also has been documented to have an adverse effect on the patient's physical state.

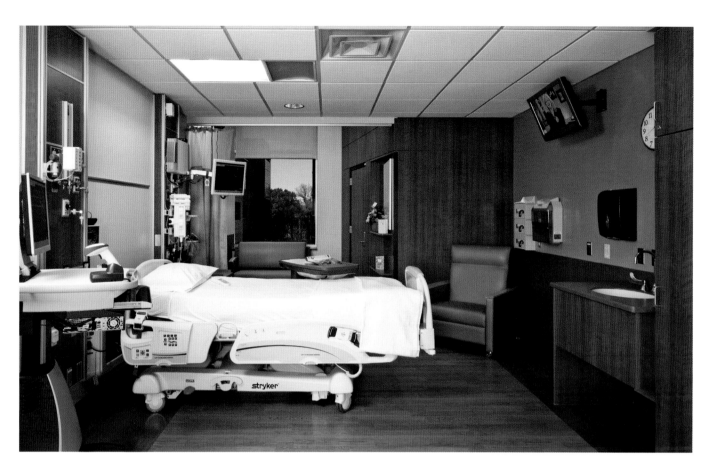

Critical Care Tower, Vanderbilt University Medical Center, Nashville, Tennessee. Patient room. *Courtesy Earl Swensson Associates and Don Blair & Partners Architects, LLP. Photo © Kyle Dreier Photography.*

This is no mere matter of designing a critical-care unit with clever little touches intended to cheer up the patients; the problems in many of the older units are far more serious. The tethered machinery makes many patients feel invaded and powerless. The sense of claustrophobia created by the clicking and pumping and beeping sounds of monitoring equipment, respirators, and IV-delivery equipment within the small space around a patient's head can dramatically increase anxiety levels. Windowed walls are often at a premium in designing any large building and windows were often absent from critical-care design, because it was sometimes assumed that CCU patients were unconscious. Even where there were windows, they were often of minimal size and offered poor views with no sightline from the bed.

A lack of windows can heighten a sense of claustrophobia inherent in these technology-packed areas, but a number of studies demonstrate that patients in windowless rooms are subject to temporal dislocation (they have, for example, an inaccurate memory of the length of their stay in CCUs) and even to what has been called the "CCU syndrome" or "CCU psychosis," which is characterized by delirium, hallucinations, and delusions. Some studies show that patients in windowless CCUs are more than twice as likely to develop delirium as those who occupy rooms with windows. In patients with abnormal hemoglobin or blood urea nitrogen levels, the incidence of delirium is almost three times greater in windowless units.

The disorienting effects of these outdated rooms without windows in older facilities are often aggravated by harsh lighting, especially from fluorescent fixtures, and by lighting that is not cyclically dimmed to correspond to the body's circadian rhythms. This can be exacerbated by noise and constant interruptions to draw blood, to monitor diagnostic equipment and the like, to administer medications, to replace IVs, and on and on. Sleeplessness, therefore, can be a common problem in critical-care units, not only due to lighting but also to the remarkably high level of noise that can prevail in such units. Some studies of CCU noise levels find that they commonly range from 45 to 90 decibels over a twenty-four-hour period. In the average domestic bedroom, most individuals would find noise levels exceeding 30 decibels incompatible with sleep.

Excessive noise is particularly stressful for cardiac patients, who exhibit increased cardiac workloads and arrhythmias in noisy environments. In addition, pain perception seems to be heightened by the presence of excessive noise. Types of noise that can occur in critical-care units are also of a particularly stressful sort—alarms, the sounds of electronic monitors, the pneumatic hissing of IV pumps, a babble of televisions, radios, and staff conversation. Interestingly, most patients say they find human noise more objectionable than machine-generated noise.

Related negative responses reported by patients include a sense that they could not "escape" their environment, a general and anxiety-provoking sense of unrelenting urgency, sensory deprivation, crowding, and a loss of privacy. Many such feelings also affect those who work in the critical-care unit, leading them to depersonalize patients, while speeding up the rate of staff burnout.

These frequently noted and intensively studied problems in critical-care environments can largely be solved through design.

A twenty-four-bed intensive care unit floor plan created by Earl Swensson Associates.

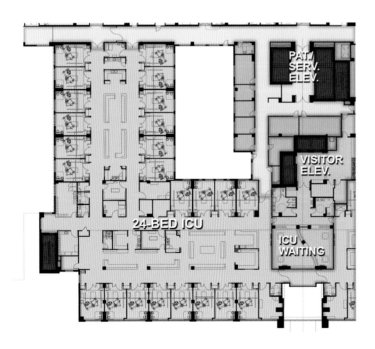

Historical Perspective

To fully appreciate the art of critical care and to evaluate recent trends, it is useful to understand the historical evolution of these units. As early as 1863, Florence Nightingale noted the existence of a recess or small room leading from the operating theater in many small rural hospitals—this was the origin of the surgical recovery room. During the two world wars, the recovery room continued to evolve to cope with patients who required extensive postoperative care and to group them to make the most efficient use of a limited number of nurses.

In the meantime, in 1930, the first ICU (intensive care unit) appeared in a German hospital. Drawing on the consolidation and intensive monitoring concept inherent in the recovery room, the German plan also called for assembling teams of the most highly skilled nurses and an experienced physician to provide a heightened degree of care for critically ill patients.

In the United States, it was the polio epidemic of the late 1940s and 1950s that spurred development of specialized units devoted to treating patients with polio-induced respiratory ailments. In 1952, in Denmark, the first formal respiratory ICU was established. When the "iron lung" was replaced by the mechanical ventilator in the late 1950s, it became logistically desirable to centralize this technology rather than distribute it throughout the hospital. In this way, technology drove the creation of the intensive care unit. The experience with polio victims suggested that patients afflicted with critical conditions could be concentrated in designated areas so that fewer nurses could provide special—intensive—care to more than one patient at a time.

During the 1960s, design for critical care diverged in two directions. ICUs located adjacent to surgical facilities, which were intended to care for and monitor patients who had undergone serious and complex surgical procedures, were designed as open wards; the beds were separated by cubicle curtains. Medical or coronary care units were designed as individual rooms or cubicles.

Planning

In all areas of hospital and healthcare facility design, the trend is toward formally including users of the facility in the design process. This is particularly important in the potential high-stress environment of the critical-care unit, where designing for maximum efficiency depends on listening to the professional staff. Architects and hospital administrators should convene a task force of representatives from the medical staff specialties, nursing, administration, planning, marketing, engineering, pharmacy, respiratory therapy, biomedicine, infection control, and operational support services (including materials management and environmental services). In consultation with the task force, the architect must develop a strong programming statement that defines the purpose and nature of the critical-care facility or facilities, including the role of specialized critical care and step-down care, discussed below.

A critical care unit floor plan created by Earl Swensson Associates.

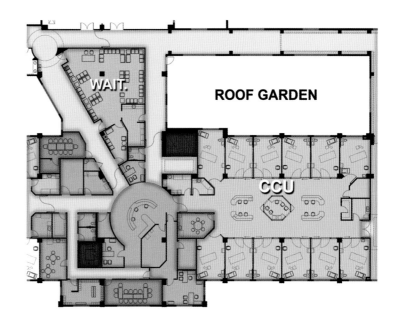

The Range of Critical Care

In programming the critical-care facility, planners, architects, and administrators are confronted with a broad range of options that are products of the evolution of medical technology, the development of managed care and

Centerpoint Medical Center, Indepen-dence, Missouri. CCU, designed by Earl Swensson Associates. *Photo © Kieran Reynolds Photography.*

cost containment, and the individual hospital's size and definition of mission. Insofar as critical care is perceived—by patients as well as staff—as a concentration of the best a hospital has to offer, there is incentive to excel in this area and offer a high degree of specialization. For these reasons, doctors sometimes perceive less acute bed units as inadequate for patient care and tend to overuse CCUs. We discuss some other aspects of these specialized critical-care facilities later in the chapter. However, intensive care is resource intensive, too. It is one of the costliest of hospital services, and, particularly in today's climate, hospitals are looking for alternatives to critical care—even as they continue to acquire and develop critical-care technologies and facilities.

The Task Force on Guidelines of the Society of Critical-care Medicine defined three levels of critical care (designated as Level I-a, Level I-c, and Level II—I-a being the highest level of care) hospitals might offer, depending on their size and the definition of their mission. Critical-care units of the first level offer delivery of care to the "desperately ill patient with complicated needs requiring the continuous availability of sophisticated equipment, specialized nurses, and physicians trained in the care of the critically ill." Within this category is Level I-c, which provides these essential services, and Level l-a, which adds a teaching and research component to these services.

Level II units are appropriate for hospitals with more limited resources. According to the Task Force, the Level II unit should be capable of delivering high-quality care to patients with single-organ failure but, in cases of complicated need or multisystem failure, patients should be transferred to a facility offering Level I care.

Even Level II critical care is expensive and increasingly subject to rationing. Often hospitals now have intermediate care units—frequently called step-down units—in cases where high-risk patients require close monitoring, but not intensive intervention. The step-down unit is often used for patients suffering from chronic ventilator failure who do not, however, require intensive respiratory monitoring or therapy.

Another step-down development is the Special Care Unit (SCU), which is designed for the chronically critically ill patient. Such a unit might have, say, eight beds in entirely private rooms. Physiologic monitoring might be limited to EKG and periodic arterial pressure monitoring. A ventilator is often in use. Whereas, most critical-care units exclude the family or accommodate family members provisionally, the SCU encourages both the family and the patient to play active roles in making healthcare decisions. Increasingly, intermediate care and SCUs have figured more prominently in critical-care design.

Because the principal focus of critical care is so often respiratory distress, many hospitals have introduced specifically designated respiratory CCUs (R-CCU) or pulmonary CCUs (P-CCU). Other specialized critical-care units include neurological CCUs, wound CCUs (often associated with a special Burn Unit), surgical CCUs, medical CCUs, geriatric CCUs, pediatric CCUs, and neonatal and high-risk obstetric CCUs. Many hospitals have tried what the professionals call acuity adaptable or universal care units, providing care to adult patients from a variety of specialty areas. And even if critical care does not occur in such an acuity-adaptable room, but in a dedicated CCU, neither may have the single focus of the units mentioned above. Instead, patients may be aggregated depending on patient type or patient acuity, such as medical or surgical. Finally, hospitals increasingly allocate critical-care space to CCUs that offer a high degree of isolation—an issue discussed later in this chapter.

Technology and Humanity: Design Priorities

One thing that creative hospital and healthcare facility design consistently demonstrates is that high technology does not need to be incompatible with humane, comfortable, patient-centered design. Effective and humane critical-care design does not need to hide technology, but it should integrate high technology into an essentially familiar—rather than an alienating—environment.

Location and Size

The location of the critical-care unit depends on such factors as the focus of the unit (whether surgical, medical, specialized) and its size. The CCU may be strategically located near the ED and surgical service for efficiency of patient transfer when necessary and for economy of sharing support services. It may also be advantageous to have the surgical recovery facilities located near the CCU to facilitate sharing of staff and common support services such as clinical lab facilities and radiology. Specialty CCUs are often adjacent

Parkwest Medical Center, Knoxville, Tennessee. CCU designed by Earl Swensson Associates. *Photo © Kieran Reynolds Photography.*

to the surgical/medical beds devoted to that specialty.

Whatever its location and adjacencies, the critical-care unit must exclude through-traffic. Some of the corridor strategies discussed in the last chapter may be applied to the critical-care unit to achieve the balance of access and isolation it demands.

As traditionally conceived, each surgical CCU has between six and twelve beds. Twelve beds are seen as the upper limit of what a CCU nursing staff and station can adequately monitor. This guideline has become less significant as CCUs have incorporated bedside computers or wireless technology that enable paperless charting and direct recording of vital signs through monitoring devices. Such technology has allowed for decentralized nursing, which lets nursing staff spend more time in patients' rooms and at mini-workstations in alcoves between rooms and other decentralized configurations. Yet even today in some localities, decentralized nursing requires either a change in building codes or a variance from existing codes.

At a minimum, the rooms need enough square footage per bed to accommodate multiple life-support equipment, while allowing sufficient room for access to all sides of the patient's bed. The 2010 *Guidelines* call for at least 200 sq. ft. of clear floor area with a minimum headwall width of 13 ft. per bed, exclusive of anterooms, vestibules, toilet rooms, closets, lockers, wardrobes, and alcoves. The CCU patient room should be planned to facilitate operation in the event of a crisis, including natural disasters and terrorist attacks.

Windows

Natural light is one of the most comforting and familiar things you can provide in a hospital. Windows must be a part of all effective ICU and CCU designs. The height of the windows should be low enough for an optimum view so that patients can see both the ground and the sky. The idea is to admit a maximum of natural light to allow patients contact and orientation with the outside world, but the light should be controllable for sleeping.

Ceilings

The intensive care patient is usually flat on her back and, therefore, spends considerable time looking at the ceiling. Ceiling material should be chosen with care to reduce glare and to provide an interesting texture that promotes a sense of orientation in the supine occupant of the room. For this reason, it is a good idea to use indirect lighting fixtures in ceilings that reflect light up, not down into the patient's face.

Other Essentials for Reality Orientation

While a view to the outside world and a thoughtful ceiling treatment are essential to maintaining reality orientation, other simple elements should not be neglected. The CCU patient room should include a clock (some state codes mandate the inclusion of one). Special "stat" clocks are available, which normally function as standard clocks but automatically become digital elapsed-time counters in a code blue (cardiac arrest) situation. The room should also have a clearly visible calendar, a radio, and a television with remote control. A simple dry-erase marker board with the day and name of the current shift nurse can be an informational amenity.

Privacy and Visibility

While contact with the outside world is important, most patients highly value their privacy. Design should allow for adequate privacy without, however, isolating the patients. The design challenge here is that patients must be visible to staff and access to the room must be unobstructed, yet a sense of privacy must also be created.

Since the critical-care unit is located apart from through-traffic areas, the trend was to use sliding glass doors or folding glass doors, which effectively seal out noise while allowing nursing staff to observe patients. Sliding doors can be detailed without bottom tracks, so that nothing impedes crash carts and other rolled equipment, but this type of door is costly and difficult to maintain. Folding doors can be entirely "break away," allowing fullest access to the patient room in emergency situations. An observation wall made of LCD blackout crystals can also be used. These panels can change from clear to opaque at the touch of a button, thereby giving the patient a significant measure of control over his privacy while still allowing for observation.

But consider this: Sliding glass doors are costly and hard to maintain. And as a result of numerous recent surveys, in which patients indicated their preference to be easily seen rather than having increased privacy, some hospitals have begun using double doors with 6-ft. openings to accommodate staff and patient needs.

Visibility of Technology

Another visibility issue deals with technology. Most life-support and monitoring devices should be kept out of the patient's range of vision. Wall-mounted and ceiling-mounted equipment helps with this.

Lighting

Where possible, general illumination should convey greater warmth and familiarity than direct fluorescent light that too often suggests commercial or institutional spaces. The challenge is to do so while maintaining green design considerations. Procedure (examination) lights should be placed directly over the patient so that staff is not working in shadows, but the sources of general illumination should be located away from the patient's prevailing line of sight to reduce fatigue and stress. Too often, even general illumination in the CCU uses over-the-bed light fixtures, which are in themselves "institutional" and alienating. Table lamps are welcome touches of familiarity, and soffits and cornices also soften the institutional effect. Wall sconces also add upscale light options.

It is vitally important that the patient, even the critically ill patient, has easy access to control of the general lighting in her room via a switch or remote control. This seemingly small measure of control over her immediate environment significantly enhances her overall sense of control—a sense that is under heavy assault during illness and, particularly, during a period of relative immobility.

General lighting levels should be kept as low as is compatible with staff efficiency. Lowering lighting levels tends to lower staff noise levels as well. Consider putting corridor lighting on a timed cycle to mesh with circadian rhythms. Thoughtful corridor lighting design might incorporate focused task lighting, so that the general lighting in traffic areas can be kept at low levels during the night.

Color and Furnishings

Color is a frequent subject of discussion in general medical/surgical patient rooms. It should also become an important consideration in the ICU/CCU. In too many existing critical-care units, the most colorful furnishings are the items of medical equipment. All too often, critical-care units appear bland as if color was bad medicine for the very ill. It would be better to manufacture medical equipment in the same neutral shades used for office machines, especially personal computers, and provide color in critical-care units through the use of well-chosen artwork, comfortable chairs, and elegant, well-made casework.

Noise

As discussed previously, noise levels in critical-care areas can be excessive. The use of sound batts (acoustic insulation), draperies, and carpeting (in corridors, not patient rooms) can significantly reduce noise levels. Hospital nursing and facilities staff prefer rubber flooring and softer vinyl flooring because carpeting makes pushing beds and heavy carts more strenuous. Laying out the critical-care suite to reduce or disperse corridor traffic is another positive step. Employing low general lighting levels during the night and evenings not only mimics circadian rhythms but also tends to signal to personnel and others that they should speak quietly. Finally, equipment alarms should be kept at the minimum number and volume consistent with safety. With two corridors, traffic on each side of the beds is cut in half—and so is the noise.

Odors

Ask most people to enumerate what they find objectionable—or anxiety-provoking—about hospitals and the "hospital smell" will be high on the list. Control of odors is not often thought of as a design issue; however, technologies now exist not only to circulate and exhaust air efficiently, but to neutralize odors and even to manipulate odors through aromatherapy, the injection of scents through the HVAC system. Providing bed pan washes in each patient room and using seamless vinyl or rubber flooring in areas prone to collecting urine or bowel matter also help to eliminate odor.

Visitor Accommodations

As in the ED, visitor accommodations are sometimes neglected in the critical-care unit, and fam-

Atrium Medical Center, Middletown, Ohio. As designed by Earl Swensson Associates, observation nursing alcoves in the CCU provide nursing efficiencies. *Photo Scott McDonald © Hedrich Blessing.*

ily and friends are sometimes actively discouraged from visiting patients in intensive care. Generally, accommodation for family and other visitors is both a humane consideration for the family and of beneficial effect to the patient. At minimum, an adequate waiting area should be made available, and the intensive-care patient room should include a comfortable chair or two for a companion.

While accommodation for family members has been seen as increasingly important in the hospital setting, especially for critically ill patients, visitation should not be forced upon ICU/CCU patients, as some express a preference for solitude. There have been studies in the past that reported both positive and negative benefits from allowing children to visit patients in ICUs.

Staff Accommodations

Intensive care of patients demands intensive effort from the professional staff. They are subject to bombardment of the senses and many emotional stresses. In general, the same design measures that reduce patient anxiety and increase patient comfort do the same for staff. This especially includes designing for the minimization of noise, careful attention to lighting (with generally low levels—at least at night—in corridors punctuated by task lighting at workstations), and the relegation of technology to the visual background while noninstitutional architectural details, furnishings, and artwork are featured in the foreground.

Staff dissatisfaction most often arises from:
- dysfunctional layouts with inadequate storage in the right spot;
- too much walking (typically six to eight miles per shift);
- lack of quiet areas in which to work;
- lifting heavy patients and other strains leading to back injury;
- poor lighting;
- cramped rooms with poor access to patients; and
- inconsistent room layouts and a lack of parity between rooms.

An adequate staff lounge area adjacent to the ICU/CCU is essential. Depending on the size of the unit, a formally designated conference/consultation/education room may be required as part of the unit. Thoughtful design will incorporate adequate space for professional conversation that is sufficiently isolated from the patient rooms. Alcoves, niches, or pockets worked into corridors provide visual interest and also offer inviting areas for consultation.

Johnston Memorial Hospital, Abingdon, VA. ICU nurses' work area.
Photo © Kyle Dreier Photography.

Staff members, particularly those who work long shifts, are subject to some of the same senses of isolation and disorientation that may afflict patients. If possible, windows should be available in staff areas and in corridors. Skylights may be used in corridors and other staff areas, while clerestory designs allow for "borrowed" daylight in corridors. The Japanese employ devices that collect sunlight and transmit it through fiber optics to living and work areas that lack direct exposure to the outside.

Achieving a Balance

In emphasizing the humane aspects of ICU/CCU design, we do not mean to denigrate technology. Not only does medical machinery save lives, but it also has the potential of actually humanizing the relation of caregiver to patient. Critical-care information systems allow for the automatic recording of vital-sign data and save each nurse valuable minutes per shift by dramatically decreasing the amount of nursing time spent collecting vital-sign data and increasing the time spent communicating with and treating patients. Bedside terminals increase the amount of data recorded on patients' charts and decrease the time spent on manual charting and general paperwork. The development of bedside laboratory technology allows immediate assessments of blood gases, electrolytes, glucose, and hematic from very small blood samples. Despite all of this, patient care suffers if the machinery itself becomes the focus of the designer's and the practitioner's attention. Many critical-care nurses complain they spend more time with machines than they do with patients, and patients express anxiety over being tied down to machines.

Good design can accommodate the machinery while also keeping it out of the way. Particular attention should be devoted to the headwall, which, especially in the critical-care environment, bristles with connections for medical gases, suction, electrical power, and terminal hookups. In general attractive casework can be used to hide all or some of the imposing hardware in the headwall. Consideration must be given as to whether the hookups should fan out from the patient to the headwall, converge at a power column, or run to an overhead rail system.

The choice of headwall, power column, or rail system is in large part determined by the layout of the room, which, in turn, is a function of overall unit design and the need to balance the demands of technology, accessibility, and aesthetics. Room layout begins with the orientation of the bed. From the point of view of the nurse, the bed should be situated to allow ready observation of the patient, especially the head. Tradition dictates that the head of the bed be against a wall, and headwalls certainly accommodate this approach. However, in a crisis, it is often essential to have access to the patient from all four sides. The bed can be pulled quickly from the wall, but tubes and monitor leads may continue to inhibit access or even present a trip hazard. Some architects have proposed a partial solution to this in unsquare rooms or rooms with one angled wall, meant to increase clearance around the bed (and to give the room greater sensory interest for the patient). However, a simpler approach is to treat the bed as an island.

If there is one thing that administrators, medical professionals, designers, and architects agree on, it is that the critical-care unit is a kind of hospital within a hospital and, therefore, a monumentally difficult design challenge, which is not reducible to a set of cut-and-dried rules. Good innovative CCU patient room designs aim at balancing the demands of high-tech medicine with high-touch humanity.

Specialized Critical Care

Most of the issues that figure in general critical care also apply to specialized critical-care units. Indeed, some authorities argue against specialized critical-care units on the grounds that most critical patients have common needs and that critical-care specialization is an arbitrary function of departmental organization rather than patient need. This view, however, does not take into account the possible cost-containment benefits of certain specialized alternatives to traditional intensive care. It is necessary for respiratory CCUs or infectious patient units to be separated from surgical CCUs to minimize infection to postoperative surgical patients. If specialized critical care is opted for, planners and architects need to consider the following uses.

Coronary Care Unit

After the medical/surgical CCU, the coronary care unit, also referred to as a CCU, is the most commonly found critical-care unit in the hospital. The central design issue in the CCU is finding a strategy to promote tranquility and even relative visual and acoustic isolation. So-called CCU psychosis is a shocking symptom of poor critical-care design. In the case of the CCU, noise and visual clutter have a readily demonstrable adverse effect on heart rates, arrhythmias, and blood pressure.

Respiratory Care and Step-down Units

The respiratory-care unit developed as an alternative to the traditional CCU in response to the constraints of managed care and cost containment. A large percentage of medical intensive care patients and surgical intensive care patients have been routinely admitted in the past to these costly units strictly for the purposes of monitoring and did not require any active intervention. The patients were not suffering from any immediate life-threatening conditions. Thus, there is a good rationale for providing more cost-effective intermediate care units for those patients in need of close monitoring rather than aggressive intervention.

Cost savings are achieved in part through reduction in the amount and nature of required equipment and, in even larger part, through reduced staffing needs. Whereas the nurse to patient ratio in the CCU may be 1:2 or even 1:1, in the respiratory or step-down unit the ratio can safely be set at 1:3 or 1:4.

Elderly Critical Care

While no radical steps need to be taken to design special critical-care facilities to accommodate older patients, certain design features can be incorporated into general CCUs to make them more friendly to the elderly.

Gerontologists speak of an "environmental docility hypothesis," which holds that as competence decreases, the probability that behavior will be influenced by environmental factors increases. We know that critically ill patients often feel at the mercy of their environment. This seems to be even more compelling among critically ill elderly patients.

Some of the design areas discussed earlier, especially noise control, light, and color, are particularly important in designing for the elderly. Noise reduction should be a high design priority. Because of diminished visual acuity in the elderly, lighting should not cause glare. This also means keeping highly reflective surfaces to a minimum. Color discrimination also deteriorates with age. Differentiating among dark shades and among pastels is a particular problem. Thoughtful use of contrast to emphasize planes and corners aids orientation. However, the elderly patient should not feel dominated by the colors in her environment.

Neurological Intensive Care

An array of neurological conditions may require intensive care. These include postoperative neurosurgical cases, stroke, subarachnoid hemorrhage, head injury, cerebral hemorrhage, Guillain-Barre syndrome with respiratory failure, medical complications of neurological disease, brain tumor, acute spinal cord trauma, status epilepticus, encephalitis-meningitis, myasthenia gravis with respiratory failure, and global brain ischemia. Many of these conditions can be treated appropriately in the general surgical or medical CCU, but the monitoring and treatment of intracranial pressure (ICP) in particular has been cited by many authorities as ample rationale for creating specialized neurological CCUs.

The best model for the neurological CCU focuses on continuous and sophisticated monitoring to achieve early detection of developing problems. Increasingly sophisticated monitoring devices have to be accommodated in neurological critical care, and these must be added to a full array of respiratory and ventilation equipment.

Perhaps the single greatest design impact of the neurological CCU is the issue of adjacency. It is desirable to locate this unit near diagnostic facilities (such as MRI and CT).

Burn Unit

Another specialized critical-care facility found in larger, often regional, hospitals is the burn unit. Some hospitals, most notably the network run by the Shrine of North America (Shriners), are devoted entirely to the treatment and rehabilitation of burn victims. For design, the single most important clinical factor in treating burns is creating structures that minimize the risk of infection. In addition to meeting the demanding clinical conditions required by the advanced treatment of severe burns, the burn CCU should project as much of a noninstitutional sense of well-being as possible. Severe burn injury is not only physically painful but is especially depressing and anxiety-provoking. Patients suffering from disfiguring injury benefit from maintenance of contact with the outside world. Tragically, it is also the case that a great proportion of burn victims are children.

Isolation Issues

In discussing the burn CCU we touched upon the issue of isolation to prevent infection. Patients admitted to the CCU have a higher risk of nosocomial infection than other hospitalized patients. Most authorities believe that design for isolation is primarily a matter of ventilation, filtering, and maintaining positive air pressure in the patient room. It is assumed that nursing the patient in a single-patient room with the door closed is the best safeguard against infection in intensive care. Yet, though hospital rooms are now virtually all exclusively private patient rooms, and the old open-ward ICU common even a decade or so ago, has all but disappeared, it is sobering to temper our assumptions about the effect of architectural design on nosocomial infections by considering the results of a 1989 study by J. Huebner and others that concluded that the difference between the incidence of infection in an old intensive care ward built in 1924 and one constructed in 1986 was slight: 34.2 percent versus 31.9 percent.

This of course underscores the benefits of hand washing and the need to provide for it. Eliminating cubicle curtains—a breeding ground for bacteria—can also help, as does using antimicrobial materials.

Women's Hospital at Centennial Medical Center, Nashville, Tennessee. NICU designed by Earl Swensson Associates. *Photo Vince Wallace/Silver Hill Images.*

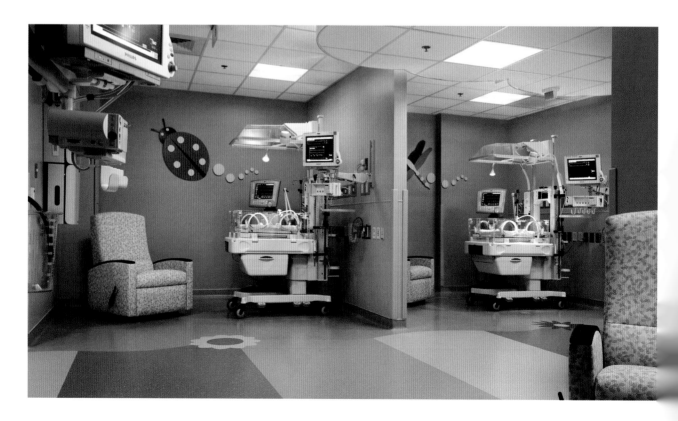

The Neonatal Intensive Care Unit

Methodist Children's Hospital of South Texas, San Antonio, Texas. NICU designed by Earl Swensson Associates. *Photo © James F. Wilson.*

The location and design of the neonatal intensive care unit (NICU) are sufficiently unique to warrant special treatment here. Pediatric critical-care medicine became a recognized discipline around 1960. Its origins are traceable to Pierre Budin, a Parisian pediatrician who created a "department for weaklings," primarily to care for and study premature neonates, and James Wilson, a pediatrician who established a four-bed negative-pressure ventilator ("iron lung") for pediatric patients at Boston's Children's Hospital in 1932.

Generally, funding for critical care has been threatened by cost-containment efforts and rationing as policymakers strive to claim more medical dollars for preventive care and fewer for critical care. However, neonatal and pediatric intensive care may well be exempt from such fund reallocation, if for no other reason than that few policymakers want to be seen as depriving children of care. Certainly, however, neonatologists and others will be increasingly confronted with caregiving decisions that balance survival, cost, and the quality of life.

General Design Issues

The modern neonatal critical-care facility is the product of two factors: (1) the understanding that the pathophysiologic phenomena associated with the newborn are so distinctive that they require an appropriate setting where the critically ill infant can be effectively managed, and (2) convergent advances in electronics and biochemistry, which make such a setting feasible. These advances include methods for continuous evaluation of numerous parameters of neonatal (and fetal) illness, methods of continuous monitoring of cardiorespiratory function, micro techniques for rapid biochemical determinations from minute blood samples, and servo-controlled radiant-heat incubators. These advances, coupled with improved methods for controlling infection, prompted the development of the NICU: a common area where all medically and surgically ill infants are treated, premature and full-term, infected and noninfected.

Even though treating all critically ill neonates in a single area allows for the cost-effective concentration of resources, neonatal intensive care is expensive and is, therefore, subject to the kind of regionalization that governs the scope and extent of emergency departments and trauma centers. On the other hand, savvy mothers often choose where they will deliver based on which facility has good neonatal care just in case delivery should put their babies at risk.

Four levels are recognized:

• Level I facilities have as their primary goal the management of normal pregnancy, labor, and delivery as well as the early identification of high-risk situations and the provision of emergency care in the event of unanticipated complications. They offer the minimum required for any facility that provides inpatient maternity care. The hospital must have the necessary personnel and equipment to perform neonatal resuscitation, to evaluate healthy newborn babies, to provide postnatal care, and to stabilize ill newborns till they can be transferred to a facility that provides intensive care.

• Level II facilities include Level I services, with the addition of a neonatal critical-care unit capable of managing most neonatal complications. They provide care to infants who are moderately sick with illnesses expected to resolve quickly and provide care for babies recovering from more serious illnesses treated in a Level III NICU.

• Level III facilities care for infants with extreme prematurity or who are critically ill or require surgical intervention.

• Level IV facilities encompass the services of Levels I, II, and III, while also offering the most advanced critical care. These are designated regional centers for neonatal intensive care.

Level III and IV NICUs perform the following functions: observe critical infants, monitor critical infants electronically and biomedically, carry out advanced therapeutic procedures, and promote maternal-child contact to the fullest extent possible. This last function reflects a growing realization that maternal handling as well as sensory stimulation (but not overstimulation or inappropriate stimulation) are crucial in the newborn's earliest hours and days—even if the infant is critically ill. Thus planners and designers of NICU facilities are faced with a set of requirements that are, in many points, contradictory. On the one hand, there is a call for a common technically sophisticated space while, on the other, there is a call for a humane environment that facilitates maternal contact.

A number of studies have suggested that humanizing the NICU may be more of a clinically urgent matter than merely a desirable goal. Some authorities have suggested that continual exposure to bright lights may contribute to retinopathy of prematurity (ROP), a leading cause of blindness in premature infants. Continual high-level illumination may also disrupt diurnal patterns at this earliest stage of development. Parents of premature infants that have been exposed to unvarying illumination twenty-four hours a day report disturbances in the infant's sleep pattern for weeks, even months, after they return home with the child. Monitoring of cardiorespiratory function demonstrates that these vital signs tend to be more stable when infants are exposed to cycled lighting that mimics diurnal patterns.

Overstimulation of cardiorespiratory function may not be solely the result of continual exposure to bright lights. When light levels are high, noise levels are commensurably high. When light levels are dimmed, noise levels also decline. Indeed, noise in traditional NICUs is often at a distressingly high level. Alarms and incubators are the biggest mechanical noise producers. These not only elevate levels of arousal, but there is evidence that protracted exposure to incubator noise levels in excess of 70 decibels may also contribute to cochlear damage and subsequent hearing loss. Since at least the early 1980s, studies have warned that the NICU is truly a high-risk environment. As in the adult CCU, sensory overload is also a threat for professional staff. In a more recent development, undertaken in part to minimize the ill effects of the traditional NICU unit, architects have moved away from the warehouse-style NICU, designing instead smaller units of four to six bassinets.

The only humanizing architectural element that most authorities argue against including in the design of the NICU is windows, primarily due to their thermal effects, which can cause potentially harmful dips or spikes in ambient temperature. In settings where fully enclosed incubators are used, it is even possible that too much sunlight can cause excessive warming due to a greenhouse effect.

LITTLETON ADVENTIST HOSPITAL-SOUTH TOWER
Littleton, Colorado

In the renovation and extension of this Colorado facility, ESa used existing structural column bays when adding two floors on top of the existing South Tower, which marks a new

Littleton Adventist Hospital-South Tower, Littleton, Colorado. Enabling patient visibility within the twenty-four-bed intensive care unit, charting alcoves are placed between every two rooms with view windows looking into the rooms. *Photo © Ed LaCasse Photography.*

trend in inpatient services. The upgrade expands the hospital's capabilities for inpatient care within a healing environment, adds a new fourth floor that contains a thirty-two-bed medical/surgical unit, and tops that off with a new fifth floor and its twenty-four-bed intensive care unit.

Each floor has designated bariatric and isolation rooms. A two-story link connects the new floors to the existing North Tower. In the ICU, charting alcoves placed between every two rooms have windows for staff to observe patients within these rooms. Supporting Littleton's "family-centered wellness" approach, the new floors include a family sanctuary and family areas. The combination of a natural color palette, texture, and lighting create timeless space that soothes and heals—a healthy environment for patients, family, and staff.

A new South Tower outpatient entrance, also part of this project, is distinctive in its visibility for wayfinding purposes. The expansion brings the hospital's total bed count to 231.

USC University Hospital, Norris Inpatient Tower, Los Angeles, California. Lee, Burkhart, Liu, Inc. designed the acute-care, ten-story Norris Inpatient Tower at the Richard K. Earner Medical Plaza as an addition to the hospital. *Courtesy Lee, Burkhart, Liu, Inc. Photo Fotoworks (Benny Chan Photography).*

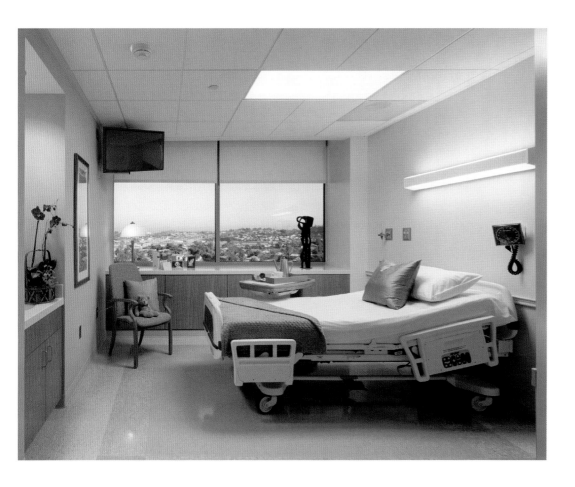

USC UNIVERSITY HOSPITAL, NORRIS INPATIENT TOWER

Los Angeles, California

Lee, Burhart, Liu designed a new acute-care tower—the Norris Inpatient Tower—at the University of Southern California's University Hospital (USCUH). Covering more than 193,000 sq. ft., the ten-story tower includes 146 patient beds; 96 percent of the beds are in private rooms and many are dedicated to the care of cancer patients. The new tower is attached to the main USCUH facility, which increases patient care efficiency by making it easily accessible to medical staff, patients, and their families.

The Norris Inpatient Tower is equipped with advanced medical technology to support the latest in clinical care. Eleven new operating rooms nearly double USCUH's surgical capacity and include three ultramodern operating suites that are primarily for minimally invasive surgeries. A fourth suite will be equipped with highly advanced intraoperative magnetic resonance imaging (MRI) equipment that will give surgeons real-time patient images and feedback, enabling them to perform even more precise neurosurgical procedures.

The Norris Inpatient Tower also includes an entire floor specifically designed for medical oncology inpatient care. Every room on this floor is equipped with a positive pressure system designed to shield immunosuppressed patients from airborne contaminants and a satellite pharmacy provides immediate chemotherapy needs to oncology patients. The facility boasts a sterile processing department, including two walk-in steriliza-

USC University Hospital, Norris Inpatient Tower, Los Angeles, California. The Norris Inpatient Tower boasts the latest in clinical care. For example, every room on the medical oncology floor comes equipped with a positive pressure system designed to shield immunosuppressed patients from airborne contaminants. *Courtesy Lee, Burkhart, Liu, Inc. Photo Fotoworks (Benny Chan Photography).*

tion chambers that are about five ft. tall and six ft. long—large enough to sterilize three operating room carts of equipment at a time. Dedicated elevators connect the sterile processing department to the surgery suite, which will improve efficiency.

As one of only two major university-affiliated teaching centers in Los Angeles, the new Norris Inpatient Tower adds to Los Angeles' capacity for advanced medical research in the ongoing search for cures and treatments for cancer and other life-threatening diseases.

MONROE CARELL JR. CHILDREN'S HOSPITAL AT VANDERBILT
Nashville, Tennessee

This hospital, designed by ESa, is discussed more fully in Chapter 11, but its Neonatal Intensive Care Unit is justly celebrated. With its NICU, the Children's Hospital provides highly specialized, family-centered care, critical for both newborns and their parents. Located on the fourth floor of the hospital, the unit has sixty-two private patient rooms equipped with the latest technology and staffed by healthcare professionals trained to treat the most complex problems facing newborns. The sixteen-bed Stahlman NICU, which is connected to the Children's Hospital NICU by a hallway, is immediately adjacent to Labor and Delivery, keeping babies close to their mothers whenever possible.

As the Regional Perinatal Center for Middle Tennessee, the NICU provides many services unavailable elsewhere in the region, including inpatient intensive care, consultative support, and neonatal transport services for critically ill infants, approximately half of whom are transported from other hospitals in Tennessee or surrounding states.

Parents, grandparents, and up to two people chosen by the parents may visit anytime. All other visitors may come with a parent. Parents are encouraged to stay in the rooms with their child. Parents also have a hospitality house for overnight stay on the same floor so they have quick access to their child but can get the rest they need from long days in the NICU. Parents may bring anyone they wish to see their baby, provided only that they are healthy and have not recently been exposed to any contagious diseases.

Monroe Carell Jr. Children's Hospital at Vanderbilt, Nashville, Tennessee. Individual NICU patient rooms allow clear sightlines for monitoring by nursing staff. *Photo Scott McDonald © Hedrich Blessing.*

Designers hoped to satisfy the major design goal of creating a quieter environment by incorporating private rooms and by using sound-absorbing materials throughout the NICU. The unit pod layout and operational flow were also elevated to decrease noise levels. Phone ringers and equipment alarms were assessed and set at appropriate levels to help keep the noise down. The deliberate placement of technology and location of staff-charting and work areas also contributed to noise control. Once the facility was occupied, the ambient noise levels proved even lower than anticipated in the design calculations. Staff and patient satisfaction increased in the new facility, and anecdotal comments point to the quiet environment as one important reason.

The pediatric critical-care unit is a thirty-six-bed unit with three twelve-bed neighborhoods. Due to the acuity of the child and adolescent patients, the critical-care patient rooms provide state-of-the-art technology with ceiling booms located centrally in the room for ease of access. Understanding and embracing the need for parents in the rooms, each room has been provided with a monitor to provide access for doctors and staff without crowding.

CRITICAL CARE TOWER AND HEART INSTITUTE
STATEN ISLAND UNIVERSITY HOSPITAL
Staten Island, New York

The Staten Island Hospital Heart Institute, a state-of-the art facility designed by Norman Rosenfeld, consulting principal at Stonehill & Taylor, is outfitted with two technologically advanced cardiothoracic operating rooms, two angiography rooms supported by four cardiac catherization labs, a ten-bed cardiac holding and recovery area, and a ten-bed cardiac surgery recovery

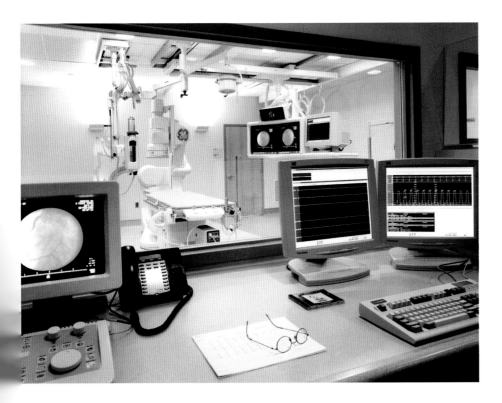

Critical Care Tower and Heart Institute, Staten Island University Hospital, Staten Island, New York. The institute houses an image-guided surgical suite with single-plane and bi-plane angiographic rooms, an intraoperative MR room, and a CT-fluoroscopy room on the ground floor that provides real-time images during surgery. *Courtesy Stonehill & Taylor Architects, P.C. Photo Whitney Cox.*

area. All these programs occupy two floors and 30,000 sq. ft. of a new, 103,000 sq. ft., six-story critical-care tower.

Other floors of the new tower include a sixteen-bed coronary care unit, a twenty-bed medical/surgical/neurological intensive care unit, and a rehab therapy and renal dialysis unit. An image-guided surgical suite houses single plane and biplane angiographic rooms, an intraoperative MRI room, and a CT-fluoroscopy room on the ground floor to provide real-time images during surgery.

NEONATAL INTENSIVE CARE UNIT
THE CHILDREN'S HOSPITAL
AT SAINT FRANCIS
Tulsa, Oklahoma

The Children's Hospital at Saint Francis hired Page Southerland Page to expand on the theme "kids come first" and design a fifty-bed neonatal intensive care unit to replace its existing open-bay facility. In the new layout, the

Neonatal Intensive Care Unit, The Children's Hospital at Saint Francis, Tulsa, Oklahoma. NICU rooms also feature indirect lighting and access to well-controlled natural light. *Courtesy Page Southerland Page, LLP. Photo DVDesign Group Inc.*

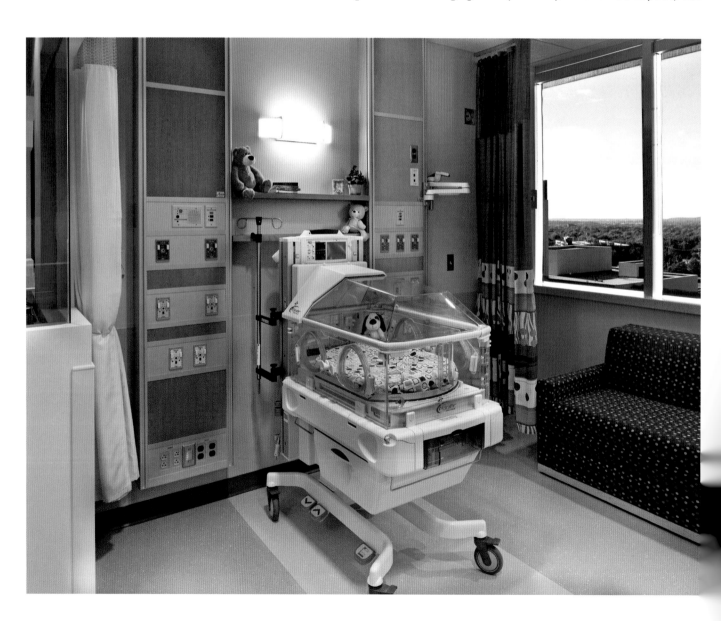

architects arranged six semiprivate and thirty-eight private rooms in pods to control ambient noise, improve access to supplies, and limit traffic through care areas, while offering family amenities and generous bedside space.

Emphasizing the role of the parent in newborn care, each room has a pull-out sofa and mother's niche with a glider, a breast-milk refrigerator, a curtain so a mother can nurse in private, drawers where parents can store their child's clothes, and shelving to help them personalize their baby's room. The rooms have dimmable wall sconces and soft, indirect lighting. The walls are decorated with a seasons theme and primary colors in a sophisticated interplay that both caters to parents and maintains continuity with the existing building.

Windows provide an important psychological relief, and every infant bed has access to well-controlled natural light, which is the most desirable illumination for nearly all caregiving tasks, including charting and evaluation of infant skin tone. Every patient room is equipped with work zones, and subcharting stations are located outside pairs of rooms. Primary team workstations are highlighted under cloudlike soffits and starry-sky domes. A central corridor facilitates the delivery of bulk services, out of view of families and visitors.

In general, it is a design that aims to create a nurturing atmosphere in the new NICU, one that also provides for exceptional clinical care for infants while accommodating the physical and emotional needs of families.

Neonatal Intensive Care Unit, The Children's Hospital at Saint Francis, Tulsa, Oklahoma. Emphasizing the role of the parent in newborn care, each NICU room has a variety of amenities. *Courtesy Page Southerland Page, LLP. Photo DVDesign Group Inc.*

NATIONAL INTREPID CENTER OF EXCELLENCE FOR TRAUMATIC BRAIN INJURY
Bethesda, Maryland

Based on its work on the Center for the Intrepid, SmithGroup designed the National Intrepid Center of Excellence, a 72,000-sq.-ft. traumatic brain injury facility for wounded soldiers returning from the war in Iraq. This world-class facility provides imaging, assessment, diagnosis, and treatment for mild to moderate traumatic brain injury (TBI) and also plays a vital role in the research and development of treatment for this disease.

Working in conjunction with the University of California, Los Angeles (UCLA) Brain Injury Research Center, designers developed the program for outpatient screening; assessment and diagnostic facilities for neurology; neuropsychology; brain imaging; electrodiagnostic assessment, treatment and rehabilitation; cognitive therapy; occupational therapy and physical ther-

National Intrepid Center of Excellence for Traumatic Brain Injury, Bethesda, Maryland. SmithGroup incorporated elements of sustainable design, including day-lighting and energy-saving controls. *Courtesy SmithGroup. Photo Maxwell MacKenzie.*

apy; pharmacological therapy; robotics and telemedicine; as well as a human blood and tissue sample repository.

Using sustainable design elements (including day-lighting, solar orientation, site reuse, alternative transportation, recycled materials, and energy-saving controls), the National Intrepid Center of Excellence will function as the center of a constellation of satellite facilities and as the primary data collection source for further research in the treatment of TBI in connection with UCLA's Brian Injury Research Center and consortium.

National Intrepid Center of Excellence for Traumatic Brain Injury, Bethesda, Maryland. Solar orientation is also one of several sustainable design elements employed by SmithGroup. *Courtesy SmithGroup. Photo Maxwell MacKenzie.*

CHAPTER 9

The Patient Care Unit

nyone who has talked with medical professionals and hospital planners or who has read the literature devoted to the future of the hospital might be tempted to conclude that hospitals have given up on their traditional principal constituent, the inpatient. But such a conclusion is unwarranted.

It is true that the inpatient market continues to shrink. It is also true that a substantial number of futurists—including staff members of Earl Swensson Associates—foresee a time, probably within this century, when the hospital will cease to exist in any form familiar to us now. Genetic engineering will radically alter the incidence and treatment of disease, and various forms of community, step-down, and home care will radically alter the management of disease. However, for the nearer term inpatient care will continue to be a significant hospital component.

With the possible exception of hospital lobby areas, nowhere is the trend toward patient-focused care more visibly evident than in the design and finish quality of patient rooms. Patient-focused room design was given its single greatest burst of momentum by the Planetree movement, which—as mentioned in Chapter 3—originated in 1978.

As we noted there, Earl Swensson Associates, notably, is one of only five charter design firms to be inducted into the Planetree Visionary Design Network. This certification establishes ESa as a specialist in evidence-based healthcare design following the Planetree philosophy and its core components of healing design. Like Planetree itself, ESa as a firm has long sought to personalize, humanize, and demystify the healthcare system with its Synergenial design. We encourage others to embrace the Planetree movement,

especially its certification process, which identifies firms that are committed to the patient-centered care philosophy for hospitals planning construction or renovations.

Midwest Medical Center, Galena, Illinois. Exterior of the first Planetree affiliate hospital in Illinois, designed by Earl Swensson Associates. *Photo Jeff Millies © Hedrich Blessing.*

Planetree units are characterized by self-responsibility and humane care. Traditional hospital rules and regulations are relaxed, and the feel of the Planetree-inspired units is generally more residential than institutional, with kitchenettes where visitors and patients can prepare their own food; indirect, full-spectrum lighting; a predominance of wood finishes rather than plastic or metal; artwork of genuine merit on loan from museums; rooms decorated with some of the patients' own belongings; a patient-visitor lounge, equipped with the latest in high-tech electronics—from televisions to MP3 players—and a library of DVDs and music; and, throughout, the maintenance of a generally "high-touch" environment.

Art, as mentioned, plays a role in new design trends for such rooms. Evidence-based design studies document that the incorporation of art in hospital environments helps reduce stress and facilitate positive feelings, supports efforts of staff, and encourages spiritual and therapeutic wellness. So, not surprisingly, a growing number of clinicians and other professionals from the medical community are working the arts into both healthcare and community settings worldwide. Nearly half of the healthcare institutions in the United States reported having arts in healthcare programming. The majority of these programs are in hospitals, with smaller numbers found in long-term care and hospice/palliative care organizations. The three most common types of arts programming are permanent display of art, performances in public spaces, and bedside activities.

According to a 2009 state of the field report, *Arts in Healthcare*, by the National Endowment for the Arts (NEA) and the Society of the Arts in Healthcare, research now "demonstrates the benefits of the arts in healthcare in hospitals, nursing homes, senior centers, hospices, and other locations within the community. Arts in healthcare programs and creative arts therapies have been applied to a vast array of health issues—from post-traumatic stress disorder to autism, mental health, chronic illnesses, Alzheimer's and dementia, neurological disorders and brain injuries, premature infants, and physical disabilities—to improve patients' overall health outcomes, treatment compliance, and quality of life."

The report goes on to claim that new evidence is emerging on the economic benefit of these programs. They result in shorter hospital stays, less medication, and fewer complications—all of which reduce healthcare costs. Still, much of this research is rich in anecdote and poor in data. That is not true, however, for the research already mentioned that connects arts in healthcare programs to an improved quality of care for patients, for their families, and even for medical staff. Here, extensive studies have established that integrating the arts into healthcare settings helps to cultivate a healing environment and support the physical, mental, and emotional recovery of patients, as well as foster a positive environment for caregivers that improves workplace satisfaction and employee retention. Art can also communicate health and recovery information. In short, art is a form of nonverbal communication reflecting an image of the mission and quality of care offered by a healthcare facility. Some firms, such as Lin Swensson & Associates, now specialize in just this area.

All things considered, this new emphasis on evidenced-based design and patient-focused care in hospital rooms offers the following medical/economic benefits: lower infection rates, reduced medical errors, reduced average lengths of stay (ALOS), reduced staff turnover, reduced staff injuries, and reduced complaints from patients and families. While all of this may seem a far cry from what is now the often-maligned concept of the "Nightingale ward," patient-focused design may actually have developed from the reforms of the Lady with the Lamp.

Elsewhere we have briefly outlined the development of the modern hospital. No less than Planetree's efforts, Nightingale's reforms were aimed at humanizing hospital conditions. The conditions Nightingale faced—filth, disorder, and a nursing "profession" held in vile repute—were the result of the absence of an efficient institution rather than overbearing institutionalism. Her reforms, therefore, were directed at bringing order to chaos; replacing dirt with cleanliness; providing natural light, ventilation, and the openness afforded by high ceilings; and creating an environment in which nurses could perform efficiently and effectively as valued medical professionals.

There was little question of housing patients in private rooms. To begin with, in the medical care system of Nightingale's day, this would have been economically unfeasible. Well-to-do patients were treated at home. Only the working poor and the indigent submitted themselves to hospitals. Medical economics dictated treatment in wards rather than rooms, and Nightingale turned this economic necessity into a patient-management asset. The design of the Nightingale ward was intended to facilitate nursing care, allowing fewer nurses to minister effectively to larger numbers of patients.

Moreover, the public nature of the ward lent moral credibility to the nurse's role by eliminating the potential intimacies of care in a private room. It might be argued that Nightingale's reforms were not focused on the patient, but had as their objective the convenience of the institution and the moral and professional rehabilitation of the nursing profession. But this view fails to take into account the historical context of her reforms. They enabled the creation of an institution in place of disorder and (at best) benign neglect. And who could deny that, by transforming nursing into a true profession, Nightingale vastly improved—humanized—patient care?

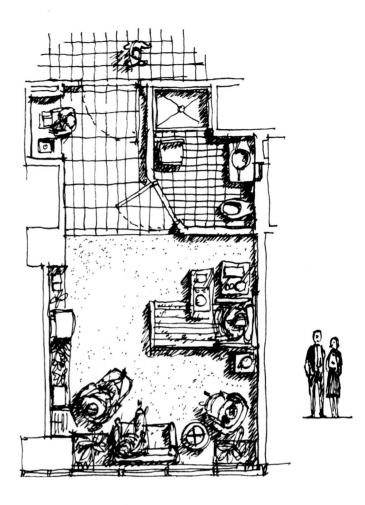

A room dedicated to patient-focused care might include a nurses' work area, plenty of seating for visitors, casework for TV/electronics and personal possessions, and handicapped-accessible bath facilities. Sketch by Earl S. Swensson.

Florence Nightingale's reforms were monumental steps toward patient-focused care. But, as we have learned most dramatically over the last thirty years, the paradigms that shape healthcare are hardly immutable and immune to change. In large part due to Nightingale's reforms, and in part due to the technical advancement of medicine, by the close of the nineteenth century, consignment to a hospital was no longer the equivalent of a death sentence. Hospitals began to emerge as places where people actually got well. With the amelioration of the hospital's image, wealthier patients began to seek hospital care, creating a demand for private rooms. While some medical authorities touted the private room as a means of reducing the potential for cross-infection of patients, the motivation for the introduction of the private room was socioeconomic rather than medical. Certainly, private rooms did not make the nurse's job easier. Quite the contrary for many years, far into the twentieth century, the open ward was looked upon as the more efficient environment for providing patient care.

At a superficial glance, the ongoing trend toward patient units with exclusively private rooms may seem nothing more than an extension of a response to a marketplace that began at the end of the nineteenth century. Both the marketplace and the medical approach to patient care have evolved.

Floyd Medical Center, Rome, Georgia. In the conversion of an existing floor, a small unit of patient suites was created and named Palatine Suites. Two feature a separate connecting sitting room, and alcove-like entries help to maintain quietness and privacy. *Photo © Kieran Reynolds Photography.*

No longer is the nurse a mere observer and practical caretaker who has charge of the patient in the doctor's absence. Nurses are now part of a patient-care team, a team whose work is increasingly facilitated by bedside diagnostic, monitoring, and medication-dispensing equipment. The team approach and technological developments have made the open ward essentially obsolete. Not since the late nineteenth century has it been the most comfortable patient environment. Now it is also no longer the most efficient means of monitoring and managing patients.

In 2006, research and analysis over the last few years of single versus semiprivate rooms culminated in the American Institute of Architects' *Guidelines for Design and Construction of Health Care Facilities* and its call for a standard of private rooms (unless the functional program requires two-bed arrangements). It was a victory for patients and for their families, but also one for nurses and healthcare professionals. With support from the U.S. Department of Health and Human Services, the latest edition of that guide was published in 2010 by the Facility Guidelines Institute of AHSRAE, which includes the American National Standards Institute (ANSI) and the American Society for Healthcare Engineering (ASHE).

From Patient Focus to Clinical Integration

By the 1990s, in an effort to adapt to the demands of managed care and cost containment, hospitals were evolving into organic components of organized delivery systems (ODS)—networks of organizations that provide a coordinated continuum of services to a defined population. The ODS, intimately linked to an insurance product, assumed fiscal and clinical responsibility for the health status of a defined population. Instead of focusing on an "illness" paradigm—stressing acute care, provider dominance, and individual patients—the ODSs were structured according to a wellness paradigm and emphasized health status prediction and management, provider-patient partnerships, and a collective population-based focus.

Through the principle of vertical integration, the ODSs came to own, manage, and coordinate such diverse health services as home healthcare agencies, hospices, group practices, rehabilitative services, acute inpatient care, and so on. If vertical integration structured the "macro" aspects of the ODS, clinical integration informed the "micro" aspects.

Clinical integration is the coordination of patient care across the functions and operating units of an organized delivery system. In a clinically integrated facility, a designated nurse may supervise a team of personnel to administer care to each patient from admission to discharge. The nurse also coordinates patient care with physicians and other healthcare consultants. Even support functions, such as dietary assistance and housekeeping, are unit-based. Clinical integration depends on "work redesign" to create a four-level patient-care team.

1. A professional registered nurse (RN) patient-care manager works with physicians and others to assess the appropriate use of resources to facilitate treatment. The RN brings patients, physicians, and others together to determine and create a plan to achieve desired outcomes. She manages staff, including hiring, scheduling, and skill-developing, for the relevant group of patients. Finally, the RN manages the financial and material resources required for achieving desired goals.

2. The patient-care nurse administers tests and medication.

3. The patient-care technician provides such care as hygiene, certain technical procedures (such as EKG), routine wound care, and so on.

4. The unit assistant provides housecleaning in the patient room, delivers supplies, and so on.

Vertical integration, with its attendant trend toward clinical integration and work redesign, makes the patient room the most intensive focus of inpatient care. Wherever possible, the team comes to the patient, instead of transporting the patient to various professionals.

Convergence and Conflict

As in many other areas of the hospital, technology and humanity often conflict in the design of the patient room and the entire patient unit. Most authorities, physicians, nurses, planners, administrators, architects, and patients agree that the patient room should be a humane environment. Yet, while the overall goal may be agreed upon, there are still many competing needs to be considered.

One suggested redefinition of the hospital's *internal* message—a sense of security, community, comprehension of the surrounding order, freedom of choice—may sometimes conflict with what *external* architectural form conveys. But while the architectural edifice may be intended to speak to any number of things—the site itself, the public, even the press—the room must speak to the patient, must, as Eric Meub (1993) said, "console the spirit."

According to the Facility Guidelines Institute's 2010 *Guidelines for Design and Construction of Health Care Facilities*, these—shall we call them—"spiritual" imperatives should include the following:

- Private rooms
- Dignity
- Peace and quiet
- Sense of being close to nurses in case help is needed
- Cleanliness
- Security
- Diversion and entertainment
- Company of other patients, when appropriate (as in rehabilitation or psychological therapy, for instance)
- Interesting area for ambulation
- Tangible goal outside the patient room to encourage ambulation
- Access to bathroom and shower with adequate space to move and turn with an I.V. pole or walker
- Easy access and control of room lighting, bed position, television, phone, and nurses' call signal
- Accessible place for personal belongings
- Accommodation for visitor(s)
- Good, glare-free light
- Outside view
- Aesthetic, pleasing environment
- Access to view diagnostic images, lab tests, etc.
- Assurance of cross-referenced medications to identify negative reactions or past allergies
- Access to CCTV or other educational topics about illness or postprocedure care
- Assurance of cleaned room from prior occupant and other infection control practices (such as air quality)
- Good food choices and flexible meal times
- IT, computer, and Internet access
- Fewer interruptions at night during sleep

Visitors' needs generally do not conflict with those of the patient, except that a high volume of visitation may disturb some patients, especially if rooms open to busy principal corridors. The patient unit should address the following visitor needs:

- Easy access and wayfinding
- Access to information
- Waiting lounge
- Privacy for conversation with staff and physicians
- Privacy for conversation with patient
- Telephone
- Designated restrooms
- Dining facility, including options to share meals with patients in room or flex hours and light meal choices (excluding vending machines)
- Accommodation for overnight stay with patients
- IT, computer, Internet access

Increasingly, hospitals are designing to accommodate family members as "care partners." Larger patient rooms permit a family member to sleep in the room.

Hospital rooms need to accommodate not only patients but also nursing and medical staff. Rooms should provide them easy access to patients, minimize the walking distances required to perform routine tasks, allow them a sense of "knowing what's going on" in the units, and assure them the ability to move beds, equipment, and supplies in and out of rooms. In addition, rooms should also account for the following nursing staff needs and offer:

Christus St. Michael Health System, Texarkana, Texas. Completed in 1994, the facility consists of a replacement hospital, two MOBs, and a rehabilitation hospital. *Courtesy Watkins Hamilton Ross Architects, Inc. Photo Richard Payne, FAIA.*

- a range of working space from bedside, to bed view, to quiet working zones off stage;
- specialty bariatric rooms with adequate equipment;
- patient lifts to eliminate staff back and strain injuries;
- the ability to accommodate differing approaches to staffing (team vs. primary);
- the ability to deal with shift in severity index (step-down);
- the ability to work effectively in day or night shifts;
- the ability to isolate a higher percentage of patients with infectious diseases;
- the ability to interact with the pharmacist and physician on the unit;
- the ability to flex beds and wings during patient to nurse ratio changes with second and third shift and during census swings;
- the ability to manage and change supplies to patients with bar-coding scanners or PAR restock systems;
- access to information retrieval and input;
- access to high-urgency/frequent-use items;
- access to supplies and safe disposal of used supplies;
- access to equipment storage in designated spaces;
- access to medication;
- ability of all care providers to confer in privacy;
- access to office and conference space;

- staff lounge facility (close but not on main visitor corridor);
- Security—personal security and secure storage for property items (well-designed provisions for security should be welcomed by patients as well as staff).

Again according to the *Guidelines for Design and Construction of Health Care Facilities*, the following physicians' needs generally do not conflict with those of the patient, so far as design is concerned:
- Bed availability
- Accommodation for all types of payers
- Accommodation for any specialty or subspecialty
- Cutting-edge care setting
- Caregivers easy to find
- Patients easy to find
- Charts easy to find
- Ability for all care providers to confer in privacy
- Quiet place for dictation or direct data entry, data retrieval, reference materials
- Access to properly equipped procedure room
- Access to clerical support
- Commercially competitive unit with attractive image

The academic physician has the following additional needs that patients may find intrusive, but good design can minimize these feelings:
- Large-enough unit to accommodate medical teaching team
- Space for teaching without getting in the way of other functions
- Co-location of specialty beds for ease of rounds
- Ability to confer with students on unit in privacy
- Access to charts/diagnostic images/texts/computer terminal/printer
- On-call facility
- Locker facility
- Resident office
- Resident workroom
- Nearby classroom

In addition, the patient unit must accommodate clerical staff, other caregivers (physical therapists, respiratory therapists, etc.), and support services (case managers, dietary, pharmacy, materials management, etc.).
The clerical staff needs the ability to perform the following tasks:
- Observe unit to control flow of visitors and ancillary support staff and keep track of patient movement
- Communicate with patients
- Communicate with staff
- Access data for retrieval and input
- Communicate with other departments
- Accommodate pick-up and drop-off of patients

Physical therapists, inhalation therapists, I.V. therapists, radiology technicians, and other caregivers require the following accommodations:

- Office space or secure work space
- On-floor storage space for supplies
- Dedicated space for patient care
- Communication with home department
- Equipment storage
- Remote monitoring capabilities

Finally, support services have the following needs:

- Access to service elevators with clear lines to support services and lower levels
- Access to patient-care unit without impinging on patient space
- Floor space for supply and dietary carts, etc.
- Satellite facilities: pharmacy, lab, reheat pantry
- Transport system for lab specimens
- Waste and soiled linen management system
- Decentralized housekeeping centers
- Low-maintenance engineering system with good access to frequent maintenance points

Maintenance operations should not impinge on patient or staff space or activities.

Patient-focused, clinically integrated design should accommodate and reconcile these potentially conflicting needs as fully as possible.

Design for Patient-Focused, Clinically Integrated Facilities

Many late-twentieth-century research projects—such as those by Wanda J. Jones and Milton Bullard for Ratcliff (Emeryville, California), The H.O.M. Group (San Francisco), and the more recent 2004 study by Habid Chaudhury, Ali Mahmood, and Michael Valente for the Center for Health Design—set out ultimately to answer the questions of how a totally patient-focused hospital would operate and what it would look like if we applied all the ideas arising from the various demonstration projects and research available. Many of the features called for by such research have already been incorporated in advanced patient-room design.

The old-paradigm wards and semiprivate rooms have no place in today's patient-focused facilities. Instead, these hospitals feature large single-patient private rooms. If the minimum standard room today is, according to the *Guidelines for Design and Construction of Health Care Facilities,* 160 sq. ft. of clear floor space exclusive of toilet rooms, closets, lockers, wardrobes, and alcoves or vestibules, then the patient-focused room will be 250 sq. ft of clear space exclusive of family alcoves, toilet rooms, closets, lockers, wardrobes, vestibules, staff charting areas, and staff hand-washing areas, with minimum clear dimensions of 15 ft.

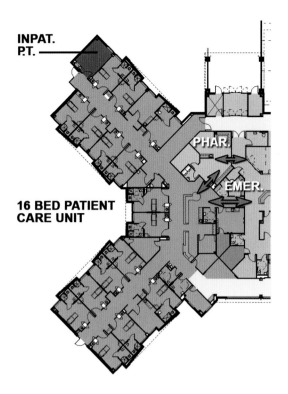

INPAT.
P.T.

PHAR.

EMER.

16 BED PATIENT
CARE UNIT

A sixteen-bed patient care unit floor plan created by Earl Swensson Associates.

The greater space is required for effective treatment by the care team, including the use of portable equipment brought to the patient and the performance of certain procedures in the room. This flexibility reduces the necessity of transporting the patient between specialists and procedures. Moreover, the larger room allows for more comfortable conferencing and counseling, and it can accommodate family members, as either visitors or care partners. (One design possibility incorporates a large window seat that can be converted into a bed).

A larger patient room can perform many of the functions of an ICU, provided that the proper equipment is brought in, thereby making it unnecessary to move the patient in and out of a separate ICU. Indeed, it may be possible to convert any number of the larger rooms to dedicated ICUs as required without major new construction. Under managed care, inpatients have been almost by definition sicker patients (those who are less ill are treated on an ambulatory or very short-term-stay basis), so the potential for ready conversion to ICU function has been very important. Stacking rooms of the same size in bed towers also allows for future conversion.

Finally, planning facilities with larger rooms makes long-term economic sense. To be sure, initial capital costs are greater, but the gain in flexibility and future adaptability can represent a substantial savings. Larger rooms are more easily adapted to such "down-program" uses as hospice, rehabilitation, elderly housing, and the like. For a while, the trend toward "acuity-adaptable" care—that is, the use of high-technology rooms to provide a means of keeping patients in the same room from admission until discharge, regardless of the patient's acuity level—promoted the use of large rooms, but that experiment may have run its course.

Sometimes called "universal care rooms," acuity-adaptable rooms are identically sized and designed for the full range of inpatient care. Although universal care rooms were once planned to be large enough to serve as LDR rooms or labor, delivery, recovery, postpartum (LDRP) rooms with sufficient space for portable computed tomography (CT) or magnetic resonance imaging (MRI) equipment to allow more invasive procedures to be performed bedside, that concept was by and large superseded by acuity-adaptable units—patient rooms within a single service line, sized and equipped to handle critical and step-down levels of care, but excluding medical/surgical acute care.

While such rooms allow patients to be moved on the same floor to a critical-care room when acuity changes and to be stepped down to a room in the medical/surgery unit from which they can be discharged, staffing them is a major challenge. They became controversial when nursing staff level per unit proved not as flexible as the rooms themselves, and hospitals simply cannot afford ICU-skilled nurses in lower-acuity rooms. Still, the flexibility of identical rooms that can be reassigned easily with no structural modifications has great appeal to most organizations. Rooms can be better sized to adapt as a unit to future needs, so that a whole unit may change.

Another step toward enhancing flexibility is to consider installing disabled-accessible bathrooms for all rooms. This will render all rooms accessible to all patients at all times, regardless of age, sex, or handicapped status. It will never be necessary for Admitting to scramble to accommodate a disabled patient.

No longer are the old "inboard" bathrooms—that is, bathrooms next to the corridor—standard in hospital patient rooms. Today bathrooms are typically located on the outside wall. These "outboard" bathrooms allow the entire room space to be available for use according to the state's code analysis; it keeps the interior wall free, which could readily be converted to glass if the room needed to be an ICU. Advocates of the inboard bathroom point out, however, that such placement provides additional privacy for patients, is a good location for hand washing and utility use by staff, creates a vestibule that accommodates the door swing, is logical from a construction cost standpoint, and makes the patient room more closely resemble a hotel room, providing space for an expansive exterior window. However, these often get trumped by the safety and visibility concerns of senior nurses.

The Jones and Bullard report recommends the design of what they called the "care suite," a cluster of beds smaller than the conventional nursing unit that can be readily supervised by a care team or "care pair" (a cross-trained pair of nurses supported by technicians). These care suites are further developments of two trends in hospital design: the triangle and the pod.

As triangle and pod plans represented a major step toward modularization from the traditional "racetrack" plan and from double-loaded (or single) corridor plans, so the care suite is a further modular departure from the triangle and pod plans.

The care suites could be designed such that the individual patient rooms do not open onto a busy corridor. These clusters are also more easily managed to accommodate fluctuating patient census. It is easier to close a six-bed cluster than a thirty- to thirty-six-bed standard nursing unit. It would also be relatively easy to assign different suites to specific types of patients, allowing programs to grow or shrink in manageable increments. Finally, rooms located at the ends of each suite could readily be transformed into isolation rooms. Each care suite could include a lounge, library, kitchenette, and conference facilities, all creating a more human scale and a sense of community, security, and serenity.

Patient focusing depends in large measure on implementation of "bedside information systems," or clinical computing. Clinical computing links all care activity in real time, handling guidelines and protocols as well as

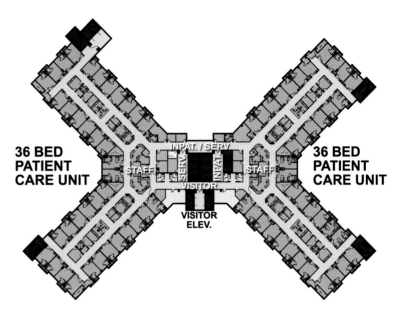

36 BED PATIENT CARE UNIT

36 BED PATIENT CARE UNIT

A thirty-six-bed patient care unit floor plan created by Earl Swensson Associates.

results obtained from tests and procedures. The most advanced systems can accept input from patient monitoring devices (such as blood pressure, temperature, EKG, and so on). Clinical computing allows for more detailed and frequently updated charting, requiring less time than manual charting. The technology also allows for the generation of checklists and quality assurance evaluations—crucial aspects of total quality management (TQM) systems. Such paperwork would be time-consuming and cumbersome in the absence of bedside computing. Studies indicate that clinical computing also significantly reduces charting and medication errors.

Most significantly for design, bedside technologies allow for the kind of decentralized care that really makes care suites and care pairs feasible. With clinical computing all patient data can be shared—in real time—by all members of the care team. With advanced data communications, data can also be shared with consultants off-site, whether they are across the street or halfway around the world.

The rapid advances in computer and wireless technology in recent years have brought clinical computing within the reach of most hospitals. But even at a time when one is accustomed to expect everything from computers, the requirements for bedside technology are especially demanding:

- Customers want systems that will add minimal per-bed capital costs.
- The system must be simple to use.
- The system must be thoroughly networked and able to share data completely and immediately with all other hospital computers.
- The system should be ergonomically located, and not in conflict with patient headwall support (medical gases, electrical outlets, etc.).
- Displays must be sharp and graphics capable.
- The equipment must be durable. In a hospital environment, the equipment will be subject to jostling, dropping, bumping, and spillage. In some settings, particularly urban hospitals, vandalism may well be a significant problem.
- The equipment must be small and unobtrusive. At its most advanced, of course, the bedside computer will replace in-room monitoring equipment and so will actually save space.
- The software must be flexible and readily capable of being customized.
- Processors must be high powered and fast.

Handheld computers address many of the issues listed above. They are naturals for many charting applications. Handheld units make expensive, space-consuming, and damage-prone bedside terminals unnecessary. They can be docked as necessary with a headwall-mounted port to interface with the hospital network. A computer monitor, complete with a port to accept output from the handheld computer, could be installed for each bed.

Robotics may also contribute to decentralized patient care. Robots can be used as an alternative method of transporting supplies and laboratory specimens from one location to another. They are usually modified industrial robots that can be programmed to follow painted lines on floors and are "smart" enough to avoid bumping into obstacles, including people.

Such bedside robotics began in Japan with a robot called Mekong that was developed for lifting, moving, and carrying patients. Nursing tasks are highly strenuous—more closely related to heavy industrial work than to domestic duties. Not surprisingly, nurses are chronically plagued by back pain related to patient handling, resulting in innumerable lost working days. Robots like Mekong are, as of now, a topic of conversation in the United States.

Two trends are clear: Patient management, from admission to discharge and even follow-up, is devolving increasingly upon a nurse or nursing teams. An increasing proportion of inpatients are the sickest individuals, who make more demands on the nurses' skill—and on their physical strength. In view of these convergent trends, it seems likely that bedside robotics will continue to develop and eventually figure as an important element of patient-care design.

MAYO CLINIC HOSPITAL
Phoenix, Arizona

As the Mayo Clinic once reported to *Commercial Building,* "William Mayo, over a hundred years ago, stated that the best interest of the patient is the only interest to consider." With that kind of tradition behind it, the Mayo Clinic and ESa created the Mayo Clinic Hospital in Phoenix, Arizona, as a showcase for patient-focused, clinically integrated facilities. It was the first hospital the Mayo Clinic designed from the ground up. Working with ESa, the hospital articulated the following principles in planning the facility:

• A design with effective, user-friendly patient flow. (For example, the planning committees looked at the episode of patient care from entrance to exit of the healthcare system and set goals from that pattern).

• An overall patient-care focus.

Mayo Clinic Hospital, Phoenix, Arizona. A thin layer of masonry veneer on the curtainwall blends with desert surroundings. *Photo © Mark Boisclair Photography, Inc.*

Mayo Clinic Specialty Building, Phoenix, Arizona. The lobby, designed by ESa, reflects geometric forms and earth tones to blend with the landscapes of the Sonora Desert and the McDowell Mountains. *Photo © Kieran Reynolds Photography.*

• A separation of clean from dirty in every hospital area, especially in the OR and Central Services.

• An effective delivery of supplies to the patient's side.

One of the first things the planning group did was conduct a needs survey to determine what was called for in the way of patient mix for physician specialty practice, patient acuity levels, and medical practical needs. Next, the group conducted a complete cost analysis, including cost of the land, structure, infrastructure, capital equipment, and staffing. Aiming to be a local, national, and international center of excellence, the Mayo Clinic opened the doors of its five-story, acute-care medical/surgical facility. With its emphasis on providing the latest medical technology in a patient- and family-friendly facility, the Mayo Clinic intended the hospital to set the standard of inpatient care within a unified, integrated, multicampus system that includes several Mayo Hospitals in the Midwest, Florida, and Arizona, and intertwines clinical practice, education, and research. The finished hospital occupies 440,000 sq. ft. on five floors. With 208 spacious private patient rooms, clustered in groups no larger than 12 beds each, it is not the largest hospital in the Phoenix area, but it is built for future expansion—up to 500 beds—as the population boom in the city moves northward.

The hospital was designed with geometric forms and earth tones to blend with the landscapes of the Sonora Desert and the McDowell Mountains. The main entry is framed in varying shades of green sandstone, contrasting with the exterior's neutral browns and echoing the colors of local vegetation. Saguaro and agave cacti, both indigenous, fill pots near the entrance. Inside, the desert landscape and dusky colors continue. The main lobby features a five-story atrium flooded with natural light and fitted with live desert greenery and a fountain flowing down a rock wall. Balconies on each floor of the hospital overlook the serene and calming environment of the lobby, which includes an information desk, registration, social services, cafeteria, and gift shop.

Patient services are conveniently and visually accessible from the main lobby and central banks of elevators. From another entrance on the first floor, the ED has fourteen examination rooms and four observation areas. The department features walk-in and ambulance/helipad entrances. Diagnostic radiology, neurodiagnostics, noninvasive cardiac diagnostics, cardiac catheterization, pulmonary testing, and a full-service laboratory and pathology lab with satellite support, all communicate with key departments in other parts of the hospital. Filmless computerized radiology is used throughout the hospital, and physicians can access X-rays on a computer screen immediately after they are taken. The main pharmacy and the central service department are located on the first floor, albeit directly below the operating rooms on the second floor, to which central services has direct access. While patients and visitors enter and leave from the same point, traffic from technicians and staff has been separated, so there is no commingled traffic pattern.

The second-floor operating rooms, fourteen of them for inpatient and outpatient surgery, are part of a 36,000-sq.-ft. surgical suite. Also located on the second floor are the ICU/CCU units, the pre- and postanesthesia care units, the short-stay recovery unit, and a sleep studies lab. The third floor is devoted to subacute care, rehabilitation, and physical therapy, as well as housing medical/surgical beds for urology, orthopedics, and neurology/neurosurgery patients. The fourth floor contains additional patient rooms, inpatient dialysis, the oncology unit, and a transplant facility. All patient rooms are private and are clustered in groups no larger than twelve each; all are wired for telemetry so that monitoring of the heart and other vital signs can be accomplished from any patient room.

Overall, the design emphasized adaptability for the latest medical technology while remaining patient and family friendly. The fifth floor is shelled to allow for future growth, in each direction horizontally and up to eight floors vertically. The interstitial floor was added for future communications so that additions can be made without interrupting existing services.

Mayo Clinic Specialty Building, Phoenix, Arizona. Exam room. Generous natural light and layers of ambient and task lighting help create a soothing environment. *Photo © Kieran Reynolds Photography.*

MIDWEST MEDICAL CENTER

Galena, Illinois

Designed by ESa, Midwest Medical Center replaced a facility that once had only linoleum floors and cement-block walls. In early 2004, it became the first Planetree Affiliate Hospital in the State of Illinois. The new organization's priority is to put the needs of patients first. The critical access hospital firmly believes that the physical environment is vital to the healing process of the patient, which means facility design should include efficient layouts that support patient dignity and personhood. Aesthetics, art, and a warm, noninstitutional design that values humans, not just technology, serve as cornerstones. Architectural barriers inhibiting patient control and privacy as well as interfering with family participation were removed. Architecture in this historic resort community informs the facility's design as, for example, cornices and a clock tower crown the entry.

For the firm's interior design team, woodwork proved an essential element in helping create the environment from the outset. They established a soothing calmness inside the building through a combination of rich maple woodwork, natural colors in the ceramic-tiled lobby floor, natural light, a copper waterfall feature, extensive molding details, and generous views of nature.

Midwest Medical Center, Galena, Illinois. The healing environment of a Planetree affiliate embraces elements found in hospitality architecture. *Photo Jeff Millies © Hedrich Blessing.*

As the first Planetree affiliate in Illinois, Midwest Medical Center incorporates all of the Planetree tenets and takes design cues from the existing architecture of the historic resort town of Galena. The interior spaces are designed to provide a calm soothing environment for patients, family, and visitors as well as nurturing spaces for staff.

While maple was the wood of choice for the project, a cherry stain was used throughout the space. ESa also used a wood-look, high-pressure decorative laminate with the natural wood in areas where durability was required. The main lobby area, wrapped by a decorative column, offers immediately warm colors, rich woods, soothing sconce lighting, vaulted ceilings, and life-size windows that showcase the Midwestern sky. The idea was to provide a healing element for every place the eye landed. From the water wall to the bubbling fountain in the healing garden, the visitor should feel that he or she has come to a place where caring counts.

After twelve months of construction, the facility's 94,000 sq. ft. feature a state-of-the-art fitness center, a resource library, a meditation suite, and the Whispering Willow

Gifts and Vista Café, which attracts community members for reasons other than illness. Patient rooms, each with a generously windowed view, offer comforting family zones. In addition to the facility's being patient- and family-centered, it nurtures its staff with such amenities as windows in the operating suites. Streamlined efficiencies include clinical adjacencies; for example, the ED is adjacent to diagnostics, and preparation for outpatient surgery is separated from recovery only by doors that allow for flexibility of space. Open spaces promote integration among staff, families, and patients. An easily expandable platform provides for future growth. The design of the twenty-five-bed, critical access replacement facility was consciously based on the Planetree tenets, which embody holistic, patient-centered care in a healing environment. As a result, a hospital that once required patients to walk a long dark corridor simply to take a bath has become a beautiful, compassionate, and patient-focused medically advanced healing facility.

Midwest Medical Center, Galena, Illinois. A combination of stone and tile provides accents to nurses' stations. *Photo Craig Dugan © Hedrich Blessing.*

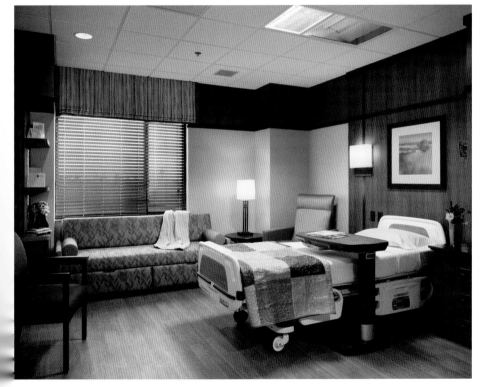

Midwest Medical Center, Galena, Illinois. Patient rooms, each with a windowed view, also include accommodations for families. *Photo Jeff Millies © Hedrich Blessing.*

OrthoColorado Hospital at St. Anthony Medical Campus, Lakewood, Colorado. The main entrance lobby has direct access to the lobby of an attached integrated medical office building. *Photo © Michael Peck.*

ESa designed this 124,587 sq.-ft., three-story "hospital within a hospital" as the first phase of the new St. Anthony Medical Campus in the City of Lakewood, not far from Denver. The second phase is the 524,500 sq.-ft. St. Anthony Hospital.

OrthoColorado Hospital's services include forty-eight private orthopedic inpatient beds and eight orthopedic operating rooms with staging and PACU spaces. A small specialty orthopedic emergency room and clinic with dedicated radiology, laboratory, pharmacy, and dietary services are also available.

The orthopedic hospital has a main entrance lobby with direct access to the lobby of an attached integrated medical office building. The design of the patient-focused facility uses hospitality-based concepts and incorporates generous accommodations for family in all patient rooms. Natural light, healing colors, and warm materials mark the facility throughout.

OrthoColorado Hospital at St. Anthony Medical Campus, Lakewood, Colorado. The interior of the main lobby. *Photo © Michael Peck.*

ST. VINCENT'S
SOUTH TOWER
Birmingham, Alabama

In this 218,000-sq.-ft. expansion to an urban medical campus, ESa designed a patient-focused, hospitality-influenced, healing environment and provided accommodations for family members. St. Vincent's recognizes the integral role families play in patient care, and its spaces were designed throughout to promote interactions among staff, families, and patients. Each of the three completed patient care floors contains thirty private patient rooms and four family suites in addition to a family lounge and family pantry. Patient rooms are equipped with writing desks and wireless Internet access. Next to the atrium overlook on each unit is a family area with a living room atmosphere. Visitors and family members can retreat to this space when they want to be outside, but near, the patient's room.

St. Vincent's South Tower, Birmingham, Alabama. Each patient room is designed to accommodate a lift system. *Photo © Kieran Reynolds Photography.*

The patient units have a slight V-shape, with nursing substations positioned at the midpoint of each arm of the V. The units are connected to allow for flexibility between units to deal with the peaks and lulls of hospital traffic. Thirty patient rooms are clustered in two groups of fifteen on either side of the substations, which creates shorter walking distances for nurses. The patient rooms are arranged in a racetrack configuration to reduce noise on the unit. "That's one of the things, after talking to the nurses, they are just very happy about—how quiet it is," says ESa principal Todd Robinson.

Supplies are stored in several nursing alcoves located along the hallway. Each alcove holds two flat-screen monitors, so physicians can view patient records and images from the hospital's picture archiving and communication system (PACS) at the same time or compare two images side-by-side. Patient records and images can also be viewed bedside. Cabinetry in each patient room opens to reveal computer systems for patient monitoring and charting. The computer monitors are at eye level, with keyboards that can be turned so caregivers can face the patient while entering information.

Medical gas outlets are also concealed inside the furnishings. The headwall, located on the nursing side of the bed, allows nurses easy access to gases or suction without their having to reach over patients or walk around to the far side of the room, which is reserved for family use. In these rooms, people do not trip over one another. The rooms have exterior windows, along an angled toilet wall. This accomplishes several things: First, patients can

St. Vincent's South Tower, Birmingham, Alabama. Angled patient beds provide privacy while allowing medical staff immediate access to the headwall. *Photo © Kieran Reynolds Photography.*

see outside or talk with people in the room's family zone without turning their heads. Second, placing the toilet area along the hallway also allows for larger exterior windows. Third, angling the bed away from the hallway increases privacy for the patient, which ESa research discovered was an important concern for the Birmingham community. Finally, the layout improves patient safety by placing the head of the bed closer to nurses, so they can reach the patient more quickly, and it makes it easy to move beds or gurneys in and out of the room.

Patient rooms are paired with toilet areas abutting one another, to take advantage of shared plumbing chases. The rooms feature family-friendly amenities such as a refrigerator, built-in hair dryer, safe, desk, flat-screen TV, and pullout bed. The flooring is a wood-look vinyl. Draperies soften the rooms and give them a homey appearance, as well.

Each room is equipped for a bedside patient lift. Initially, eight rooms had lifts subject to evaluation by hospital staff for possible installation in additional patient rooms.

Closely related to the VIP suites discussed below are the South Tower's four family suites. Visiting hospitalized family members has long been a dreary and uncomfortable affair, especially for those spending the night. With all the new research underscoring the importance of family in patient care, hospitals are now making every effort to accommodate the families of patients. Single-patient rooms with distinct family zones and convertible furniture suitable for rooming-in have become standard in new hospital design. Here ESa took this idea a step further. The four suites range from 691 sq. ft. to 724 sq. ft. in size, and they are stacked above one another on every patient floor, taking advantage of an angle at one end of the building's floor plate to gain extra square footage. The patient rooms of the suites are nearly identical to all other patient rooms in the facility, but, like hotel suites, a doorway connects these rooms to separate rooms offering sleeping and seating areas for family members and other guests. The suites have proven especially useful for patients in the hospital's orthopedic and oncology programs.

A Fading Trend: The Premium Suite

If the general medical/surgical patient room now borrows much from the hospitality industry, a number of hospitals took analogy a step further by introducing what used to be called "VIP suites," which correspond to the concierge floor or executive level of many upscale hotels. They are a waning trend, and indeed their old designation might these days spark a class warfare debate in healthcare facility design circles. The premium suite is a fully self-contained environment designed to provide a high level of creature comforts. Such suites characteristically include a separate kitchen that serves twenty-four hours a day; a separate, private waiting lobby for visitors; private consultation rooms for family and patients; lounges and reading areas; game rooms; and even dining rooms (although present experience suggests that these are underutilized; most patients prefer to dine in their suites). Decor tends to be traditional, since the assumption is that the clientele who occupy the suites will be older patients, whose tastes lean toward the traditional.

The Camellia Pavilion was designed by HOK for the University of Alabama at Birmingham Hospital. Rooms in the Georgian-styled pavilion offer a minimum of 390 to 400 sq. ft.—and that is just bedroom space. True suites, which include a sitting room, double the square footage. As in a hotel, such amenities as televisions and DVD players are concealed in armoires rather than suspended, hospital-fashion, from the ceiling. Desks feature data ports for the patient's personal computer, and there is a full bath with a tub and a shower. The larger suites have two full baths, the second one meant to accommodate the assistants or security people who might be part of an entourage. The bathroom also sports a refrigerator and juice bar.

Entry to the Camellia Pavilion's premium suites is separate from, but close to, the main hospital entrance. The pavilion entrance opens into a private room that functions as a small lobby, from which visitors can take elevators to the suites. Cart and service traffic are separated from visitor and patient traffic to reduce corridor bustle and noise. The Camellia Pavilion shares a fitness center with other parts of the hospital. Although physical therapy is performed in the fitness center, the facility is also open to staff and visitors. This in itself minimizes the clinical feel of the rehabilitation facility.

Hospitals that offer such suites have reported a very high rate of occupancy, on average 10 percent higher than the rate for standard rooms. In creating them, architects and designers face the technical and aesthetic challenges of making high-tech equipment work in settings that, as in the Georgian-inspired Camellia Pavilion, are not only traditional but even historical in inspiration.

In another example, as part of a phased expansion and renovation of the Floyd Medical Center in Rome, Georgia, ESa included the conversion of an existing floor to a small unit of patient suites to support growing services and to better position the hospital in its market. These new patient accommodations with special amenities are named The Palatine Suites, after one of Rome, Italy's seven hills. Three of the seven suites feature a patient bedroom and a separate sitting room for the benefit of family members. Four others have no adjoining sitting room, but retain the amenities of the other suites, including vinyl plank flooring emulating hardwood and porcelain tile bathrooms. Other upgrades help maintain a low level of noise and provide a sense of more luxurious accommodation. These rooms have proved very popular and maintain a high occupancy rate.

A New Alternative for Patient Accommodation: The Wellness Environment

In keeping with their evidence-based design, a typical Wellness Environments patient room follows a four-zone design principle in every room—a zone for the patient, for the caregiver, for the family, and for hygiene. *Courtesy Wellness Environments. Photo Paige Rumore Photography.*

Let us turn to a new concept in patient accommodation that we think may revolutionize the way hospitals in the future deal with patient rooms—Wellness Environments. The concept was first formulated back in 1996 in Nashville, Tennessee, when Earl Swensson, convinced that patient rooms had become too provider focused, envisioned a new kind of patient room, an environment devoted to wellness rather than a room built merely to warehouse and care for the sick. Eight years of research and development and four more of production led to Wellness Environments, a company dedicated to creating the perfect patient room for the future.

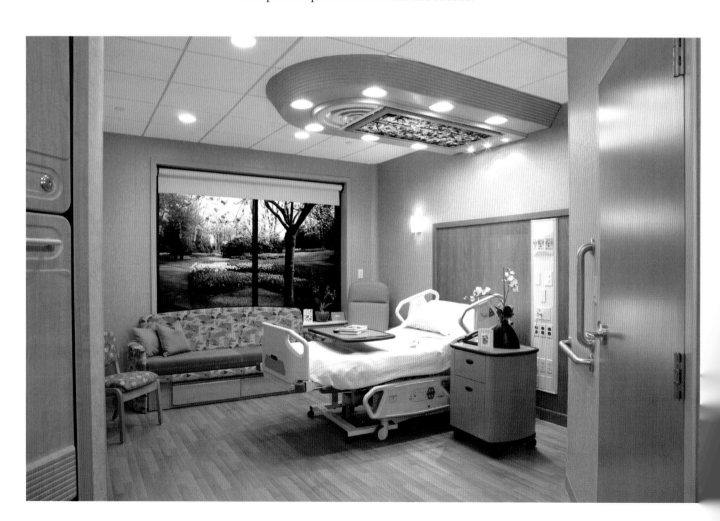

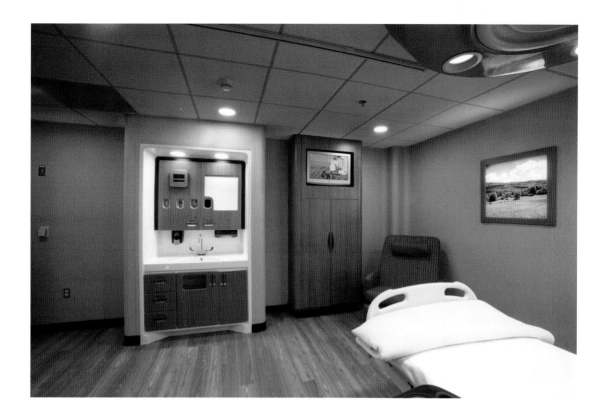

To meet this challenge, Earl Swensson Associates asked themselves such questions as: Can the design of a hospital room actually speed the recovery process? Do patients feel more relaxed when they can look out a window on a scenic view? Can staff efficiency increase based on the design of the patient room? Since they knew from years of experience with hospital and healthcare design that the answer to all was a resounding yes, they geared their company to the design and installation of turnkey modular patient rooms for renovation and new construction. The company's revolutionary total-room package incorporates a four-zone design principle in every room—a zone for the patient, for the caregiver, for the family, and for hygiene. The design delivers improved patient care, promotes faster healing, and provides patient comfort and safety, while creating an efficient workplace for healthcare professionals.

The firm's use of evidence-based design is quite apparent in the patient zone, which features radius corners in both the wall system and in the furniture and grout-free accessories that help reduce the risk of hospital-acquired infections. Historically, 90-degree corners and grouted sinks and showers have proved a breeding ground for bacteria and germs. The radius corner, and one-piece molded acrylic sinks and showers, eliminate the crevices that germs can inhabit. The rooms advance patient safety with abundant grab bars to help avoid falls and rounded corners to reduce the risk of injury. Wellness rooms include a signature multifunctional overbed canopy with an air diffuser that directs airflow away from the patient and an abundance of lights—exam lights for attending physicians, patient-controlled reading lights, and backlit nature scenes—which aid in healing by helping to reduce patient anxiety and stress.

The Wellness caregiver zone employs a workstation for charting, documentation, and communications within each room—a recessed clinical information unit at which doctors and nurses can quickly obtain patient information. The station's antimicrobial keyboard can be cleaned with bleach and folds into the wall when not in use. As more diagnostic and therapeutic procedures are performed bedside, more equipment and supplies will be needed within patient rooms; Wellness rooms are larger to accommodate these needs. The nurse task center offers ample storage for the most frequently used supplies while creating a standardized location for stored supplies in every room. In short, the rooms are designed to promote nursing efficiency. Such units also encourage, among other things, frequent hand washing to prevent the spread of healthcare associated infections (HAIs) as well as increasing staff efficiency.

The importance of a dedicated space for a family member who can aid in the healing process has become increasingly evident, and the room's family zone features a sofa sleeper with built-in storage for personal belongings, an armoire with a built-in television niche, a comfortable recliner, and shelves to keep special gifts and the like. Indeed, one reason the rooms are larger is precisely to provide families with furnishings such as sleeper sofas and armoires.

Finally, the Wellness hygiene zone incorporates one-piece molded acrylic showers and vanities with the radius corners mentioned above that provide a germ-free, easy-to-clean environment. Wellness, with its one source provider concept, installs even the smallest details such as the tissue holders, glove dispensers, plumbing fixtures, a built in bedpan cabinet, and even the robe hook. Every surface in the hygiene zone can be cleaned in a 10 percent bleach solution to help disinfect and to kill germs and bacteria.

The Wellness room is also designed to make business sense. It can reduce costs in a number of ways. Modular construction speeds the installation process, provides a faster turnaround resulting in improved cash flow, and is flexible since components are movable. A leasing option allows facilities to use operating expenses rather than capital funds to pay for the rooms, and depreciation on the rooms can be accelerated. Wellness rooms never need painting, patching, or sanding. Because of the system's flexibility, behind-the-wall problems—leaks, rewiring, and so forth—can be addressed in hours, not days. Wellness rooms can be cleaned in about half the time of traditional rooms. Wellness rooms help with doctor and nurse recruitment. Finally, Wellness rooms also offer facilities a tangible marketing tool—a better patient room that promotes healing.

Departing from the clinical atmosphere of traditional rooms, the Wellness room environment is comfortable and soothing. Using research that incorporates patient satisfaction, proven healing therapies, and medical staff input, Wellness Environments integrates the latest technology to build an efficient, high-quality, task-centered patient room that also provides a comfortable setting for the patient and family. In short, as facilities such as the Self Regional Medical Center in Greenwood, South Carolina, the Sumner Regional Medical Center in Gallatin, Tennessee, and the North Sunflower Medical Center in Ruleville, Mississippi, can testify, the Wellness room provides an innovative alternative to traditional construction.

MISSION HOSPITAL ACUTE CARE TOWER

Mission Viejo, California

The new 100,000-sq.-ft. acute-care tower at Mission Hospital expands the Orange County campus in Southern California and redefines the facility as a technologically advanced acute-care center with high-quality patient services and a good work environment for staff. RBB Architects used Building Information Modeling (BIM) to help coordinate this complex project and deliver it ahead of schedule. In fact, the project garnered a Gold ConstrucTech Vision Award for its high level of BIM-inspired innovations in the exterior design. The tower also earned the national Marvin M. Black Award for achieving Excellence in Partnership.

The tower design focused on patient-centered design and next-generation innovations in healthcare, including imaging, diagnostics, and critical-care services. The tower, which is connected to the existing hospital by a pedestrian bridge, proffers a new aesthetic for the hospital, one aimed at establishing a more modern identity for the campus and at setting a new standard for future expansion.

The tower's exterior features an exposed braced-frame structural system that provides superior seismic performance in compliance with California's stringent regulations for hospitals. The unique system reduces the size of columns and beams. Main vertical systems such as elevators, stairs, mechanical

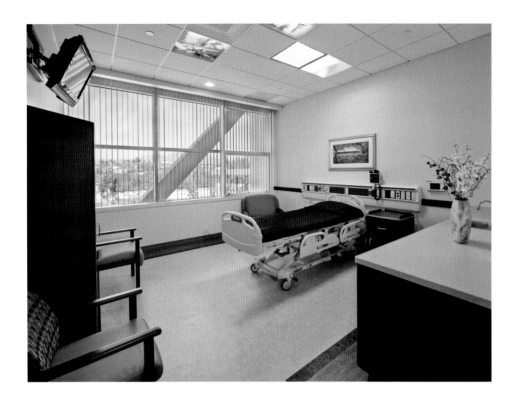

Mission Hospital Acute Care Tower, Mission Viejo, California. The focus on patient-centered care is evident in the design of its patient rooms. *Courtesy RBB Architects Inc. Photo Solar Eye.*

and electrical shafts are positioned outside the braced-floor area. These features maximize the floor area and flexibility to accommodate growth. The exterior appearance, with its unique aluminum cladding, seeks to convey the state-of-the-art medical services contained within. Strong radial shapes at both ends of the building and concentric framing along the front present a distinctive appearance from every angle.

In keeping with the St. Joseph's Health System religious pedigree, a forty-five-seat chapel, located at the entrance to the hospital, plays a prominent role in the design and offers easy access to patients, visitors, and the community. Its essential form is a half cylinder with an inclined glass roof supported from the top by radial trusses. Natural light floods the space and inspires its visitors and, along with the adjacent healing garden and its soothing water displays, offers a serene setting for meditation. The low radiating walls from the chapel define the garden, which is partially visible from the outpatient corridor of the imaging department.

NEW PAVILION AT PAOLI HOSPITAL
PATIENT CARE UNIT
Paoli, Pennsylvania

Already mentioned in Chapter 5 for its model emergency facilities, the new pavilion is an innovative patient care facility, a unique combination of the latest technologies and therapeutic healing environments. It was designed by architect EwingCole as part of the Center for Health Design's Pebble Project and built on evidence-based design to promote the healing process, enhance patient safety, enable nurses to focus more of their time and attention on patients, increase comfort and lessen patient and family anxiety, minimize the spread of infection, improve patient satisfaction, and create a better work environment for doctors, nurses, and staff.

While its ground floor houses the new ED and its first floor a new surgical department, its third and fourth floors are dedicated to patient care. The critical-care unit is located on the third floor, where all patient rooms are private. The patient rooms themselves are designed flexibly to accommodate various levels of care. They use specific zones for staff, family, and patients, which minimizes cross-circulation between staff and visitors. The floor's multiple nursing stations and staff charting areas cut down staff travel. Some

90 percent of patient care areas are exposed to natural light with large, oversized windows. And the expanded CCU boasts state-of-the-art technology.

The bed orientation and angled patient rooms on the fourth floor allow nurses to easily monitor patients. The floor's decentralized nursing stations place nurses closer to patients, and its identical patient room layouts enhance patient safety and increase efficiency of caregivers. Medical gases, electrical outlets, and patient monitoring are located for ease of access. Direct and indirect lighting enhances the environment by evenly diffusing and distributing light. And floor patterns separate staff work zones from the public corridor.

In general, the facility recognizes the profound influence of environments upon health, and is built to reduce the cost of healthcare delivery through energy-efficient design that enhances the performance of its caregivers.

New Pavilion at Paoli Hospital, Patient Care Unit, Paoli, Pennsylvania. The new pavilion is an innovative patient care facility, blending the latest technologies with therapeutic healing environments. *Courtesy EwingCole. Photo Matt Wargo.*

New Pavilion at Paoli Hospital, Patient Care Unit, Paoli, Pennsylvania. Decentralized nurses' stations place nurses closer to patients, and the identical patient room layouts enhance patient safety and increase efficiency of caregivers. *Courtesy EwingCole. Photo Matt Wargo.*

SACRED HEART MEDICAL CENTER AT RIVERBEND
Springfield, Oregon

The Sacred Heart Medical Center, located in Oregon's Willamette Valley, wanted to establish a new standard of healthcare facility that both represented a pronounced regional aesthetic and—using leading-edge, evidence-based design—made for exemplary patient care. It had the site, 181 acres of gorgeous undeveloped land in the Eugene-Springfield area, and Anshen+Allen architects helped it come up with the design. Sacred Heart Medical Center at RiverBend—as the site was dubbed—would be a state-of-the-art, $367 million, 1.2-million-sq.-ft. medical complex devoted to patient-centered care and focused on quality clinical outcomes and patient safety.

Sacred Heart felt that, with its stunning setting, easy access, and ample space, RiverBend would prove the perfect spot for an inspiring, technologically advanced, twenty-first-century hospital. The project team worked with sixty-two user groups, focus groups, and a patient-and-family council. Consulted over five years, the groups were engaged at key project milestones including the executive review during schematics and design development, the functional mock-up walk-through, and the flow review workshop.

Planners conceived of the new hospital as a healing destination that would uplift and transform the patient and staff experience through exemplary patient care. In addition to the rigorous attention they wished to place on patient safety, they also wanted to focus on arrival and reception, and on patient and family spaces. Ultimately, too, the design—including the interior detailing and artwork—would clearly connect to the natural setting.

The architects nestled the facility in a bend of the McKenzie River, surrounded by groves of Douglas firs and a meadow, taking advantage of the site's natural beauty to create a distinct sense of place and offer inspirational

Sacred Heart Medical Center at RiverBend, Springfield, Oregon. A porte cochere, constructed of natural stone and timber, signals your arrival, followed by a two-story atrium, with a stone fireplace at its center that serves as a natural area for congregation and connection. *Courtesy Anshen+Allen, part of Stantec Architecture. Associate Architect: WATG. Photo David Wakely.*

views. Though the placement of the hospital provides an avenue for future expansion, it was also designed to maintain responsible stewardship of the surrounding land and become part of a community where healthcare and wellness are wholly integrated into the area's culture. The campus includes walking or running trails, and the center has reserved parcels of land for housing, hotels, restaurants, a conference center, assisted-living facilities, and medical retail operations.

The emphasis on the emotional and intellectual as well as the physical needs of its patients and their families, friends, and visitors (and the well-being of staff, too) helped shape the aesthetics of exterior and interior design. Crafted in warm brick and framed by rolling grass-covered hills, the hospital recalls the grand lodges of the Pacific Northwest and connects the campus to the history of the land and the design traditions of its community.

The designers intended the hospitality-inspired features of the center to extend from a visitor's arrival through his or her travel to the deepest clinical areas, creating what the architects call in their promotional literature "a seamless interior language." A porte cochere, constructed of natural stone and timber, signals arrival and opens into a two-story atrium with a stone fireplace at its center that serves as a natural area for congregation and connection.

The interior detailing—such as custom lighting, hand-crafted wrought iron railings, crown molding, and natural stonemasonry—carry through into

Sacred Heart Medical Center at River-Bend, Springfield, Oregon. The architects nestled Sacred Heart in a bend of the McKenzie River, surrounded by groves of Douglas firs and a meadow. Crafted in warm brick and framed by rolling grass-covered hills, the hospital recalls the grand lodges of the Pacific Northwest and connects the campus to local history and the design traditions. *Courtesy Anshen+Allen, part of Stantec Architecture. Associate Architect: WATG. Photo David Wakely.*

247

Sacred Heart Medical Center at River-Bend, Springfield, Oregon. Aimed at lowering stress and offering a tranquil refuge, the design of the private patient rooms offers family accommodation and striking views of the river and surrounding landscape. *Courtesy Anshen+Allen, part of Stantec Architecture. Associate Architect: WATG. Photo David Wakely.*

the patient rooms, nursing stations, waiting alcoves, and even the emergency department. The aim was a wholly integrated design that demonstrated Sacred Heart's dedication to patient comfort and patient-focused care.

The designers emphasized this nowhere more clearly than in the patient room, the nexus of the patient experience. Aimed at mitigating stress and offering a tranquil refuge, the design of private patient rooms provides family accommodation and striking views of the river and surrounding landscape. Custom wood casework and molding contribute to creating a homelike experience in the rooms, all of which offer sleeping accommodations for family members.

The hospital conducted a retrospective study on the effects of mechanical ceiling lifts on the number and severity of work-related muscular and skeletal problems, which led to the integration of mechanical patient lifts in every patient room. And because the hospital placed much importance on reducing medical errors, it called for including other features such as decentralized nursing stations and in-room bar-coded medication. Private patient rooms, carpeted corridors, abundant natural daylight, and garden roofscapes were integrated into the design to help create a positive environment, good experiences for patients, and comfortable working conditions for the staff.

Finally, Sacred Heart commissioned local and national artists to celebrate the facility's regional identity and elevate the healing experience through carved glass panels and bas-relief limestone carvings. The chapel's 60-ft. carved glass mural, for example, represents the McKenzie River as opalescent-colored glass suggests its undulating waters and spills soft light into the atrium, helping reinforce the sense that Sacred Heart Medical Center at RiverBend is a good place to be for patients and their families.

ST. JOSEPH'S HOSPITAL-PATIENT BED TOWER

St. Paul, Minnesota

Seeking to underscore the recommitment of St. Joseph's Hospital to its location in downtown St. Paul, the architectural firm HOK used the hospital's new patient bed tower to establish, as the firm says, "a strong relationship between the patient tower and the State Capitol," one that "represents a reconnection and recommitment to the city."

The new patient tower, which spans 86 ft. across a city street, anchors the northern edge of the downtown area and repositions future hospital expansion

St. Joseph's Hospital-Patient Bed Tower, St. Paul, Minnesota. Designers shaped the new patient bed towers to capture dramatic views of St. Paul, including a commanding look at the State Capitol. *Courtesy HOK. Photo Paúl Rivera-archphoto.*

westward. HOK shaped the building to capture dramatic views of the city. Intersecting arcs in the curved forms of the lobby and tower create a garden plaza, giving visitors a commanding look at the State Capitol. The firm also strategically positioned family waiting rooms in projecting bays at the north and south ends of the tower to offer unique views of the town.

The project allows for a continuum of inpatient care. Patients from critical care to medical/surgical status remain on one floor and perhaps in one room for their entire length of stay. Each forty-five-bed floor, one for cardiovascular and one for neuroscience patients, is self-contained, offering their own therapy and rehabilitation spaces to decrease patient movement. The private patient rooms are same-handed and canted. They are equipped with outboard toilets to allow the staff more accessibility to and better visibility of the patients.

The patient floor space allows for the appropriate amount of support, with a wider footprint by the most acute beds, allowing even more support. The cardiology diagnostic and treatment areas combine all aspects of outpatient care on the third floor.

St. Joseph's Hospital-Patient Bed Tower, St. Paul, Minnesota. Intersecting arcs in the curved forms of the lobby and tower at the de Paul Patient Tower create a garden plaza for visitors and easy wayfinding for patients. *Courtesy HOK. Photo Paúl Rivera-archphoto.*

CHAPTER 10

Ambulatory Care Design, Professional Offices, and Bedless Hospitals

Not so very long ago, the medical world was neatly divided into hospitals and doctors' offices. Sometimes, for the sake of convenience, doctors' offices were housed in a medical office building (MOB) attached to or adjacent to a hospital. Some doctors performed minor surgical procedures in their offices, but aside from this, surgery was the province of the hospital. A doctor's office was primarily a place for examination, evaluation, and relatively simple routine procedures (inoculation, drawing of blood for lab tests, and so on). Anything beyond this was generally referred to a hospital, and that usually meant admittance to a bed, even if the condition or procedure did not absolutely necessitate an overnight stay. For the simple reason that most people grew up—as professionals or as patients—under that system, it seemed natural, inevitable, and right. Given the course of past changes in healthcare—cost containment and managed care, for example—and those likely to come, the system has become less and less viable.

There are two broad ways of looking at the continuing paradigm shift dissolving the barriers between private practice and the realm of the hospital. From the perspective of hospital professionals, the past three decades have seen periods of boom in hospital construction, yet the more sustained trend has been toward vacancy of beds. Many administrators have viewed this trend with alarm; others have rethought the hospital beyond the overnight stay and successfully restructured it for increased ambulatory care. Back in the early 1980s, according to the American Hospital Association, fewer than

Samaritan North Health Center, Phase II, Englewood, Ohio. The brick detailing and standing-seam metal roof give a residential character to this satellite facility of a major Dayton, Ohio, hospital. The center offers diagnostic services and a MOB. *Photo © 2000 Gordon K. Morioka.*

12 percent of total hospital revenues in the United States were outpatient-related. By mid-decade that figure had increased to 23 percent, reflecting a 92 percent growth in that segment of the market. By the beginning of the 1990s, a significant number of hospitals had reported that 40 to 60 percent of their revenues resulted from outpatient services. By the mid-1990s, the revenue mix for the majority of hospitals remained around half outpatient revenue, half inpatient revenue. In this century, the split of the ratio of the late 1980s became nearly the reverse—30 percent inpatient and 70 percent outpatient. Although the vacancy rate in hospital beds slowed considerably in the early 2000s, the changes it wrought in the ratio of outpatient versus inpatient revenue may be permanent.

For example, from the point of view of the physician, the day of the solo practitioner—the iconic norm in American medicine—is virtually over. Increasing competition among physicians, cost-containment pressures leading to more restrictive reimbursement practices, and the cost of maintaining malpractice liability protection have all contributed to a precipitous decline in the number of solo practitioners and a concomitant explosion in the number of group practices. Group practices—usually three or more physicians who share patient care and the business aspects of a practice—often have the combined financial clout to purchase equipment and office facilities for services that were once exclusively the province of hospital-based ambulatory care. During the 1980s, entrepreneurial physicians (and others) began to further challenge hospitals—as well as solo practitioners—by creating freestanding facilities to provide urgent, episodic, and primary medical care. In 1980 there were fewer than 300 such facilities nationwide. Seven years later this number increased 400 percent to over 3,000. By the early 1990s, some 5,500 freestanding facilities were in operation, handling about 63 million patient visits annually—compared with 5 million in 1980. By the beginning of the twenty-first century, says AHA, 22 percent of facilities were freestanding outpatient centers. Despite this phenomenal growth, such freestanding facilities have rarely attained financial viability. In the 1990s, only some 30 percent were operating in the black, and they continue to struggle with profitability. But this has not discouraged the concurrent development of freestanding ambulatory surgery facilities, which continue to crop up around the country.

Increasingly, hospitals have shown an interest in affiliating with group practices or even acquiring them. Hospitals have also been expanding outpatient programs to offer the same kind of "convenience" care available from freestanding facilities. Since freestanding urgent care centers were originally perceived as direct competition for the hospital ED, EDs were expanded to include additional space for less acute urgent care and upgraded to increase efficiencies and make an emergency visit a more pleasant and less time-consuming experience. More and more, EDs evolved into two separate and discrete operations: one to handle emergency care (trauma, sudden severe illness) and another for urgent and primary care (for patients who commonly visit a private physician or a freestanding convenience facility). In many hospitals nowadays, ambulatory convenience care is entirely separate from the ED. Finally, an increasing number of hospitals and hospital corporations are building freestanding community-based convenience facilities of their own. Beyond this, hospitals and hospital corporations are creating discrete ambulatory surgery departments within the hospital or even building freestanding ambulatory surgery centers.

Other freestanding facilities that witnessed considerable growth beginning in the 1980s were diagnostic—or imaging—centers and various treatment centers specializing in treatment of the eye, the heart, the elderly, cancer patients, women, and so on.

For the architect, designer, and planner, the proliferation of hospital-based and freestanding ambulatory services has resulted in a medical landscape more varied than ever before. With the increasingly innovative business relationships that have developed among hospitals, insurance providers, hospital corporations, group practices, and individual physicians, the demand for ambulatory care facilities, both hospital-based and freestanding, continues to grow.

MOBs/POBs

Other than the hospital, the most familiar healthcare building is the medical office building (MOB) or physicians' office building (POB). As traditionally designed, however, these were suited to solo practice and not easily adaptable to the increasingly larger single- and multispecialty group practices. For example, each practitioner shared central building support services, including elevators, toilets, HVAC, and so on, which was perfectly adequate for individual doctors, but limited options for group practice. The rigid design of traditional MOBs cannot readily support the sharing of clinical areas (exam, consultation, nurse support, procedure area), diagnostics, reception, administrative and support services, and office and conference space.

The advanced MOB must boast not only a design for sharing facilities but also one that appeals to patients by meeting the following criteria:

• It should accommodate a focus on wellness by providing space for fitness services and health maintenance, as opposed to the exclusive treatment of disease.

• It should appeal to today's more sophisticated and better-informed patients.

• It should incorporate elements of universal design, particularly with the elderly in mind. This reflects the trend toward an aging patient population. Design elements to consider include lighting to eliminate glare, avoidance of strong contrasts, design to compensate for reduced color perception, furnishings that properly support an aging body, crystal-clear wayfinding cues, and the like.

• It should be designed with women in mind. Women make most of the healthcare decisions in the United States, including where to "shop" for their family's medical care.

As discussed earlier, consumer and shopping metaphors have been incorporated into the medical mall concept. It is possible to conceive the MOB in these terms, and, in fact, some hospitals have renovated facilities as outpatient medical malls. In any case, the medical mall need not be taken too literally, but it is a design option that several hospital-related MOBs have placed in the suburbs as an alternative to traveling to a busy medical campus for outpatient services. The consumer model is also useful for keeping MOB design from degenerating into what noted medical interior designer Jain Malkin calls a "formula fast-food restaurant." Retail merchants long ago learned the value of good design in marketing, and, certainly, prospective patients find an aesthetically attractive, distinctive design appealing and reassuring as a visible projection of an attitude toward quality and excellence.

Effective design in medical office space goes deeper than this. For example, the office suite of an allergy practice should not be decorated with heavily textured surfaces, shag rugs, or nubby upholstery—no matter how elegant or residential looking. For this market, such harborers of allergens are not only inappropriate, but they are also unpleasant and even harmful. Similarly, a suite designed for a neurological specialty should avoid sharply contrasting surfaces, busy patterns, and vivid colors—design elements that may exacerbate the disorientation neurologically afflicted patients may have. Then there are certain specialties that employ equipment requiring special design

Samaritan North Health Center, Phase II, Englewood, Ohio. The main lobby has physicians' offices above and a courtyard below. The detailing of the railings and millwork references regional Prairie School design. *Photo Craig Dugan © Hedrich Blessing.*

provisions. Magnetic resonance imaging (MRI), discussed in Chapter 6, is one such specialty. If MRI equipment is to be housed in the MOB, shielding and other provisions must be integrated within the design if the equipment is not self-shielded.

Whereas hospitals tend to follow a relatively small number of design approaches, Jain Malkin identifies nine distinct approaches—"gourmet recipes"—to MOB design:

1. Retail—the galleria or mall concept.

2. Hospitality—the luxury hotel approach.

3. Cultural—facilities designed with respect for the ethnicity of the patient community; for example, the use of indigenous materials or design motifs.

4. High technology—facilities that emphasize rather than disguise the high-tech nature of treatment.

5. Intellectual—architecture that expresses the patient's struggle against disease.

6. Entertainment or theater—an approach that is especially appropriate for pediatric practices, it entertains, amuses, distracts, and educates through decor.

7. Comfort—design that emphasizes amelioration of intimidation; this would be especially appropriate, for example, in facilities that use ultra-high-tech equipment: MRI, linear accelerators for cancer treatment, and so on.

8. Corporate—businesslike and no-nonsense.

9. Residential—homey, familiar, comforting.

Some of these approaches invite a design so daring it gives many hospital administrators pause. For example, the Starbright Pavilion, designed by Kaplan McLaughlin Diaz for the Los Angeles County USC Medical Center, is a radical healing environment for children with life-threatening diseases. The design is based on the findings and assumptions of the emerging research field of psychoneuroimmunology (PNI). The goal was to create an environment that would make children happy and thereby boost their immunologic systems. Starbright used bright, primary colors, simple geometric shapes, and Erector set–like structural members to create a dazzling, brilliant, and mega-toylike environment. Provisions for video and live entertainment as well as imaginative play environments were also included.

In California's Simi Valley, a children's dental group designed an office facility around an outerspace concept. Patients arrive at a "Pre-Flight" check-in counter and then are led by a space-suited dental technician through a metallic "Time-Warp Tunnel" to procedure rooms equipped with "flight chairs."

Wild as some approaches are, they are easily accepted in a pediatric context. No parent enjoys taking his or her child to the doctor or dentist, and these medical consumers welcome design strategies that allay their children's anxieties. Designs for adult facilities that convey strong messages are far more controversial.

Of course, all architecture speaks, although sometimes it is in confused and contradictory mumbles and shouts. As explored in Chapter 2, the hospital design vocabularies most of us now think of as "traditional" evolved as an expression of a very powerful message, proclaiming, among other things, the majesty and supremacy of the institution over the individual. Given sufficient thought, this message seems as outrageous as any; it is just that familiarity and custom have inured us to the significance of that message. New messages that depart sharply from the old institutional message are far more acutely sensitive.

The proliferation of MOBs, whether associated with hospitals or not, certainly affords architects, designers, administrators, and caregivers more opportunities for expression. Indeed, care providers are likely to demand increasingly greater levels of thoughtful expression from architects, thereby multiplying the risks and rewards of design.

Freestanding Clinics

Freestanding ambulatory care centers—for urgent and primary care—now dot the American landscape. For the most part, these are not upscale facilities, and few of them are distinguished architecturally. This need not be the case, since the population served by such facilities is sufficient and patients look for an attractive care environment.

A freestanding ambulatory care center near Jackson, Mississippi, for example, designed by Thomas Goodman, balances economy, user-friendliness, and architectural flair. The 2,600-sq.-ft. facility combines the geometric planes of Modernism, the wit of Postmodernism, architectural details of the Old South, and a residential touch in the use of clapboard. The same blend of styles is repeated indoors, with traditional black-and-white checkerboard vinyl tile, a Southern plantation–type column, and a sleek, modern nursing station and registration desk. The result is a visually reassuring as well as interesting general-purpose suburban clinic.

There are any number of variations on the outpatient freestanding clinic, many of them creating innovative combinations of services that greatly extend a hospital's ambulatory outreach. Taking their cue from the proliferation of freestanding physician-owned-and-operated ambulatory centers, hospitals will likely build more of these modest, humanly scaled neighborhood facilities in the years to come.

Freestanding Diagnostic Centers and Hospital Satellite Facilities

Chapter 6 covers design considerations for diagnostic imaging and includes some freestanding as well as hospital-based facilities. Physician-owned freestanding diagnostic facilities have become common; another trend is toward satellite facilities operated by hospitals. Examples of each follow.

SAMARITAN NORTH HEALTH CENTER, PHASE II
Englewood, Ohio

The Samaritan North Health Center, designed by ESa, is located in the affluent Englewood suburb of Dayton, Ohio. The 220,000-sq-ft. facility is a combination of diagnostic center and MOB and is a satellite facility of Dayton's 560-bed Good Samaritan Hospital. "Just what makes you think you will be able to successfully compete with freestanding, for-profit centers?" a board member of Good Samaritan demanded when the project was first proposed.

The question captured much of the skepticism surrounding the notion of the traditional downtown hospital branching into the ambulatory arena, a skepticism perhaps justified by the fact that the hospital's physicians had virtually abandoned outpatient services in favor of their own, privately held surgical, imaging, and rehabilitation enterprises.

For many years Dayton had had no accessible facilities northwest of town. The new satellite facility extended the healthcare reach of Good Samaritan into these suburbs, and Samaritan North quickly became one of

Samaritan North Health Center, Phase II, Englewood, Ohio. The dropped cloud-shape ceiling of the café makes the space more intimate and absorbs sound. *Photo Craig Dugan © Hedrich Blessing.*

Samaritan North Health Center, Phase II, Englewood, Ohio. The sports medicine/rehab center has its own entrance so it will eventually become a private fitness club. *Photo Craig Dugan © Hedrich Blessing.*

the country's fastest-growing medical facilities. Built in two phases, the hospital provides a fast-lane, one-stop, convenient, in-and-out healthcare service suitable to the needs of its new users.

When phase one was complete, the hospital offered diagnostic services, cancer therapy, rehabilitation, and sports medicine, plus fifty physicians' offices integrated on the top floors, linked by computer and pneumatic tubes to the services below. Its focus on wellness and service was further enhanced by a fully staffed community health information library and community education center, child care for patients, a pharmacy, and a café featuring heart-friendly meals. Phase two created a 30,000-sq.-ft. "bedless" outpatient surgery center, a wellness health center, and an expansion of the existing physical therapy, cardiac rehabilitation, and occupational therapy areas. A second linear accelerator vault for the oncology department was also added.

Designed to blend into a residential neighborhood, the multilevel building is organized like a mall around a central three-story skylit area and looks far more residential than institutional. The site of Samaritan North is sloped, and ESa designed the facility to take full advantage of this challenge, creating separate entrances at varying levels. The visible layout, together with the circulation plan, simplifies patients' wayfinding. The principal areas, including imaging, community education, pharmacy, cafeteria, and administrative areas, are at the highest level. Patients entering the main lobby can easily see the receptionist, central registration, and signage for diagnostic testing, which helps make wayfinding intuitive. The next lower level houses the oncology service and the physical therapy/rehabilitation/ sports medicine facilities (intentionally styled like a private fitness club). The plant-filled courtyard on this ground level, where a fountain muffles sound, is a soothing prelude to the adjacent cancer department. Its treatment room looks out on the greenery through a glass wall frosted for privacy. At the lowest level is a dedicated staff parking area and staff entrance to the facility. The physicians' offices comprise three stories in addition to the first story of outpatient services. Because they share this first story with the imaging center, physicians can send patients directly for diagnostic procedures without obliging them to reenter the system and register at a main desk.

Samaritan North developed new holistic strategies in training management and staff, carefully vetting its personnel and teaching them customer service and teamwork. Single teams are responsible for a patient's experience, thus giving new life to the health center's touted goal of patient-focused care. Teamwork is rewarded with earned bonuses to all employees rather than individuals, and self-managing task forces address such issues as customer satisfaction. Patient and physician surveys are commonplace. There are no physical barriers between departments. Indeed, Samaritan North represents a tight integration of individual physician, hospital facility, and medical consumer that is a strong current trend and likely to prevail.

MIDTOWN MANHATTAN AMBULATORY CARE OUTPATIENT CENTER
New York, New York

According to Cathryn Bang + Partners, hospitals need to meet service line growth and market expansion. In addition to inpatient bed additions, hospitals need to expand diagnostics, treatment, and outpatient services spaces to accommodate increasing volume of high-acuity care services within the hospital and to relocate ambulatory outpatient care services in separate buildings away from the hospital.

Cathryn Bang designed this new, 240,000-sq.-ft. ambulatory care outpatient center to meet such needs, and for the first time, a modern, patient-centered, state-of-the-art healthcare facility will be available in the heart of midtown Manhattan. The outpatient center offers access to the medical profession's top specialists, as well as the hotels, restaurants, and shopping that draw visitors to Manhattan from all over the world. Patients will be able to receive their treatment and return to their normal schedule in the city in the same day.

Midtown Manhattan Ambulatory Care Outpatient Center, New York, New York. CATHRYN BANG + PARTNERS Architecture Planning Interiors designed the center to accommodate the increasing volume of high-acuity-care service within the hospital and to relocate ambulatory outpatient care services in separate buildings away from the hospital. *Courtesy CATHRYN BANG + PARTNERS Architecture Planning Interiors. Photo CATHRYN BANG + PARTNERS Architecture Planning Interiors.*

Vanderbilt Bill Wilkerson Center for Otolaryngology and Communications Sciences, Nashville, Tennessee. The curving center serves as a first-impression, gateway building for the Vanderbilt University medical campus. *Photo Scott McDonald © Hedrich Blessing.*

Vanderbilt Bill Wilkerson Center for Otolaryngology and Communications Sciences, Nashville, Tennessee. Highly specialized spaces within the center include a two-story anechoic chamber. *Photo © Kieran Reynolds Photography.*

VANDERBILT BILL WILKERSON CENTER FOR OTOLARYNGOLOGY AND COMMUNICATIONS SCIENCES
Nashville, Tennessee

This new outpatient center, designed by ESa, is a distinctive 318,000-sq.-ft. curving medical facility on a tight, urban site that serves as a first-impression, gateway building for the Vanderbilt University medical campus. The new facility consolidates services formerly housed in four separate locations. These services include a speech-language pathology clinic, the Scottish Rite Masons Research Institute for Communication Disorders, the new center for childhood deafness and family communication, the voice center, a clinic for otolaryngology and head and neck surgery, the audiology clinic, new administrative offices, faculty offices, classrooms, research treatment rooms, and laboratories.

Concrete, masonry, and curtain walls create an eclectic blend of the hospital campus vocabulary. ESa used the program components to create the elegant curved curtain wall with the smallest components on the top floors, avoiding the typical "stepped box" effect of many such designs. The designers used low roofs for outdoor therapy spaces for children's programs and rehab space. The design called for building over the existing parking garage, which required a blended structure made of concrete on the lower two floors with steel above to achieve the benefits of lighter weight. ESa's design staggered—rather than stacked—connectors across the street from the existing hospital.

The highly specialized spaces within the center include a two-story anechoic chamber (the first in the country), a reverberation chamber, acoustically isolated sound testing booths, a therapy tank, and an indoor track. The teaching space includes an eighty-eight-seat lecture hall, computer training suite, and multipurpose classrooms designed to flex for lecture or interactive training programs.

EISENHOWER GEORGE AND JULIA ARGYROS HEALTH CENTER
La Quinta, California

As the interior designer for architectural firm Boulder Associates, Jain Malkin sought to ensure that, in keeping with its green building aesthetic, the 96,000-sq.-ft. Eisenhower George and Julia Argyros Health Center was a celebration of the healing power and natural beauty of the desert air and hot springs in the surrounding Coachella Valley.

A fountain with three granite stones pays tribute the San Bernardino, San Jacinto, and Santa Rosa mountain ranges that shelter the valley. The entry to the building includes a dramatic sweeping tensile structure suspended over a broad arc, expressed in the cobblestone paving that unifies and curves through the interior space. The building's façade includes among its materials the traditional stucco so common to desert architecture, and this reference is complemented by the unique terra cotta and aluminum panel rain screen.

The architects situated the building to take advantage of dramatic views of the foothills and mountains beyond. They minimized glare and overheating by using such design features as fins, louvers, and screens to shade the building and add to its desert look. The main lobby features a "rain" sculpture above a lush garden oasis, which includes water cascading over granite boulders. The oculus at the end of the lobby offers a dramatic focal point against the desert sky beyond.

Eisenhower George and Julia Argyros Health Center, La Quinta, California. The designers intended to express the desert wind in the textures and sinuous curves that flow through the ceiling. *Courtesy Jain Malkin Inc. Photo Ed LaCasse Photography.*

The designers hoped to express the desert wind in the textures and sinuous curves that flow through the ceiling. An illuminated sculpture of bright orange silk anemones above circular seating offers patrons a visual reminder of the desert sun. The first floor of the building contains a lab and suites for express care radiation, oncology, and imaging, all including in their interior design an element or two of the overall concept. The Center for Healthy Living suite provides a medical library and computers for patients.

The design of the first floor flows upward to the second through an open mezzanine. The second floor includes a conference and education center that hosts wellness and community services and events. The suites for women's wellness, primary care, and orthopedic medicine are located on this level, all with their unique identities and entrances.

References to the light, color, and texture of the desert are woven into finishes and design features on the third floor, where physicians' offices take up most of the space. The lobby includes two reception desks flanked by stone-clad walls, several computer stations, an entertainment center, a children's play area, and a television with a digital aquarium.

The upscale Executive Health Center continues the design theme of the building and provides spalike amenities such as walk-in rain showers and adjacent private dressing areas. The reception area of this suite opens to

Eisenhower George and Julia Argyros Health Center, La Quinta, California. References to the light, color, and texture of the desert are woven into finishes and design features of the Ambulatory Care Center. *Courtesy Jain Malkin Inc. Photo Ed LaCasse Photography.*

sweeping views of the mountains with club chairs beneath a ceiling dome enhanced by LED lighting that sequences through the colors of the rainbow.

Inside the treatment spaces and waiting areas, television monitors feature images from nature and music from the Continuous Ambient Relaxation Environment (C.A.R.E.) channel, developed specifically for healthcare environments.

Ambulatory Surgery

Traditionally, physicians have performed minor surgical procedures in their offices, and it was only after World War II that a sizable number of such procedures were taken over by hospitals. Major procedures, of course, had been the province of hospitals since at least the later nineteenth century, and the prevailing philosophy of treatment placed great emphasis on postoperative recuperation. For example, the great surgeon William Halsted prescribed a twenty-one-day period of bed rest for hernia repair. However, it was anticipated that most of these long periods would be spent in bed at home, not in the hospital. As the twentieth century progressed, recuperative times shortened, but it was expected that the patient would be cared for during recuperation in a hospital bed. Thus postsurgical stays often occupied several days of uneventful hospital bed rest. Even relatively minor procedures carried out in a hospital mandated at least an overnight stay—whether or not it was strictly necessary for medical reasons.

In 1961, the first modern ambulatory surgery program began at Butterworth Hospital in Grand Rapids, Michigan, and was followed the next year by a program at the University of California at Los Angeles. A decade later Drs. Wallace Reed and John Ford opened Surgicenter in Phoenix, Arizona. Planned, built, and run by these two anesthesiologists, Surgicenter was a freestanding, totally self-sufficient unit. It sparked the development of additional such units nationwide. By the later 1980s, as cost containment and DRGs began to dominate medical reimbursement, ambulatory surgery (whether in a hospital outpatient department or in a freestanding independent or hospital-affiliated setting) became commonplace. And even for procedures where a period of in-hospital recovery is still deemed necessary, the trend is toward short-stay surgery and early discharge.

As a consumer society, we are accustomed to expect that cost-saving measures must come at the expense of quality or convenience. The delivery of medical care has been challenged, perhaps more than most industries, to contain costs. The positive aspect of this pressure, however, is that the cost efficiencies do not necessarily come at the expense of the patient. Regarding

Eisenhower George and Julia Argyros Health Center, La Quinta, California. Note that the light, color, and texture are also a part of the finishes and design features of the Ambulatory Care Center at Eisenhower Medical Center in La Quinta, California. *Courtesy Jain Malkin, Inc. Photo Ed LaCasse Photography.*

the trend toward ambulatory and short-stay surgery, costs are substantially reduced, and patient care may actually be enhanced:

• Rather than experience a major, albeit temporary, change in lifestyle, ambulatory surgery patients are minimally inconvenienced. The same holds true for their families—especially in the case of procedures performed on children and infants.

• Postoperative care is handled, to a great extent, by family members. This not only saves money, it almost certainly benefits the patient, especially children and infants, who do not have to endure anxiety-provoking separation from parents. No matter how dedicated a professional nursing staff may be, it is difficult to compete with a family member's loving care.

• The patient receives more individual attention—not only from family members/caregivers, but from the staff of a center specifically set up to treat ambulatory surgery patients.

• Anxiety is reduced, and the stress of a hospital stay is eliminated.

• There is less risk of nosocomial infection. Unfortunately, hospitalization exposes patients to hospital-borne infections. This is greatly reduced in same-day surgery.

• The perception of disability or helplessness is decreased, and patients return to normal life more quickly.

• Costs are reduced.

There are disadvantages to ambulatory surgery, but none are insurmountable:

• The patient may not follow preoperative instructions. This needs to be addressed through careful preoperative education. The most serious problem is failure to heed instructions about ingesting nothing the night before a procedure. Under general anesthesia, this could result in vomiting and aspiration of vomitus, followed by asphyxiation or pneumonia.

• The patient must ensure that she has transportation to and from the facility.

• Ambulatory surgery assumes that the patient has competent at-home assistance available. If such care is not available, professional home care is still probably less costly than an overnight stay in the hospital. Advanced planning is required, however.

• Although the circumstances, setting, and implications of ambulatory surgery usually act to reduce patient anxiety, some individuals may be concerned that ambulatory units, especially those that are physically independent of a major hospital, lack the advanced resuscitative support available in a hospital setting. Careful patient education is required to address these understandable concerns.

Ambulatory surgery is commonly performed in four types of settings:

1. Hospital-based integrated units. These are in-hospital units that share facilities with inpatient surgery. For smaller hospitals, this may be the only economically viable ambulatory surgery option available. Capital costs are, of course, relatively low for an integrated unit, but this must be weighed against the potential loss of market share among medical consumers who require or want ambulatory surgery independent of the hospital setting. Treated in a setting that integrates them with inpatients, outpatients tend to feel that inpatients have priority. Actual operating costs may also be high, since major surgical facilities and personnel are used for any number of relatively minor procedures. However surgeons may be willing to undertake more types of surgery than they would in freestanding ambulatory units, given the immediate availability of full hospital surgical support.

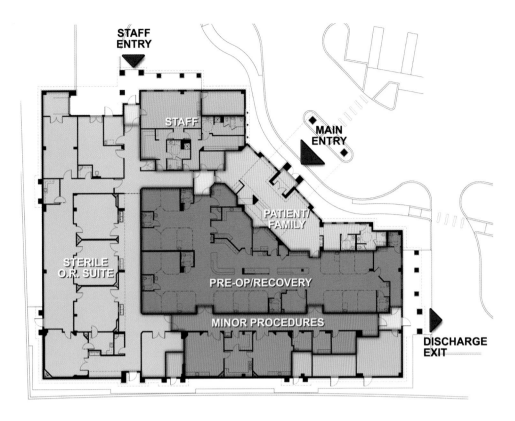

A floor plan for a facility offering ambulatory care created by Earl Swensson Associates.

2. Hospital-based autonomous units. Located within the hospital but explicitly designed for ambulatory surgery service, such units allow the hospital to capture important ambulatory markets while providing the backup of a fully equipped hospital (should these facilities be necessary). Licensing, code compliance, certificate of need (CON) issues for the particular community and related costs must be addressed.

3. Hospital satellite units. These freestanding units are located off the main hospital campus but are owned by the hospital. Using the staff expertise, resources, and good name of the hospital, these units can provide important outreach into areas more or less remote from the main hospital. As we have seen, ambulatory surgery may be integrated into fairly large satellite facilities that function as virtual hospitals without beds to provide such services as primary care (often in an integral or adjacent MOB facility), urgent care, diagnostic imaging, wellness, fitness, and rehabilitation along with ambulatory surgery. Satellite units extend the suburban reach of established hospitals sited in downtown locations.

4. Freestanding ambulatory surgery units. These are independent facilities and can often offer the same surgical services at lower cost. Depending on the patient and the type of procedure, such units are increasingly attractive in the present medical environment. However, some individuals may feel hesitant about undergoing a surgical procedure in a facility that has less extensive resuscitative equipment and perhaps a less specialized staff than a major hospital. Yet, the actual performance record of freestanding ambulatory surgical facilities has been excellent.

THE HEART CENTER OF INDIANA
Indianapolis, Indiana

Designed by ESa, the Heart Center of Indiana, which is the first free-standing heart hospital to open in the Indianapolis area, boasts four surgical suites (one for vascular procedures) and ambulatory services. Its additional cardiovascular services include an emergency care chest pain center, general radiology, CT scanning, ultrasound and MRI, three cardiac catheterization labs, an EP lab, a postanesthesia care unit, and a laboratory and blood bank.

The 168,594-sq.-ft., four-story center opened initially with 60 beds (and with shelled capacity to double that number to 120). The hospital's first floor contains administrative offices, the operating rooms, the cath labs, the blood bank, testing, MRI and CT services, foodservice, maintenance, and house-keeping. Patient care rooms are on the second and one-half of the third floor.

The Heart Center of Indiana, Indianapolis, Indiana. Designed by ESa to reflect a hospitality approach, the center's interior is flooded with natural light from a two-story atrium. *Photo © Robt. Ames Cook.*

Shell space is available in the other half of the third floor as well as in the entirety of the fourth floor. The 50,920-sq.-ft. medical office building is connected to the heart center by an enclosed walkway.

The interior spaces reflect the hospitality approach of the design. The reception desk resembles and functions as a concierge desk. Natural light floods the two-story atrium, which is filled with foliage arranged in built-in planters. A meditation courtyard, located between the hospital and medical office building, offers quiet solitude.

The Heart Center of Indiana, Indianapolis, Indiana. The first free-standing heart hospital to open in the Indianapolis area. *Photo © Robt. Ames Cook.*

SPIVEY STATION OUTPATIENT SURGERY CENTER
Jonesboro, Georgia

Located next to other healthcare facilities at Spivey Station, the surgery center seeks to make medical visits even more convenient for patients. It offers a wide range of outpatient surgical procedures within walking distance from medical offices, digital imaging centers, and a women's hospital.

CDH Partners, Inc., say innovativeness was crucial to their design. They opted to use integrated operating rooms aimed at meeting the specific and

Spivey Station Outpatient Surgery Center, Jonesboro, Georgia. Located next to other healthcare facilities at Spivey Station, this outpatient surgery center seeks to make medical visits even more convenient for patients. *Courtesy CDH Partners, Inc. Photo CDH Partners, Inc., staff photographer.*

Spivey Station Outpatient Surgery Center, Jonesboro, Georgia. The design, by CDH Partners, Inc., enhances the patient experience with an illuminated reception desk that serves as a focal point for the entire space. *Courtesy CDH Partners, Inc. Photo CDH Partners, Inc., staff photographer.*

immediate needs of each surgical procedure, so that ear, nose, and throat procedures; orthopedic surgery; and various types of breast surgery can all be performed on an outpatient basis.

The design enhances the patient's experience with an illuminated reception desk that serves as a focal point for the entire space. A trellis stretches across the ceiling from the reception desk, reinforcing its centrality as it adds visual interest. Backlit acrylic panels cover the front of the desk, illuminated by the indirect light that characterizes the entire waiting area. Partial height partitions help keep down noise and offer some privacy, while curved translucent panels create what the architects intended to be a calming, wavy line for the eye to follow across the space.

Concepts in Specialized Ambulatory Care

While the bedless hospital has emerged as a very important trend in health-care facilities, freestanding and hospital-associated ambulatory facilities devoted to a single specialty are also in significant demand. Within the given area of specialization, such facilities offer the level of care traditionally found in a hospital setting only.

TEXAS CHILDREN'S HOSPITAL CLINICAL CARE CENTER
Houston, Texas

Years ago, says FKP Architects, ambulatory care meant the kind of out-patient care you got in an add-on, defined facility with limited services to relieve stressed inpatient departments. Little thought was given to conve-nience, cost control, or amenities. All that has changed, and the demand for

Texas Children's Hospital Clinical Care Center, Houston, Texas. FKP Architects' design won the first *Businessweek* "Good Design is Good Business" award given to a hospital. *Courtesy FKP Architects. Photo © Hedrich Blessing Photographers.*

special ambulatory environments now drives the healthcare market. So it is no longer enough to just build space and shift services out of the hospital and hope for success. Since well-positioned outpatient care can enhance profitability, identify the competition and best capture and hold market share, maximize flexibility, and create brand recognition and customer loyalty, these specialty facilities must be as cutting edge as their inpatient competitors.

They must be, in fact, the kind of facility FKP created in the clinical care center of Texas Children's Hospital, where the firm designed a high-performance, high-impact outpatient pediatric hospital of 2 million sq. ft. that handles 3 million patients a year. As a result, the design of this sixteen-story center not only increased the use of exam rooms from 41 to 60 percent, it became the first hospital to win *Businessweek* magazine's Good Design Is Good Business award.

SPARTANBURG REGIONAL CANCER CENTER
Spartanburg, South Carolina

Spartanburg Regional Cancer Center (SRCC), an architectural joint venture by the firms of ESa and McMillan Smith & Partners, is an example of a medical building type intended to house a comprehensive multiplicity of treatment modalities directed against one type of disorder. Until the mid-1970s, outpatient cancer treatment centers were essentially stand-alone radiation therapy buildings. Today, they are comprehensive facilities that offer screening and educational services, diagnostic services, and treatment services. Diagnostic services include endoscopy, minor surgery (biopsy and needle aspiration), colonoscopy, cystoscopy, and imaging (CT, MRI, and chest X-ray). Treatment modalities include chemotherapy, blood transfusion, radiation therapy, phototherapy, laser therapy, and others. For disorders such as cancer, the one-stop approach that integrates treatment programs and research tracking makes for efficient, less stressful treatment, creating a sense that energy is being directed toward treating the patient rather than bouncing him or her from one hospital department to another.

Housed in an understated and architecturally dated two-story building, the original SRCC was typical of earlier such facilities—it was a radiation oncology department with a small chemotherapy suite. To take a more aggressive role in the treatment of cancer, the center was expanded and transformed into an integrated four-story center that includes an expanded radiation oncology program, a new medical oncology group practice and twenty-station chemotherapy suite, a stem-cell treatment program, a new education and family media resource center, expanded oncology research and tumor registry services, a patient and family common area with open seating, a juice and pastry bistro, a children's activity area, an indoor/outdoor fountain and meditation garden, an art exhibit area, an upscale prosthetics retail space, and professional office space (on the upper two floors).

Anchoring the new facility's design is a four-story cascading atrium entrance. Three equal steps in the atrium structure are symbolic of the "steps of healing" in cancer care (diagnosis, acceptance, treatment/cure). Radial segmented portions of the atrium roof focus on the main entrance. At night, the illuminated atrium establishes an after-hours presence on the SRCC campus. To reinforce light as a therapeutic fundamental in healing, the interior atrium has been incorporated as a four-story conditioned lightwell.

Not only does the atrium serve as interior relief for a large footprint, but it also becomes an easily recognizable reference point for patients and families who need access to multiple floors. With mezzanines looking down into the atrium lobby, filled with arbors and seating areas within a shaft of sunlight, the effect resembles that of a hotel. The atrium also overlooks an extensive garden, walled with trees and including an organically shaped pool as a centerpiece that appears to flow along a flagstone walk.

Spartanburg Regional Cancer Center, Spartanburg, South Carolina. An outdoor meditation garden, walled with trees, includes an organically shaped pool with a fountain centerpiece to lend a sense of calmness to the setting. *Courtesy Earl Swensson Associates and McMillan Smith & Partners Architects, P.A. Photo Bob Harr © Hedrich Blessing.*

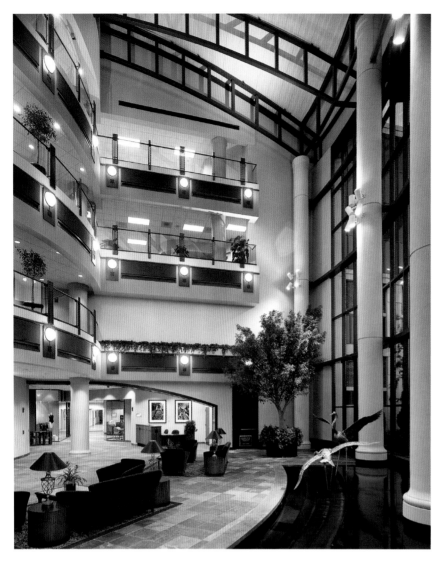

The garden blots the view of the parking lot and along with the elements of light, water, and music, it helps make the entire entry experience pleasant and calming.

To assist in efficiency and improved patient care, the design synchronizes the management of large treatment suites with zoning for appropriate nursing ratios. In the chemotherapy suite, for instance, patient treatment bays are clustered in pods of three with nursing substations located at the edge of each pod. Each patient pod includes a bathroom as an integral patient amenity. Physician access to the patient is emphasized in a number of ways, such as the dual doors in the examination rooms in the radiology/oncology treatment area. As with light, water, and music, private rooms with private spaces and visual cues of concern are important to chemotherapy patients, because they help decrease the stimuli of traditional hospital environments that can cause nausea and apprehension.

SRCC, as a case study, represents the direction cancer care will be following. Freestanding cancer centers may still be viable specialized entities, but today's trend seems to be leaning toward more comprehensive and less segregated facilities.

Spartanburg Regional Cancer Center, Spartanburg, South Carolina. As in a hotel, mezzanines overlook the sunlit lobby filled with arbors, seating areas, and sculptures in a stepped fountain, all of which serve to soothe fears associated with cancer treatment. *Courtesy Earl Swensson Associates and McMillan Smith & Partners Architects, P.A. Photo Bob Harr © Hedrich Blessing.*

PARK NICOLLET MELROSE INSTITUTE

St. Louis Park, Minnesota

Designed by Ellerbe Becket, an AECOM company of architecture interior design, the Melrose Institute was the first of its kind in the Midwest: a medically based facility dedicated solely to the treatment of eating disorders. As such, the institute is an important addition to the region's healthcare community. The new building consolidates the services of the former Park Nicollet Eating Disorders Institute and provides inpatient, outpatient, and residential care.

Park Nicollet has long been an advocate for using lean methodologies to improve healthcare quality and efficiency, so to kick off the project Ellerbe Becket held a weeklong 3P ("production," "preparation," "process") workshop that included staff, administrators, patients, and design team representatives. The workshop analyzed the flow of the practice, identified its strengths and weaknesses, and discussed eliminating unnecessary waste. Participants helped develop a new model of care for eating disorders, which in turn shaped the building's planning and design.

The facility's first floor contains most of what could be called the more public elements of its program, such as its triage and assessment area, its chapel, its bookstore, and its fitness and dining rooms. The second floor contains what might be dubbed the more private elements, which include individual and group therapy rooms as well as two experiential kitchens. The third floor houses inpatient and residential programs.

Given the lovely natural setting, incorporating natural and sustainable materials and design principles became of great importance both to the institute and to the designers. To that end, the building offers views of a neighboring nature preserve and boasts special therapeutic healing gardens.

Occupancy has far exceeded initial expectations, and user feedback has been a testament to the facility's success. According to Ellerbe Becket, families and staff alike have with some frequency called the Melrose Institute a perfect setting for the treatment of eating disorders.

Park Nicollet Melrose Institute, St. Louis Park, Minnesota. The lobby reflects designer Ellerbe Becket's commitment to natural light and materials. *Courtesy Ellerbe Becket. Photo © 2009 Don F. Wong.*

Park Nicollet Melrose Institute, St. Louis Park, Minnesota. Designed by Ellerbe Becket, the building offers notable views of a neighboring nature preserve and incorporates natural and sustainable materials. *Courtesy Ellerbe Becket. Photo © 2009 Don F. Wong.*

Meadville Medical Center, Oncology Wellness Institute, Meadville, Pennsylvania. The 19,000-sq.-ft. Oncology Wellness Institute is the first freestanding cancer care facility in Crawford County, Pennsylvania. *Courtesy Astorino. Photo CRAIGTHOMPSONPHOTO.COM.*

Meadville, Pennsylvania

Recognized with an award from the Pennsylvania Tri-State region's chapter of the Design Build Institute of America (DBIA), this 19,000-sq.-ft. center, designed by Astorino, is the first freestanding cancer care facility in Crawford County.

A state-of-the-art facility that provides outpatient treatments, radiation oncology, and improved access to local physicians, the center also includes a women's diagnostic component that offers mammography, ultrasound, and

Meadville Medical Center, Oncology Wellness Institute, Meadville, Pennsylvania. The extensive use of glass provides plenty of natural light and beautiful outdoor views to help create a calming and relaxing environment for stressed patients receiving lengthy treatments at the Oncology Wellness Institute. *Courtesy Astorino. Photo CRAIGTHOMPSONPHOTO.COM.*

bone density testing. The center's infusion area includes two private treatment rooms and ten open bays with moveable storage modules that can be used to create a semiprivate environment.

The extensive use of glass provides plenty of natural light and beautiful outdoor views—along with the patio's fountain of water—create a calming and relaxing environment, for stressed patients receiving lengthy treatments.

An innovative, functional plan couples each of four doctors' offices with an adjoining exam room to allow for more direct and personal interaction with patients. Two auxiliary exam rooms accommodate patient overflow and visiting physicians.

The radiation oncology suite offers the latest in computer tomography scanning and radiation treatment. Other amenities include a meeting room, a patient library, and a mobile imaging docking station.

THE CENTER FOR CANCER CARE AT GRIFFIN HOSPITAL
Derby, Connecticut

This S/L/A/M Collaborative project in Connecticut's smallest municipality (located in New Haven County) consisted of a 48,000-sq.-ft. addition to Griffin's ambulatory services building and cancer center and included 22,000 sq. ft. of renovations to the existing hospital emergency department and clinical laboratory. Planetree's patient-centered care philosophy served as the guidepost of the design and infused all aspects of its image, brand, and identity.

Creating this healing environment in a tranquil setting was complicated, however, by the site itself. On the corner junction of five busy, mixed business and residential streets, surrounded by hospital and clinic parking areas,

The Center for Cancer Care at Griffin Hospital, Derby, Connecticut. *Courtesy The S/L/A/M Collaborative. Photo Robert Benson Photography.*

275

The Center for Cancer Care at Griffin Hospital, Derby, Connecticut. S/L/A/M Collaborative used Planetree's patient-care philosophy in all aspects of this design. *Courtesy The S/L/A/M Collaborative. Photo Robert Benson Photography.*

OPPOSITE TOP The Hansen Center, Margaret Mary Community Hospital, Batesville, Indiana. Designed by BSA Lifestructures this oncology center received a *Modern Healthcare* design award in 2005. *Courtesy BSA Life-Structures. Photo Stephen B. Ruemmele (former BSA LifeStructures employee).*

OPPOSITE BOTTOM The Hansen Center, Margaret Mary Community Hospital, Batesville, Indiana. The bays at this oncology center have amenities for family members and views of a healing garden. *Courtesy BSA Life-Structures. Photo Jeff Millies © Hedrich Blessing.*

and sloping upward from the street at a fairly steep pitch, the site required a great deal of preparation and grading. And the building needed shielding from street noise. Construction was complicated further when the excavation of the site revealed a ledge of igneous rock that rose along the interior corner of the site. Huge glacial boulders, some weighing more than 20,000 pounds, were also exposed.

S/L/A/M incorporated both the rock ledge and the boulders into the building's design, blasting away enough of the ledge to make room for the building, and then using the rock shattered by the explosion and the remaining rock face to construct a waterway and a fountain in the center of the new structure. Thus the architects embodied the connections between the town and the river.

The unique project won a 2010 *Real Estate Exchange*, Best In Class, Healthcare award; a 2009 ASLA Connecticut Honor award, and a 2009 Center for Healthcare Design/*Contract Magazine* Healthcare Environments award in Landscape Architecture.

THE HANSEN CENTER, MARGARET MARY COMMUNITY HOSPITAL
Batesville, Indiana

Designed by BSA Lifestructures to be a nurturing environment, this oncology center received a *Modern Healthcare* design award in 2005. Not only does it nurture its patients, the facility also offers them high-quality treatment close to home.

The warm, inviting interior has floating wood ceilings, textured and curved walls, hardwood floors, water features, and art glass. The unique infusion suite design was inspired by focus groups the designer held with patients.

The patients can close textured glass screens for privacy or open them for interaction with others during chemotherapy treatment. The bays have amenities for family members and views of a healing garden.

According to BSA Lifestructures, one oncology nurse described the individual infusion bays as "Very nice. They allow," she said, "for privacy, but the ability to talk to patients next door if they want. Patients love the view, too. They love to be able to look outside at the pond, the flowers and the fountain. It helps take their minds off their treatment and encourages them to focus on their healing."

A community room and a kitchen provide space for support groups, cooking demonstrations, and classes. Salons for massage therapy, a resource library, and a boutique for wigs, prostheses, and other specialty items meet a range of needs for patients at the center. The second floor is an outpatient center with its own entrance.

The Hansen Center has some of the more precise radiation therapy treatment available. Radiation oncology and medical oncology are located in one spot, which encourages collaboration among oncologists.

MCGHealth Cancer Center, Augusta, Georgia. De-institutionalizing cancer care became the first and foremost of the design team's goals. *Courtesy Heery | design. Photo Dave Dawson Photography.*

MCGHEALTH CANCER CENTER

Augusta, Georgia

According to Patricia Sodomka, a fellow of the American College of Healthcare Executives (ACHE) and the senior vice president of Patient Family Centered Care for MCGHealth, the clinical delivery arm of the Medical College of Georgia, the willingness of the architects to listen to what patients had to say about this new facility's needs was key to its design. A cancer center patient herself, she watched with approval as spirited survivors such as Nettie Engels were asked to join a design team that included architects Heery | design, interior designers from CAMA Inc., builders from the construction firm RJ Griffin & Company, and physicians and other professionals from the MCG system to discuss and plan a leading-edge cancer treatment center.

An initial orientation meeting, according to interior designer Rosalyn Cama, helped focus the entire team on the baseline design features whose impact would affect the facility's wayfinding, its stress levels, its comfort and privacy, its communications and knowledge sharing, its spirituality and community support, its delivery of care, and its reduction of infection.

Deinstitutionalizing cancer care became the first and foremost of the design team's goals. The dark, cramped feel of the old 11,000-sq.-ft. space MCG devoted to cancer care was replaced by a spacious 60,000-sq.-ft. metal, brick, and stucco structure that serves as a one-stop shop for cancer patients.

As the sharply angled metal rooftop points toward the sky above, the spacious two-story floor-to-ceiling glass atrium beckons patients and their families into the building. The atrium spreads warmth and light, and the concierge-like check-in desk with an etched glass sign above it greets patients in numerous languages, including the southern "hey y'all." Light wood paneling, soft colors, gently curved soffits and comfortable hotel lobbylike chairs are intended, say the planners, to enhance the peaceful ambiance.

The space, which was designed to permit vertical expansion, includes a family resource center and café, and supportive amenities extend down a well-lit corridor with a quiet meditation area, a small outdoor garden, and a boutique. The atrium also houses a grand glass, steel, and limestone stairway. Two elevators are clearly visible for easy use after checking in. An additional private elevator near the infusion suite was added for those patients who may require ambulance transport to and from the facility. In the support services area, patients are matched with a nurse to guide them through the consultation and treatment process. Conference rooms, which did not exist in the former location, allow patients to gather with their team of physicians to discuss care strategies.

Beyond the patient support and waiting area, the first floor houses four pods with exam and treatment rooms arranged by cancer diagnosis. These exam suites are named and colored after native flora and fauna. The magnolia corridor, for example, is for OB/GYN oncology patients. Each wing also houses a procedure room and physician-intern team area.

At first the professionals had intended to place the bathrooms in this corridor outside patient treatment rooms, but team member Nettie Engels worried about the resulting loss of privacy and the impact it would have on

MCGHealth Cancer Center, Augusta, Georgia. The second-story infusion area serves both traditional chemotherapy patients and those participating in clinical trials. *Courtesy Heery | design. Photo Dave Dawson Photography.*

MCGHealth Cancer Center, Augusta, Georgia. The reception area. *Courtesy Heery | design. Photo Dave Dawson Photography.*

patients, and the group sacrificed a consulting room to gain the additional space needed to put the OB/GYN wing's bathrooms inside the treatment rooms. They called them "Nettie's bathrooms."

Sink placement in exam rooms was another concern. Typically, doctors enter a room and, because of the location of the sinks, wash their hands with their backs to the patient. According to Heery | design architect and project executive Jim Kukla, the cancer center "sinks are placed to encourage interaction."

Such detailed concern proved typical of the design team's efforts, and its members ultimately used an existing room in the neighboring hospital along with an off-site warehouse to create mock-ups, which led to changes in floor coloring, casework laminates, and the placement of spaces for better lighting.

Each wing, which receives ample indirect light from the windows at the far side of the building, opens with consulting rooms, followed by exam and then procedure rooms. The nursing stations at this facility are centrally located and offer additional waiting space for family or friends. Physician offices and meeting spaces are located along the back side of the facility at the edge of each corridor.

Without question, says Heery, the second story infusion area was the feature of which the entire team was most proud. Two sets of patients use this area—traditional chemotherapy patients and those participating in clinical trials. So one of the first considerations was to separate them, and the designers created two waiting areas, a more public space for traditional patients and a quieter, more private area for those engaged in clinical trials. Although the infusion area—whose check-in desk is visible from both the stairs and elevators—is open, there is a clear delineation between the two sections in the form of a curvilinear, communal sitting nook that can accommodate patients and family members.

Soft curves, like that of the sitting nook, define the space from floor to ceiling, and a personal touch is evident in every nook and cranny. Four patients can be assigned to each infusion "surfboard," as the curved modules have come to be known at MCGHealth, and patients have the option of socializing with their neighbors or pulling the curtain for privacy. Each individual space affords a personal light switch, built-in med gases, a flat-screen television, a lockable cabinet for storage, a moveable infusion chair, and a room for visitors. While a centrally located nurses' station allows good visibility throughout the open space, there are nurse workstations and sinks at individual surfboards, which encourages nurses to spend as much time as possible with their assigned patients.

Because infusion chairs are mobile, patients have the flexibility to wander around and visit other patients at their surfboards or in the sitting nook. They also have easy access to the cedar-plank-enclosed rooftop garden, a favorite feature in the new space. A separate nutrition area is another critical component, requested by the patient advisors.

Not only, then, is the center a state-of-the-art facility, it also underscores the importance of the patient and family experience in treating cancer.

KAISER FOUNDATION HEALTH PLAN, INC.
NEW CANCER TREATMENT CENTER
South San Francisco, California

In response to the increased need for high-quality radiation treatment facilities, architects at Ratcliff designed this new 20,000-sq.-ft. cancer center featuring four vaults—three with linear accelerators and one with cyberknife radiotherapy—and twelve exam rooms.

The exterior center appears modern, crisp, and cutting edge, reflecting the latest technological advances in medical treatment. To balance the sharpness of the exterior, Ratcliff softened the interior with natural shapes and earth tones. Wood panels offer aesthetic warmth, and organic shapes echo the calming effect of the nearby shoreline. In spite of site restrictions and urban density, daylight plays a distinct role here, which is unusual in radiation departments. Linear skylights and glazing provide visual cues and a clear and inviting path of travel. Room finishes, selected to ensure good indoor air quality,

Kaiser Foundation Health Plan, Inc., New Cancer Treatment Center, South San Francisco, California. To balance the sharpness of the exterior, architects at Ratcliff softened the interior by using natural shapes and earth tones. *Courtesy Ratcliff. Photo © 2009 Tim Maloney, Technical Imagery Studios.*

are low-emitting, recycled, rapidly renewable, and easily maintained. Walls in critical locations are free of miscellaneous devices and are rich in botanical-themed artwork.

As an open area for patients and family members to take a break from the intensity of the care environment and to take respite in the natural elements, the waiting room courtyard is a key element of the design. Outfitted with data outlets and a wide-screen television, the waiting room coffee bar accommodates access to the outside world for family members of patients undergoing treatment and care.

Fitness and Sports Medicine Centers

As paradigms of caring shift from remediation to prevention, hospitals and other healthcare providers have called with greater frequency for health and fitness centers. Perhaps given the need of hospitals to increase revenues, such facilities can become similar to commercial health and fitness clubs—although with stronger education programs and ties to rehabilitation and cardiac departments and sports medicine programs. In any case, the hospital fitness center is emerging as part of a holistic program, which includes exercise and recreation as well as nutrition and wellness education. Perhaps we may yet see partnerships and joint ventures among hospitals, health clubs, and even country clubs, as well as such community organizations as the YMCA/YWCA.

ST. VINCENT'S ORTHOSPORT CENTER & MEDICAL TOWER
Birmingham, Alabama

The cylinder-like, three-story rotunda front entry lobby mimics that of St. Vincent's Hospital's North Tower, with which it is connected, as it continues the seamlessness of architectural standards established during the recent decade of expansions. This new, 176,582-sq.-ft., six-story, brick

St. Vincent's OrthoSport Center & Medical Tower, Birmingham, Alabama. Rehabilitation is located on the ground floor. *Photo © Viscom Photographics.*

facility, designed by ESa, houses Dr. James Andrews' OrthoSport Center, as well as a variety of specialty services.

Rehabilitation is located on the ground floor and is easily accessed from the same level of the parking garage for those on crutches and in wheelchairs. Natural light plays an integral role in this space featuring an all-glass northern wall. A walking track surrounds a central exercise space, and a plyometrics area sits behind the rehabilitation space.

The first-floor clinic contains the destination orthopedic services of Dr. Andrews, the internationally renowned surgeon. The placement of Dr.

St. Vincent's OrthoSport Center & Medical Tower, Birmingham, Alabama. *Photo © Viscom Photographics.*

Andrews' office space drove the rest of the clinic's design. The doors to Dr. Andrews' office open directly off the main lobby. The layout of exam clusters, diagnostic services of the clinic, and access to patients were designed to create the most efficient use of the physicians' time. A less public, back entry from the parking garage is available for nationally recognized athletes and other VIPs. The second and third floors are devoted to orthopedic surgeries, both inpatient and outpatient. The remaining floors house medical office space.

Saint Anthony Medical Center, Franciscan Point Health Complex, Crown Point, Indiana. Design Organization, Inc., created a bold, easily identifiable entrance. *Courtesy Design Organization, Inc. Photo Design Organization, Inc.*

Saint Anthony Medical Center, Franciscan Point Health Complex, Crown Point, Indiana. Design Organization, Inc., used brick and stone for the human-scale design vocabulary. *Courtesy Design Organization, Inc. Photo Design Organization, Inc.*

SAINT ANTHONY MEDICAL CENTER FRANCISCAN POINT HEALTH COMPLEX
Crown Point, Indiana

Saint Anthony Franciscan Point Health Complex combines an outpatient care center (express care, diagnostics, primary care, and specialties) with a sports medicine institute (advanced sports training, orthopedics, physical and occupational therapy). The facility offers a continuum of care and services from fitness to fixing physical-health problems.

Design Organization, Inc. came up with a 68-acre master plan for the 86,000-sq.-ft. building with the focus on family-centered ease of service and patient-centered care. This focus is reinforced by the facility's bold, easily identifiable entrance and the transparent lobby that looks into a healing garden. The lobby incorporates quotes from St. Francis and a crucifix, both recalling the caregiving mission of the Sisters of St. Francis.

The architecture uses brick and stone for its human-scale design vocabulary. The vaulted roof invokes a traditional field house, reflecting the athletic development functions of the building.

Saint Anthony Medical Center, Franciscan Point Health Complex, Crown Point, Indiana. Windows are maximized for great views, good daylight, and efficient solar energy use. *Courtesy Design Organization, Inc. Photo Design Organization, Inc.*

The building was designed with a long east-west access, which maximizes windows on the south elevation along the main corridor and allows for great views, good daylight, and efficient solar energy use. Other sustainable features include highly reflective roofing, a restored habitat outside the building, storm water quality and quantity controls, and the use of recycled and low-emitting materials.

ONE NINETEEN HEALTH AND WELLNESS

Hoover, Alabama

ESa designed One Nineteen Health and Wellness under the umbrella of Birmingham's St. Vincent's Health System to introduce an all-encompassing healthcare approach to the surrounding medical campus. The center houses the region's only integrated medical and holistic healthy lifestyle program promoting well-being through education, fitness, diagnostic services, and related programs.

It includes a diagnostics center, a rehabilitation clinic, a fitness center, a spa, physicians' offices, and a health education center with a full demonstration kitchen. When designing the 154,645-sq.-ft. project ESa was faced with the challenge of creating functional adjacencies. For example, because fitness and rehabilitation programs use the same equipment it made sense to have

One Nineteen Health and Wellness, Hoover, Alabama. A circular monumental stair encased in a cardio theater serves as an anchor for the oval three-lane indoor track that connects all areas of the fitness center.
Photo Scott McDonald © Hedrich Blessing.

One Nineteen Health and Wellness, Hoover, Alabama.
Photo Vince Wallace/Silver Hill Images.

one registration desk serve both departments, which reduces square footage and redundancy and allows sharing of staff. In addition, direct connections from each area permit fitness members and patients to use the entire facility.

Because the facility was built in a suburb of Birmingham, planners from the start wanted the character and feel of a hospitality spa, turning what is traditionally considered an area for the "sick" into something healthy, something that did not have the clinical feel of a hospital. ESa was asked to draw on both its healthcare and hospitality design experience to create a spot where the practice of great medicine had the look and feel of a weekend get-away rather than a hospital stay. The master plan for One Nineteen Health and Wellness also positioned the facility for expansion in the future with the first priority being outpatient surgery.

The Workplace-based Healthcare Facility

Industrial plants and other industries have long maintained on-site clinics to treat work-related injuries, to evaluate worker's compensation claims, to perform insurance-mandated physicals, and so on. Many companies of all kinds have developed partnerships with healthcare providers—either on-site or off-site—or maintained their own medical personnel to treat not only work-related injuries and ailments but also to provide primary medical care with a very strong emphasis on preventive care and wellness programs.

The movement toward employer-promoted healthy lifestyles is spurred in part by the high and ever-rising cost of providing insurance coverage. But it is also a movement to promote wellness, thereby decreasing insurance claims (some providers rebate a portion of premiums in response to reduced claims) and increasing worker productivity. Employees who participate in a fitness program are absent fewer days in a year than workers not enrolled in such programs. Wellness programs have also been credited with reducing employee tardiness.

Homecare

As hospitals and other healthcare providers reach out into the workplace, they also reach out into the home. These days hospitals nationwide have extensive homecare programs, and the trend continues to grow. Although hospital homecare departments do not always generate a lot of revenue, in an epoch of cost containment, homecare can be extremely cost-effective.

Currently, the more significant trend is toward decentralization and community outreach, including homecare. The continued development of electronic monitoring, treatment, and telemetry technologies will only encourage this trend. For planners and administrators who suffer from what Laurence J. Peter once called an "edifice complex," this can only seem disappointing and deflating. For those who look beyond the physical edifice, however, it is apparent that hospitals are on their way to becoming, in varying degrees, virtual entities: not so much buildings to which patients are brought, but networks delivering care through many venues, including hospitals with and without beds, freestanding clinics (some specialized, some providing general or family practice), workplace clinics, and the homes of individual patients. If this seems difficult to visualize, just think of the rapid evolution of the bank from a Greek—or Roman—revival edifice surrounding a vault to a financial network of branches, ATMs, point-of-purchase cash registers, and home computers. For architects, designers, planners, administrators, and healthcare providers, the virtual hospital is an emerging reality that is at once wonderful and challenging in its implications.

System Planning

In recent years, the same pressures that led to a growing demand for ambulatory care have also created a demand for organized delivery systems (discussed in Chapter 8). One of the more significant of those pressures is perhaps the major shift from inpatient to outpatient services, which—fed by technological advances that allow all sorts of procedures to be done on an outpatient basis—has created a partially consumer-driven medical marketplace. While healthcare providers now recognize the importance of environment to healing, the fact is that patients respond more favorably to a hospital that looks friendly and feels comfortable, making design central in the current economy where there is increasing competition for patients.

Financial pressures also have driven change, as much or perhaps even more than the drive to provide a more personal, patient-friendly space. When payers began organizing into HMOs and other managed-care organizations, the emphasis on cost containment put the pressure on providers, who had to find unaccustomed efficiencies in their operations. To counter the effect of such cost-conscious payment, provider systems began merging and acquiring (or being acquired) in a new networking drive to survive. Networking and integration of services offered provider systems at least the chance to weather the squeeze brought on by managed care and sometimes even to emerge with new opportunities. (These trends are not likely to be reversed even by new federal healthcare reforms, which while they may change the payer, are still going to emphasize economic frugality and cost cutting in medical care.)

In any case, historically this consumerism and competition for payers combined with urban sprawl and demographic shifts to change the landscape of healthcare facility planning. In cities across the country, urban hospitals faced not only stiff competition from burgeoning suburban facilities but also issues of quality healthcare and security. In addition, older hospitals in downtown areas are frequently "landlocked" by other businesses and developments; even if they are able to attract new customers from the suburbs, they sometimes experience difficulty handling the new outpatient traffic since they were designed for acute, inpatient care. The ambulatory facilities are also frequently cheaper to build because design requirements and building codes are less restrictive and they do not have to incur the higher costs associated with mechanical/plumbing/electrical (M/P/E) systems. The final tolling of the bell may come with the technological advances, especially communications technology, that make telemedicine more achievable. Smaller and more remote facilities can now draw on the depth of expertise at larger facilities for diagnosis, for example, which further encourages networking. And once a system of facilities is up and running, the initial focus of the larger, more complex medical center becomes higher-acuity care, while less-acute care is provided in the rural affiliate sites.

As such demographics and pressures began to play out over the last thirty-five years or so, the bedless hospitals we have mentioned frequently in this chapter proliferated as sort of suburban branches of larger, urban medical centers to better serve the clientele in outlying areas of large urban markets. But as these facilities themselves—and/or the networks with which they were associated—have matured and as the larger, less friendly facilities in the urban centers have begun to retrench or shut down, providers are once again thinking about adding beds, if not full-time acute-care beds then at least observation beds. In short, the bedless trend seems to be already undergoing a trend of its own to include at least observation beds or twenty-three-hour beds.

In the current environment, providers almost naturally seek greater efficiency through elimination of redundancy. Many hospitals and medical centers join together not only to ensure market share but to create a stronger whole systemwide, combining strengths, streamlining operations, and looking for economies of scale. Here again, integration and networking play their special roles. Integrated systems provide one-stop shopping with many amenities to prospective patients, while networking allows larger medical facilities to buy up smaller ones and achieve efficiencies, broaden their markets, and strengthen their positions vis-à-vis managed-care companies. At this point, networks may consist of as little as two hospitals working together, but they can also involve twenty facilities, each offering a specialized kind of care.

All of this requires architects to think in terms of system planning, rather than planning for individual facilities. Smaller networks may not be able to achieve all the economies of scale that, say, an HCA (Hospital Corporation of America) or Kaiser Permanente can, but they can maximize them by conducting the same kind of coordinated analysis that looks at life cycle and maintenance as well as initial costs. More important even to smaller networks is the care integration of facilities. No longer can they afford to simply throw up a bedless hospital in an outlying neighborhood to grab market share. System planning means making sure that such a facility—and all the facilities in the network—serves the system as a whole, does not duplicate services that can be better handled in other areas of the system, and is flexible enough to handle its own maturing, so that it can expand as other parts of the system contract.

To summarize, bedless hospitals—birthed by a range of factors including mergers that decrease inpatient beds, managed-care penetration of the market, a growing emphasis on outpatient care, changes in urban demographics and in medicine and medical technology, and a growing consumer consciousness and competitive market—offer the complete range of medical services, usually to outpatients only, although they may have short-stay beds as well. In any case, they do not include services for intensive care or long-stay acute patients, although they may belong to networks that do. Indeed, they are increasingly part of a healthcare network that most often comprises primary care practices, small neighborhood facilities, and the regional outpatient center (usually located in a high-growth area). This network offers a wide range of services, including primary and secondary physicians, diagnostics, imaging, ambulatory surgery, and birthing centers. The design challenge for these networks is system planning, to look at not just the building currently under construction but at its place and function within the system presently and in the future.

ELMHURST MEMORIAL CENTER FOR HEALTH
Elmhurst, Illinois

As in many urban areas, Elmhurst's main hospital could not expand due to a lack of available land, and it also suffered from the accessibility problems associated with inner-city facilities. Meanwhile, outpatient demand in the surrounding region was growing by leaps and bounds, and the hospital could not meet that demand. An extensive land search was conducted,

Elmhurst Memorial Center for Health, Elmhurst, Illinois. With its noninstitutional brick exterior, the center blends in with the surrounding residential setting. *Photo Craig Dugan © Hedrich Blessing.*

and the designers at ESa were led to a site that required several homes to be relocated to clear a large-enough area for the planned outpatient and physicians' office facility. It was a good site with high visibility but for that very reason much community outreach work was required before building could get underway. Ultimately positioned on 15 acres, the facility was designed to harmonize with the community with a Prairie-style exterior carried out in warm brick and a slate roof—a design that consciously pays homage to Frank Lloyd Wright and simultaneously announces that this hospital is more hotel or home than institution.

The integration of physicians' offices with diagnostic services offers immediacy of care with one-site convenience for patients and doctors alike. ESa also employed the following special design features:

• Parking areas for patients and visitors, and convenient ingress and egress for employees and physicians

• A covered drop-off and pick-up point on the north side of the building for surgery, physical therapy, and cardiac rehabilitation patients

• Specialized outpatient departments located on the perimeter of the building, allowing for future horizontal expansion with access from a central waiting area

• A walking trail that encircles the building as a community amenity and additional element of the facility's rehabilitation program

Because the facility was not a full-scale hospital, cost savings were realized through lower expenditures in such areas as electrical and plumbing systems, despite the fact that the hospital walked a tightrope due to the high retail costs associated with "comfort" amenities, such as a health education resource center; a pharmacy; a gift shop; an optical shop; the large, elegantly appointed public areas; and retention lakes, fountains, and a waterfall. Future expansion of the center allows for integration with a planned new inpatient facility.

Elmhurst Memorial Center for Health, Elmhurst, Illinois. The built-in sofas just outside the resource center offer patients and their family members comfortable seating. *Photo Craig Dugan © Hedrich Blessing.*

CHAPTER 11

Women's and Children's Healthcare Facilities

We have grouped women's and children's healthcare facilities into a single chapter to reflect a leading-edge trend of family-centered care in planning such facilities. Increasingly today, administrators, planners, and caregivers are asking for facilities in which maternity and pediatric care are delivered as a continuum. Let us begin with the example of a type of facility that has become familiar to the healthcare landscape.

CENTRAL DUPAGE HOSPITAL— WOMEN AND CHILDREN'S PAVILION
Winfield, Illinois

In an expansive, complex, campuswide expansion and renovation of Central DuPage Hospital in phases that spanned a period of eight years, ESa first created a new neonatal intensive care unit, a renovated emergency department, and an expanded employee parking garage. Then, in 2004, the Women and Children's Pavilion was added.

The new pavilion is an addition to an existing wing and has its own dedicated entry. Patient-centered improvements incorporated state-of-the-art technology and design efficiencies that enabled Central DuPage to better deliver advanced, comprehensive healthcare services for women and infants.

Centers of excellence were established that align physicians with their inpatient and outpatient services for women's health, cardiology services, and surgical services. The portals-of-care approach enables patients to conveniently

Central DuPage Hospital—Women and Children's Pavilion, Winfield, Illinois. An elegant sculpture in the atrium signifies the nature of the facility. *Photo Scott McDonald © Hedrich Blessing.*

park adjacent to the services they seek. The adjacency of women's health to surgery provides backup and support for the caesarian ORs from surgery.

The project was phased to create minimal disruptions and throughout construction—which included a new ambulatory services pavilion, also with a dedicated entry, in 2005 and a new surgery pavilion in 2006—the facility remained in operation.

Marketing Epiphany

Late in the twentieth century a movement focusing on women's health began. Traditionally, obstetrics and gynecology departments have concentrated on women's reproductive needs. This new movement includes a more holistic approach to women's health, including preventive care as well as a focus on the growing body of research addressing how diseases and drugs act differently in women than in men.

After the age of fourteen, women visit the doctor more often than men do. They are hospitalized more often, and the surgical procedures specific to women—such as hysterectomies, tubal ligations, and caesarean sections—account for more than half of the most frequently performed surgeries. Perhaps even more significantly, women make the great majority of the health-care decisions for all U.S. households. If the female patient is satisfied with the care she receives, and the facility or its affiliates offer other kinds of care,

Central DuPage Hospital—Women and Children's Pavilion, Winfield, Illinois. The pavilion adds 135,000 sq. ft. to the medical center's maternal-child-care facilities. *Photo Scott McDonald © Hedrich Blessing.*

she is likely to bring in other members of her family to the facility for their healthcare needs.

Certainly by the 1980s, many had recognized the size of the women's healthcare population and its significance. But many of the answers that emerged from the 1980s were cosmetic: the same old programs in more attractive settings. To be sure, such cosmetic improvements were important—both in terms of attracting patients and making them feel more comfortable and empowered—but they were hardly the whole answer. Yes, women wanted healthcare delivery in an attractive setting, but their needs were also more complex, more profound, and more sophisticated.

To begin with, there is no single female patient. Needs vary with socio-economic status, level of education, plans for a family, and age. So the first thing any facility offering women's healthcare must do is become sensitive to the range of needs and desires that exist in what may seem, superficially, a narrowly specialized segment of healthcare. Even so, certain common trends continue to motivate planning and design for women's healthcare programs and facilities.

Convenience

• In the vast majority of households, both husband and wife work outside the home. Yet since 1960, when only one out of three women (aged twenty-five to thirty-four) worked outside the home, men have picked up only about one-quarter of the domestic workload. This means that women are busy—at work and at home.

- Effective women's healthcare must accommodate difficult and demanding schedules, not only by offering extended hours of availability but by decentralizing care through community-based programs and facilities and through self-help programs.
- Childcare should be available on-site.
- Comprehensive, one-stop care will have the edge. There is a marketing opportunity for women's health facilities associated with internal medicine or family practice in addition to obstetrics and gynecology (OB/GYN). There is also an opportunity for association with pediatrics; the entire family can be cared for in a single visit.
- Medical mall designs may offer appealing convenience to these patients.

Reasonable Cost

Ads in popular women's magazines and on television characteristically portray professional women as holding high-paying, high-prestige jobs. It is undeniable that the majority of women now work outside the home. But it is also undeniable that, on average, women are paid less than men. They are also frequently the heads of one-parent families. All of this adds up to a necessarily cost-conscious patient.

Access to Information

- On average, all patients today are better educated and better informed; nowhere is this more true than for women.
- Women are taking—and will continue to take—a more active role in healthcare decisions. Patient education and access to information is an essential element in the design of women's healthcare facilities.

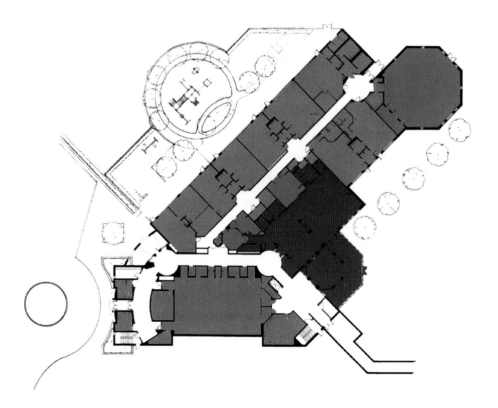

Condell Intergenerational Day Care Center, Libertyville, Illinois. Floor plan, first floor. A convenience for busy women (and men), this center combines daycare for children and adults in the same facility. *Courtesy OWP&P.*

Green Daycare space for children
Blue Shared space
Rust Older adult space
Olive Community/hospital space

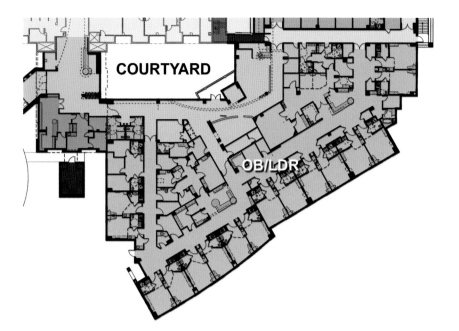

An obstetrics/labor/delivery/recovery floor plan created by Earl Swensson Associates.

COURTYARD

OB/LDR

• Women are looking for a wide range of healthcare alternatives and are requesting information to make the most informed healthcare decisions.

Wellness and Fitness

• In general, women are more willing than men to participate in preventive, wellness, and fitness programs.

• In general, women are far more likely than men to participate in health education programs, including nutritional information programs.

Do-It-Yourself

The self-help market is particularly active among women, providing opportunities for educational outreach programs.

Older Women

• The healthcare needs of women change as women age.

• The healthcare needs of older women are currently underserved, especially where health education is concerned.

• Like other care providers, women's healthcare professionals must consider an aging population.

Hospital-based Women's Centers

In the last few decades, a number of hospitals rushed to get on the women's healthcare bandwagon with too often merely cosmetic renovations of existing OB/GYN spaces, which they then dubbed "Women's Centers." Because so many of these failed to generate anticipated revenues, some reached the conclusion that women's health centers should be freestanding. Yet reputable studies and national surveys indicated that what a woman really wanted in a healthcare center was not a separate facility. To the contrary, the majority of women actually wanted a facility connected physically to a larger hospital. However, women did clearly indicate that they also wanted a center with a separate identity from the hospital, and most of them wanted access to such a center through a separate entrance.

The message was plain. Hospital-based women's centers could succeed, provided they were legitimate entities with an individually established identity. Today, a comprehensive, hospital-based women's center should be a true wellness environment that actively promotes health and the prevention of disease as well as caring and curing. It should include all of the elements below:

- Complete OB/GYN services, with access to LDR/LDRP (labor/delivery/ recovery or labor/delivery/recovery/postpartum; i.e., single-room maternity care) rooms
- Diagnostic screening services (mammography, bone-density screening, etc.)
- Fertility clinic services
- Fitness and exercise programs (in a dedicated space)
- Education programs (in a dedicated space)
- Psychological/sociological counseling service (in a dedicated space); this service includes general psychological counseling as well as intervention in cases of child abuse or domestic violence
- An avenue to other hospital services such as plastic surgery (the third most widely used medical service for women) and cardiology (the fourth most widely used medical service for women)

When talking about access to surgery in regard to women's centers and hospitals, it is important to mention fetal surgery. Fetal surgery is the surgical treatment of a fetus to correct certain life-threatening congenital abnormalities before birth. Highly specialized skills and training are required, and, for this reason, fetal surgery programs are associated with larger, academic medical centers.

ST. DAVID'S WOMEN'S CENTER OF TEXAS
ON CAMPUS OF ST. DAVID'S NORTH AUSTIN MEDICAL CENTER
Austin, Texas

In this 221,568-sq.-ft. addition to an existing hospital, ESa provided a new, separate entrance through a three-story atrium to the facility dedicated to women's services at the St. David's Women's Center of Texas. The atrium seamlessly connects inpatient care spaces and physicians' offices, and this integration influenced the final form the building took, a form that incorporates lease space efficiencies while maintaining the primary purpose as the new labor and delivery wing for the hospital.

The Women's Center also connects to the hospital via a sky bridge to the second floor of the main building, where renovations to the existing second floor added twenty neonatal intensive care unit (NICU) positions, sixteen new positions in the well-baby nursery, and an expanded postpartum unit. Below the sky bridge lies

St. David's Women's Center of Texas, on campus of St. David's North Austin Medical Center, Austin, Texas. The spaciousness of the labor/delivery/ recovery/post-partum rooms provide zones for families and accommodate equipment maneuverability. *Photo © James F. Wilson.*

a garden focused on a stone fountain, which provides space for relaxing and reflection and adds ambiance to the clinical setting.

The atrium allows for a dramatic lobby, filled with natural light that illuminates a curved curtain wall, accentuated by a grand spiral staircase and adorned with a bold contemporary art mobile. The staircase connects to family waiting areas, which overlook the lobby on all levels. Close by are twenty-nine LDRP rooms, five C-section OR suites, and a women's diagnostic imaging center.

Finally ESa designed the women's center to accommodate a future expansion of four more floors, for a total of seven stories, as well as horizontal expansion on the ground level.

WOMEN'S CENTER AT DEKALB MEDICAL CENTER
NORTH DECATUR CAMPUS
Decatur, Georgia

Designed by CDH Partners, the new 163,000-sq.-ft. Women's Center at DeKalb Medical Center in a suburb of metropolitan Atlanta offers an array of obstetric, gynecological, and maternity services, with an emphasis on family-centered, maternity care.

The center's rooms—designed to resemble lodge rooms with soothing colors, natural stone accents, antique brick, amber lighting, lobby fireplaces, and mission-style furnishings—are all private.

The five-story facility includes eighteen private LDR hotel-like suites, which allow expectant mothers to stay in the same room before, during, and after delivery. There are eight private family waiting areas next to the LDR suites. The center is also equipped with large antepartum rooms for expectant mothers requiring hospitalization before delivery. Finally, there are sixty-two postpartum mother-baby rooms with high-speed Internet access, refrigerators, private bathrooms, and window seat couches to accommodate guests.

Women's Center at DeKalb Medical Center, North Decatur Campus, Decatur, Georgia. *Courtesy CDH Partners, Inc. Photo CDH Partners, Inc., staff photographer.*

Other features at the center include a new bistro, a business center, a 100-seat auditorium, classrooms, a boutique, and underground parking with an underground elevator that takes patients directly to the admissions department.

ST. LUKE'S SUGAR LAND HOSPITAL

Sugar Land, Texas

Located on greenfield campus in a suburb of Houston, St. Luke's Sugar Land Hospital has a full floor dedicated to women's services, including a newborn nursery and a Level III neonatal intensive care unit. The 220,000-sq.-ft., five-story hospital also offers a wide spectrum of other inpatient and outpatient services. Another full floor is dedicated to critical-care services, which

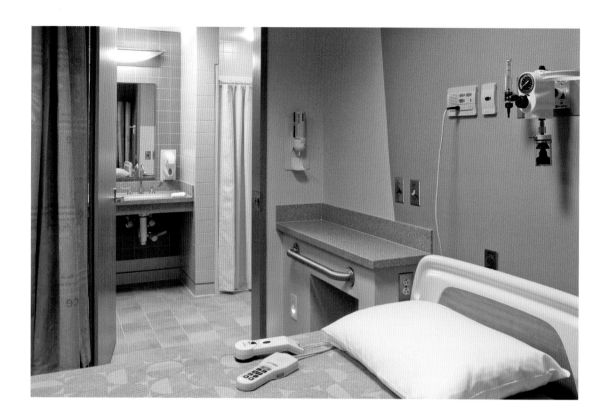

St. Luke's Sugar Land Hospital, Sugar Land, Texas. Aiming to design a safer hospital, architect Page Southerland Page, LLP, reduced the transfer distance between the patient bed and the bathroom to an eight-foot journey aided by a continuous handrail. *Courtesy Page Southerland Page, LLP. Photo Carl Mayfield Photography.*

include a sixteen-bed adult intensive care unit, eight surgical suites, two cardiac catheterization labs, and an eleven-room emergency department with five pediatric observation rooms. Adjacent to the ED is a full-service imaging department, which provides MRI, CT, nuclear medicine, angiography, mammography, ultrasound, and general radiography and fluoroscopy services.

Since architect Page Southerland Page aimed to design a safer hospital, the transfer distance between the patient bed and the bathroom was reduced to an eight-foot journey aided by a continuous handrail. All of the hospital's 100 private rooms were designed to be same-handed, and, thanks to this same-handed design with its offset, corridor-side (inboard) bathrooms, all of the rooms are handicap-accessible. The design also allowed for larger windows, increasing the natural light in the rooms, which also include family zones.

The two patient floors include bariatric rooms that can be converted to VIP rooms when required. A large two-story rotunda connects the hospital to the campus's five-story, 125,000-sq.-ft. medical office building. Both the hospital and the MOB are constructed with steel framing and a glass curtain wall system using highly energy-efficient glass.

KATZ WOMEN'S HOSPITAL
LONG ISLAND JEWISH MEDICAL CENTER
New Hyde Park, New York

This building, designed by Skidmore, Owings & Merrill (SOM), is both a medical facility and the centerpiece of a revitalization plan for the 48-acre campus. Acting as a new front door to the hospital's main tower, the

250,000-sq.-ft. structure consolidates women's services and provides health-care to expectant mothers through the creation of spaces for diagnostic and treatment services, labor and delivery, ante- and postpartum care, C-section operating rooms, 102 replacement beds, and a nursery for sixty newborns.

These facilities improve efficiency and provide a high degree of comfort for patient- and family-focused care in a soothing and humane environment. The building infrastructure and all building systems allow for future vertical expansion of two additional stories, accommodating thirty medical/surgical beds each, for uses that will be determined by the client in response to the rapidly changing needs of the healthcare marketplace.

SOM used Revit software to create a comprehensive Building Information Model (BIM) that allowed them to incorporate limited outsourced BIM services and take advantage of remote collaboration with consultants.

Katz Women's Hospital, Long Island Jewish Medical Center, New Hyde Park, New York. The women's lounge. *Courtesy Skidmore, Owings & Merrill. Photo © SOM.*

Freestanding Women's Hospitals

While there are many hospitals that offer special services to women, fewer hospitals are entirely devoted to women's care in the United States. Some are affiliated with acute-care hospitals; others are independent facilities. As might be expected, obstetrics is the core of the women's hospital, account-ing for a high percentage of patient discharges. However, as Mark Wietecha of Hamilton/KSA (an Atlanta-based consulting firm) once observed, wom-en's hospitals' reliance on obstetrics could prove disastrous for them if no changes occur. More acute-care hospitals are getting back into the birthing business, and that may draw patients away from some women's hospitals. On the other hand, as more women's hospitals offer increasingly comprehensive care, such as plastic surgery and cardiology—two specialties extensively used by women—it is likely that competition between acute-care and women's hospitals will intensify even further. At minimum, some women's hospitals are branching into such services as high-risk pregnancies, perinatology, neonatology, breast and uterine cancer detection and treatment, in vitro fertilization, urodynamics (focusing on urinary incontinence), urinary reconstructive surgery, cosmetic surgery, and behavioral health. A few of these hospitals also offer general surgery, cardiology, and other mainstream services.

BAPTIST MEMORIAL HOSPITAL FOR WOMEN
Memphis, Tennessee

ESa designed the 260,000-sq.-ft. women's hospital with an MOB as part of its system planning for Baptist Memorial's network of facilities in western Tennessee.

This freestanding facility designed exclusively as a women's hospital is also considered an extension of Baptist Memorial East. While all of those services associated specifically with women's care have been relocated from Baptist Memorial East, the facility does not have the ED usually associated with a new hospital. Instead, emergency cases are handled at Baptist Memorial East (though the women's hospital does have an ambulance entry for patients arriving after hours).

The design of the Baptist Memorial Hospital for Women sought to provide maximum functionality and flexibility while balancing the demands of women's healthcare within the restricted space of its site. To purchase the land for the project—which was to include a 100,000-sq.-ft. MOB and a parking garage large enough to accommodate nearly 700 cars—Baptist Memorial had to secure the approval of two suburban neighborhood associations. Located on 9 acres bordered by a lake, the site posed several design challenges due to space limitations created by existing buildings, utility easements, and local height restrictions and setback requirements.

Nevertheless, Baptist Memorial Hospital for Women houses under one roof most of the services and resources

Baptist Memorial Hospital for Women, Memphis, Tennessee. Main lobby with its fountain focal point. *Photo Scott McDonald © Hedrich Blessing.*

Baptist Memorial Hospital for Women, Memphis, Tennessee. Typical labor/ delivery/recovery/post-partum room. *Photo Scott McDonald © Hedrich Blessing.*

necessary for the treatment of female patients, with the exception of cardiac and oncology surgical services. The 140-bed hospital provides a comprehensive program for women supported with advanced technology. It includes twenty-three LDR rooms, thirteen antepartum patient rooms, twenty-six women's medical/surgical rooms, forty-seven postpartum patient rooms, forty neonatal intensive care beds, three C-section rooms, three GYN/surgical operating rooms, four ICU beds, and nine OB triage spaces. Educational programs are provided for in a 180-seat educational forum, and a dining area seats a hundred staff, patients, and visitors. The connector hallway leading from the lobby to the physicians' office building doubles as a patient mall, offering such amenities as retail and a women's resource library.

The prevailing look is noninstitutional, with residential-style furnishings, ample natural light, and extensive outdoor landscaping. Because of the shared services with Baptist Memorial East, exterior signage design proved critical in clearly directing hospital patients and visitors to the appropriate facilities.

Baptist Memorial Hospital for Women offers the birthing, surgical, acute-care, and medical and diagnostic services—mammography, ultrasound, and lab—appropriate to women in a gracious, comfortable, and even luxurious home ambiance that allows the Baptist Memorial network to meet the needs of a large and now well-established portion of the healthcare facility market.

WOMEN'S HOSPITAL AT CENTENNIAL MEDICAL CENTER
Nashville, Tennessee

ESa integrated West Side Hospital into a new medical center, transforming the hospital into the Women's Hospital at Centennial Medical Center, a center of excellence in women's care. The facility provides a patient-focused, family-oriented birthing unit as well as the entire range of women's services. This includes gynecology and a women's imaging center that is separate from the hospital proper but adjacent to it. In addition, the Women's Hospital offers counseling programs, educational programs, minor ambulatory surgery, plastic surgery, a breast center, urology services, and diagnostic services that target heart disease, stroke, and cancer—leading causes of death among women that are not encompassed in the traditional gynecological practice. The Women's Hospital directly interfaces with a cancer treatment center. As part of the services offered, the hospital maintains one of the most successful

Women's Hospital at Centennial Medical Center, Nashville, Tennessee. The redesigned entrance has been redefined by a glass and steel canopy. *Photo Bill LaFevor.*

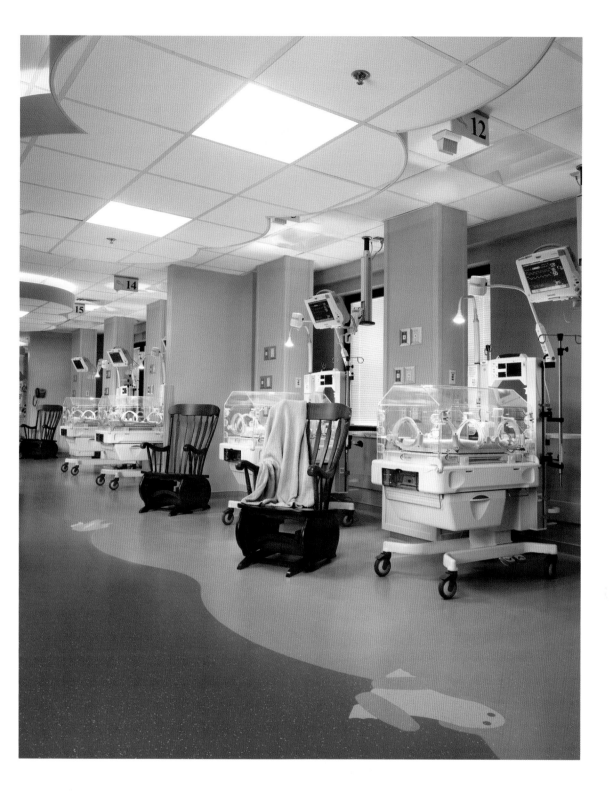

in vitro fertilization programs in the country. A women's resource library is located in an adjacent MOB and offers books, videotapes, and pamphlets that can be examined at the center or at home. Since the Women's Hospital is part of the Centennial Medical Center, a pediatric unit is located nearby, which, like the Women's Hospital itself, is family-oriented.

The Women's Hospital has two floors of residential-style LDR rooms. All of the rooms feature birthing beds, a stabilization bed for the newborn, designer decor, and soft lighting. The eighth-floor LDR rooms are larger,

Women's Hospital at Centennial Medical Center, Nashville, Tennessee. NICU. *Photo Vince Wallace/Silver Hill Images.*

and they are equipped with such luxury features as whirlpool baths. After recovery, mothers are transferred to fourth-floor post-delivery rooms that are also designer-decorated and feature whirlpool baths. The room eventually becomes the setting for a candlelight dinner for the mother and father. The average length of stay is only 1.5 to 2.1 days for vaginal deliveries.

A well-baby nursery is located on the same floor as the post-delivery suites, and the NICU—discussed in Chapter 8—is located on the seventh floor for adjacency to the LDR rooms and other birthing facilities. A lactation clinic completes the menu of birthing services. This is an important service because it promotes the health of the newborn (no artificial formula is superior to mother's milk), enhances the mothering experience, and strengthens the bond between mother and child, yet it is also highly cost-efficient.

In the summer of 2000, ESa expanded and renovated parts of the already thriving hospital to add more services and larger, more comfortable room accommodations. For convenience and easy accessibility, the entrance drive-through was redesigned and then redefined with a new glass and steel canopy. The first-floor program now includes a new, natural light-filled lobby, waiting area, admitting space, retail stores, and a coffee shop. The second-floor dining area was renovated and rearranged to include a new, dedicated children's dining room. Finally, the fifth floor was totally reworked for enlarged LDRP suites—every three former patient room spaces were converted into two room spaces, allowing for family members, additional storage, and the latest technology.

Park Ridge Hospital, Fletcher, North Carolina. The birthing center, called The Baby Place, features a spa room. *Photo © Kyle Dreier Photography.*

Freestanding Ambulatory and Birthing Centers

Although many caregivers, administrators, and entrepreneurs believed during the 1980s that women wanted women's services outside of a hospital setting, more recently they have learned that women actually prefer women's healthcare centers that are within a hospital setting, but retain a separate identity from the hospital, including a separate entrance. Meanwhile, however, many freestanding women's healthcare centers were built across the nation. The most successful of these freestanding ambulatory and birthing centers offer the following convenient and cost-effective qualities:

- Flexible and extensive office hours
- Readily available parking
- Minimum wait time
- A community-based approach
- Advance notice for fees/services, including lab tests
- Female staff

Piedmont Fayette Hospital, Fayetteville, Georgia. The labor/delivery/recovery/patient rooms in the women's health center are spacious, with zones for the newborn, family, and caregivers. *Photo © Rion Rizzo/Creative Sources.*

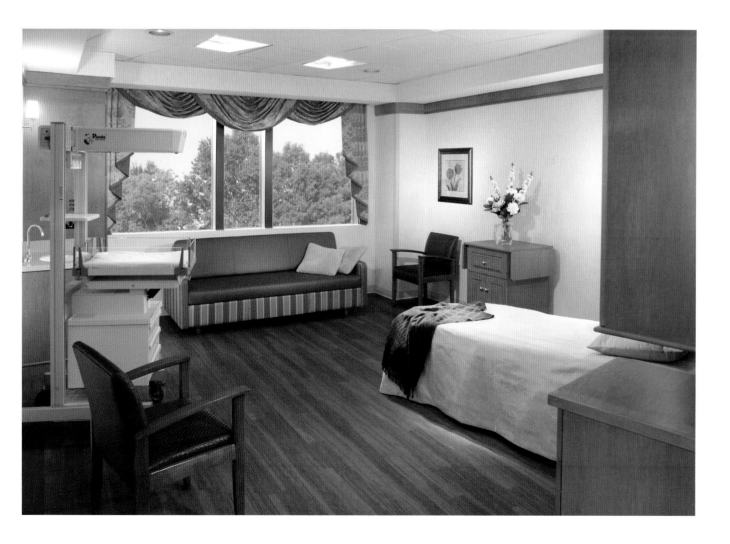

It is possible to design a freestanding women's center primarily as OB/GYN space, but the trend is to make such centers genuine centers—devoted to traditional OB/GYN functions, but with educational materials, programs, imaging, and psychological counseling available, including dedicated space for women's support groups.

Here are some design considerations for the freestanding women's center:

- *Sophisticated decor.* It is a mistake to assume that designing for women automatically means a faux French provincial look with ruffles and lace. The typical women's center client is likely to be sophisticated and non-traditional. Color and design, accordingly, should be both comfortable and sophisticated and fit well within the local community.

- *Space for education.* Provide a few private study carrels and, perhaps, a multipurpose room for lectures and seminars. Such programs not only serve the community, but they also focus attention on the facility as a genuine center for women's health concerns. If possible, allocate modest library space with electronic access to information.

- *Examination rooms.* Emphasize comfort and amenities here. Provide private dressing spaces and a mirror. Use attractive casework to store away medical instruments. Display artwork.

- *Consultation room/office.* Furnish this private room with a desk, lounge chairs, and a coffee table to encourage a relaxed, inviting space for consultation.

- *Specimen pass-through between the patient restroom and the lab.* This obviates the necessity of walking through a public area with a specimen.

- *Countertop height.* Bear in mind that the facility will be used by women and, likely, in large measure staffed by women. Make sure that countertop heights are appropriate for a 5-foot-4 woman, not a 6-foot man. Average countertop height is 36 inches; consider 32 to 34-inch heights instead for adjustable work counters.

Even before freestanding women's centers appeared, alternative birthing centers commanded a good deal of press coverage. In the early 1990s, more birthing centers opened and accounted for one-third of nonhospital births, or less than one-half of 1 percent of births in the United States. By the mid-1990s, there were 135 birthing centers in the United States with another 60 under development. By the late 1990s, birthing centers had become fashionable in American healthcare. These primary-care facilities are devoted to women who wish to experience a natural childbirth. If any medical complications arise during labor, the patient is rushed to the hospital.

The Future of Obstetrics

While hospital-based and freestanding women's health centers increased in popularity in the last several decades, they also came to no longer represent

LeConte Medical Center, Sevierville, Tennessee. The Health Unit Coordinator station of the Dolly Parton Birthing Unit features a photograph of its benefactor, while birch twigs sandwiched within composite inlay panels grace the front of the desk. *Courtesy Earl Swensson Associates and BarberMcMurry Architects. Photo © Kyle Dreier Photography.*

the radical alternative to conventional hospital-based OB/GYN care that they once had. The conventions of traditional OB/GYN care changed to embrace the kinds of choices that alternative health centers offered.

Nowhere has this been truer than in birthing. Despite the proliferation of birthing alternatives, including home births, most births continue to occur in hospitals and are likely to do so for some time to come. Yet hospital obstetrical practices and accommodations have continued to evolve, according to the birthing center model. After all, a hospital-based birthing center offers mother and child the best of the alternative and conventional worlds: a comfortable, homelike setting that encourages natural childbirth and instant access to the emergency backup available in an acute-care setting.

Hospitals moved in these directions, in large part, because of market demand. It is also the kind of service many quite deliberately shop for, seeking not just medical competence but also the most supportive and attractive setting for what is always a momentous experience, and one that should be joyful.

Hospitals have trended toward two variations on homelike birth: LDR rooms and LDRP rooms. The second alternative, which is single-room maternity care, is the more radically patient-focused of the two, and it has steadily gained in popularity over the last two decades. In the LDRP setting, labor, delivery, recovery and postpartum recovery and care all take place in the same room.

LDRP rooms are essentially larger patient rooms with additional space and services. We have already reviewed some examples of the headwall that conceals medical gases and electrical outlets, the bed that converts to a delivery chair, equipment that can readily be wheeled in and out, and the ceiling-mounted, fully adjustable examination light. For the postpartum function, the LDRP room must be spacious enough to accommodate family members; it might include a window seat, which can be quickly converted to a bed for overnight family stays. A wall-mounted, fold-down table for in-room dining encourages the mother to get out of bed more quickly. If the room is large enough, a small standalone table can be included for dining. In general, the hospitality or residential model is quite appropriate for LDRP rooms.

NORTH CENTRAL BAPTIST HOSPITAL

San Antonio, Texas

When this once rural, 190,000-sq.-ft. hospital expanded by some 240,000 sq. ft. to accommodate the population growth in San Antonio, it renovated its surgery and recovery spaces and added a new adult and pediatric emergency department, outpatient staging, a cardiac center, and a women's center.

Designed by ESa, the new two-story atrium connects the new 140,000-sq.-ft. medical office building with the patient care tower and the Women's Center. Designed as a healing, patient-friendly addition to the existing hospital, the two-story lobby is filled with natural light from skylights and floor-to-ceiling curtain walls. This addition is structured for future vertical expansion of six more floors, for eight floors total, as the site cannot handle further horizontal growth.

The exterior aesthetic pays homage to the existing four-story brick hospital and to the vernacular and material textures found in the "hill country" architecture of central Texas. A Texas limestone-clad tower element adjacent to the Women's Center entry lends a sense of arrival. The hospital addition is designed for centers of excellence to be located on horizontal platforms. So the Women's Center, located on the second floor, is aligned with the obstetric physicians and the hospital's own in vitro fertilization lab on the second floor of the medical office building.

The hospital's LDR rooms are large, with their headwalls angled adjacent to the patient's bathroom, which orients the foot of the bed away from the door and offers more privacy for the expectant mother. It also orients the patient toward the

North Central Baptist Hospital, San Antonio, Texas. The headwalls of the large labor/delivery/recovery rooms are angled adjacent to the patient's bathroom, orienting the foot of the bed away from the door and toward the exterior window for unobstructed views of the outside. *Photo © Kieran Reynolds Photography.*

family area of the room and toward the exterior window for unobstructed views of the outside. Support spaces are decentralized to minimize staff travel and provide for quick access. The corridors have equipment alcoves outside each pair of rooms, to cut staff travel distances.

The NICU is an open ward to provide visibility throughout the unit and allow for ease of staff coverage. It is convenient to the C-section and LDR beds and to the public entry into the OB unit to allow easy access for family members. The postpartum unit mimics a hospitality suite. Nursing workstations and alcoves were decentralized throughout the unit in an effort to keep staff closer to the patients.

AVISTA ADVENTIST HOSPITAL
Louisville, Colorado

"Patients are anxious to have a quality experience," John Sackett, chief executive officer of Avista Adventist Hospital in Louisville, Colorado, told ESa. The facility was expanded and renovated by some 100,000 sq. ft. The hospital, located in a high-population-growth area (in the child-bearing age group especially) in Louisville, Colorado, near Boulder, extended and improved its obstetrics program.

Called the "New Life Center," the number of birthing suites grew from nineteen to twenty-eight, medical/surgical rooms increased by nineteen, and the emergency department was enlarged with the inclusion of a children's play area. ESa created a new front-door lobby for the hospital and added a gift shop and informal dining area, turning the existing lobby into an entry for the medical office building.

Avista Adventist Hospital, Louisville, Colorado. The spacious patient rooms in the New Life Center allow necessary space for medical personnel and equipment during labor and delivery. *Photo Scott McDonald © Hedrich Blessing.*

The hospital had, of course, always provided accommodations for mothers needing labor, delivery, recovery and postpartum care, and it did so traditionally in one room. So Avista Adventist opted to continue that tradition in its expanded obstetrics program, after interviews with mothers and pregnant women showed they preferred it that way— remaining in one room for their entire stay.

Avista Adventist's decision to build a twenty-eight-bed unit for LDRP, something of a departure from the national norm, grew out of the fact that the hospital's heaviest patient volume lay

Avista Adventist Hospital, Louisville, Colorado. The tranquility of the New Life Center spa room provides respite for new mothers. *Photo Scott McDonald © Hedrich Blessing.*

in obstetrics, where its doctors delivered an average of 210 babies a month. In the first year, the number of mothers delivering children exceeded the number of new beds more than a dozen times, and the overflow had to be accommodated in the old center's space, so, clearly, the hospital had understood its market.

In Avista Adventist's New Life Center, the LDRP rooms are oriented so that beds lie along angled walls, facing windows. The configuration affords patient privacy and allows the beds to be closer to the doors of the rooms, providing convenient access to the patient for the nursing staff. The angled beds also prevent passersby from seeing patients, which, in turn, eliminated the need for curtains, so no cubicle curtain tracks were installed.

Each pair of maternity rooms has a front-door "porch," that is, an inset with a large column that keeps out hallway noise. In addition, the floor and wall finishes make the entire New Life Center much quieter than the old space. And LDRP rooms have an area for neonatal resuscitation. The Center has a storage supply closet for every two rooms within the setback room entry, which cuts down clutter, and a locked cabinet built into each patient-bed footwall provides for minor medication storage.

The New Life Center also boasts C-section rooms and well-baby nurseries, situated with a mind toward traffic flow. Next to the central nursing station sit four triage or antepartum rooms, which allow mothers in early stages of labor to be observed. At first, staff worried that the center was too large, but they soon saw that the circular arrangement of rooms around the central core made for better efficiency than the old linear arrangement. A nurses' lounge behind the central station allows the nurses to stay within the unit while taking breaks.

Instead of installing tubs in every patient room, the designers opted for a more efficient but quite luxurious spa within the center, which provides a space for mothers to be pampered. (An art glide on the wall conceals available medical gases in case of emergency).

The new construction flows so seamlessly into the existing hospital that patients coming to the medical campus for the first time have been unable to tell where the new expansion begins and the old facility ends.

THE WOMAN'S HOSPITAL OF TEXAS

Houston, Texas

The four-story west tower addition to the existing four-story hospital, designed by ESa, adds ninety-six patient beds, twenty-six NICU positions, and 175,583 sq. ft. Since the goals were to not only increase patient capacity but also to enhance functional efficiencies and patient flow, ESa strategically placed the new services and renovated areas.

Intending to create a welcoming ambiance, the designers used warm woods, a neutral color palette, and an abundance of natural light in the addition. They redid the main entrance and lobby to provide a larger drop-off area and a weather-protected walkway from the hospital to the main parking structure. Within the new patient rooms, every bed is in a monitored position and has a computer at the bedside for documentation. The spacious rooms provide family members with comfortable furniture to encourage overnight stays. The facility is equipped for wireless Internet access.

The project's multiple phases began with a full powerhouse replacement and upgrades to the emergency department, radiology, and utilities. The new addition, which includes the drop-off entrance, lobby, loading dock, kitchen, dining, post- and antepartum units and NICU positions, was completed next. Renovations of the C-section recovery, LDR rooms, laboratory, medical records, and the balance of the radiology department were completed in the final phase.

The Woman's Hospital of Texas, Houston, Texas. Intending to create a welcoming ambiance, ESa used warm woods, a neutral color palette, and an abundance of natural light in the new addition. *Photo James F. Wilson.*

The world of childhood naturally invites daring, fantasy, and innovation. Childhood and its needs are, by their very nature, anti-institutional. The enlightened children's hospital does more than deal with a child's medical and surgical problems. It creates an environment that addresses physical, social, developmental, and emotional needs. Moreover, it takes into account not only the child's needs but those of his family. More and more children's hospitals and pediatric facilities encourage family participation in the treatment and healing process, not as just a matter of policy, but by providing for families in the design of the facility.

Indeed, most healthcare facilities are now awakening to the importance of providing for families. In the case of children's healthcare facilities, providing for the family should not be considered an add-on design feature, but rather the starting point. This means making parental sleeping accommodations part of the design from the beginning, providing a family lounge and, perhaps, a meditation room—a quiet place to take a break from the emotionally and physically draining demands of caring for a seriously ill child. Sleeping accommodations may be as simple as a chair that opens into a bed in a patient room large enough to accommodate it or as extensive as full guest suites. The needs of siblings, too, should be remembered. Child-care resources for siblings might be made available in a dedicated space. At the very least, a playroom should be part of the family accommodations.

Having made sure to include both patients and parents in the design process, here are other key design goals:

- *Easy access to information and technology for patients and parents.*
- *Interaction with peers.* The inclusion of playrooms, lounges, and classrooms enhances social interaction among children. Even well-designed corridors, especially those with bays or alcoves, invite such interaction. Depression and a sense of isolation are major psychological factors in any seriously ill person. They may be quite intense in a child or adolescent. Peer interaction does much for morale and, therefore, promotes healing.
- *Control of territory.* Anyone who has children knows how they feel about their rooms. To the child, her room is a nest, a refuge, a special place that empowers her in ways denied her in other parts of the house. Patient-room design should enhance this sense of territoriality. This begins with the orientation of furniture. The child's back should be against the wall, not toward the center of the room. When people enter the room, they should face the child, not approach her from behind. Children have the same privacy needs as other patients—it's just that, in an adult world, this need is not always respected. Finally, it is useful to provide pediatric rooms with space—a shelf, an alcove—for a child's treasures and toys. A closet or some other secure place to keep belongings also adds to her sense of security, a feeling that the item she loves and is familiar with will be safe.
- *Independence.* The environment should promote a sense of independence, including (as much as possible) freedom of movement and a sense of

competency. Color coding and carefully placed art features can aid both by assisting wayfinding.

- *Access to outdoors.* Children love to play outdoors. Include such amenities as a patio, deck, solarium, or healing garden. As the National Association of Children's Hospitals and Related Institutions (NACHRI) resource guide makes clear, evidence-based design hails the many benefits of access to nature.

- *Stimulation of imagination/fantasy.* The NACHRI resource also touts the clear benefit of positive distraction for children's health. Art is especially useful in this regard, and some facilities, such as the Vanderbilt University Medical Center—whose children's facility, Monroe Carell Jr. Children's Hospital at Vanderbilt, we discuss below—has deployed fine art to aid the healing of its patients.

ROCKY MOUNTAIN HOSPITAL FOR CHILDREN
PRESBYTERIAN/ST. LUKE'S MEDICAL CENTER
Denver, Colorado

ESa's design of this "children's hospital within a hospital" addition to the Presbyterian St. Luke's Medical Center relates contextually to the surrounding area and projects a warm, familiar, healing environment to the patients and families it serves throughout the Colorado region. The scale of the exterior harmonizes with the surrounding urban residential neighborhood. Its restricted height preserves views of the Rocky Mountains from regional parks and residences.

Rocky Mountain Hospital for Children, Presbyterian/St. Luke's Medical Center, Denver, Colorado. The lobby relates to the natural beauty of the surrounding area while projecting a warm, cozy, healing environment. *Photo © Michael Peck.*

Rocky Mountain Hospital for Children, Presbyterian/St. Luke's Medical Center, Denver, Colorado. Staircase in the lobby. *Photo © Michael Peck.*

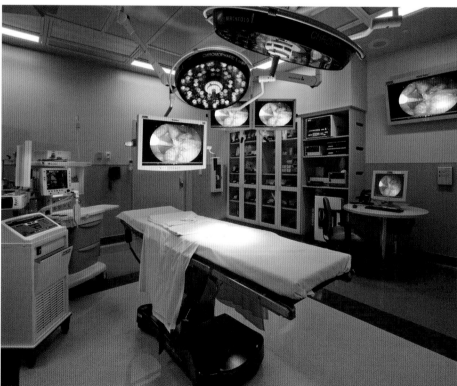

Rocky Mountain Hospital for Children, Presbyterian/St. Luke's Medical Center, Denver, Colorado. An operating room. *Photo © Michael Peck.*

The hospital includes thirty-six private pediatric medical/surgical beds, ten PICU beds, eight pediatric oncology beds, a pediatric surgery center, outpatient services, and an adult/pediatric emergency department. Amenities include a fireplace in the lobby; interactive artwork and play areas; a family resource center; chapel, family laundry, and shower facilities; a Ronald McDonald House; and spacious patient rooms with desk areas and wireless technology. Nature themes are integrated throughout the spaces. To provide for future growth, the design allows the ability to add two more floors.

ESa faced a major challenge in designing a separate identity for the children's hospital on an established urban healthcare campus. The entrance to the site, situated on a road perpendicular to the existing main hospital entrance, permitted the designers to create a unique children's campus entry with appropriate scale and identity. Tying the children's hospital's new construction to the existing hospital played a significant role in the overall design. Although there is a variation between existing and new floor-to-floor heights, ESa created a dedicated circulation tower between the two structures to allow a seamless transition when traversing from one to the other.

CHILDREN'S HOSPITAL OF PITTSBURGH OF UPMC

Pittsburgh, Pennsylvania

Located in Pittsburgh's Lawrenceville neighborhood and situated on 10 acres, this new children's hospital, internationally recognized for its outstanding clinical services, research programs, and medical education, boasts a new design that distinguishes itself as a model for pediatric healthcare. The architectural firm Astorino brought together research, design, and conceptual thinking in a process that took into account the thoughts and feelings of parents, patients, and hospital staff and arrived at a design grounded in family-centered care, the latest technology, the environmental sustainability of a green campus, a quiet building, the safety of the facility's patients, and the quality of their stay.

The focus on family-centered care led to the inclusion of private rooms that create a more homelike environment, bright colors and soft fabrics, comfortable sleeping spaces for parents, a desk with data ports and Internet access in each patient room, caregiver stations located closer to patient rooms, and a playroom fully equipped with toys, movies, games, and books. The facility's 20,000-sq.-ft. resource center includes an atrium, a chapel, a library, a healing garden, and a business center for working parents. In the atrium area, the hospital can feature movies and large group activities.

Throughout the hospital, easy-to-follow directional signs and electronic messaging boards make wayfinding simple for patients and visitors. The hospital also offers in-room entertainment, as well as group events and a wide variety of food in a spacious cafeteria or as room service. There is a gift shop in the main lobby and ample, convenient parking. Other family-friendly features include a sibling center, outdoor garden areas adjacent to the cafeteria, daycare, and a central conference center. The hospital's large waiting areas are furnished with child-friendly pieces and play tables. There are teen lounges with computers, videos, games, and music. The hospital also offers family laundry facilities.

The hospital's 1.5 million sq. ft. of usable space includes nine floors of inpatient and outpatient care areas, the aforementioned spacious, private rooms designed with kids in mind, the 20,000-sq.-ft. family resource and activity center (one of the largest in the world), and 296 licensed beds, 41 of them in the emergency room and trauma center, 79 in the CCU, 36 in the pediatric ICU, 12 in the cardiac ICU, and 31 in the neonatal ICU. There are thirteen operating suites, six of them equipped with leading-edge minimally invasive equipment. State-of-the-art technology, including a nursing workstation for every two patient rooms in addition to computer and communications equipment, enhances communication within teams of caregivers. The hospital's paperless information management system allows physicians to place nearly all inpatient care orders electronically, eliminating handwritten and verbal orders.

The technological sophistication, however, is broader than that, incorporating a high level of technology to improve patient care, reduce human error, and improve patient, visitor, and staff safety, while providing operating efficiencies to manage costs effectively. Children's Hospital of Pittsburgh was among the first fully digital hospitals in the country, and its infrastructure services include a campuswide wireless data network that enables access to electronic health records, prescription writing, and other clinical and nonclinical applications. Its power service cannot be interrupted, and the facility offers 100 percent access to the Internet. The cell-phone friendly facility has a campuswide wireless phone system, soft phones, and a centralized call center for billing inquiries, staff scheduling, and patient inquiries. There is a housewide patient tracking and child abduction system and a provider (nurse) call (inpatient and outpatient) system integrated with patient equipment, to monitor any patient and family communications and send calls directly to care provider wireless phones to allow a more timely response.

Children's Hospital of Pittsburgh was designed as a green campus, meaning it uses key resources such as energy, water, materials, and land more efficiently than buildings erected simply to building code. The hospital's environmentally sustainable buildings, with their natural lighting and better air quality, contribute to the improved health, comfort, and productivity of their residents. The hospital's commitment to green practices extends beyond its bricks and mortar and is reflected in its new operating policies and procedures regarding facility maintenance, housekeeping, food service, and waste management. Children's clinicians, academicians, and community members also conduct research on sustainability and its health effects on children.

As part of its green profile, Children's is resolutely friendly to the environment and offers easy access to public transportation, bike racks and showers, preferred parking for van pools, discounted parking for car pools, and water-efficient landscaping. The hospital uses recycled building materials (including recycled postconsumer structural steel), local and regional construction materials to reduce transportation issues, and low volatile organic compound (VOC) materials such as sealants, adhesives, paints, and carpets.

It installs air-filtration systems that increase indoor air quality and water fixtures that reduce water use. The hospital also offers a green education program for staff, patients, and visitors.

Since research shows that a quiet hospital environment enhances patient healing and satisfaction among healthcare providers, Children's Hospital of Pittsburgh was designed to be one of the quietest hospitals in existence. Its scheme to reduce noise in patient areas, public spaces, conference rooms, lounges, and consultation rooms included: masonry exterior walls for most patient rooms; floor-to-deck full-height partitions, sealed and insulated; multilayer drywall partitions in patient rooms; acoustic ceiling tile in lieu of hard ceilings; extensive carpeting and door seals; remote locations for staff work areas and consult rooms; sound-deadened elevator cab enclosures; extensive vibration isolators; a remote central plant location that eliminated noise from boilers, chillers, and generators; cast iron piping for storm and sanitary stacks; the use of personal communication devices in lieu of overhead paging; the silent notification of nurse call through integration of wireless communication devices; the silent notification of alarms from monitoring equipment through integration to wireless communication devices, and soft wheels on mobile carts.

To keep patients and their families safe and to enhance the quality of their stay, Children's Hospital considered everything from such obvious touches as offering separate garages and elevators for patients to more subtle improvements such as including pass-through nurse servers between corridors and

Children's Hospital of Pittsburgh of UPMC, Pittsburgh, Pennsylvania. Located in Pittsburgh's Lawrenceville neighborhood and situated on 10 acres, this facility boasts a distinguished new design grounded in the environmental sustainability of a "green campus." Courtesy Astorino. Photo Alexander Denmarsh.

patient rooms to restock supplies or dispose of dirty linens and dietary trays. Aimed at improving infection rates, patient privacy, and noise level, nearly half of the operating rooms in the new hospital are designed to accommodate minimally invasive procedures. All operative services are located on one floor including operating suites, a catheterization lab, interventional radiology, a procedures center, and an infusion center. The hospital's catheterization lab is designed to mimic the operating room environment, so if a more invasive procedure is required, the patient does not have to be moved to a different location. Specialized units, such as cardiac intensive care and oncology, are located close to the labs and other services often used by these specialties. An onsite linear accelerator and PET/ CT scanner eliminate the need for patients to travel to other buildings for these services. And the hospital's isolated rooms and playrooms ensure containment of contagious disease.

Children's Hospital of Pittsburgh of UPMC, Pittsburgh, Pennsylvania. The focus on family-centered care led to a more homelike environment by using bright colors and soft fabrics. In the atrium area, the hospital can feature movies and large group activities. *Courtesy Astorino. Photo Alexander Denmarsh.*

Finally, the new building cuts a playful shape against the horizon and is bathed in vibrant hues like blue, yellow, and red. This friendly looking and iconic building is visible from miles around and acts as a welcoming beacon, putting children and their parents at ease. Justly touted, Children's Hospital of Pittsburgh is one of eight pediatric hospitals in the United States named to *U.S. News & World Report*'s Honor Roll of America's "Best Children's Hospitals" for 2010–2011. It is ranked tenth in total dollars and seventh in number of awards from the National Institutes of Health for the NIH's 2008 fiscal year. It was named a 2009 Top Hospital for the second straight year by the Leapfrog Group, an independent patient safety organization. It is the first pediatric hospital in this country to achieve Stage 7 recognition from HIMSS Analytics for its electronic medical records. And it has been recognized by KLAS, an independent healthcare research organization, as the number one pediatric hospital in its use of healthcare information technology.

PEDIATRIC SUB-SPECIALTIES SUITE, OVERLOOK HOSPITAL
Summit, New Jersey

Designed by Buckl Architects, Inc., Overlook Hospital's pediatric sub-specialties office suite in the Medical Arts Center 2 opened in March 2010. The new medical arts center project includes four distinct pediatric specialty units: one for eating disorders, one for pediatric surgery, the Valerie Center for oncology treatment, and a multispecialty clinic with distinct areas for neurology, cardiology, gastrointestinal disorders, and general patient visits.

The main waiting area of the sub-specialties clinic provides a bright, open space with natural light and views to the east of the New York City skyline. Patients check in at an automated kiosk inside the front door and provide the details of their visit at registration stations on both sides of the waiting area, from which staff monitors the waiting room and its visitors. An intake room on both sides of the waiting room channels the flow of patients from waiting to intake to exam room.

Buckl designed the suites to flex up and down into each other for variations in scheduling loads. They made room finishes very lively to keep in tune with the playfulness and energy of pediatric patients, creating a sense of fun to help distract kids even as they go to see the doctor. The exam rooms combine areas for exams and consults and provide comfortable banquettes for family and sibling seating.

As part of the comprehensive pediatric specialty services, the hospital's eating disorders clinic found a new location for its unique services to a special group of children and young adults suffering from obesity and other food-related problems. The reception and waiting areas of the eating disorder's clinic offer what the architects call "a fresh yet sophisticated palette intended to soothe rather than excite."

Pediatric Sub-specialties Suite, Overlook Hospital, Summit, New Jersey. Buckl Architects, Inc., designed the suite with very lively finishes—as at this nurses' station and intake and exam rooms hallway—to keep in tune with the playfulness and energy of pediatric patients. *Courtesy Buckl Architects, Inc. Photo Greg Benson Photography.*

Pediatric Sub-specialties Suite, Overlook Hospital, Summit, New Jersey. The waiting area of Overlook's sub-specialties clinic provides a bright, open space with natural light. *Courtesy Buckl Architects, Inc. Photo Greg Benson Photography.*

The eating disorder's suite includes weigh-in and exam areas, private meeting and group rooms, and a flexible meeting space for group dining, art therapy, and other interactive group activities. The sliding-glass partition maintains a sense of openness, even when the room is divided, and provides a cost-effective, operable wall system that is easy for staff to operate.

MONROE CARELL JR. CHILDREN'S HOSPITAL AT VANDERBILT
Nashville, Tennessee
Ranked by *Child* magazine as one of the top ten pediatric hospitals in the United States one year after opening its new freestanding facility, the Monroe Carell Jr. Children's Hospital at Vanderbilt also won the *Buildings'* Interior Design Award as not only a visually stunning, but also a cutting-edge facility that gives children a place to hope and heal.

The children's facility was formerly located on three floors within the adult Vanderbilt University Hospital. This "hospital within a hospital," was created in 1980 to support Vanderbilt's growing pediatric programs. Its patient rooms were small, which made it difficult to accommodate parents who needed to stay with their children. The pediatric programs were growing and spread out in multiple buildings across the medical center campus. There was a need to consolidate these programs into one facility and improve patient and family access.

With the aspirations to become a national model for family-centered care, Vanderbilt decided to construct a freestanding children's hospital that would free up badly needed space for adult services in the existing hospital and allow Vanderbilt to create a facility designed for children following certain specific guiding principles—the building's design was to be viewed from the eyes of a child, it was to enhance patient and family access, it was to establish clear lines of sight between patients and staff, it was to create spaces with flexible use, and it was to incorporate a Tennessee theme encompassing nature and water.

The architect, ESa, adhered to these principles throughout the project. A total of twenty-eight committees—including physicians, staff, former and current patients, parents, and donors—met with the architects throughout the design process. The end result was an eight-story, 206-inpatient-bed children's hospital and attached doctors' office tower as part of Vanderbilt University Medical Center's campus.

Consolidating this 660,000-plus-sq.-ft. building onto its designated 2-acre site was no easy task. The hospital required certain services to be located on the ground floor (such as the emergency room and main entrance) and other services built off of these particular points (placing the imaging center, for example, next to the emergency room). Vanderbilt wanted to use

Monroe Carell Jr. Children's Hospital at Vanderbilt, Nashville, Tennessee. The curving canopy and serpentine wall surrounding the healing garden allude to the hospital's theme of "Ribbons of Hope and Rivers of Healing." *Photo Scott McDonald © Hedrich Blessing.*

this children's healthcare facility to convey its dedication to the well-being and comfort of not only its patients, but of physicians, staff, and family members as well. A third of its space would eventually be devoted to the patients' families—comfortable places to sleep close by, places to eat, family lounges with kitchen and laundry facilities, a fully equipped business center (with computers, fax machines, and telephones), even places to sit and reflect.

The idea was to create a hospital that doesn't feel like a hospital, vital to making children feel at ease in unfamiliar environments. ESa designed both the inside and outside of the building to welcome children. To make the hospital seem a place like their own, Vanderbilt constructed the facility of granite rather than the brick used on its medical campus and surrounding buildings. The hospital's name is displayed with paper dolls as part of

Monroe Carell Jr. Children's Hospital at Vanderbilt, Nashville, Tennessee. *A playful sculpture, a butterfly garden, curving ceiling elements, and color help soften the public "Main Street" on the second level leading from the parking garage. Photo Craig Dugan © Hedrich Blessing.*

325

its logo in letters that look as if they have been cut out of sheets of colored construction paper. Whimsical cones and cylinders are featured for young eyes to enjoy, but they truly house spaces for families. The hospital's public areas boast cheerful, interactive art—acrylic butterflies that can be set to fly, an operable train village, and playful sculptures. Bathroom fixtures, windowsills, and countertops are all set at a child's level to allow patients to see what goes on around them.

Drawing from a local natural resource—the rivers of Tennessee—the theme "Ribbons of Hope and Rivers of Healing" recurs abstractly throughout the hospital to simulate flowing water. Ribbonlike elements continue the theme at the top of the landing of the grand staircase, in the railing, and in the curving metal ceiling treatment on the main street. This helps children who are too young to read to navigate the halls on patient floors without getting lost. Additionally, floors and wings are organized as neighborhoods designated with colors and distinctive animal signage that allows children to make their way through the space. (Learning from the children's hospital experience, Vanderbilt hired a graphic designer to come in, review the entire medical complex, and help with its global wayfinding system).

Centered on evidence-based design, the facility offers patients exposure to nature though rooftop gardens, natural light, and outdoor scenery. It provides the positive distractions of interactive art displays and access to music, such as live performances on a theater-like stage. It allows patients to control their environments by managing their room lighting, and simplified wayfinding helps control anxieties. It places an emphasis on safety, on durability, and on ease of cleaning. Nothing too hard or complicated, familiar materials provide a comfortable environment, decrease anxiety, and promote healing. Vanderbilt set the goal that the design should respond to what the children see and what gives them joy, a design that should address the needs of children of all ages, heights, and developmental levels.

That did not mean designing the pediatric facility just for toddlers and no one else. The facility would be used by children and adolescents of all ages up to eighteen and—because of the nature of some illnesses—perhaps even on into their early twenties. It was necessary, then, to include imagery at many different physical levels and to try to avoid alienating older patients.

In the end, of course, it came down to designing for family. Families are crucial to the continuum of treatment, hence Vanderbilt's allocation of so much of its total square footage to family-centered space, as mentioned earlier. But to offer family members the best environment for supporting and comforting sick children and for working with physicians to make often hard but necessary decisions, the hospital also provided communal support areas especially for families. These include a chapel, a resource center, a room for children filled with information to explain illnesses, and supervised playrooms for patients and siblings. Finally, the hospital provides a convenient outpatient pharmacy and gift shop.

Physicians and staff also suffer some of the same pressures facing patients and their family members. Vanderbilt understood it was important to provide space for employees, too, to decompress—a rooftop garden, located on the

fourth floor, for example. Plus the design of the entire facility also allows natural light to pierce the core of the hospital, providing staff a span of sunlight they might not otherwise see in the course of a normal working day.

Other design elements also help physicians and staff, including access to the latest technologies in providing precision and convenience in patient care. Nurses' stations and team workrooms enjoy clear lines of sight into patient rooms, thanks to design configurations using open or glass enclosures to improve patient observation. Critical-care patient areas surround staff work areas, which afford staff a full view of all rooms. Screens viewing individual patient rooms hang from the ceiling above nurses' control centers and provide for more monitoring. Each private patient room has a "staff zone," which allows space for nurses and doctors.

In the end, Vanderbilt Children's Hospital creates an environment that makes it easier for children to get well. For, as the architectural and medical fields now recognize, the physical environment is as important to the healing process as any medical advance.

Monroe Carell Jr. Children's Hospital at Vanderbilt, Nashville, Tennessee. Configuration and placement of nursing control centers and glassed work areas allow nursing staff to be in full view of patient rooms. *Photo Scott McDonald © Hedrich Blessing.*

CHAPTER 12

Design for the Elderly

Subacute and Long-Term Care

F or centuries, old age has meant a period of seemingly inevitable, distressing, sometimes horrifying decline. Even those who managed to survive into their dotage faced years of pain, debilitation, and dependency. But science now believes that much of the physical deterioration brought on by age is far from inescapable, and fast-paced developments in physiological and biomedical research have given us some hope that old age could at last lose some of its dread. Perhaps the golden years may indeed be more golden than in the past and become years of healthier, more active living for millions.

The statistics certainly hint so. In modern Western societies, medical breakthroughs and healthier lifestyles have helped to increase life expectancy a couple of years each decade since the beginning of the twentieth century. In the United States today, according to the U.S. Census Bureau, the average life expectancy is 77.8 years; back in 1900, it was 47 years. The over-sixty-five crowd has been growing nearly twice as fast as younger folks. They now encompass 38.5 million or 12.6 percent of the general U.S. population, and that number will more than double in the next fifty years. Demographers warn that when the first baby boomers hit what in the twentieth century was considered retirement age in 2011, those numbers will explode and people sixty-five and older will account for one in five of all Americans by 2050. Not only that, they are not necessarily retiring at that age any longer, which means they are not looking for retirement homes as soon as they once did. Given this trend to stay in the workforce, even when older folks find the community in which they plan to spend their sunset years, they may now live there *and* go to work—at another type of job, perhaps, yet still going to work rather than enjoying leisure time.

There's more. Seniors eighty-five and older now constitute the fastest-growing segment of the country's population. According to the U.S. Census Bureau, these oldsters will grow to some 9 million by 2030 and then swell to 19 million by midcentury. Some demographers, not employed by the government, put that number at more like 48 million. And while most of the experts cap average life expectancy at eighty-five, some have argued that American newborns can count on living, on average, to one hundred years of age. Many medical professionals believe the maximum possible lifespan to be somewhere between 115 and 120 years, and not a few are determined to see folks reach that maximum. Medical advances have already had a profound effect on the quality of life among the aging. A federal survey, conducted yearly, revealed that the 20,000 sixty-five-and-older people it tracked enjoyed a steady decrease in chronic disabilities of all kinds, with the most dramatic reductions experienced by those over eighty-five.

In the past, added years have not always been a blessing. As twentieth-century medicine often extended life mechanically, the elderly sometimes learned new fears with the increasing frequency of such diseases as prostate cancer, Alzheimer's, and macular degeneration. Drawbacks were not always physiological—seniors were often concerned that their extra years might make up a life not worth living, but one spent neglected or forgotten in a nursing home where indifferent care was aimed at merely maintaining their bodies rather than improving their existence. To ensure that a longer life does not make for a painful and expensive curse, gerontologists are pursuing two different strategies to stave off the aging process. The first strategy accepts that aging is a biological given but that attendant disease, disability,

Freedom Pointe at The Villages, The Villages, Florida. Central courtyard of the Continuing Care Retirement Community. *Photo © Kieran Reynolds Photography.*

329

Massachusetts General Hospital, Center for Aging and Neurodisorders—Building 114, Charlestown, Massachusetts. The architects at Payette restored the four-story building to house Alzheimer's, Parkinson's, and aging research in the Department of Neurology. *Courtesy Payette. Photo © Bruce T. Martin.*

and decline can be retarded through exercise, diet, and advances in medicine. A more radical strategy, adopted by many geneticists, wishes to challenge nature directly and halt—or even reverse—degeneration in the body's cells.

Many medical breakthroughs have already had an impact on aging. The elderly see better today than ever before, thanks to the millions of cataract procedures performed each year. Ophthalmologists can now implant a new, artificial lens behind the iris, if needed, in a once cutting-edge procedure now so routine that it is done on an outpatient basis. Injured body parts and worn-out joints that once severely limited the mobility of senior citizens are now often surgically repaired: the number of hip and knee replacements has increased by tens of thousands annually. Most fractures can now be restored to the original state of mobility. New medicines slow the onset of osteoporosis, alleviate the dangers and distress of menopause, inhibit bone loss, and boost the waning sex drive. All of this makes for a healthier, happier, less fragile, and more mobile old age.

But doctors and medical researchers also warn of the dangers of overselling the miracles medicine can work. Alzheimer's, AIDS, cancer, heart disease, Parkinson's, and diabetes all remain problems for the elderly; cures—despite the advances in gene therapy and biotechnology—dance tantalizingly just out of reach. While architects and designers, no less than medical professionals, need to prepare for the nascent "elderly boom," they also need to keep in mind that, for the moment at least, while advancements in medicine promise us healthier, longer lives, unfortunately, "healthier" and "longer" still tend, at some point, to become mutually exclusive goals. Thus, designing for elderly patients sooner or later involves some kind of long-term, subacute care.

The long-term care facility most familiar to the elderly even today is the freestanding skilled nursing facility (SNF), once more commonly called a nursing home. Nursing homes today hold much of the same horror for the average patient that hospitals held in centuries past (as we discussed in Chapter 2). The very words "nursing home" conjure up the fears of a lonely old age and an undignified death, which is one reason the number of nursing-home residents continues to drop, despite an aging population. In some ways, this image is unfair since, as we make clear below, many SNFs provide high-quality care, and—with the right design and attention to purpose—they can be nicer places than the popular imagination allows.

As fears of losing control and of giving up privacy and independence for institutionalized healthcare drives more and more seniors to consider options, millions have begun to demand—and to get—a growing array of alternatives to the nursing home. Thus, eldercare design today runs the gamut from freestanding SNFs offering subacute care to assisted-living complexes to rehabilitation and wellness centers to independent-living communities, with some facilities that include a continuum of all of the above and are called continuing care retirement communities (CCRCs).

Though some 1.8 million of the elderly still live in nursing homes, according to the most recent census, the percentage of Americans seventy-five and older in nursing homes has been declining steadily despite the graying of the nation—from more than 10 percent in 1990 to around 8 percent in 2000 to about 7.4 percent in 2006. Upper-income elderly whites have been moving increasingly to assisted-living facilities—private apartments staffed by care providers—or are being otherwise cared for by their baby boom children. More often now, too, they live on their own, in independent apartments, usually in retirement communities, that come with simpler services than those available through assisted living. Finally, seniors increasingly also live in CCRCs that provide all levels of care for residents as they age, from independent-living to full-fledged nursing care.

While the federal or state governments pay for nearly 60 percent of nationwide nursing home costs (45 percent of it through Medicaid), they won't pick up much of the tab for the newer forms of long-term care. A few dozen states pay for some assisted living, but their programs are usually small, and they cover very few poor people. Instead, seniors are increasingly paying for their long-term care costs—which can amount to tens of thousands of dollars a year—out of their own or their families' pockets and through private insurance. At the turn of the twenty-first century, nearly 40 percent of the beds in assisted-living facilities could be found in three states—California, Florida, and Pennsylvania—although the number of such facilities has continued to increase, especially in Sun Belt retirement areas.

There are, then, many other factors entering into the design equation stemming from the major population shift that drives the demand for new eldercare and senior living options:

- The residences and communities must be pleasing not only to the prospective residents but to their families as well.
- Technologies are rapidly emerging and have major impacts on lifestyles and services.
- Reimbursements and the insurance industry are continually undergoing changes.
- Codes and regulatory agencies are becoming stricter regarding design for varying levels of care.

The eldercare and senior living options that succeed will offer a high quality of life and be affordable. And that's precisely where research, planning, and design come in.

Subacute Care

Medicine has learned to cure many diseases once thought incurable, and, even more, it is learning to manage those illnesses it cannot cure. Some chronically ill patients can be cared for on an outpatient basis or through homecare programs. Most medical experts see this trend continuing. Yet, as medicine extends the lives of patients who are chronically ill, ambulatory services and homecare are often insufficient. Therefore, a growing segment of inpatient healthcare is "subacute care." Traditionally—that is, before the arrival of DRGs (diagnosis-related groups)—chronic care was the province of freestanding skilled nursing facilities, while subacute care was the responsibility of the acute hospital. After the introduction of the DRG model, freestanding skilled-nursing facilities continued to operate, but, increasingly, acute hospitals began admitting only genuinely acute patients. While the chronic patient requires, on average, one to two years of supportive care, the subacute patient usually requires some fifteen to twenty days of restorative and rehabilitative care. In many areas, this patient's needs are being served inadequately. It is possible for freestanding SNFs and even longer-term chronic-care facilities to meet such needs.

The fastest-growing market for SNF care is, naturally enough, among elderly patients. Oftentimes, community nursing homes are not equipped to treat patients requiring tube feedings, those with new colostomies (and associated complications) or serious decubitus ulcers (bed sores), those depending on a ventilator, or those with stroke-related disabilities, chronic pulmonary complications, complications of joint and hip procedures, and other disorders. Many AIDS patients, too, have a need for subacute care, particularly as various therapies have extended survival without, however, curing the underlying disease. Finally, advances in the treatment of neonates with severe disorders mean that more patients who in the past would have died in infancy now survive for longer periods, albeit frequently with disabilities that require either long-term care or more-or-less protracted episodes of skilled-nursing care.

What all of these groups have in common is a requirement for eight to nine hours of nursing per day, compared to four to six hours in an acute setting and twelve to twenty-four hours in an ICU.

The literature devoted to long-term care environments, especially for the aged and those afflicted with Alzheimer's disease and other forms of dementia, is vast. This in itself is a significant indicator of changing demographics and the healthcare community's recognition of these changes.

In eldercare, the traditional distinctions between long-term and sub-acute care grow increasingly blurred as the emphasis in all levels of care shifts from maintenance to rehabilitation. The term "nursing home" has been heard less and less often as SNFs have stressed living over nursing. This emphasis applies generally to all emerging skilled-nursing, rehabilitation, and psychiatric/neurological facilities, regardless of the age group they serve. Perhaps the single overriding concept that informs SNF and long-term facility design is still best expressed in the title of a classic book by Uriel Cohen and Gerald D. Weisman from back in the 1990s on planning environments for people with dementia: *Holding on to Home*.

Holding on to home may mean creating noninstitutional, homelike environments. Indeed, this is often deemed desirable, as are environments fashioned after the hospitality model. On a deeper level, however, designs that facilitate holding on to home are designs that enable optimum functioning.

The challenge to the architect and designer is to change focus from creating merely aesthetically satisfying structures to creating aesthetically satisfying structures that are barrier-free and that make wayfinding crystal clear by facilitating cognitive mapping. Nowhere is the paradigm shift from standardized design for a healthy thirty-year-old male to standardized design for a frailer seventy-year-old woman more apparent than in effective layout and detailing for the skilled-nursing facility. Consider the following key issues:

• In regular care facilities, architects customarily conceal functional items, especially toilets. In an extended-care facility, such items must be clearly indicated and marked. Patients with Alzheimer's and other ailments have difficulty remembering the location of architectural features they cannot see. Clearly situating the toilet demonstrates how thoughtful design can promote health, a sense of well-being, and independence, and facilitate holding on to home. If a patient cannot readily find the toilet, the likelihood of incontinence increases and, with that, the patient's sense of dignity and independence diminishes. Furthermore, since the average facility with incontinent patients generates a staggering seventy pounds of soiled laundry per day, careful design for wayfinding saves patient time and money and staff costs, not to mention stress on the environment. Many such homelike elements contribute to advanced SNF design.

• Architects and designers must balance the perceptions and expectations of a patient's family on the one hand with building features that benefit the patient on the other. For example, glare is a considerable problem for aged eyes. Not only should lighting be designed to minimize glare, but shiny surfaces, which produce glare, should be avoided. This means that unwaxed, matte-finished flooring is best for patients—even though their families may equate "shiny" with "elegant," "new," and "clean." Again, glare-free design actively encourages patient mobility, while a pleasing shiny floor discourages it.

• The kind of color palette that appeals to most designers for a residential, hospitality, or even acute hospital environment may be inappropriate for long-term care facilities. As eyes age, the ability to distinguish violets, blues, and greens diminishes, while colors at the other end of the spectrum—red, orange, and yellow—remain much more distinct. Common sense suggests that these latter colors will not contribute to a serene interior environment—and this is perfectly true, if design is standardized for the healthy thirty-year-old. For the seventy-year-old, however, such vibrant colors create an environment that encourages mobility, facilitates wayfinding, and, therefore, promotes well-being.

THE CUMBERLAND AT GREEN HILLS
Nashville, Tennessee

In tune with the architectural vernacular of the upscale neighborhood, ESa kept the design of this 121,726-sq.-ft. assisted-living/memory care complex traditional and elegant. Its elevated suburban site looks down on the city's skyline, a view ESa made the most of with generous window space.

The Cumberland at Green Hills, Nashville, Tennessee. Sunrooms with casual furniture are provided for residents so they can enjoy abundant natural light. *Photo © Kieran Reynolds Photography.*

Extensive use of wood-paneled wainscoting, mouldings, columns, and trim give the residence its English manor style, enhanced by the two-sided, stone-surround fireplaces in the lobby reception area and main parlors. Arched transoms over the expanse of windows in the lobby, conservatory, skyline room, and dining room emphasize the high-coffered ceilings. A covered terrace with columns allows outdoor dining in good weather.

Of the 110 residences, 17 are secured memory care units in a separate, attached building. Among its services, The Cumberland provides a physical therapy suite, beauty salon, multipurpose room, game room, billiards room, library, ice cream parlor, tearoom, activity room, and private dining.

THE DEUPREE COMMUNITY
Cincinnati, Ohio

The Deupree Community is one of two communities in Cincinnati operated by Episcopal Retirement Homes. Previously, the Deupree campus did not provide nursing care, so those needing that level of care had to be moved to a sister campus.

With the goal, then, of providing nursing care for twenty-four residents in private rooms but in a residential environment, the architects at SFCS

The Cumberland at Green Hills, Nashville, Tennessee. The skyline lounge provides a dignified, quiet area for residents to enjoy conversation, cocktails, and a spectacular view of the city's distant skyline. *Photo © Kieran Reynolds Photography.*

335

The Deupree Community, Cincinnati, Ohio. The Deupree Community is one of two communities in Cincinnati operated by Episcopal Retirement Homes. *Courtesy SFCS Inc. Photo Michael Houghton Photography.*

The Deupree Community, Cincinnati, Ohio. SFCS Inc.'s design provides nursing care for twenty-four residents in private rooms, and a small house residential environment consisting of two, twelve-resident "small cottages." A small connector runs between them, and the front door of each faces in opposite directions so that they appear detached. The south cottage was designed in craftsman style, the north cottage in colonial. *Courtesy SFCS Inc. Photo Tom Uhlman Photography.*

designed two twelve-resident cottages with a small connector between them. The front doors of the cottages face opposite directions, so they look detached. The south cottage was designed in a craftsman style, the north cottage in colonial. A shared courtyard and garden with connecting walking paths between the cottages encourage residents to interact and enjoy the outdoors.

Each cottage boasts a garage that provides for deliveries of food and other supplies, essential since these cottages are not supported by a central kitchen.

Each of the twenty-four rooms has a full shower. The planners used a special offset toilet layout to improve the ability of the staff to assist residents and to make the toilets more accessible.

The resident rooms are located in a private area, but are connected with very short hallways to the central household, where there is a living room, a dining room, and a resident kitchen. Off to the side are a den and library, with natural light spilling in from two sides and direct access to the garden patio.

Behavioral Health (Psychiatric) Facilities

JOHN GEORGE PSYCHIATRIC PAVILION

San Leandro, California

Architects at Ratcliff created a 71,000-sq.-ft., five-building campus that incorporates a short-stay acute-care hospital for eighty patients and a full outpatient treatment center. The goal was to design a noninstitutional, village-like environment that would encourage social interaction among patients and between patients and staff. At the same time, the designers sought to promote maximum efficiency of staff operations.

The site, a prominent hilltop location in an area featuring Mediterranean-style structures, suggests an Italian hill town. Accordingly, the "village" incorporates such themes as residential neighborhoods clustered around piazzas. A symbolic clock tower marks the main entrance to the facility and is connected to an administrative building by a large plaza. This building acts as the town center, with regular daytime activities (occupational and recreational therapy) concentrated here. Inside the "city wall," a village green provides space for outdoor community activities for residents. It affords both quiet and active areas. Under a curved arcade within the exterior courtyard, individual front doors mark entrances to three "neighborhoods" of living units.

The interior spaces are designed to enhance the flow of patients through the facility and present a transition from public to private spaces. Each of the three groupings of informal patient neighborhoods has a private courtyard, which projects into a secluded valley on the far side of the hilltop. All patient bedrooms feature vaulted ceilings and 16-sq.-ft. windows that look out onto the hillside.

Day rooms provide open spaces for social interaction. Structural frames and carpeted seating groups subdivide the day rooms into more intimate spaces, yet visibility is maintained for staff supervision. Windows are large,

John George Psychiatric Pavilion, San Leandro, California. The design is organized around a central courtyard in a campus setting. A colonnade connects the buildings, all of which give the Pavilion a strong feeling of community. *Courtesy Ratcliff. Photo Jane Lidz.*

but an intimate scale is maintained through the use of small panes. Skylights offer additional contact with the outdoors. Warm-toned wall treatments, an abundance of natural lighting, and the maintenance of residential scale have created a relaxed atmosphere that, according to staff, has had a noticeable effect on reducing the incidence of violent behavior in patients transferred from older facilities.

Rehabilitation Facilities and Wellness Centers

Inpatient rehabilitation facilities share many of the design characteristics of SNFs. Indeed, the trend in all long-term care is to emphasize rehabilitation, to the maximum extent possible, over maintenance. As is also true of SNFs, the prevailing trend in design is always to connect with the outside world. Such considerations also play a central role in the design of outpatient or resident wellness centers. Sparked in part by the emphasis of baby boomers on wellness in their desire to stave off aging, the trend is having a major impact on long-term-care design.

For much of the twentieth century, few would have thought to associate the word "spa" with either nursing homes or retirement communities. But today, discussions between architects and providers are frequently laced with such terms as "holistic," "massage," and even "feng shui." And there is certainly more than enough research to show that exercise, spiritual faith, and social contact do wonders for a person's health, regardless of age. A true wellness program addresses at least five aspects of health, according to the nonprofit National Wellness Association of Stevens, Wisconsin: physical, social, emotional, intellectual, and occupational. Most long-term healthcare wellness projects include the following components:

- *A wellness center.* Most holistic-minded providers have a fitness or exercise center at the heart of the program. Leading architects and providers use these centers to help reinvent the space for senior communities and—as an example of one innovation—unite wellness and therapy areas into one well-designed workout room. Particularly on a campus or at a facility that offers varying levels of care, such a central, integrated space can help ease the social isolation felt by many nursing-home residents. Bringing the programs together in one space or in adjacent rooms can also improve staffing efficiency, outcomes, and resident satisfaction. Finally, the close proximity fosters a kind of communication and cooperation that might be missing if the programs were shut off in separate rooms.

- *A connection with nature.* Rooms with a view are another design feature essential to good wellness programs. They let in natural light, and they allow the residents to connect with nature. Therapeutic gardens, with quiet corners for meditation, foster spiritual wellness. An atrium or some other year-round enclosed garden brings the outdoors inside.

- *A pool.* A popular amenity associated with wellness programs, a pool offers physical, social, and recreational benefits. Designers should take care, however, in specifying the right materials. A pool lined with slippery mosaic glass tile might look wonderful, but it would be unsafe for the elderly. Since senior residents also tend to have poor immune systems, it is important to select the right filtration and chemical control system. Bacteria grow rapidly in water kept at a temperature warm enough to suit an older population; this can quickly turn a spa into a health hazard.

- *Multipurpose rooms.* Rooms that may serve many purposes can also support a holistic approach. They can be used for anything from holding memorials to watching movies, they are great for lectures and continuing education classes, and—especially if such flexible space is located near the exercise room—they can be used for such comforting purposes as massage therapy and aromatherapy.

Assisted Living

Two types of senior housing designed to offer autonomy for active residents have lost ground in the current competition for senior residents: independent-living apartments and congregated housing with shared dining and community facilities for singles. Assisted-living facilities are replacing them, partly because they provide more comprehensive services. The vast majority of all new housing construction for the elderly includes an assisted-living component.

Reinvent the nursing home and you might think of assisted living.

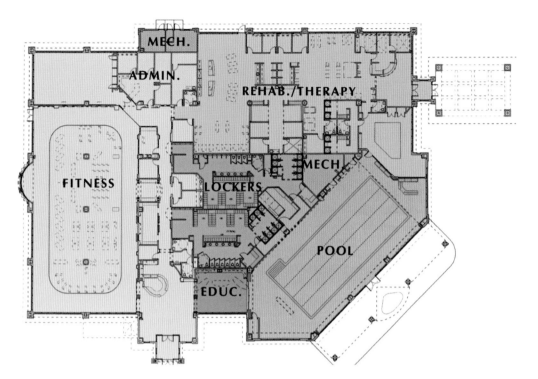

A wellness facility study floor plan designed by Earl Swensson Associates.

Serving seniors over seventy years old, assisted-living facilities offer private apartments, usually with kitchenettes and bathrooms, instead of the shared rooms of a nursing home. These single-occupancy resident rooms are grouped into units according to the level of assistance needed. There is staff available to help residents eat, bathe, and dress. Some meals are often included as are services such as house-cleaning, laundry, and transportation. Although assisted-living facilities do not provide medical care, they do offer—depending on individual states' licensing regulations—a wide range of medical-related care. Staff often supervises medications, for example, and a medical nurse might well administer rehabilitation treatments. Many assisted-living facilities incorporate a special wing or other unit for those who have Alzheimer's or other forms of dementia and memory disorders.

The move to such a facility is usually precipitated by a major change in one's life, such as the death of a spouse or the onset of a physical condition that limits one's ability to live alone. While the latter might make a person dependent on others for some help in daily living, it may not require medical care. The rule of thumb is that those seniors who require assistance in two or more activities of daily living qualify as potential residents for assisted living. In any case, moving from an independent living situation to assisted living can be a traumatic change psychologically for the resident and for the resident's family members. Architects should take this stressful change into account in designing assisted-living communities and campuses by creating pleasant environments that are residential in nature and feature the individuality of each resident.

More homelike than nursing homes, some assisted-living properties are designed to resemble upscale hotels, complete with marble lobbies and concierge desks, following the hospitality model of some healthcare facilities, but the real emphasis is usually a homelike environment. Residents get help remaining independent as long as possible, and it is also harder for them to get lonely in a spot with a range of social interaction, exercise classes, and trips by van to museums and malls. In addition to providing such residential appeal and to being easily accessible for residents, assisted-living communities must also be operationally functional. Planning and design should incorporate staffing patterns and caregiving needs, but the operational model has tended toward minimal staffing. Dining services should be designed for efficiency, but they should also be provided in comfortable surroundings, since meals in particular become focal points in an aging resident's life.

One of the real attractions of assisted living is its sociability—single women make up the majority of assisted-living residents. Assisted-living units can, therefore, be smaller than some more luxurious options. These are frequently homelike living spaces sharing common areas with a feel not unlike a sorority house in the way it encompasses social interaction. One of the real challenges, however, is how to accomplish all this with the minimum of staff. Assisted-living facilities look for what they call a "universal worker"; they do have a nurse available but much of the actual help for the residents comes from such workers.

As we've mentioned, homes for the memory-impaired are a specialized subgroup of assisted living for residents with various forms of dementia. They should be designed with simple, functional layouts, easy wayfinding, and carefully treated surfaces that eliminate confusion for disoriented residents. Once again, relieving stress is essential, which means placing special emphasis in the design on respect for privacy of the individual and their safety.

THE SUMMIT AT LAKEWAY— SKILLED NURSING
Lakeway, Texas

A new component of the Summit at Lakeway campus, designed by ESa, the 60,000-sq.-ft., ninety-eight-bed skilled nursing facility lies adjacent to the facility's assisted-living housing and memory care units. The two buildings are connected by a breezeway.

Located on a heavily sloping hill, the design and placement of the facility takes full advantage of sweeping views of Lake Travis and the Texas Hill countryside. Leading off a parlor on the first level, a sunken terrace area, flanked by a retaining wall and landscaping, is shaded by a wood arbor.

The Summit at Lakeway—Skilled Nursing, Lakeway, Texas. In an effort to achieve a Texas-Spanish feel for the interiors, ESa used natural colors, including greens, golds, and ambers. *Photo © Kieran Reynolds Photography.*

The Summit at Lakeway—Skilled
Nursing, Lakeway, Texas. Lighter-
toned paint colors make the interiors
light and airy. *Photo © Kieran
Reynolds Photography.*

In an effort to achieve a Texas-Spanish feel for the interiors, natural colors, including greens, golds, and ambers were used. Intricate "ironwork" patterns grace the carpets and textiles. While lighting and finishes appear rustic,
lighter-tone paint colors make the interiors light and airy.

THE SUMMIT AT LAKEWAY—
ASSISTED LIVING AND MEMORY CARE
Lakeway, Texas

This four-story, 77,000-sq.-ft. assisted-living and memory care facility,
designed by ESa, provides sixty-six assisted-living residential units and up
to fifteen beds of memory care. Specially designed to meet the senior living
needs of the Lakeway resort community on Lake Travis, the facility—as mentioned earlier—sits on a heavily sloping hill to take full advantage of views of
Lake Travis and a Texas-size stretch of open land to the north. ESa also paid
careful attention to the overall height of the facility to maintain such views
for future construction planned uphill.

Built from a combination of native Austin limestone and synthetic
stucco, the facility melds seamlessly into the picturesque landscape of the
Texas Hill Country. It offers both public and private gardens at three of its
four levels and separate entrances for public, staff, and service personnel.
Interior spaces are as aesthetically pleasing as they are efficient. The aide
station is clearly visible and accessible to those entering the building. In

the assisted-living areas, common spaces include entry alcoves and hallway nooks with seating areas and desks for residents.

The Summit at Lakeway—Assisted Living and Memory Care, Lakeway, Texas. *Photo © Paul Bardagjy.*

THE BLAKEFORD AT GREEN HILLS

Nashville, Tennessee

In this 8,000-sq.-ft. renovation, designed by ESa, thirty-nine skilled-nursing beds were added to the senior living community as were seventeen assisted-living apartments and an additional 4,000 sq. ft. to the rehabilitation center. Residential areas, which include the existing health center, program and activity spaces, lobby, and dining, were renovated.

Special features within skilled nursing include a spalike bathing suite designed to maintain the dignity of the residents. Elongated stone tiles at the vanity and a gilded mirror framed in wood and complemented with sconces help create a soothing space. A fireplace serves as the focal point of each dining room, which has built-in breakfronts with pocket doors that shield an opening in the wall to the kitchen. Plates can be passed through the breakfronts to the serving staff, much as they are in a restaurant, without exposing views of the kitchen.

In keeping with the rest of The Blakeford community and the well-established neighborhood surrounding it, the facility's interior design is traditional with a transitional twist. A calming neutral background palette relies on upholstery and art for color.

Though the trend in elderly care has been toward freestanding assisted-living facilities, the elderly have in recent decades also been attracted to continuing care retirement communities or CCRCs, which some experts believe will have greater appeal for the consumer-driven baby boomers now reaching what used to be considered the retirement years. This type of community combines different kinds of care in a single setting, so residents can live independently for as long as possible, and then move to an assisted-living facility when their needs grow greater or even switch to a full-time nursing facility if needed. A CCRC can be a single high-rise building close to an urban center or it can be a complex of buildings on a bucolic campus.

Paying an entry fee, residents usually move in to an apartment or condo, but some continuing care communities offer small houses. All-inclusive or life-care facilities frequently cover all long-term healthcare costs, but some charge less in the beginning when a resident can live independently and more as the resident's healthcare needs grow. At the independent apartment or condo, some healthcare services, such as a nurse on call, are provided. The next step is to an assisted living facility, when the residents need help in two or more areas called "activities of daily living" or ADLs, which these days are specifically governed by regulators—help, for example, in providing meals, in getting dressed, or in bathing and personal hygiene. In any case, the central concept of the CCRC is continuity of care for residents progressing into old age.

Though in the past most CCRCs were run by nonprofit groups, private facilities have become increasingly more common. CCRCs offer residents peace of mind, since all forms of long-term care are guaranteed and nearby, which is especially appealing to couples who often worry about what will happen to their spouse should they fall too ill to care for themselves. Since these facilities run the gamut of possibilities, however, they may be more complicated to design effectively. In addition, many of the units must be pre-sold before the construction can begin, which means they take time to build.

THE GARDENS AT FREEDOM VILLAGE AT BRANDYWINE
West Brandywine, Pennsylvania

ESa designed is three-story 60,000-sq.-ft. assisted-living facility containing fifty-seven apartment units as an addition to an existing continuing care retirement community. This expansion enabled the community to relocate assisted-living residents who were in an existing facility to the new spaces, which freed-up space for conversion to additional skilled-nursing beds.

Architectural design references the materials and elements that were already present in the community and familiar to the region. Interior design promotes a comfortable elegance.

Amenities and services included are typical of CCRCs—a monumental stone fireplace in the main lobby, an ice cream parlor, private dining, a multipurpose/AV entertainment room on the second level with access to an outdoor veranda overlooking the activity lawn, arts and crafts space, physical

The Gardens at Freedom Village at Brandywine, West Brandywine, Pennsylvania. The second level's veranda offers covered respite and overlooks the courtyard's activity lawn. *Photo © Kieran Reynolds Photography.*

The Gardens at Freedom Village at Brandywine, West Brandywine, Pennsylvania. A skylight crowns the library, which features stained wood wall panels and a fireplace, evoking a Philadelphia law library. *Photo © Kieran Reynolds Photography.*

therapy, and a beauty salon with spalike decor. The third-floor library evokes a Philadelphia law library setting with stained wood wall panels, fireplace, and a long library table.

The project also included renovation and upgrading of the existing activity courtyard with accommodations for shuffleboard and croquet.

FREEDOM POINTE
AT THE VILLAGES
The Villages, Florida

ESa designed a new independent-living component to complement the existing assisted-living and memory care facilities (and a future skilled-nursing facility) to form a continuing care retirement community within The Villages retirement community. The CCRC campus is conveniently across the street from The Villages Regional Medical Center, also designed by ESa.

Two-hundred and forty-one apartments are housed in the seven-story,

Freedom Pointe at The Villages, The Villages, Florida. Balconies and a patio are available for outdoor dining. *Photo © Kieran Reynolds Photography.*

Freedom Pointe at The Villages, The Villages, Florida. The main lobby boasts the quiet elegance of wood accents and muted colors. *Photo © Kieran Reynolds Photography.*

Freedom Pointe at The Villages, The Villages, Florida. A resident room (skilled-nursing facility). *Photo © Kieran Reynolds Photography.*

Freedom Pointe at The Villages, The Villages, Florida. The lap pool. *Photo © Kieran Reynolds Photography.*

Spanish-styled structure, which conforms to the Villages' downtown community and to the other components of the CCRC. ESa achieved its low-rise feel with a massing of steps of four to five to seven stories. A red concrete mission-tile roof crowns the facility. Surrounded by large water oaks in a parklike setting, the building overlooks a lake and a golf course.

Extensive amenities provided include a bank, a pharmacy, a business center, and administrative offices. Its multifunction facilities also boast a kitchen, a dining pub and tea shop, a day spa, a meditation room, and physicians' offices. There are also other support facilities—physical therapy, a woodshop, and an arts and crafts area. A 140,000-sq.-ft., three-story garage contains 250 parking spaces, each of them one-and-one-half spaces wide to accommodate both a car and a golf cart. A freestanding pool house/multipurpose facility is located in the adjacent courtyard.

THREE CROWNS PARK

Evanston, Illinois

After over a century of providing care to its senior population, Three Crowns Park decided its facility needed upgrading so it could reposition itself in the marketplace and continue its mission. After researching other skilled-nursing facilities and CCRCs, Three Crowns decided to adopt the household model for its skilled-nursing care to change the physical environment and make its community more competitive.

Three Crowns Park, Evanston, Illinois. To upgrade the more than century-old Three Crowns Park, AG Architecture created three sixteen-bed households, each with a distinctive point of entry and strictly limited crossover. *Courtesy AG Architecture. Photo © Tricia Shay Photography.*

Three Crowns Park, Evanston, Illinois. A sunroom and sitting room offer additional private spaces that provide access to the outdoors and space to meet with family. *Courtesy AG Architecture. Photo © Tricia Shay Photography.*

To achieve this goal, AG Architecture created three, sixteen-to-eighteen-bed households. Each household has a distinct point of entry, with crossover between households strictly limited. AG expanded the existing third floor to include the third floor above new independent-living apartments.

The new environment for each household begins at the elevator lobby entries. Using a simulated front porch design, each entry creates a distinct residential experience. This sets the tone for the household experience as you enter into the great room with a living room, dining area, and activity kitchen. A sunroom and sitting room offer additional private spaces that provide access to the outdoors and space to meet with family. As in all homes, bedrooms are placed in more private areas of the house and are encouraged to be spaces for personal expression. Though highly personalized, these spaces were still designed with the appropriate safety features such as call lights and visual access to a nursing nook.

To best accommodate the residents and staff and not disturb daily operations, this project required a strategic phasing schedule. In the first phase, the new addition was completed and some of the residents were relocated; they then enjoyed a more personalized level of care. Though the existing wings created significant physical obstacles to work around, thoughtful planning and finish upgrades aimed to create a more homelike environment. The nature and delivery of long-term care would be forever changed on this campus.

Long-Term Living Magazine honored Three Crown Parks with its 2009 DESIGN/Environments for Aging Best in Show award and the Society for the Advancement of Gerontological Environments (SAGE) judged the facility a forward-thinking, resident-centered community.

NEWCASTLE ESTATES

Mequon, Wisconsin

To meet growing market demands, Milwaukee Protestant Home decided to expand its existing Mequon senior living community (Newcastle Place). The result was Newcastle Estates, 107,141-sq.-ft. of private residences and common spaces comprising unique amenities to support this distinct market segment within the greater Mequon community.

After raising a family and developing strong community ties, retirees in the area sought housing options that allow them to remain in the

Newcastle Estates, Mequon, Wisconsin. Luxury was the key word for the design of the carriage homes and apartment units. *Courtesy AG Architecture. Photo © Tricia Shay Photography.*

community they loved and enjoyed. Newcastle Place, and now Newcastle Estates, offer Mequon's senior population the opportunity to do so by creating a variety of housing options and amenities. Newcastle Estates provides fifty independent-living apartments as well as nineteen single-family carriage homes to support a variety of lifestyle needs. The location provides residents with a residential neighborhood surrounded by a serene natural environment in the heart of their familiar community. In addition, it provides access to upscale supportive living options in the existing Newcastle Place as well as medical services via the nearby hospital and medical complex should the need arise.

Designed by AG Architecture, Newcastle Estates followed current facility trends that favor residential units over retail space. The first level of the new independent-living apartment building incorporates intimate common areas to encourage socialization. Fine dining is an option for residents on both of the facility's campuses. A high-end restaurant atmosphere (located on

Newcastle Estates, Mequon, Wisconsin. A high-end restaurant located on the ground floor incorporates a general dining area, a terrace view dining area, an intimate bar, and a chef's table in the kitchen. *Courtesy AG Architecture. Photo © Tricia Shay Photography.*

the ground floor) incorporates a general dining area, terrace view dining, an intimate bar setting, and a "Chef's Table" in the kitchen.

Luxury was the key word for the design of the carriage homes and apartment units. The cottage-style carriage homes offer five different floor plans with eight different facades and color schemes. The residential apartment units also offer a variety of floor plan options, each with a covered, screened-in porch. All unit and housing amenities are senior-friendly. The structural framing for the apartment units (exterior wall-to-corridor framing and load-bearing walls) offers residents the opportunity for interior unit customization for increased personalization. Furthermore, this structural design supports the longevity of the building, allowing the building owner to modify unit designs to follow future market trends.

The carriage homes were also designed to meet the needs of the growing, educated senior market. All of the homes address energy-efficiency standards, and six homes are recognized as Wisconsin ENERGY STAR® Homes. With the help of Kings Way Homes, Five Star Energy Corp., and Milwaukee Protestant Home, AG was able to take their specifications and building standards to the next level to benefit both the client and the environment.

To receive the Wisconsin ENERGY STAR Homes label, a home must meet guidelines for energy efficiency established by the U.S. Environmental Protection Agency. Below is a list of energy-efficient features that are considered to receive this recognized standard:

- Effective insulation
- High-performance windows
- Tight construction and ducts
- Efficient heating and cooling equipment
- Efficient products
- Third-party verification

Newcastle Estates supports the aging population of Mequon while preserving a historical and environmentally significant site.

CASCADES VERDAE
Greenville, South Carolina

CJMW Architecture, along with GMK Interior Design, designed this independent-living neighborhood for Verdae, a mixed-use retirement community. The project's developer, Banyan Senior Living, sought to incorporate best practices learned from its years of experience operating other CCRCs.

Front-line staff from other communities played an important role in the design process, and the plan called for 166 independent-living apartments, forty-three cottages, a 53,000-sq.-ft. clubhouse, and a healthcare center. The healthcare center is not only large, but it also provides all care in small household settings and is built to the same high standard of finish quality as the rest of the project.

The independent-living apartment buildings center on a lawn with the clubhouse at its end. Covered parking is provided below each apartment building. Residents can get to the clubhouse through a series of one-story

Cascades Verdae, Greenville, South Carolina. CJMW Architecture designed this independent-living neighborhood as a mixed-use retirement community. *Courtesy CJMW Architecture. Photo Warner Photography, Inc.*

connectors. The cottages that make up the rest of the neighborhood sit along the perimeter, and all have alley access to two-and-one-half-car garages (the one-half is for golf carts). The clubhouse includes multiple dining rooms, meeting spaces, a ballroom, and a movie theater. A large wellness center on the lower level of the clubhouse includes an exercise pool, fitness equipment, aerobics rooms, and other amenities. The healthcare center, connected to the lower level of the clubhouse, offers healthcare residents the chance to use the wellness center. All the buildings come in the regional red-brick Georgian style, and the designers paid great attention to classical proportions and details throughout the neighborhood.

The Health Care Center at the Cascades includes forty-four nursing, forty-eight assisted-living, and twenty-four special-care beds, all in private rooms arranged in eight households. Each assisted-living or special-care household consists of twelve resident rooms clustered around a central living/dining/kitchen area. Each nursing unit consists of twenty-two rooms clustered around a central common area. All households are interconnected for ease of staff circulation and to enable residents to go indoors to the Wellness Center, located in the lower level of the independent-living clubhouse, and to the Health Care Clubhouse, which includes a therapy suite and spa. The arrangement combines the intimacy and homelike settings of the households with efficiency of operation.

Long-Term Living Magazine awarded the Cascades Verdae a citation of merit in its 2010 DESIGN/Environments for Aging Architectural Showcase. A jury appointed by SAGE (The Society for the Advancement of Gerontological Environments), CHD (The Center for Health Design), and ASID (The American Society of Interior Designers) selected six citation winners from among projects submitted from across the country. The jury was made up of experts in the field of aging including facility operators, architects, interior designers, gerontologists, and regulatory officials.

Cascades Verdae, Greenville, South Carolina. The interior design of the Cascades Verdae combines the intimacy and homelike settings of a household with efficiency of operation. *Courtesy CJMW Architecture. Photo Warner Photography, Inc.*

CHAPTER 13

Trends in the Twenty-First Century

At the beginning of this book, we mentioned two plays by the great nineteenth-century dramatist Henrik Ibsen: *An Enemy of the People* and *The Master Builder*. The hero of one is a physician; of the other, an architect. Both men find themselves faced with similar tasks: to diagnose and heal the ills of their community and their society. Both the physician and architect promote the health of humanity and civilization. For us, this concept drives our practice as architects, especially as healthcare architects—and it has driven us as authors of this book. But it is more than a talisman or metaphor. It is a reality. If there is one trend that overrides all others in shaping the future of hospital and healthcare facility design, it is the emergence of architects and designers as full partners in planning and delivering medical care.

A Catalog of Trends and Developments

Throughout this book, we have tried to balance on the cutting-edge, delineating trends for which those concerned with hospitals and healthcare facilities are currently building or currently planning (or should be currently building or planning). In this final chapter, we take an extended view and attempt to outline the trends and developments likely to shape healthcare and, therefore, the practice of healthcare architecture for the future. The discussion naturally falls into three broad areas: (1) a catalog of medical trends and developments, (2) how architecture will address and facilitate these trends and developments, and (3) the practice of architecture as the practice of medicine.

With some justification, medical historians regard all healthcare prior to the later 1930s as the Dark Ages. For the most part, until an arsenal of

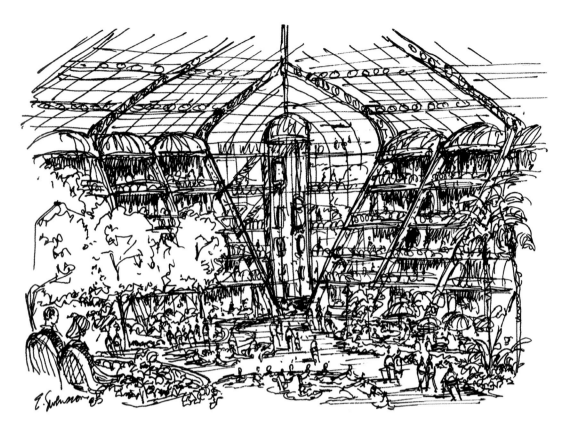

antibiotic drugs became available, doctors really could do relatively little to combat disease. They could palliate and they could support, but they could offer little in the way of aggressive, effective treatment. Antibiotics cured an array of illnesses, and, back in the 1960s and 1970s, public health officials felt that they had pretty much triumphed over infectious diseases. Smallpox had been virtually eliminated, and polio was all but vanquished, thanks to vaccines. Antibiotics improved sanitation, and pesticides conquered such age-old scourges as tuberculosis, cholera, and malaria. One by one, it seemed, the maladies that plagued humanity were being wiped off the face of the earth.

Then came the counterattack—HIV, Ebola, Marburg virus, Lassa fever, Legionnaire's disease, hantavirus, hepatitis C, anthrax, West Nile virus. In all, a few dozen newly identified pathogens, most of them out of the newly inhabited and exploited rain forests of Africa and South America, made the interspecies jump from animals to humans and swooped down on various populations during the last couple of decades of the twentieth century. At the same time, human defense perimeters began to crumble. Underfunded prevention programs and the overprescription by doctors and misuse by patients of former "miracle drugs" such as penicillin and tetracycline led pathogens to develop immunities and create mutant strains of themselves. Antibiotic-resistant strains of TB, dengue fever, bacterial meningitis, yellow fever, cholera, malaria, and even the dreaded plague have cropped up again. This resistance resides in hospitals, where the high concentration of powerful antibiotics has led these diseases to develop ways to survive against them.

Meanwhile, the sense that modern medicine had relieved much suffering and given us all the feeling that we are no longer helpless in the face of disease gave way by the 1990s to a panicky feeling that microbes were taking

Extended-Care Center of the Future. Perspective. Incorporating all the activities necessary for rehabilitation and recuperation, this facility accommodates not just the patient but the spouse as well. Each patient's living quarters includes a balcony that overlooks the therapy facilities and amenities on the ground floor. *Sketch by Earl S. Swensson.*

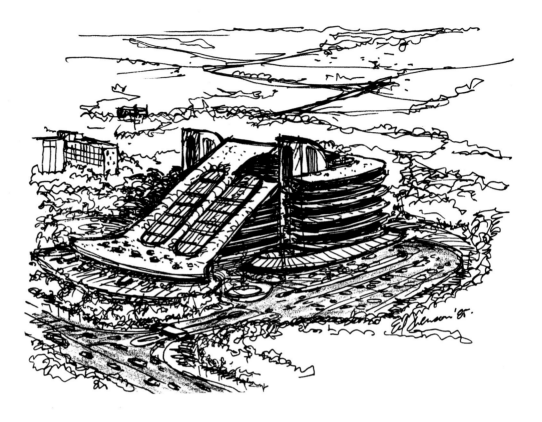

Acute-Care Center of the Future. Perspective. Upon entering the registration area (the small building at the driveway in the foreground), patients present their personal data card containing all the information needed for check-in. An attendant directs the patients to the appropriate department. Patient rooms occupy the periphery of the building. Ancillary areas are located in the core. The sloped area at the front of the facility houses shafts for the transport of supplies; mechanical, electrical, and plumbing lines; and staff circulation. Supplies are received at the base of the sloped area, and then distributed as needed. The building is organized vertically by department—one floor for cardiology, one for neurology, etc. Floors can be reconfigured as needed. *Sketch by Earl S. Swensson.*

their revenge, and there was little humanity could do about it. Even the belief that modern medicine had done much to lengthen the span of human life came under scrutiny. No one doubted the fact that, in 1940, the average American life expectancy was sixty-three years and that it was now more than seventy-eight years. However, many authorities began to ascribe this increase, not to medical science alone, but also to such wealth-linked factors as improved sanitation, better nutrition, better housing, improved working conditions, and even the virtually universal use of household refrigeration, which has greatly reduced the incidence of food-borne bacteria contamination. Looked at from a world perspective, rather than that of one wealthy industrial nation, the human population is not, in fact, getting healthier. The failure of medicine—if that is how one chooses to view it—was not just a failure to defeat disease once and for all, but a failure even to treat disease at a reasonable cost by not providing cost-effective healthcare.

The emotional pendulum has swung back some in this century. While doctors accept the fact that new illnesses and new, potentially devastating strains of familiar diseases like influenza will continue to threaten human life, they also know that the right strategies can contain the damage. New technology and new discoveries fuel medical confidence. While the war against infectious diseases has become something of a guerrilla conflict, the long-maintained fronts against hereditary and lifestyle diseases—diabetes, cancer, heart disease, and Alzheimer's—in the industrialized Western world, at least are advancing, as in more traditional warfare, with the massing and deployment of newer, better weapons. Two megatrends have and will continue to shape the future of medicine in the United States:

1. Medicine now addresses the causes of disease, which means that medicine digs to the roots—or, more properly, the seeds—of life itself by engineering human genes, chromosomes, and molecules to eliminate rather than attempt to cure disease. This century will continue to be a century of biology, fueled by the massive pools of information formed by the Human Genome Project and other genetic and immunologic studies. Genetic engineering promises in the long run to be the most cost-effective way of dealing with disease, because it prevents rather than patches and repairs.

2. For those diseases and disorders that cannot be engineered out of existence and in the case of injury and accident, noninvasive treatments and minimally invasive procedures will continue to extensively replace surgery. Thus, this century will be a century of technology, driven by the confluence of computing power, robotics, and nanotechnology.

The pace of innovation that drives these trends is astoundingly swift and will only accelerate in coming years. One reason is that the tools of invention are much improved these days. Pharmacologists now manipulate three-dimensional portraits of drug molecules on-screen like Legos, shaping them to match targets in the human body. Biologists, many of whom scoffed back in the 1980s at the suggestion of cataloging the billions of DNA pairs in the human genetic makeup, were instead able to deliver the rough draft of the human genome in 2000, well ahead of schedule thanks to robots and high-speed computers. Neurologists use MRIs to watch the brain at work as thoughts and emotions light up a screen with a strange new grammar of light and impulse. This marriage of machinery and computational muscle has yielded—and will continue to yield—amazing advances. These days, surgeons routinely deploy robotic arms for open-heart surgery, minimizing incisions and drastically reducing recovery time. Researchers have built transistors so small they can hide under a virus, and machines keep getting smaller. The era of nanotechnology is upon us, an era in which invisible devices mere atoms wide will perform tasks mundane and vital, adjusting the lighting in a room, say, or hunting down cancer cells. Having pushed the silicon chip nearly to the limits of its capacity, researchers are working on a true microprocessor, one built not on wires and chips, but on quantum particles or perhaps DNA.

Telecommunications and the Internet have had an immense impact on society and healthcare in a world that has gone wireless. As bandwidth has stretched and been stitched together with fiber-optic cable and wireless technology to bear ever heavier traffic, the advances in electronic communications (storage and retrieval) and data processing have transformed the environment in which medicine is practiced. Medical records, billing, and patient charting take up less room, are handled with greater speed, and pose fewer frustrations. Patients can be checked in at their bedside; doctors can diagnose, communicate, and even conduct surgery from remote locations. The Picture Archiving and Communication System (PACS), which began as a hospital-based image management tool, can now be used in teleradiology to transmit and view radiologic images in any number of locations. Caregivers and patients in separate locations now often communicate daily without the need to meet in a hospital setting. Individuals use the Internet, placed in the palms of their hands by dozens of new devices, not just to text, tweet, and gossip but as a means of access to all kinds of medical information and care. "All digital" hospitals are no longer just a dream but also a possibility.

Then there is the revolution going on in biology with the new ability to manipulate human genes and cells at the molecular level. As early as 1998, researchers had persuaded a few cells from a human embryo to grow in the lab. From this beginning, stem cells became a promising way of growing tissue to repair damaged hearts and other organs—or to replace them altogether (and from the beginning were a source of political controversy because their procurement might involve harvesting them from fetuses). Electrodes lodged in the brains of paralyzed stroke victims let them guide computer cursors with their thoughts, raising the possibility of efficacious melding of humans and machines that remind us of science fiction. And the Human Genome Project jump-started our understanding of heredity and disease while giving us an ever clearer vision of what it means to be human.

Still, if more slowly than we once hoped, the manipulation of human genes together with the use of special new drugs are unlocking a future where the human body might be able to confound and defeat its ancient enemies. Cancer, perhaps, has seen the most advances in treatment, with hundreds of new drugs coming off advanced clinical trials that target the disease (or more properly, the range of diseases) like smart bombs, especially the all-too-familiar cancers such as brain, liver, colon, lung, skin, prostate, and ovarian. Cancer vaccines are being tested that boost the immune systems of patients to kill new cancer cells, not preventing the onset but stopping its spread. There are likely to be new vaccines for malaria, Lyme disease, and others. We still hope to see gene therapy for obesity, for baldness, and for clogged arteries. Researchers are attempting to treat Parkinson's with a special gene implant to produce the dopamine its victims' brains need to replace. Some continue to predict that gene therapy may yet revolutionize medicine and that virtually every disease will one day be treated by it.

While these advances are certainly mind-boggling, they can also be sobering, raising issues of control and privacy that trouble many even as they give hope for extended, healthier lives. A few years ago, people raised moral questions about genetic advances. If diseases can be engineered out of genes, can't other qualities be engineered in? What will genetic engineering do to the human gene pool? How will it affect human ecology and evolution? Will such engineering create new "super" strains of disease, just as the indiscriminate use of antibiotics has created new strains of resistant bacteria? Finally, is human genetic engineering morally desirable?

Laws are now on the books that outlaw human cloning, but you would be hard pressed to find anyone who believes that will prevent it. Private drug companies that have already trademarked individual DNA strands with unknown functions expect huge profits from genetically engineered cures for a myriad of diseases. The morality of genetic engineering now takes on legal, economic, and political hues as well. Can a gene, present in your body, actually belong legally to a corporation? Do government prosecutors and insurance companies invade our privacy when they work up genetic profiles upon which they then make policy decisions to prosecute individuals or deny them healthcare coverage or medical benefits? Laws have been passed to prevent the sharing of such information with insurance companies. Similar concerns have constantly cropped up with telecommunications and the Internet. Once your life and your medical history is digitized, can it ever truly remain private, no matter what the laws say?

Scarcely less disquieting are the implications of these megatrends for the constantly increasing cost of medical care. The physician's vaunted Hippocratic Oath harmonizes with the Judeo-Christian ethic of universal charity and a revulsion from putting a price of any kind on human life. However, the Hippocratic Oath is the product of an age of cheap—and, in any case, limited—medical treatment. Until rather recently, to do everything possible for a patient cost very little more than to do nothing at all, simply because there was not much that could be done. The ambition to do all one could to save a life was and remains a noble one, but it has proved costly. Medical science continued to expand what could be done for any given patient and each of these procedures, drugs, and interventions came with a price tag. For decades the inflation of medical costs far outpaced that of the economy and those costs continued to rise dramatically even as the economy sputtered. Employers have been cutting back on the premiums they are willing to pay, and the whole system feels the threat of the new—often miraculous but always expensive—therapies and cures, creating a situation that even the public policy of healthcare reform will find difficult to address.

New technology has freed healthcare from the bed-centered hospital of the old paradigm and any cost-versus-benefit analysis of it must go beyond dollars and cents. Healthcare consumers who are savvy and well informed are weighing the prospective benefit of a given treatment against the quality of life they may expect as a result of it, and more patients may more frequently opt out of treatments that prolong misery merely to prolong basic life processes.

These megatrends may embody wonders and worries, but they are no longer a true surprise—they are extensions. Within these are lesser trends, which are part and parcel of these megatrends, representing continuing developments of current technological and demographic facts. Let's turn to a few of them.

Genomics

As mentioned earlier, genetic engineering may provide the most profound alternative to conventional medical treatments by obviating the need for treatment altogether. Genetically engineered agriculture has now long been a reality and just recently the project to map the entirety of human chromosomes was completed, yielding a picture of our genetic makeup that

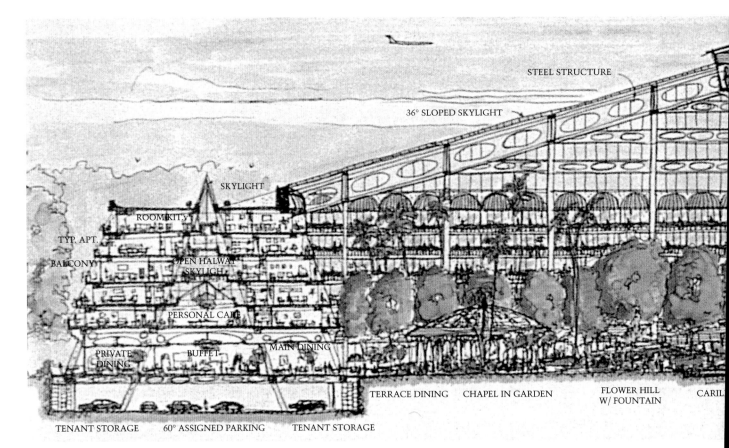

Labels on image: STEEL STRUCTURE, 36° SLOPED SKYLIGHT, SKYLIGHT, ROOM/KIT.v, TYP. APT., BALCONY, OPEN HALWAY SKYLIGHT, PERSONAL CARE, PRIVATE DINING, BUFFET, MAIN DINING, TERRACE DINING, CHAPEL IN GARDEN, FLOWER HILL W/ FOUNTAIN, CARIL, TENANT STORAGE, 60° ASSIGNED PARKING, TENANT STORAGE

Synergenial Continuing Care Retirement Community (CCRC) Complex. This design for the future integrates a healthcare-oriented facility for the elderly in a community that includes 1.3 million sq. ft. of office space; an 800-room hotel; a covered shopping galleria; a medical center with 320 acute-care rooms; a medical office building; a diagnostic center and outpatient services; and educational, fitness, cultural, and recreational facilities. *Sketch by Earl S. Swensson.*

surprised many by its lack of complexity. Fewer chromosomes determined more biological destiny than almost anyone had imagined. For the practice of preventive medicine, the first major step in genetic engineering has already been taken with screening for certain genetic markers that indicate susceptibility to various diseases. These tests proliferate, and, as the markers are identified, it has become possible to take a look at the genetic "fingerprint" of an individual and prescribe preventive measures—drugs, lifestyle changes, and so on—to head off disease before it actually manifests itself. Beyond this, techniques are being developed to manipulate genetic material on the level of the gene, chromosome, and even molecule to produce desired results.

Today, immunologic and genomic researchers are scrambling not only to produce new antibiotics but also to create entirely new ways of attacking pathogens. Some of these include antibiotic peptides, which are natural substances manufactured by humans and animals. Another strategy is based on peptide nucleic acids (PNAs), using these synthetic polymers to mimic and bind to genes and RNA more strongly than even DNA itself. All these genetic tactics are aimed at getting beyond dependence on antibiotics, but hospitals are also addressing the antibiotic crisis directly. Hospitals have instituted controls on antibiotic use, especially those used for prevention, and they have become fierce about sterilizing clinical environments. Healthcare facilities that can promise low rates of infectious diseases gain a market edge.

Researchers also see the immune system as a means of taking us safely beyond the "antibiotic era." Once driven in part by HIV research, immunologists have now long been studying the complex interactions within cells and between cells. They propose to use genetically engineered recombinant

AN ROOM

STRUCTURAL
TENSION RING

EXERCISE
ROOM   ATRIUM   ART ROOM   OUTDOOR
                                          ART ROOM

MMER PORCH   SNACK
            LAP POOL   TENNIS COURT BEYOND   BAR

TENANT STORAGE   60° ASSIGNED PARKING

viruses and "naked" DNA—DNA stripped of its active ingredients, the accompanying peptides—as both preventive and therapeutic vaccines. They are also investigating new drugs that stimulate or block interactions with the receptors on the surfaces of targeted cells and are looking for ways to stimulate the body's immune response by using elements of its immune system.

The implications of this research for healthcare and healthcare facility design are clearer than antibiotics research. The likely proliferation of specific vaccines underscores the focus on early identification and prevention of disease. These have implications that contribute toward the large-scale reduction of the type of care offered by more traditional hospitals, including surgery and nontraumatic, high-intensity acute care. At the same time, they push hospitals toward the kind of services that might be offered in outpatient care: genomic screening, vaccinations, and general preventive care.

The impact of genetics on life expectancy can be enormous. As we have mentioned a number of times, the average life expectancy in America has increased dramatically over the last century. Some researchers have hopes of also increasing the maximum life span. These hopes hinge on researchers who are exploring methods of turning back the clock for specific organs and body systems. For one thing, we may soon be able to replace organs more routinely than with human organ transplantation, which requires both a rigid and extensive regimen of drugs to repress the immune system's rejection of "foreign" tissue and the availability of usable donor organs that match the recipient's body tissue. Both xenographs (genetically engineered organs and tissue grown in animals or in the lab) and artificial organs are a possibility. Companies have conducted human trials with implanted mechanical replacement hearts, and some companies offer artificial livers—mechanical gadgets seeded with human or pig cells cultured in a lab—that would sustain patients until a transplant was possible or until they recovered.

Both stem cells and cloning also hold the promise of growing new tissues or organs in the lab. Researchers are isolating telomerase, an enzyme that rebuilds telomeres on the ends of chromosomes after each cell division. When a body's telomeres are depleted, its cells cannot divide anymore: they die. Using telomerase to rebuild them might stop the clock on specific organs, even entire systems. There are also promising studies of glycosylation (the process whereby glucose binds to protein), which is implicated in the formation of cataracts, in the denaturing of nerve tissue in the heart, in the cross-links that reduce flexibility in aging arteries, and in the plaques that form on the brains of Alzheimer's patients.

Finally, there is cloning, associated in the popular imagination with genetic engineering. Cloning caught the attention of the world press in 1998, when scientists reproduced genetically identical sheep and cattle. A lot of people got the notion, fed by sci-fi movies, that cloning was some kind of photocopying process. A clone was an instant twin, sprung full-blown in the lab like Venus from the half shell. This created a storm of ethical protest and a legislative fury on the topic. But a clone is simply a genetically identical being a generation younger than its parent that is gestated in a different womb and nurtured from birth in a different environment, not the eerie exact facsimile in word and deed of science fiction.

Despite the sound and the fury, reproductive cloning may become accepted one day just as in vitro fertilization and surrogate motherhood have become accepted, even if it is unlikely to become common or popular. Meanwhile, therapeutic cloning and research cloning are already important. Cloning of cells has long been a basic tool of biotechnology and has helped, over the last three decades, to create vaccines and breakthrough drugs for heart attacks, kidney disease, diabetes, various cancers, hepatitis, multiple sclerosis, cystic fibrosis, and other ailments. Researchers are now cloning human cells in the lab to produce, for example, new skin for burn victims and new cartilage and bone for accident victims.

Researchers have attempted to use human stem cells to grow proteins, hormones, and such tissue as myocardium to strengthen bad hearts. The goal is routinely to grow entire replacement organs, and it has met with some success—for example, in growing new hearts. But since stem cells are fetal cells that have not yet specialized, the research has come under condemnation from right-to-life groups. Cloning may offer an out, since scientists in recent experiments have been able to convert mouse brain cells into blood-producing bone marrow cells and have converted human tumor cells into nondividing neurons to treat stroke victims. If, as these experiments imply, ordinary somatic cells can be reprogrammed to different functions, there would be no need to use fetal stem cells at all.

In addition to the implications for design we have already talked about, genetic engineering to lengthen life will have a major impact on future facility planning. While invasive surgery and acute care would be de-emphasized, there would be an increased need for testing and observation areas and an increased emphasis on wellness centers instead of skilled-nursing facilities. In short, the advances in genetics fuel the momentum toward flexible, outpatient, short-stay, high-tech, integrated facilities.

Nanotechnology

Nanotechnology—the ability to create minuscule, artificially intelligent machines one molecule at a time and then mass-produce them—is fast becoming a reality. To make such machines, researchers are breaking down the walls between organic and inorganic chemistry to give inorganic materials, which tend to be hard and brittle (like glass) some of the typically soft and rubbery qualities of organic materials (like skin) and vice versa. The results might be, for example, a big, flat-panel display for handheld computers that folds up, or polymer-based paints and coatings that contain ceramic particles to defy scratching, or improved catalysts that spawn new pharmaceuticals. Metal-composite car-body panels might pop back into shape after minor fender-benders. Turbofans in jet engines might self-repair tiny stress cracks. All manner of smart materials that emulate biological systems would enable them to adapt to changing conditions, compensate for wear, and warn of impending trouble.

Synergenial Continuing Care Retirement Community (CCRC) Complex. The Synergenial community of the future is standardized for a seventy-five-year-old female rather than the customary thirty-year-old male. *Sketch by Earl S. Swensson.*

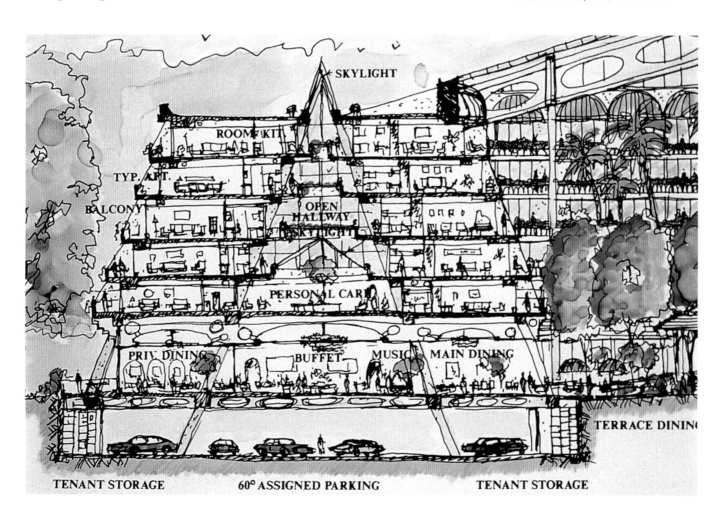

TENANT STORAGE   60° ASSIGNED PARKING   TENANT STORAGE

Inorganic-organic hybrids are nothing new. Fiberglass-reinforced plastics have been around for years. But they are essentially physical mixtures, often suffering from weak chemical bonds that delaminate beyond certain stress levels and suffer structural failure. Nanoengineering promises to cure these problems by tailoring the surfaces of components so that they have chemical hooks designed to glom on to each other. And to do that, you have to get down to the scale at which molecules mingle to create DNA and proteins, the building blocks of life, where things are measured in nanometers. A nanometer is a billionth of a meter. Individual atoms are a few nanometers in diameter. Using exotic tools such as a scanning-probe microscope with supersharp tips, physicists can create new molecules that extend the performance of organic materials to unprecedented levels. Consider the nanotubes first created in 1991 by Sumo Ijima, a scientist at the NEC Corporation. They are elongated versions of carbon Bucky balls, discovered in 1985 by Richard E. Smally (who earned a Nobel Prize for the find in 1996). The nanotubes are at least 100 times stronger than steel, but only one-sixth as heavy.

Other scientists have coated silicon atoms with chlorine atoms one atom thick to create a lubricating film that allows microelemental systems (MEMS)—little machines carved into silicon chips—to include parts that move across the surface. Still others have discovered that nanoparticles sandwiched between a polymer that conducts negative charges and one that conducts positive charges can create light-emitting diodes (LEDs) spanning the visible spectrum and making possible, say, fold-up displays for pocket computers or "wallpaper" TV screens for home. Such feats indicate that materials science is now reaching a point analogous to genetic engineering in biology. Molecules will be engineered at the atomic level and then replicated with biologically modeled processes to produce bulk quantities.

We are on the verge of handheld biosensors capable of detecting a wide range of diseases within minutes from a drop of blood, urine, or saliva. It will only be a while, maybe, before nanotechnologists build a nanoscale "universal assembler," the basic building block of a molecular-scale factory, although researchers associated with Molecular Manufacturing, Xerox PARC, and NASA–Ames have already come up with the blueprints for many of the pieces that would make up such nanomachines. Within a generation, nanomedicine should emerge with nanomachines designed to do specific tasks—for example, scour buildup in an artery or blast a tumor into oblivion—and then self-destruct after they have finished. Data storage of unbelievable density will be possible. Electronic devices 100 to 750 times smaller than those in current computer chips could be used not only to compute but to sense and mend tissue inside the body. "Smart" materials that sense their environment and respond to it much like living tissue would have a wide array of medical applications within the body, the least of which would be greatly enhancing diagnostic abilities. The "lab on a chip"—miniature chemical laboratories a millimeter square—already speeds up analysis of blood and gene samples. Future minilabs might well form the core of a diagnostic system that is handheld or even implanted in the body.

In any case, as biosensors become more sophisticated and are linked with nanoscale internal body monitors, their use will greatly reduce the need for laboratory space in the hospital. Once true nanomachines arrive, their use will combine with biotechnology to turn medicine on its head. By the third decade of this century, instead of palliating, curing, and restoring the human body, we may well be enhancing it.

Pharmacology

Beginning in the 1990s, pharmacology radically changed its tactics. As a result of gene-mapping techniques already underway, the search for new drugs widened and speeded up. Under the old paradigm, common when the 1990s began, academic research labs, funded by the National Institutes of Health (NIH), carried out basic research. Large pharmaceutical companies looked over that research for the best leads, then tried to develop new drugs that worked. Today, the advance work is often carried out by biotech companies who get their funds from venture capitalists, private investors, investment banks, and the stock market. The giant pharmaceutical companies sniff out those biotech firms with the most promising lines of research and hook up with them in joint partnerships.

This rapid-fire development has resulted in a plethora of new and promising drugs that streak through the FDA-approval process. Hundreds of biotech drugs have already hit the market. In cancer treatment alone, new drugs have spilled onto the market from hundreds of clinical trials. With hundreds more in development, there will soon be an increase in our pharmacology armory unlike anything we've experienced. And because many if not most of these drugs were developed by studying specific changes in genes accompanying particular diseases, they proved far more targeted and successful than before.

As a result, we have seen a quite swift shift from surgery, especially of the more invasive type, toward a greater dependence on a much wider array of drugs. Among other things, this has lead to decreases in the length of stay, a reduced need for surgical suites and support services, and an increased need for home health services and electronic, Internet-mediated home contact with patients about their compound pharmaceutical regimens.

Treatment Modalities

In general, old-style surgery has come to be considered very invasive. Lasers—already extensively used in neurosurgery, vascular surgery, ophthalmology, laparoscopic procedures, and dental surgery—have expanded into orthopedic surgery and angioplasty. Photodynamic therapy, using site-specific dyes to color a tumor so that only it (and not surrounding tissue) is destroyed by laser light is available. Endoscopic surgery has developed as a minimally invasive alternative to conventional surgery.

Wherever possible, wholly noninvasive alternatives will continue to replace even minimally invasive surgery. Lithotripters, an acoustic alternative to surgery in the treatment of kidney and gall stones, are not likely to find their way out of hospitals due to cost; however, the procedure is becoming an outpatient treatment. As mentioned, a panoply of new drugs has reduced the necessity of surgery for dissolving vertebral disks, reducing coronary artery blockages, dissolving blood clots, and dissolving gall stones.

The therapeutic effects of electromagnetic fields (EMFs) are emerging. Until fairly recently, medical attention was focused exclusively on the potentially harmful effects of EMFs generated by such items as household wiring and power transmission lines. At selected frequencies, however, EMFs can accelerate the healing of fractured bones; stabilize irregular heart rhythms; aid in the control of seizures; accelerate healing of skin, tendons, and nerves; retard bacterial growth; and so on.

Robotic Surgery

As early as the mid-1990s, robotic devices were already being used in rigid endoscopy. About that time IBM and Integrated Surgical Systems of Sacramento, California, created Robodoc, a robot-surgeon designed to perform a highly specialized task in a very common kind of surgery: precisely milling out a cavity in the thigh bone to fit the prosthesis used in hip replacement. The tolerances involved are better suited to a precision machine shop than an operating room: a few thousandths of a centimeter. Robodoc, which is linked to a CT scanner, uses a CT image to mill out the required cavity with twenty times the accuracy of even the best human orthopedic surgeon.

Other robots appeared at the beginning of the twenty-first century, and what's new is that the surgeon hardly has to touch the companion robots that do the initial cutting through muscle and the stitching afterward. We have discussed the impact of robotic surgery on OR design in Chapter 7 since the FDA approved the da Vinci Surgical System robots for use in laparoscopic surgery in July 2000 and for noncardiac surgery in March 2001. Computer Motion, da Vinci's major rival, took a more modular approach, developing one-, two-, and three-armed versions of its robotic product, the ZEUS Surgical Robotic System.

The major economic argument for robots is probably in cardiac surgery in conjunction with three-dimensional digital imaging devices. In many operations, the surgeon is not even in the room for much of the procedure. Instead, a scrub nurse and sometimes a scrub tech attend the surgery physically, while the surgeon monitors the operation through three-dimensional head mounts from a nearby surgery command center, thus keeping the number in the sterile surgical field to a minimum. Most of the surgery is minimally invasive, done with miniature instruments through tiny incisions into arteries or through natural orifices, or noninvasive, using gamma knives or focused ultrasound devices. As a result, recovery times are shorter, outcomes better, and infections fewer. As the technology matures, robots are becoming especially useful in critical and exacting tasks like heart surgery and neurosurgery, where the robot's cutting is clean and precise, unperturbed by even the slightest tremor of a human hand that might make all the difference to a patient.

Decentralized Care and Self-Care

Forbidden Planet, a popular science-fiction movie of the 1950s, featured a lost civilization of an advanced race that had developed a technology free from "instrumentality"; they had only to think into existence whatever item they wanted or activity they wished to perform. Unlike the Krell (the name of

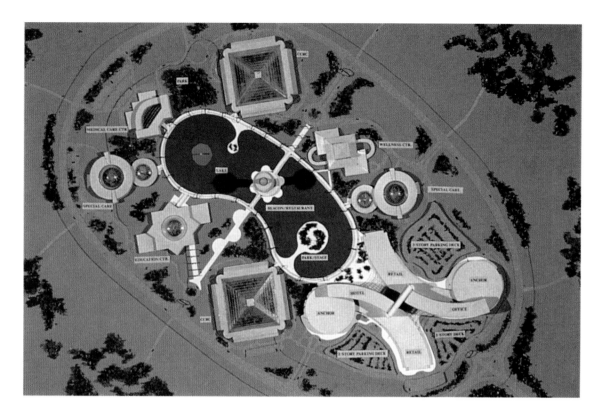

the extraterrestrial people in the movie), we have not yet eliminated instrumentality. But, since the invention and subsequent proliferation of the silicon chip, we have certainly made instrumentality small.

In 1946, ENIAC, the first fully electronic computer, was unveiled at the University of Pennsylvania; it weighed in at thirty tons and occupied 3,000 cubic feet of space. Running on 18,000 notoriously undependable vacuum tubes and costing millions to develop, it required highly trained specialists to operate it. Today's handheld devices (let alone even modest desktop or laptop personal computers) easily outstrip ENIAC's calculating power. Transistors are already microscopic; millions of them are arrayed on the central processing chips of all computers. The size of the individual transistor will continue to shrink, even down to the molecular level, so that billions and billions of transistors might be accommodated on a single chip. The result will be further miniaturization and enhancement of computing power, making electronics-intensive medical equipment ever more portable and affordable.

At the very least, smaller, less costly electronics and the development of wireless technology and the Internet will continue to feed the decentralization of sophisticated diagnostic imaging equipment. Few doctors these days even need to be on-site to interpret the results of such equipment, since data can be transmitted anywhere. At some point, monitoring devices will likely be so portable that they could be attached to, implanted in, or perhaps even injected into the body. A computer could monitor vital signs and other data continuously and in real time, alerting caregivers as well as the patient to any problems. This means that the patient being monitored could be physically independent of any central facility. Most likely, many of the problems

Synergenial Continuing Care Retirement Community (CCRC) Complex. The plan includes a chapel, lap pool, activity center, carillon, small pond, and various amenities such as a restaurant and pub, a research library, a computer center, and an investment club.

369

to which the monitoring system may alert him will be treated at home. These developments will give real impetus to the Medical Home models of healthcare. Also known as the Patient-Centered Medical Home (PCMH), it hails an approach to providing comprehensive primary care based on a partnership between individual patients and their personal providers facilitated by home scales and other equipment that read data and transfer it to the doctor for evaluation.

We could go on listing developing and likely-to-develop devices, but the point is that miniaturization, exponential increases in computing power, decreasing cost, and the universal ease of data transmission (both wireless and through fiber-optic lines), new genetic and biotechnical therapies, and the rapid marketing of powerful new drug treatments, all lead inexorably to the decentralization of care. This creates a continued decrease in inpatient care, a concomitant increase in ambulatory care, an increase in visitation to freestanding and satellite clinics, and an increase in self-care administered at home—perhaps the greatest growth market of all.

A Caveat

The aforementioned trends are real, but they are contingent, for healthcare needs can sometimes change radically and so can the designs of healthcare facilities. Consider the implication for healthcare architecture of some of the trends we discussed—we predicted that acute-care hospitals may grow fewer in number and, in general, smaller in size. But most of the new acute-care hospitals being built are often "megaplexes"—very large regional facilities. Yet there is an effort now to address rural markets with critical access hospitals; community hospitals that receive cost-based reimbursement from the government may feed the trend. We predict a trend toward fewer and smaller acute-care operations. If so, as acute-care hospitals shed beds, they will also convert significant portions of their operations to ambulatory care.

But what if—and that is always the controlling question in formulating scenarios—a disease epidemic surfaces, something akin to the recent Ebola outbreaks, that requires a high volume of protracted traditional acute care? In the rush to get rid of empty beds, it is possible that we may find ourselves critically short of acute-care facilities.

We have seen the economic and technological logic pushing hospitals away from inpatient care, but, indeed, we may also have already seen the "overbedded" phenomenon run its course. Certainly, more and more architectural clients are asking for more inpatient capacity. The period of greatest vulnerability will be whatever transitional span may stretch between the ongoing reduction of acute-care beds and the development of the preventive, diagnostic, and treatment techniques discussed earlier.

Consider another example—the critical condition of America's EDs. In a typical scenario, hallways are packed with "boarding" patients, stuck in healthcare limbo, who can't be sent home because they are too sick and can't be moved to an inpatient unit because the hospital is full. Waiting rooms are full of the sick and injured and ambulances are diverted to other facilities because there is no doctor, no nurse, no inch of space available to deal with another patient. The situation is acute in all types of hospitals—academic, public, and private—in both urban and rural areas.

Certainly, as we discussed in Chapter 5, emergency rooms have been in crisis before, but the overcrowding going on today is not confined to emergency medicine. It cannot be explained away by a heavy flu season; it is a direct result of less staff, fewer available beds, and patients going to the ED for primary care. Furthermore, when telemetry or intensive care units (ICUs) are filled, the ED becomes the de facto ICU. The situation has potential for danger, as the ED staff becomes overwhelmed with caring for critical or high-risk patients who have no hospital bed, while ambulances continue to arrive with seriously ill or injured patients.

But what if changes in medical insurance coverage fostered by healthcare reforms have a major impact on how patients use EDs? That would certainly have an impact on how we design them.

The downturn in the economy, the public disclosure of information required of hospitals, the increasingly savvy public on healthcare issues, the workforce shortages, the competition for patients, the customer-service orientation of hospitals, and the need for efficient operations are all factors we have touched on earlier that today have an impact on hospital design. Healthcare facility design trends now toward flexibility for future needs and to new technologies. We try these days to take into account such trends as medical tourism, a term originally coined to describe the rapidly growing travel across international borders to obtain healthcare; wellness care, which involves the physical, social, emotional, and occupational well-being of the patient; and alternative care, which considers healing practices that may not fall within the realm of conventional medicine.

And that, too, may change.

New Roles for Architects

Designers of future healthcare facilities will probably be asked to create whole healthcare communities, especially as a larger percentage of the population ages. By 2020 almost one-third of the U.S. population will be at least fifty-five years old, and some 9 million Americans will be over eighty-five. Planned communities focused on wellness and providing various levels of assisted living—a mega Continuing Care Retirement Community (CCRC)—for a significant segment of the population, may take the place of hospitals, skilled-nursing facilities, and retirement villages.

Such communities, as exemplified by the "Synergenial Suburban Village" designed by ESa, may become as pervasive in this century as the development of planned suburban communities was in the early post–World War II period. The Synergenial Suburban Village integrates healthcare-oriented eldercare into the heart of a community that would include 1.3 million sq. ft. of office space; an 800-room hotel; a covered shopping galleria; continuing education and conference facilities; recreational, fitness, cultural, and amusement facilities; and a medical center with 320 acute-care rooms, a medical office building, a diagnostic center, and full outpatient facilities. The entire Synergenial Suburban Village would be standardized for a seventy-year-old, 5-foot-4 female rather than the customary thirty-year-old, 5-foot-10 male.

Maybe, at some point in the future, anything even remotely resembling today's hospitals will have ceased to exist. But for at least much of this century there will be hospitals—in addition to other, smaller healthcare facilities. What will administrators and planners look for in hospital buildings that are built in the next twenty-five years? The key word will be flexibility.

As Thomas F. Frist, Jr., then chairman of HCA Healthcare Corporation, once observed, "The hospital for the twenty-first century will serve as a nerve center for a fully integrated health delivery system. As a template, it must have built-in flexibility to adjust to its ever-changing network."

The concept of flexibility extends beyond what the architect designs to the architect himself. The architect will provide a range of services beyond the traditional architecture and engineering (A&E) tasks, including strategic business planning, evaluation of lease-versus-build options, financial planning, mechanical and electrical systems evaluation, space planning inventories, furniture inventories, long-range planning, and master planning. Once the building is completed, the architect will remain in contact with the owners for the life of the facility, providing a full range of services on a contractual basis. These services will include ongoing evaluation and planning for expansion, contraction, and adaptation to changing needs.

Practice Architecture, Practice Medicine

Architects will be called in on planning processes earlier, they will be asked to contribute a very broad range of expertise, and they will be active during the entire lifespan of the building. In this sense, then, architects will serve as caregivers, practitioners of medicine, and members of the patient-care team. But there is a more profound dimension of this new role.

The present cutting-edge and future of healthcare architecture are being driven by economics, as well as by two imperatives usually assumed to be antagonistic: high technology and high humanity. We hope this book, especially with its emphasis on "green" design and evidence-based, patient-centered design—has demonstrated that these need not be mutually exclusive. Quite the contrary, as high technology can be used to foster a higher and higher degree of humanity in healthcare. Still, two imperatives do lead us to a paradox, which, we believe, penetrates to the heart of the future of hospital and healthcare facility design.

In ancient Egypt, Greece, and India—and in other venerable cultures as well—healing was associated with temples and magical spaces. We who have built our own temples to science and technology and commerce have long looked on such magical, mystical notions with a mixture of wonder, envy, and contempt, judging them as the nineteenth-century British critic and essayist Matthew Arnold judged them: the delightful products of humanity's "childhood." Yet, as they say in fairytales, "lo and behold!"

Our science has led us, through a long and meandering course, back to a concept similar to those healing temples of old. We now know that places can make you sick and can also help to make you well. The hospital can no longer be thought of as a shelter—a mere shell—within which some healing activity takes place. The healthcare environment is integral to that healing, an instrument of that healing as surely as is a scalpel, a laser beam, an electromagnetic field, or the human touch of a dedicated caregiver. The commitment of ESa's use of sustainable design—and its enthusiastic participation in the Planetree process—points to the company's twofold commitment. First, we believe in creating healthy environments that incorporate the ideals of high-performance architecture. Second, as a company, we are proactively responsible with our own work habits as well as our outreach efforts to the communities we inhabit and serve. Combined, we are actively working to conserve and improve the environment around us.

In short, we believe the healthcare environment of the future, and that is why ESa incorporated sustainable, green-building initiatives in its designs well in advance of industry trends. As a member of the U.S. Green Building Council (USGBC), ESa supports the concept of creating spaces that are environmentally responsible, high-performance, profitable, and healthy. We feel that sustainability and the basic principles of good design are synonymous and, therefore, use them as a basis for design in our projects—from front-end site selection and building placement to the final selection of finishes and furniture.

So whatever directions the healthcare design of the future may take, it will include an expression of what we have long called Synergenial design and practice now as part of the Planetree Visionary Network: a new direction in architecture based on human-inspired, evidence-based design, state of-the-art engineering and sustainable environments, and sound economics to create spaces that can evoke positive human responses, appeal to the senses, are task-oriented, and function well both physically and emotionally. In fact, Earl Swensson first coined the term *Synergenial* to illustrate what he saw as architecture's movement beyond a structure's technical makeup and toward its potential for inspiring wellness. Synergenial design has always been healing design: the orchestration of all elements for the purpose of bringing about well-being. This is a holistic approach to healthcare and a holistic approach to architecture as the facilitator of health. We do not intend it to be our prescription for the future. Instead, we earnestly believe and we ardently hope it is a *description* of the future.

Synergenial Continuing Care Retirement Community (CCRC) Complex. Within the CCRC complexes, all design accommodates the physical, social, and emotional needs of residents, who would range in age from 75 to 110. The two CCRC structures are six stories tall and situated on 10 acres; they offer 320 apartments to accommodate a population of approximately 800 individuals.

Selected Bibliography

Academic Emergency Medicine (February 2001).

"Acute Care Stacked on Public Uses: Marin General Hospital Addition," *Architectural Record*, vol. 178, no. 7 (June 1990), 94–97.

Aging America: Trends and Projections, U.S. Senate Special Committee Report on Aging. Washington, D.C.: Department of Health and Human Services, 1991.

Aging Design Research Program: Design for Aging: Strategies for Collaboration Between Architects and Occupational Therapists. Washington: ADRP (1993).

Ahuja, Jan, et al. "IRIS: An Experimental Multimedia Workstation Linking the Departments of Emergency Medicine and Radiological Sciences," *Journal of Emergency Medicine*, vol. 11 (1993), 219–28.

Aker, Jenna M. "Healthcare Meets Hospitality," *Buildings Magazine* (October 2008).

Alati, Danine. "Health Building," *Contract* (October 2009), 2–4.

Aldridge, Eva, et al. "VIP Suites: A New Trend," *Journal of Health Care Interior Design*, vol. 3 (1991), 85–95.

Allen, David, and Margaret Davis. "A Computerized CIS Enhances Bedside Intensive Care," *Nursing Management*, vol. 23, no. 7 (July 1992), 112I–12P.

Allen, Floyd. "The Special Concerns of Healthcare Facilities," *Commercial Building* (August/September 1999), 16–18.

Altenhoff, Jenifer. "Hospes," *Ekriture*, vol. 3 (July 1993), 18–23.

Alt-White, Anna C., et al. "Selection and Development of a Critical Care Bedside Computer," *Nursing Management*, vol. 23, no. 7 (July 1992), 112A–12H.

AHA Hospital Statistics, 2011 Edition. Chicago: American Hospital Association.

An Introduction to Evidence-Based Design. Concord, CA: Center for Health Design (2008).

Anderson, Howard J. "Are Hospitals Prepared for More Growth in Ambulatory Care?" *Trustee*, vol. 44, no. 9 (September 1991), 16–17.

_____. "Improving Access to Care Drives Updated ED Designs," *Health Facilities Management* (March 1993), 42–46.

_____. "Survey Identifies Trends in Equipment Acquisitions," *Hospitals* (September 20, 1992), 30–35.

_____. "Survey: Equipment Budgets Up; Use in Outpatient Areas Growing," *Hospitals* (September 20, 1992), 38–44.

Anderson, John W. "Nursing Facility Design Offers Residential Look, Feel—Inside and Out," *Health Facilities Management* (November 1993), 14–15.

Anderson, Neil. "The Medical Office Building: A Strategic Key to the Future," *Trustee*, vol. 42, no. 2 (February 1989), 15, 19.

Anderson, Rebecca Cogwell, and Kim Edward Anderson. "Worksite Health Promotion," *AAOHN (American Association of Occupational Health Nurses) Journal*, vol. 39, no. 2 (February 1991), 57–61.

Aoun, Andre. "Developmental and Family-Centered Care," *Designing for Child Health: Institute for Family Centered Care*, vol. 3, no. 1 (Spring 1995), 14–15.

Apallas, Alexa K. "Building on Success," *Healthcare Construction and Operations*, vol. 4, no. 1 (January/February 2006).

Aquavella, James V. "Ambulatory Surgery in the 1990s," *Journal of Ambulatory Care Management*, vol. 13, no. 1 (1990), 21–24.

Aragone, Joan. "Planning Around Technology," *Healthcare Business, Facility Design* (April 2001).

Archer, Benjamin R., et al. "Protective Barriers for X-Ray Facilities," *The Construction Specifier*, vol. 46, no. 8 (August 1993), 82–90.

"Architectural Showplace, Community Hospital: Central DuPage Hospital, Winfield, IL," *Healthcare Design*, vol. 6, no. 5 (September 2006).

"Architectural Showplace, Community Hospital: Floyd Medical Center, Rome, GA," *Healthcare Design*, vol. 6, no. 5 (September 2006).

"Architectural Showplace: St. Vincent's One Nineteen Health and Wellness Center, Birmingham, AL," *Health Care Design*, vol. 5, no. 4 (September 2005).

Arcidi, Philip. Linear Nursing Unit: Cardiac Patient Tower, St. Luke's Medical Center, Milwaukee, Wisconsin," *Progressive Architecture*, vol. 72, no. 3 (March 1992), 94–95.

Ardron, M. E., and A. Finneston. "Use of Rehabilitation Apartments for Elderly Patients," *Age and Aging*, vol. 19, no. 3 (1990), 195–98.

"ASC Design, Development and Construction, Part 1," *Today's SurgiCenter*, vol. 4, no. 6 (June 2006).

Ashley, Mary Holt. "Discharge Holding Area: Using Inpatient Beds More Effectively," *Journal of Nursing Administration*, vol. 19, no. 12 (December 1989), 32–35.

"Atrium Medical Center, Middletown, OH," *Modern Healthcare* (September 22, 2008).

Bailey, Laura, et al. "Wellness Centers," *Journal of Healthcare Design* (September 1993), 105–14.

Baker, Carol F. "Discomfort to Environmental Noise: Heart Rate Responses of SICU Patients," *Critical Care Nursing Quarterly*, vol. 15, no. 2 (August 1992), 75–90.

Balsano, Armand E., and Frances J. Fowler. "Subacute Care as a New Source of Revenue," *Healthcare Financial Management*, vol. 47, no. 7 (July 1993), 56–62.

Bame, Sherry I. "Design Research: Ambulatory Clinic Design: The Case of Dialysis Facilities," *Journal of Healthcare Design*, (September 1993), 125–33.

Bantle, Anita. "Automated Workforce Tracking Keeps You Flexible," *IT Solutions* (September 2007), 29–32.

Barber, Janet M. "Key Considerations in Emergency and Trauma Unit Design," *Critical Care Nursing Quarterly*, vol. 14, no. 1 (1991), 71–82.

Bardoczi, Stephen J. "Dual Alzheimer's Unit Sensitively Carved Out of X-Shaped Floor Plan," *Health Facilities Management*, vol. 3, no. 10 (Spring 1990), 14–15.

Barillo, David J., et al. "Utilization of the Burn Unit for Nonburn Patients: The 'Wound Intensive Care Unit'," *Annals of Plastic Surgery*, vol. 23, no. 5 (November 1989), 426–29.

Barista, Dave. "Healthcare Embraces Hospitality," *Building Design and Construction* (November 2000).

Barker, David. "Design Guide—Radiotherapy," *Hospital Development*, vol. 24, no. 9 (October 1993), 19–22.

Barker, Kenneth N., et al. "Effect of Technological Changes in Information Transfer on the Delivery of Pharmacy Services," *American Journal of Pharmaceutical Education* (Winter Supplement 1989), 27S–40S.

Barton, Anne K. "Mainstreaming Inpatients and Outpatients: Modifying Systems to Everyone's Advantage," *AORN (Association of periOperative Registered Nurses) Journal*, vol. 41, no. 2 (February 1985), 386–88.

_____. "Swing Beds: A Nursing Challenge," *Nursing Management*, vol. 21, no. 8 (August 1990), 34–35.

Bauer, Suzanne. "A Sense of Wonder: Interiors at a Children's Hospital Spark the Imagination of Its Patients," *Hospitality Design*, vol. 14, no. 8 (September 1992), 36–38.

Beale, Craig. "Medical Mall Conveys a 21st Century Image with Room to Expand," *Health Facilities Management*, vol. 1, no. 1 (September 1988), 16–17.

Beck, Melinda, et al. "State of Emergency: Hospitals Are Seeking Radical Solutions to Ease Walk-In patient Overload," *Newsweek*, vol. 118, no. 16 (October 14, 1991), 52–53.

Becker, Cinda. "Imaging: The Next Generation," *Modern Healthcare* (November 27, 2000), 48–52, 61.

Becker, Cinda. "Look, No Hands—With Surgical Robots, Industry Embraces Cutting-Edge Technology," *Modern Healthcare, Special Report* (April 30, 2001), 36–46.

Beckham, J. Daniel. "Beating the Box: Those Who Have Predicted the Demise of the American Hospital Have Missed the Point—They Are Focused on a Hospital as an Edifice," *Healthcare Forum Journal*, vol. 35, no. 2 (March/April 1992), 55–58.

Beckwith, Deanne. *The Coherence of Color: A Palette for Health Care Designers.* Zeeland, Michigan: Milcare (1993).

Begley, Sharon. "AIDS at 20," *Newsweek* (June 11, 2001).

Behar, Richard. "Medicine's $10 Billion Bonanza: Fitness Centers," *Forbes*, vol. 141, no. 13 (June 13, 1988), 101–6.

Behar, Susan. "Making Accessibility Easy on the Eye," *The Construction Specifier*, vol. 45, no. 6 (June 1992), 114–19.

_____. "Universal Design Blends Function with Form," *Group Practice Journal*, vol. 40, no. 4 (July/August 1991), 87–88.

Bell, Susan. "Earl Swensson Associates, Inc., Creating Environments for the 21st Century," *Builder/Architect, Middle Tennessee Edition* (May 1995).

"Belmont University, The Gordon E. Inman Center—College of Health Sciences and Nursing," *Learning by Design*, Washington, D.C.: National School Boards Association (2007).

Benya, James R. "Advanced Health Care Facility Lighting Design," address delivered October 15, 1993.

_____. "Lighting for Healing," *Journal of Health Care Interior Design*, vol. 1 (1989), 55–58.

_____. "The Lighting Design Professional," *Architectural Lighting*, vol. 3, no. 1 (January 1989), 44–48.

Bergman, Rhonda. "Integrated Information Paves the Way to Better Decision Making on Patient Care," *Hospitals and Health Networks*, vol. 68, no. 1 (January 5, 1994), 56.

_____. "Quantum Leaps: A Look at the Health Care Delivery System in Twenty Years," *Hospitals and Health Networks*, vol. 67, no. 19 (October 5, 1993), 28, 31–35.

_____. "Letting Telemedicine Do the Walking," *Hospitals and Health Networks*, vol. 67, no. 20 (October 20, 1993), 46–48.

Bergoust, Donald G. "St. Patrick Hospital: Innovations in HVAC and Plumbing," *The Construction Specifier*, vol. 40, no. 10 (October 1987), 101–7.

Bergstrom, Ebba. "Bathrooms Designed for the Disabled," *Nursing Mirror*, vol. 160, no. 5 (June 19, 1985), 21–24.

"Big Punch in a Small Package: The Emerging Nanotechnology Revolution," *Medical Construction and Design* (May/June 2008), 22–23.

Biner, Paul M., et al. "Inside Windows: An Alternative to Conventional Windows in Offices and Other Settings," *Environment and Behavior*, vol. 23, no. 3 (May 1991), 359–82.

Birdsong, Craig, and Cynthia Leibrock. "Patient-Centered Design," *Healthcare Forum Journal*, vol. 33, no. 3 (May/June 1990), 40–45.

Birkmeier, Tom. "Reskinning the Aging Building: A Hot Option for the Facility Master Plan," *Healthcare Design*, vol. 6, no. 2 (February 2006).

Birren, Faber. *Color Psychology and Color Therapy.* New York: Carol (1992).

"Birth of Universal Health, Inc.," *The Economist*, vol. 330, no. 7856 (March 26, 1994), 73–74.

"Birthing Centers Gain Market Share," *Healthcare Building Ideas* (April 5, 2007), 87–93.

Black, Cherie. "To Build a Better Hospital, Virginia Mason Takes a Lesson from Toyota Plants," *Seattle Post-Intelligencer* (March 15, 2008).

Blaese, R. Michael, et al. "Gene Therapy: Sci-Fi No Longer," *Patient Care*, vol. 27, no. 11 (June 15, 1993), 24–27, 30, 35, 38–39, 42.

Blatterman, Joan. "The Future: Health Delivery and Design: 2000 to 2040," *Architectural Record*, vol. 185, no. 5 (May 1997), 304.

Bleeker, Nick. "Well-Lighted: Health-Care Environments Can Benefit from Technology That Delivers High-Quality Light at Low Cost," *Construction Specifier*, vol. 46, no. 8 (August 1993), 92–95.

Blignaut, John D. "The Fetal Care Center: Designing a Center to Meet Advances in Medical Care," *Medical Construction and Design* (November/December 2007), 42–44.

Blyth, Pamela L., ed. *Health Care Interior Finishes: Problems and Solutions—An Environmental Services Perspective.* Chicago: American Society for Healthcare Environmental Services of the American Hospital Association (1993).

Bodnar, James. "Prescription Flooring," *The Construction Specifier*, vol. 44, no. 8 (August 1991), 74–81.

Boerger, John, and Mardelle Shepley. "Mental Health Design: A Case Study," *Journal of Health Care Interior Design*, vol. 3 (1991), 149–57.

Bonine, Bruce R. "Alternative Futures in Health Care," *Health Care Strategic Management*, vol. 8, no. 1 (January 1990), 12–15.

Borzo, Greg. "New Hospitals May Resemble Malls," *Health Care Strategic Management*, vol. 10, no. 11 (November 1992), 17–19.

_____. "Patient-Focused Hospitals Begin Reporting Good Results," *Health Care Strategic Management*, vol. 10, no. 8 (August 1992), 1, 17–22.

Bosker, Gideon. "Architecture as an Asset in Health Care," *Architecture*, vol. 76, no. 1 (January 1987), 35–39.

Brantley, Angela. "Rising Violence in ERs Cause Hospitals to Redesign Security," *Modern Healthcare*, vol. 22, no. 40 (October 5, 1992), 44–45.

Bray, Karen A., and Kathryn Hearn. "Critical Care Unit Design, Part I: Organizing Plans," *Nursing Management*, vol. 24, no. 1 (January 1993), 80A–80H.

_____. "Critical Care Unit Design, Part II: Monitoring Operations," *Nursing Management*, vol. 24, no. 2 (February 1993), 80J–80O.

_____. "Critical Care Unit Design, Part III: Establishing Operations," *Nursing Management*, vol. 24, no. 3 (March 1993), 64A–64H.

Bridgers, Mark, Peggy Lawless, and Blake Church. "How Changes in Healthcare May Affect Your Strategy," *Fails Management Institute (FMI) Quarterly*, issue 3 (2007), 112–33.

Brinkley, James. "An Environment of Caring," *Designing for Child Health: Institute for Family Centered Care*, vol. 1, no. 1 (Summer 1993), 1–3.

Brock, John E. "Solving Difficult Site Problems for MRI and PET," *European Journal of Radiology*, vol. 16 (1992), 30–34.

Brown, George. "Construction Alternatives for Free-Standing Facilities," *Radiology Management*, vol. 12, no. 1 (Winter 1990), 27–30.

Buckley, Jean Amerault, et al. "Medical Office Design: Brigham West Medical Office Campus," *Journal of Healthcare Design*, vol. 4 (1992), 87–92.

"Building a Caring Community: Freeport Hospital Health Care Village," *Architectural Record*, vol. 178, no. 7 (June 1990), 90–94.

Building Design for Handicapped and Aged Persons: Council on Tall Buildings and Urban Habitat. New York: McGraw-Hill (1992).

Bunke, JoAnn. "Selecting Lifts for Patients with Special Needs," *American Nurse Today* (March 2007), 54–55.

Bunker-Hellmich, Lou Ann and Terri Zborowsky. "The Inside Scoop on Safety: Hospital Interiors Must Keep Patients and Staff Secure from Injury," *Medical Construction and Design* (May/June 2009), 42–45.

Burda, David. "Total Quality Management Becomes Big Business: But All the Hype May Actually Be Adding to Hospitals' Operating Costs," *Modern Healthcare*, vol. 21, no. 4 (January 28, 1991), 25–29.

Burke, Marybeth. "New Surgical Technologies Reshape Hospital Strategies," *Hospitals*, vol. 66, no. 9 (May 5, 1992), 30–42.

Burmahl, Beth. "Facilities of the Future," *Health Facilities Management*, vol. 13, no. 2 (February 2000).

———. "Facility Profile: Fayette Focuses on Family, Flexibility," *Health Facilities Management*, vol. 11, no. 9 (September 1998).

Burnett, Linda. "Designed to Heal," *Contract* (March 2001), 82–84.

Burnette, Sam. "Gearing Up for the Outpatient: A Masterplan for the Year 2000," *Nashville Medical News* (February 1994), 13–15.

———. "Physical Connection to Hospital Provides Tennessee Outpatient Center with the Best of Both Worlds," *Today's SurgiCenter* (July 2005).

Burns, Jenny. "New Hospital, Middle Tennessee Medical Center, Breaks Mold: Patient-room Layout, Construction Method s Girst in Region," *Nashville Business Journal* (October 9, 2009).

Burns, John. "Long-term Chains Post Strong Growth in Subacute, Specialty Care," *Modern Healthcare*, vol. 23, no. 21 (May 24, 1993), 63–69.

———. "Market Opening Up to the Non-Traditional," *Modern Healthcare*, vol. 23, no. 9 (August 9, 1993), 96–98.

———. "Move to Outpatient Settings May Boost Medical Hotels," *Modern Healthcare*, vol. 22, no. 23 (June 8, 1992), 57–58.

———. "Special Units Aim at Dementia," *Modern Healthcare*, vol. 22, no. 46 (November 16, 1992), 26–30.

———. "Subacute Care Feeds Need to Diversify," *Modern Healthcare*, vol. 23, no. 50 (December 13, 1993), 338–343.

Bush-Brown, Albert, and Dianne Davis. *Hospitable Design for Healthcare and Senior Communities*. New York: Van Nostrand Reinhold, 1992.

Butler, Darrell L., et al. "Wayfinding by Newcomers in a Complex Building," *Human Factors*, vol. 35, no. 1 (1993), 159–73.

Bynam, Jim, and Gary Justice. "Shhh … It's Quiet Time: Hospital Designers Find Innovative Ways to Reduce Noise at Healthcare Facilities," *Healthcare Construction and Operations* (July/August 2008), 12–13.

Calkins, Margaret P. *Design for Dementia: Planning Environments for the Elderly and the Confused*. Owings Mills, MD: National Health Publishing (1988).

———. "Designing Cues for Wanderers," *Architecture*, vol. 78, no. 10 (October 1989), 117–18.

———. "Designing for an Aging Population," *Healthcare Forum Journal*, vol. 35, no. 5 (September/October 1992), 22–23.

———. "Executive Forum: The Corinne Dolan Alzheimer Center," *Journal of Healthcare Design*, vol. 4 (1992), 17–23.

Cannman, Sheila F. "The Changing Face of Critical Care," *Healthcare Design*, vol. 8, no. 11 (November 2008), 48–54.

Canter, Eric W. "Structuring Freestanding Diagnostic Imaging Centers for Profitability," *Radiology Management*, vol. 12, no. 2 (Spring 1990), 29–34.

Carlson, Leanne Kaiser. "Creating Designs That Heal," *California Hospitals*, vol. 6, no. 3 (May/June 1992), 12–14.

Carpman, Janet R. "Wayfinding in Health Care: 6 Common Myths," *Health Facilities Management*, vol. 3, no. 5 (May 1991), 24, 26–28.

Carpman, Janet R., and Myron A. Grant. *Design That Cares: Planning Health Facilities for Patients and Visitors*, 2nd ed. Chicago: American Hospital Publishing, Inc. (1993).

Carr, Tony, and Carolyn S. Webster. "Recovery Care Centers: An Innovative Approach to Caring for Healthy Surgical Patients," *AORN (Association of periOperative Registered Nurses) Journal*, vol. 53, no. 4 (April 1991), 986–95.

Carter, Edward, et al. "Acute Care Design: San Diego Children's Hospital and Health Center Addition," *Journal of Healthcare Design* (September 1993), 25–31.

Castilla, John. "The Contractor's View: Welcome to the Neighborhood," *Healthcare Design*, vol. 7, no. 9 (August 2007), 16–21.

Ceder, Ken. "Design Technology: Lighting for Health," *Journal of Healthcare Design*, vol. 4 (1992), 145–48.

"Center for Cancer Care at Griffin Hospital, Derby, CT," *Architectural Stone And Landscape Design* (Winter 2008), 8–12.

Centers for Disease Control. "Healthy People 2000: National Health Promotion, Disease Prevention Objectives for the Year 2000," *Journal of the American Medical Association (JAMA)*, vol. 264, no. 16 (October 24/31, 1990), 2057–58.

Ceol, Dawn Weyrich. "Total Quality Management," *Provider*, vol. 19, no. 9 (September 1991), 35–48.

Cerne, Frank. "Homeward Bound: Hospitals See Solid Future for Home Health Care," *Hospitals*, vol. 67, no. 4 (February 20, 1993), 52–54.

Chartbook on Health Data on Older Americans: United States, 1992. Hyattsville, MD: U.S. Department of Health and Human Services; Public Health Service; Centers for Disease Control and Prevention; National Center for Health Statistics (1993).

Chapman, Robert H. "Thoughts for the Day: The Shift Towards Day Surgery . . . ," *Hospital Development*, vol. 24, no. 8 (September 1993), 21–22.

Chaudhury, H., A. Mahmood, and M. Valente. "The Effect of Environmental Design on Reducing Nursing Errors and Increasing Efficiency in Acute Care Settings: A Review and Analysis of the Literature," *Environment and Behavior*, vol. 41, no. 6 (2009), 755–86.

Chernow, Bart. "The Bedside Laboratory: A Critical Step Forward in ICU Care," *Chest*, vol. 97, no. 5 (May 1990 supplement), 183S–84S.

"Child Kingdom," *Contract*, vol. 31, no. 2 (February 1989), 110–11.

"Children's Hospital Design Promotes Hope and Healing," *Design Solutions: Journal of the Architectural Woodwork Institute* (Winter 2005), 2–8.

Chu, Stephen. "Part I, Clinical Information Systems: A Fourth Generation," *Nursing Management*, vol. 24, no. 10 (October 1993), 59–60.

Cline, Marilyn, and Kava Maasih. "Renovated Satellite Clinics Brighten a Neighborhood," *Designing for Child Health: Institute for Family Centered Care*, vol. 2, no. 2 (Fall 1994), 5–7.

"Clinic Plus Doctor's Office," *Architectural Record*, vol. 173, no. 12 (October 1985), 132–133.

Coe, Rodney M. *Sociology of Medicine*. New York: McGraw-Hill (1978).

Cohen, Robert C. "When Care is Denied, Bureaucracy and Cost Controls are the Culprits ... Two Patients' Story: Battling the System," *Los Angeles Times*, Part A (August 27, 1995), 16.

Cohen, Uriel, and Gerald D. Weisman. *Holding On To Home: Designing Environments for People with Dementia*. Baltimore: Johns Hopkins University Press (1991).

Cohen, Uriel, and Kristen Day. *Contemporary Environments for People with Dementia*. Baltimore: Johns Hopkins University Press (1993).

Coile, Russell C., Jr. "The Megatrends—and the Backlash," *Healthcare Forum Journal*, vol. 33, no. 3 (March/April 1990), 37–41.

————. "Six Predictions for the Nineties," *Healthcare Forum Journal*, vol. 33, no. 3 (May/June 1990), 69–70.

Coker, Robert H. "Modular Facility Grafts Speed with Lower Costs in Customized Skin Clinic: University Medical Center Dermatology Clinic, Tucson," *Health Facilities Management* (April 1992), 18–19.

Collett, Howard M. "1990 Helipad Survey," *Journal of Air Medical Transport*, vol. 9, no. 8 (August 1990), 20–21.

Comer, Billie and Ryan. "When Care is Denied, Bureaucracy and Cost Controls are the Culprits ... Two Patients' Story: Experimental Problem," *Los Angeles Times*, Part A (August 27, 1995), 16.

Condon, Marian. "Environment, Health, and Safety," *American Nurse Today* (April 2007), 50.

Conlin, D. Walters. "Future Health Care: Increasing the 'Alternatives'," *The Futurist*, vol. 22, no. 3 (May/June 1988), 15.

Cooper, Helene. "Offering Aerobics, Karate, Aquatics, Hospitals Stress Business of 'Wellness'," *Wall Street Journal* (August 9, 1993), B1.

"Cosmetic Surgery: Remedy for Hospital's Dated-Looking Façade Is New Rain Screen Curtain Wall Cladding System," *Metal Architecture* (January 2004).

Coster, Ronald L. "Substance-Abuse Centers," *Journal of Health Care Interior Design*, vol. 2 (1990), 55–63.

"The Course for Health Care," *Florida AEC Trends*, vol. 1, no. 4 (November 1998).

Cowan, Timothy J., et al. "Intensive Care Design," *The Construction Specifier*, vol. 46, no. 8 (August 1993), 48–59.

Cowley, Geoffrey, and Pat Wingert. "Trouble in the Nursery: Are Hospital Lights Blinding Premature Babies?," *Newsweek*, vol. 114, no. 9 (August 1989), 52.

Cox, Anthony, and Philip Groves. *Hospitals and Health-Care Facilities: A Design and Development Guide*. London: Butterworth Architecture (1990).

Craig, Sanna. "Consumer Clout: Healthcare Customers," *Healthcare Forum Journal*, vol. 31, no. 2 (March/April 1988), 10–20.

Cramer, Carol, and Virginia R. Renz. "Preoperative Care Unit: An Alternative to the Holding Room," *AORN (Association of periOperative Registered Nurses) Journal*, vol. 45, no. 2 (February 1987), 464–72.

"Creating a Healing Environment," Design Solutions: Journal of the Architectural Woodwork Institute (Winter 2009).

Croshie, Michael J. "Universal Hardware: Simplicity Is the Key to Specifying Hardware for the Disabled," *Architecture*, vol. 80, no. 7 (July 1991), 88–89.

Croswell, Camille L. "Building New Strategies," *Modern Healthcare* (March 12, 2001), 23, 36.

Cruz, Laurie D. "Ambulatory Surgery—The Next Decade," *AORN (Association of periOperative Registered Nurses) Journal*, vol. 51, no. 1 (January 1990), 241–47.

Culley, James D., Ph.D., et al. "Digital Radiography Systems: An Overview," *Radiology Management* (November/December 2000), 24–33.

"Cumberland at Green Hills, Nashville, Tennessee," *Design Environments for the Aging* (March 2008).

Currie, John Michael. *The Fourth Factor: A Historical Perspective on Architecture and Medicine*. New York: American Institute of Architecture (2007).

Dancer, Gail E. "Automated Transport Systems," *Hospital Management International* (1991), 264–65.

Davidson, Stuart N. "Tomorrow's Medicine," *Healthcare Forum Journal* (July/August 1996), 16–19.

Davis, James E., "Ambulatory Surgery . . . How Far Can We Go?," *Medical Clinics of North America*, vol. 77, no. 2 (March 1993), 365–75.

Deliganis, Sam G. "Maternity-wing 'Face-lift' Becomes Big Renovation to Recoup Market Share," *Health Facilities Management*, vol. 3, no. 12 (December 1990), 10–11.

DeLong, Deanna L. "Preoperative Holding Area: Personalizing Patients' Experiences," *AORN (Association of periOperative Registered Nurses) Journal*, vol. 55, no. 2 (February 1992), 563–66.

Dennery, Phyllis A. "Shattered Dreams: Impressions of a Neonatologist as the Parent of a Preemie," *Designing for Child Health: Institute for Family Centered Care*, vol. 3, no. 1 (Spring 1995), 7–8.

Derlet, Robert W., M.D., et al. "Frequent Overcrowding in U.S. Emergency Departments," *Academic Emergency Medicine*, vol. 8, no. 2 (February 2001), 151–55.

Design Considerations for Mental Health Facilities: American Institute of Architects, Committee on Architecture for Health. Washington, D.C.: American Institute of Architects Press (1993).

Designing Healthy Buildings: Indoor Air Quality: American Institute of Architects Building Performance and Regulations Committee/Committee on the Environment. Washington, D.C.: American Institute of Architects (1992).

Devlin, Ann Sloan. "Psychiatric Ward Renovation: Staff Perception and Patient Behavior," *Environment and Behavior*, vol. 24, no. 1 (January 1992), 66–84.

DeWitt, Paul Mergenhagen. "The Birth Business," *American Demographics*, vol. 15, no. 9 (September 1993), 44–49.

————. "In Pursuit of Pregnancy," *American Demographics*, vol. 15, no. 5 (May 1993), 48–54.

DiMotta, Susan, et al. "Long-Term Care Design: Blazing New Territory—Code Reform and Beyond," *Journal of Healthcare Design*, vol. 5 (1993), 197–203.

Donovan, Michelle Regan. "The Changing Face of Emergency and Trauma Centers: Promoting Efficacy with Design," *AHA Healthcare Facilities Management Series*, 055350 (October 1992).

————. "An Endangered Resource: Hospital Emergency Departments Are Threatened by Closures and a Reduction in Services," *Health Progress* (May 1991), 50–53.

Dorn, Suzanne. "The Beat Goes On: Heart Center of Sarasota Florida," *Hospitality Design*, vol. 15, no. 1 (January/February 1993), 46–49.

————. "Fresh Start: Imaginative Interiors Lift the Spirits of Young Patients at This Children's Burn Hospital," *Hospitality Design*, vol. 15, no. 5 (June 1993), 40–44.

————. "Separate But Equal: A New Women's Hospital in San Diego Offers State-of-the-Art Care with a Warm and Cheery Look," *Hospitality Design*, vol. 15, no. 8 (October 1993), 54–59.

Downes, John J. "The Historical Evolution, Current Status, and Prospective Development of Pediatric Critical Care," *Critical Care Clinics*, vol. 8, no. 1 (January 1992), 1–23.

Downey, Jessica. "Hospital(ity) Corners: Taking Hotel Know-how on the Road, a Tennessee Firm Brings Inspiration to Hospitals," *Lodging: The Official Magazine of the American Hotel and Lodging Association* (April 2004).

Downing, Jack W. "Hospital Doubles Size of Emergency Center—Without Disrupting Care," *Health Facilities Management*, vol. 5, no. 12 (December 1992), 12–13.

Dubbs, Dana. "The New Generation: Efficiencies, Added Services and High-End Touches Are Priorities in Today's Rural Hospital Designs," *Health Facilities Management*, vol. 18, no. 9 (September 2005).

Dubin, Fred S. "Intelligent Buildings: HVAC, Lighting and Other Design Trends," *The Construction Specifier*, vol. 43, no. 8 (February 1990), 51–57.

Dubnicki, Carol, and James B. Williams. "The People Side of TQM," *Healthcare Forum Journal*, vol. 35, no. 5 (September/October 1992), 54–61.

DuBose, Jan and Terry Donahue. "Taking the Pain Out of Patient Handling," *American Nurse Today* (December 2006), 37–43.

"DuPont/HFM Forum on Carpet in Health Care Facilities," *Health Facilities Management*, vol. 7, no. 2 (February 1994), 38–46.

Dyer, Dorothy. "Rehab Center Offers Hotel-Like Comforts for Injured 'Guests'," *Health Facilities Management*, vol. 2, no. 5 (May 1989), 14–15.

Dyer, Ian D. "Meeting the Needs of Visitors—A Practical Approach," *Intensive Care Nursing*, vol. 7 (1991), 135–47.

Eagle, Amy. "Back to Nature: Using Natural and Recycled Materials to Give Hospitals a Fresh Look," *Health Facilities Management*, vol. 22, no. 9 (September 2009).

_____. "Fit for Life: New Facility Helps Alabama Hospital Serve the Wellness Market," *Health Facilities Management*, vol. 19, no. 8 (August 2006), 2–7.

_____. "Platform for Success: Spacious Site Inspires Design Team's Imagination," *Health Facilities Management*, vol. 21, no. 9 (September 2008).

_____. "Southern Charm: Mississippi Patient Tower Combines Past and Future," *Health Facilities Management*, vol. 20, no. 8 (August 2007).

_____. "Strong Finish: New Patient Tower Tops Off Alabama Hospital's Master Plan," *Health Facilities Management*, vol. 20, no. 6 (June 2007).

Eastman, A. Brent. "Blood in Our Streets: The Status and Evolution of Trauma Care Systems," *Archives of Surgery* (June 1992), 677–81.

Eaton, Kate. "Industrial Rehabilitation—A Win/Win Outpatient Program," *Trustee*, vol. 44, no. 2 (February 1991), 22.

Eckert, Marvina Kay, and Lorene Newberry. "A Look at Our New Emergency Department: Kennestone Hospital Emergency Center, Marietta, Georgia," *Journal of Emergency Nursing*, vol. 18, no. 3 (June 1993), 29A–33A.

Eckholm, Eric. "Study Links Paperwork to 25% of Hospital Costs," *New York Times* (August 5, 1993), A14.

"Eco-Friendly Hotel of 2020," *Lodging: The Official Magazine of the American Hotel and Lodging Association* (February 2006).

Ehlinger, Edward P. "Access to Health Care and the Year 2000 Objectives," *Minnesota Medicine* (January 1991), 15–17.

Elbe, John, and Don Altemeyer. "The Future of Clinical Lab Design," *Medical Construction and Design* (May/June 2007), 29–33.

Elliott, Victoria Stagg. "3-D Imaging Could Replace Invasive Tests," *American Medical News* (December 18, 2000).

Elmer-Dewitt, Philip. "The Genetic Revolution: New Technology Enables Us to Improve on Nature. How Far Should We Go?" *Time*, vol. 43, no. 3 (January 17, 1994), 46–53.

Engelking, Constance. "The Human Genome Exposed: A Glimpse of Promise, Predicament, and Impact on Practice," *Oncology Nursing Forum*, vol. 22, no. 2, (1995 supplement), 3–9.

Eubanks, Paula. "Chronic Care: A Future Delivery Model," *Hospitals*, vol. 64, no. 6 (March 20, 1990), 42–46.

_____. "Wayfinding: More Than Just Putting Up Signs," *Health Facilities Management*, vol. 2, no. 6 (June 1989), 20, 22–23, 25.

_____. "Wellness Programs Pay Off for Hospitals and Their Employees," *Trustee*, vol. 45, no. 1 (January 1992), 15.

Evans, Melanie, and Vince Galloro. "Growth Amid Signs of Strain," *Modern Healthcare* (June 11, 2007), 24–28.

Exter, Thomas G. "The Baby Boomers Turn 40: Implications for Healthcare Marketing," *Healthcare Forum Journal*, vol. 32, no. 1 (January/February 1989), 19–22.

Fairchild, Susan. *Perioperative Nursing Principles and Practice*. Boston: Jones and Bartlett (1993).

Farris, Bain J. "Converting a Unit to Patient-Focused Care," *Health Progress*, vol. 74, no. 4 (April 1993), 22–25.

Fegelman, Andrew. "New Cook Hospital Gets Lift from Study," *Chicago Tribune* (December 10, 1993), sec. 2, 1, 7.

Fendrick, Stephanie, Mike Kotzen, Tejas Gandhi, and Amy Keller. "Process-driven Design," *Healthcare Design*, vol. 7, no. 6, 16–20.

Ferguson, Tom. "Patient, Heal Thyself: Health in the Information Age," *The Futurist*, vol. 26, no. 1 (January/February 1992), 9–13.

Field, Roger. "Surgeons Perform From a Remote Location," *Medical World News*, vol. 34, no. 2 (February 1993), 35.

Findlay, Steven. "Help! This Is an Emergency!: Despite Heroic Rescues, Ambulance Service and Trauma Centers Are Hurting," *U.S. News & World Report*, vol. 107, no. 19 (November 13, 1989), 28, 33–34.

_____. "Portrait of a Hospital: Boston's Massachusetts General," *U.S. News & World Report*, vol. 108, no. 17 (April 1990), 63–67.

Findlay, Steven, et al. "No More Knives," *U.S. News & World Report*, vol. 110, no. 19 (May 20, 1992), 76–78.

Fitzgerald, Joan. "Architects and Builders Optimistic, Even in the Face of Healthcare Reform," *Modern Healthcare*, vol. 24, no. 12 (March 21, 1994), 41–54.

Fitzgerald, Sharon H. "Pituitary Center Offers Patients 'One-Stop Shopping'," *Nashville Medical News* (February 1999), 6.

_____. "Wireless Revolution Hits Health Care," *Nashville Medical News* (February 1999), 5.

Fletcher, Jim. "Interactive Video in Health Care," *International Hospital Federation 1988 Official Yearbook*, 157–158.

Flower, Joe. "The Way It Is, Is Not The Way It Will Be," *Health Forum Journal* (July 1999).

Forsythe, Paula. "Changing the Ecology of the NICU," *Designing for Child Health: Institute for Family Centered Care*, vol. 3, no. 1 (Spring 1995), 11–14.

Forty, Adrian. *Objects of Desire: Design and Society Since 1750*. New York: Thames and Hudson (1992).

_____. *Words and Buildings: A Vocabulary of Modern Architecture*. New York: Thames and Hudson (2000).

Fox, Renee C. *The Sociology of Medicine: A Participant Observer's View*. Englewood Cliffs, NJ: Prentice Hall (1989).

Franta, Gregory. *Environmentally Sustainable Architecture in a Health Care Facility*. Washington, D.C.: American Institute of Architects (1992).

Franz, Julie. "Triangle Design Saves Time, Money," *Modern Healthcare*, vol. 14, no. 3 (March 1984), 127–28.

Frayer, William W. "Neonatal Intensive Care Unit Renovation: The New York Hospital-Cornell Medical Center, 1975–76," *Clinics in Perinatology*, vol. 10, no. 1 (February 1983), 153–65.

Frick, Mathis P., et al. "Considerations in Setting Up a Positron Emission Tomography Center," *Seminars in Nuclear Medicine*, vol. 22, no. 3 (July 1992), 182–88.

Friedman, Eliot, ed. *The Hospital in Modern Society*. Glencoe, IL: The Free Press (1963).

Friedman, Emily. "The Sagging Safety Net: Emergency Departments on the Brink of Crisis," *Hospitals*, vol. 66, no. 4 (February 20, 1992), 26–35.

Gabel, Linda. "Trends in Culture and Lifestyle: The Impact on Healthcare Environments," *Medical Construction and Design* (May/June 2007), 42–46.

Gaerig, Chris. "When Lean and LEED Intersect," *Health Care Design*, vol. 9, no. 10 (October 2009), 14–17.

Gappell, Millicent. "Design Technology: Psychoneuroimmunology," *Journal of Healthcare Design*, vol. 4 (1992), 127–30.

————. "Hospice Facilities," *Journal of Health Care Interior Design*, vol. 2 (1990), 77–80.

Gardner, Elizabeth. "A Direct Line Between Buyer and Supplier," *Modern Healthcare*, vol. 19, no. 11 (March 17, 1989), 26–28.

————. "Hospitals Not in a Hurry to Plug in Computers by the Bedside," *Modern Healthcare*, vol. 20, no. 28 (July 16, 1990), 31–55.

————. "Hospitals on Road to Data 'Highways'," *Modern Healthcare*, vol. 23, no. 23 (June 7, 1993), 32.

————. "Hospitals Put Wireless Terminals to the Test," *Modern Healthcare*, vol. 23, no. 14 (April 5, 1993), 38.

————. "Revamping Hospitals' Approach to Renovation," *Modern Healthcare*, vol. 19, no. 15 (April 14, 1989), 34–46.

————. "Telemedicine Goes the Distance: Advancing Technology Allows Transmission of Data to Practitioners in Remote Locations," *Modern Healthcare*, vol. 20, no. 32 (August 13, 1990), 25, 28–32.

Gaskie, Margaret. "Kindly Light: Lighting for a New Hospital Contributes to Both the Image of Hospitality and the Real Thing," *Architectural Record Lighting*, vol. 6, no. 55 (May 1992), 56–61. 1

Geboy, Lyn. "The Evidence-Based Design Wheel: A New Approach to Understanding the Evidence in Evidence-Based Design," *Healthcare Design*, vol. 7, no. 3 (March 2007), 41–46.

Geunther, Robin, and Gail Vitorri. *Sustainable Healthcare Architecture*. New York: John Wiley and Sons (2008).

Gilbert, Fred I., Jr. "Health Care in the United States: The Need for a New Paradigm," *Hawaii Medical Journal*, vol. 52, no. 1 (January 1993), 8, 10, 12–13.

Gill, Kenneth E. "Hospital Retrofit: Dual-Duct HVAC Systems," *Heating/Piping/Air Conditioning*, vol. 65, no. 11 (November 1993), 31–40.

————. "HVAC Design for Isolation Rooms," *Heating/Piping/Air Conditioning*, vol. 66, no. 2 (February 1994), 45–52.

Gill, Kenneth E., and Alan L. Wozniak. "Hospital Gets IAQ Checkup," *Heating/Piping/Air Conditioning*, vol. 65, no. 8 (August 1993), 43–51.

Glick, Deanna. "When Care is Denied, Bureaucracy and Cost Controls are the Culprit . . . One Patient's Story: A Diabetic's Dilemma," *Los Angeles Times*, Part A (August 27, 1995), 15.

Godfrey-June, Jean. "Cross-Dressing: How Are Residential Looks Finding Their Way into Offices, Hospitals, Department Stores, and More—at the Same Time Contract Design Is Going Home?," *Contract Design*, vol. 34, no. 7 (July 1992), 70–71.

————. "Powerful Medicine: Design Speeds Up the Medical Learning Curve in Dramatic Ways in Schaetzel Center for Health Education at Scripps Memorial Hospital, La Jolla, Calif.," *Contract Design*, vol. 35, no. 10 (October 1993), 59–62.

————. "What Do the Aging Want?," *Contract Design*, vol. 34, no. 3 (March 1992), 55–57.

Goffman, Erving. *Asylums: Essays on the Social Situation of Mental Patients and Other Inmates*. New Brunswick, NJ: Aldine Transaction (2007).

Goldsmith, Jeff C. "Keynote Address: The New Generation of Healthcare and Design," *Journal of Healthcare Design*, vol. 5 (1993), 3–9.

————. "A Radical Prescription for Hospitals," *Harvard Business Review*, vol. 89, no. 3 (May/June 1989), 104–11.

————. "The Reshaping of Healthcare: Part 1," *Healthcare Forum Journal*, vol. 35, no. 3 (May/June 1992), 19–27.

————. "The Reshaping of Healthcare: Part 2," *Healthcare Forum Journal*, vol. 35, no. 4 (July/August 1992), 34–41.

Goldsmith, Jeff C., and Richard Miller. "Restoring the Human Scale: Healthcare Facilities Will Be Designed as Living Spaces for Families, Not Warehouses for Sick People," *Healthcare Forum Journal*, vol. 33, no. 6 (November/December 1990), 22–27.

Goldsmith, Marsha F. "Long-Term Care for Older Americans: The Institutionalization of Senescence," *Journal of The American Medical Association (JAMA)*, vol. 269, no. 18 (May 12, 1993), 2331.

Goodman, John, and Dianne Ward. "Satisfied Patients Lower Risk and Improve Bottom Line," *Patient Safety and Quality Healthcare* (March/April 2008), 32–38.

Gorman, Jean. "Critical Condition: What Is the Role of Design in the Transformation of a Health Care System Undergoing Financial Crisis and Flux?," *Interiors*, vol. 151, no. 12 (December 1992), 28, 32, 36, 96.

Gorner, Peter, and Ronald Kotulak. "Gene Therapy Poised to Reinvent Medicine," *Chicago Tribune* (April 13, 1990), sec. 1, 1.

Gottschalk, Mark A. "Sensors Add Smarts to Medical Products," *Design News*, vol. 15, no. 3 (August 2, 1993), 58–63.

Graham, Todd. "Surfacing Solutions for Healthcare Facilities," *Medical Construction and Design* (May/June 2007), 48–54.

Graven, Stanley N., et al. "The High-Risk Infant Environment: Part 1. The Role of the Neonatal Intensive Care Unit in the Outcome of High-Risk Infants," *Journal of Perinatology*, vol. 12, no. 2 (1992), 164–72.

————. "The High-Risk Infant Environment: Part 2. The Role of Caregiving and the Social Environment," *Journal of Perinatology*, vol. 12, no. 3 (1992), 267–75.

Green, Robert. "Well Equipped: Architects Who Specialize in Equipment Increasingly Must Specialize to Keep Abreast of Changing Technology," *The Construction Specifier*, vol. 45, no. 6 (June 1992), 78–88.

Greene, Jay. *Health-Care Policy Reform: Issues and Implications. A Report of the AIA Academy of Architecture for Health Conference*. Washington, D.C.: American Institute of Architects (1993).

————. "If You Can't Stem the Tide, Try Diverting a Trickle: More Hospitals Are Taking to Strategies Like Fast-Tracking to Direct Non-Emergency Cases to more Appropriate Settings for Care," *Modern Healthcare*, vol. 22, no. 15 (April 13, 1992), 49, 52–61.

————. "Paying Attention to Emergency Care: Hospitals Look Internally to Raise Revenues Through Better Billing, Pricing Practices," *Modern Healthcare*, vol. 21, no. 13 (April 1, 1991), 27–33.

Gregerson, John. "Regrouping for Reform," *Building Design and Construction*, vol. 37, no. 12 (December 1996), 38–40.

Gregory, Mary M. "Concepts in Headwall Selection and Design," *Critical Care Nursing Quarterly*, vol. 16, no. 3 (November 1993), 51–55.

————. "On Humanizing the Critical Care Environment," *Critical Care Nursing Quarterly*, vol. 16, no. 3 (November 1993), 1–6.

Griffin, Don. *Hospitals: What They Are and How They Work.* 3rd ed. Sudbury, MA: Jones and Bartlett (2006).

Griffin, Mary. "Hospital-Based SNFs: A Good Bet for Institutions?" *Health Care Strategic Management*, vol. 8, no. 6 (June 1990), 1, 20–22.

Grumet, Gerald W. "Sounding Board: Pandemonium in the Modern Hospital," *New England Journal of Medicine*, vol. 32, no. 6 (February 11, 1993), 433–37.

Guerin, Thomas B. "Materials Management Considerations in Critical Care Areas," *Critical Care Nursing Quarterly*, vol. 15, no. 3 (1992), 56–62.

"Guidelines and Levels of Care for Pediatric Intensive Care Units," *Pediatrics*, vol. 92, no. 1 (July 1993), 166–75.

Guidelines for Design and Construction of Health Care Facilities. Chicago: The Facilities Guidelines Institute (2010).

"Guidelines for Establishment of Gastrointestinal Endoscopy Areas," *Gastrointestinal Endoscopy*, vol. 37, no. 6 (1991), 661–62.

Guidelines for Perinatal Care: American Academy of Pediatrics and The American College of Obstetricians and Gynecologists. 6th ed. Elk Grove Village, IL: American Academy of Pediatrics; and Washington, D.C.: American College of Obstetricians and Gynecologists (2007).

Guinn, Robert M. "Good Design Is Good Medicine," *Hospital Management International 1991*, 210–11.

Gulak, Morton B. "Architectural Guidelines for State Psychiatric Hospitals," *Hospital and Community Psychiatry*, vol. 2, no. 7 (July 1991), 705–7.

Gunby, Phil. "Adult Day Care Centers Vital, Many More Needed," *Journal Of The American Medical Association (JAMA)*, vol. 269, no. 18 (May 12, 1993), 2341–42.

Guynes, David A. "Physical Rehabilitation Centers," *Journal of Health Care Interior Design*, vol. 2 (1993), 37–46.

Hadfield, Robert W. "Custom Ceilings: Acoustical Ceilings Offer a Number of Innovations for Unique Installations," *The Construction Specifier*, vol. 45, no. 3 (March 1992), 134–41.

Hager, Douglas E., and Christopher C. McClave. "LDR v. LDRP: A Comparison," *Frontline Planning*, vol. 8, no. 9 (1990).

Hahn, Ted, and Elizabeth Whitbeck. "Smart Pumps and Synergy: A Forward Thinking Conversion Is Helping One Hospital Reduce I.V. Medication Errors and Enhance Staff Collaboration," *IT Solutions* (September 2007), 27–28.

Hajworonsky, Michael, and Joanne M. Conway. "Trends in Radiology: Part I," *Radiology Management*, vol. 14, no. 1 (Winter 1992), 46–57.

Hall, Brenda, et al. "Designing a Critical Care Unit: Description of a Multidisciplinary Process," *Nursing Clinics of North America*, vol. 27, no. 1 (March 1992), 129–39.

Hall, Jill H. "Child Health Care Facilities," *Journal of Health Care Interior Design*, vol. 2 (1990), 65–69.

_____. "Signs—What Do They Say," *Designing for Child Health: Institute for Family Centered Care*, vol.2, no. 1 (Spring 1994), 1–3.

Halm, Margo A., and Michele A. Alpen. "The Impact of Technology on Patients and Families," *Nursing Clinics of North America*, vol. 28, no. 2 (June 1993), 443–57.

Hamilton, Kirk, ed. *Unit 2000: Patient Beds for the Future.* Houston: Watkins Carter Hamilton Architects (1993).

Hansell, Heidi Nerwin. "The Behavioral Effects of Noise on Man: The Patient with 'Intensive Care Unit Psychosis'," *Heart and Lung*, vol. 13, no. 1 (January 1984), 59–65.

Hanson, Margaret, and Richard L. Kobus. "Medical Office Design: Brigham and Women's Hospital Ambulatory Services Building II," *Journal of Healthcare Design*, vol. 4 (1992), 93–98.

Hard, Rob. "More Hospitals Move Toward Bedside Systems," *Hospitals*, vol. 66, no. 19 (October 5, l992), 72–73.

_____. "Robots: Can They Help Solve the Technologist Shortage?," *Hospitals*, vol. 65, no. 12 (June 20, 1991), 56–57.

Hardy, Jeff. "No Hidden Patient: Facility Design for Safety," *Patient Safety and Quality Health Care* (September/October 2006), 22–25.

_____. "Rethinking the Emergency Department," *Healthcare Design*, vol. 7, no. 3 (March 2007), 49–52.

Hardy, Jeff, and Ron Lustig. "No Hidden Patient," *Health Care Design*, vol. 6, no. 4 (July 2006).

Hardy, Owen B., and Lawrence P. Lammers. *Hospitals: The Planning and Design Process.* 2nd ed. Rockville, MD: Aspen (1986).

Harrell, James W. "User Driven Design Process," *Critical Care Nursing Quarterly*, vol. 14, no. 1 (1991), 21–29.

Harrell, Michelle F. "Designing Critical Care Units: An Overview," *Critical Care Nursing Quarterly*, vol. 14, no. 1 (1991), 1–8.

_____. "Headwall Considerations for Critical Care Unit Designs," *Critical Care Nursing Quarterly*, vol. 14, no. 1 (January 1991), 50–53.

Harriman, Marc S. "Clean Rooms: Contaminant-Free Workspaces Require a Design and Mechanical Synthesis," *Architecture*, vol. 80, no. 7 (July 1991), 83.

Hathorn, Kathy, and Upsli Nanda. *A Guide to Evidence-Based Art.* San Diego: The Center for Health Design (2008).

Hayes, John C. "Film and Digital Tie Again in Breast Cancer Detection," *DiagnosticImaging.com, In Review* (January 2001), 3–4.

"A Healing Place: Kaneko Ford and Bobrow Thomas Team Up to Create an Oasis for Children in L.A.'s Inner City," *Contract Design*, vol. 31, no. 2 (February 1989), 106–7.

Health Facilities Review 2003–2004: American Institute of Architects Academy of Architecture for Health. Mulgrave, Victoria, Australia: Images Publishing Group (2004).

Hemmes, Michael, comp. *Managing Health Care Construction Projects: A Practical Guide.* Chicago: American Hospital Publishing (1993).

Hemperly, Stephen W. "Hazardous Materials and Waste Program: Chemical Exposure, Evaluation, and Control," *AHA Technical Document Series*, 055941 (February 1991).

Henderson, John A. "Surgery Centers' Success Challenges Hospitals," *Modern Healthcare*, vol. 19, no. 22 (June 2, 1989), 78–80.

Henderson, John. "Hospitals Seek Bigger Cut of Outpatient Surgeries," *Modern Healthcare*, vol. 23, no. 26 (June 28, 1993), 82–85.

Henderson, Justin. "Quiet Compassion: A Comforting Refuge for Terminally Ill AIDS Patients," *Interiors*, vol. 151, no. 12 (December 1992), 62–63.

_____. "Tendering Care: The Northlake Cancer Treatment Center Places High Tech Medicine in a Soothing Environment," *Interiors*, vol. 150, no. 5 (December 1991), 60–63.

Herbig, Paul, and William Koehler. "Implications of the Baby Bust Generation upon the Health Care Market," *Health Marketing Quarterly*, vol. 10, nos. 3–4 (1993), 23–37.

Hiatt, Lorraine. "Breakthroughs in Long-Term Care Design," *Journal of Healthcare Design*, vol. 4 (1992), 205–15.

_____. "Long-Term Care Facilities," *Journal of Healthcare Design*, vol. 5 (1993), 195–205.

_____. "Long-Term Care: Future Possibilities," *Journal of Healthcare Design*, vol. 4 (1992), 55–63.

_____. *Nursing Home Renovation Designed for Reform.* Boston, MA: Butterworth Architecture (1991).

Highton, Marybeth. "Putting the Focus on Health: Wellness Centers Energize Hospital and Community," *Trustee*, vol. 46, no. 10 (October 1993), 4–6.

Hiltzik, Michael A., and David R. Olmos. "Emergency Rooms, HMOs Clash Over Treatments and Payments," *Los Angeles Times* (August 30, 1995), A12.

_____. "'Kaiser Justice System's Fairness Is Questioned," *Los Angeles Times* (August 30, 1995), A1–A4.

_____. "A Mixed Diagnosis for HMOs," *Los Angeles Times* (August 27, 1995), A1–A7.

_____. "Are Executives at HMOs Paid Too Much Money?" *Los Angeles Times* (August 30, 1995), A13.

_____. "Pressure Is Mounting for Better Oversight of HMOs," *Los Angeles Times* (August 31, 1995), A1–A3.

_____. "State Widely Criticized for Regulation of HMOs," *Los Angeles Times* (August 28, 1995), A1–A7.

Hinton, William, C.N.M.T., M.S. "Planning for PET," *Architect Newsletter*, 1st.quarter (2001).

Hinz, Christine A. "Aging Population Gives Hospitals Potential Focus," *Health Care Strategic Management*, vol. 9, no. 4 (April 1991), 1, 19–22.

_____. "PET Offers High-Tech Tool—But with High Price Tag," *Health Care Strategic Management*, vol. 9, no. 12 (December 1991), 1, 18–22.

_____. "Recovery Centers Rx for Excess Beds in Hospitals," *Health Care Strategic Management*, vol. 9, no. 1 (January 1991), 1, 19–22.

_____. "Sports Medicine Centers Offer Marginal Profits," *Health Care Strategic Management*, vol. 8, no. 11 (November 1990), 1, 23–26.

"Historic Town's Hospitals Brings Best of Old and New," *Health Facilities Management*, vol. 21, no. 1 (January 2008).

Hoffman, Thomas. "Hospital Robots Have the Rx for Efficiency," *Computer World*, vol. 27, no. 114 (January 11, 1993), 69, 72.

Hogue, Kerry. "Kid-centric: Children's Hospital of Atlanta Promotes Kid-friendly Care in Award-winning Space," *Medical Construction and Design* (May/June 2008), 42–47.

"A Holistic Healing Environment," *Buildings Magazine* (October 2007).

Holmes, Scott, and Dan Showengerdt. "Removing 'Waste': Getting Down to Essentials Through a Lean Design Process," *Health Facilities Management* (March 2008), 41–44.

Holness, Gordon. "Breathing Easy: Approaches to Hospital HVAC Design Are Numerous and Conflicting," *The Construction Specifier*, vol. 45, no. 6 (June 1992), 63–77.

Honaker, Charles. "Home Health Care Renaissance: A $16 Billion a Year Industry by 1995," *Group Practice Journal*, vol. 40, no. 3 (March/April 1991), 8–12.

Horn, Miriam. "Hospitals Fit For Healing: Designers Are Proving That Medical Institutions Need Not Be Sickeningly Dreary," *U.S. News & World Report* (July 22, 1991), 48–50.

Horwitz-Bennet, Barbara. "Leading LEED: BIM to Take LEED to the Next Level," *Contract Magazine* (January 2008), 48–50.

"Hospitals and Physicians in the Year 2000," pamphlet. Chicago: Hospital Research and Educational Trust (1990).

"Hospitals Emphasize Hospitality: High-Tech and High-Touch Changing Hospital Design," *Southeast Construction* (July 2006).

The Hospital of the Future: Can the Patient Focused Model Really Work? Chicago: Chicago Health Executives Forum (1991).

Hoss, Jeff. "A Look at Our New Emergency Department: St. Luke's Hospitals Meritcare, Fargo, North Dakota," *Journal of Emergency Nursing*, vol. 18, no. 4 (August 1992), 36A–40A.

Hoyt, Jeffrey. "Immediate Care Facilities: Designing Convenient Medicine," *The Construction Specifier*, vol. 40, no. 10 (October 1987), 78–79.

Hubner, J., et al. "Endemic Noscocomial Transmission of Staphylococcus Bacteria Isolates In Intensive Care Unit Over 10 Years," *The Journal of Infectious Diseases* (1994).

_____. "Influence of Architectural Design on Nosocomial Infections in Intensive Care Units—A Prospective 2-year Analysis," *Intensive Care Medicine*, vol. 15 (1989), 129–83.

_____. "Influence of Architectural Design on Nosocomial Infections in Intensive Care Units—A Prospective 2-Year Analysis," *Intensive Care Medicine* 15 (1989), 179-183.

Huelat, Barbara J. "Current Trends in Cancer Center Design," *Journal of Health Care Interior Design*, vol. 3 (1991), 9–16.

_____. *Healing Environments: Design for the Body, Mind and Spirit.* Alexandria, VA: Medezyn (2003).

Huff, Charlotte. "Leaps and Bounds: A Nationwide Building Boom Among Children's Hospitals Is Dramatically Changing the Pediatric Landscape," *Hospital and Health Networks Magazine* (October 2007), 37–42.

Hulle, Elizabeth. "Highlights of Current Construction Projects," *Designing for Child Health: Institute for Family Centered Care*, vol. 2, no. 2 (Fall 1994), 11–13.

Humphreys, H. "Infection Control and the Design of a New Operating Theatre Suite," *Journal of Hospital Infection*, vol. 23 (1993), 61–70.

Ilg, Deann. "Senior Communities," *The Construction Specifier*, vol. 45, no. 2 (June 1992), 120–23.

Inglesby, Tom. "Asset Tracking and Beyond," *Patient Safety and Quality Healthcare* (November/December 2006), 60–62.

_____. "Reading Within the Lines," *Patient Safety and Quality Healthcare* (November/December 2006), 63–65.

Jacobson, John S. "Patient Relations Program Eases Construction's Inconvenience," *Health Progress*, vol. 76, no. 10 (December 1986), 101.

James, W. Paul, and William Tatton-Brown. *Hospitals: Design and Development.* London: Architectural Press; New York: Van Nostrand Reinhold (1986).

Janower, Murray L. "Patient-Focused Care: Radiology Department Beware," *Radiology*, vol. 187 (1993), 313–15.

Jaspen, Bruce. "Mayo, Deere Join Forces to Spread Plan to Des Moines," *Modern Healthcare*, vol. 23, no. 49 (December 6, 1993), 18.

Jenna, Judith K. "Toward the Patient-Driven Hospital," parts 1 and 2, *Healthcare Forum Journal*, vol. 9, no. 4 (May/June 1986), 8–18; (July/August 1986), 52–59.

Johnson, Donald E. L. "Integrated Subacute Care: 20% of Your Patient Days," *Health Care Strategic Management*, vol. 11, no. 8 (August 1993), 2–3.

_____. "Window of Opportunity for Subacute Services Is Small," *Health Care Strategic Management*, vol. 11, no. 7 (July 1993), 2–3.

Jones, Wanda J. "Acute Care Design: The New Generation," *Journal of Healthcare Design* (September 1993), 33–38.

Jones, Wanda J., and Milton Bullard. *New Century Hospital: Patient-Focused Planning and Design.* San Francisco: New Century Healthcare Press (1992).

_____. "Translating Operational Change into Facility Design: Measuring the Feasibility, Cost-Effectiveness, and Space Requirements of Patient-Focused Facilities," *Healthcare Forum Journal*, vol. 36, no. 1 (January/February 1993), 67–69.

Jurow, Alice, and Marc Schweitzer. "Planetree Patients Come First in Health Care Design," *California Hospitals*, vol. 6, no. 3 (May/June 1993), 14–16.

Kaiser, Leland. "The Hospital as a Healing Place," *Healthcare Forum Journal*, vol. 35, no. 5 (September/October 1992), 39–40.

Kalb, Paul E., and David H. Miller. "Utilization Strategies for Intensive Care Units," *Journal Of The American Medical Association (JAMA)*, vol. 261, no. 16 (April 28, 1989), 2389–395.

Kalymun, Mary. "Relationships Between Sensory Decline Among the Elderly and the Physical Environment: Implications for Health Care," *Rhode Island Medical Journal*, vol. 72 (May 1989), 161–67.

Kanaly, George W., Jr. "Systamodule: Hospital Environments for Today, Tomorrow, and Beyond," *Mississippi Pharmacist* (May 1975).

Kane, Robert E., and Rosalie A. Kane. "A Nursing Home in Your Future?" *New England Journal of Medicine*, vol. 324, no. 9 (February 28, 1991), 627–29.

Kania, Alan J. "Hospital-Based Home Care Integral to Seamless Service," *Health Care Strategic Management*, vol. 11, no. 8 (August 1993), 1, 19–23.

————. "Hospital-Health and Fitness Centers Promote Wellness," *Health Care Strategic Management*, vol. 11, no. 6 (June 1993), 1, 18–23.

————. Trauma Centers Form a Health-Care System," *Health Care Strategic Management*, vol. 11, no. 3 (March 1993), 1, 20–23.

Kantrowitz, Min. *Design Evaluation of Six Primary Care Facilities for the Purpose of Informing Future Design Decisions.* Martinez, CA: Center for Health Design (1993).

Kasper, Susie. "The Philanthropy That Makes Design Possible," *Healthcare Design*, vol. 7, no. 9 (August 2007), 48–53.

Kay, Bruce G., et al. "Designing a Modern Hospital Pharmacy," *American Journal of Hospital Pharmacy*, vol. 43 (February 1986), 339–43.

Keenan, Linda A., and Ellen F. Goldman. "Positive Imaging: Design as Marketing Tool in Diagnostic Centers," *Administrative Radiology*, vol. 8, no. 2 (February 1989), 36–41.

Keep, P. J. "Stimulus Deprivation in Windowless Rooms," *Anaesthesia*, vol. 32 (1977), 598–600.

Keep, Philip, et al. "Windows in the Intensive Therapy Unit," *Anaesthesia*, vol. 35 (1980), 257–62.

Kellman, Neil. "History of Health Care Environments," *Journal of Health Care Interior Design*, vol. 1 (1989), 19–27.

Kelly, Joyce. "Going Wireless," *Hospital and Health Networks* (November 2000), 65–68.

Kelly, Lucie S. "High Tech/High Touch—Now More Than Ever," *Nursing Outlook*, vol. 32, no. 1 (January/February 1984), 15.

Kenkel, Paul J. "Companies Sweeten Wellness Plans," *Modern Healthcare*, vol. 22, no. 47 (November 23, 1992), 49.

————. "Financial Incentives in Wellness Plans Aimed at Reducing Insurance Costs by Helping Workers Shed Unhealthy Habits," *Modern Healthcare*, vol. 22, no. 3 (January 20, 1992), 38.

Kennedy, Randy. "The Pablo Picasso Alzheimer's Therapy," *The New York Times* (October 30, 2005).

Kight, Douglas. "Hospital Women's Centers That Work," *Health Care Strategic Management*, vol. 6, no. 10 (October 1988), 12–13.

Kile, Denise. "Tom Landry Sports Center Takes Wellness, Physical Performance to High-Tech Levels," *Dallas Business Journal* (August 30–September 5, 1991), 28–29.

Kim, Howard. "Trauma Networks Look for Rescue: Hospitals Dropping Out as Uncompensated Costs Mount," *Modern Healthcare*, vol. 20, no. 5 (February 5, 1990), 33–35.

Klaus, Marshall H., ed. *Care of the High-Risk Neonate.* 4th ed. Philadelphia: Saunders (1993).

Klebs, Pamela, and Julie Kent. "Journey of Transformation to an Optimal Healing Community," *Health Care Design*, vol. 10, no. 9 (September 2010), 18–22.

Klein, Susan. "Respite Program Gives Care Givers a Break," *Health Progress*, vol. 70, no. 12 (November 1989), 64–68.

Kleman, Marie, et al. "Physiologic Responses of Coronary Care Patients to Visiting," *Journal of Cardiovascular Nursing*, vol. 7, no. 3 (April 1993), 52–62.

Knowles, E. W. (Bucky). "In a Time of Change, Construction Planning Takes on Complex New Dimensions," *Hospitals*, vol. 66, no. 4 (February 20, 1992), 42–51.

Knowles, Fred T. "ADA's Signage Rules: Significant, Strict, Specific," *Health Facilities Management*, vol. 5, no. 11 (November 1992), 44–53.

Kobus, Richard L., et al. *Healthcare Facilities.* 2nd ed. New York: John Wiley and Sons (2008).

Koch, Richard M. "Design Considerations for Electrical Power, Lighting, and Auxiliary Systems in Critical Care Areas of Hospitals," *Critical Care Nursing Quarterly*, vol. 14, no. 1 (1991), 54–59.

Kohn, Linda T., Janet M. Corrigan, and Milla S. Sonaldson, eds. *To Err Is Human: Building a Safer Health System.* Washington, D.C.: National Academy Press (2000).

Kolanowski, Ann M. "The Clinical Importance of Environmental Lighting to the Elderly," *Journal of Gerontological Nursing*, vol. 18, no. 1 (1992), 10–13.

Koska, Mary T. "Patient-Centered Care: Can Your Hospital Afford Not to Have It?" *Hospitals*, vol. 64, no. 21 (November 5, 1990), 48–54.

————. "Total Quality Improvement: A Hospital Case Study," *Trustee*, vol. 43, no. 8 (August 1990), 16–17.

————. "Urgent Care/Primary Care Concept Proves Profitable," *Hospitals*, vol. 63, no. 17 (September 5, 1989), 74–76.

Kovner, Anthony R., et al. *Healthcare Delivery in the United States.* New York: Springer (2005).

Kowalczyk, Liz. "Beyond X-rays: A Pricey Picture," *The Boston Globe* (January 12, 2001).

Kreiss, Kathleen. "The Sick Building Syndrome in Office Buildings—A Breath of Fresh Air," *New England Journal of Medicine*, vol. 328, no. 12 (March 25, 1993), 877–78.

Kuhn, Thomas S. *The Structure of Scientific Revolutions.* Chicago: University of Chicago Press (1996).

Kuspan, Joseph F., and George J. Mann. "Truly Groundbreaking: Dell Children's Medical Center of Central Texas," *Medical Construction and Design* (September/October 2007), 34–38.

Lamprecht, Loren J., and Ann B. Kulik. "Through a Child's Eyes," *The Construction Specifier*, vol. 46, no. 8 (August 1993), 38–47.

Land, Karen Brumley. "Activity Room Design, Equipment Impact Programming Success," *Provider*, vol. 19, no. 9 (September 1993), 95.

Landro, Laura. "Hospitals Beef Up Pediatric ERs: New Facilities, Training Aim to Address Shortcomings That Lead to Uneven Care," *Wall Street Journal* (September 9, 2006).

————. "Pediatric ICUs Make Headway Against Infection," *Wall Street Journal* (April 18, 2007).

Lane, Mary Rockwood. "A New Paradigm for Holistic Nursing Practice," *Journal of Holistic Nursing*, vol. 24, no. 1 (March 2006), 1–6.

Larson, Tom. "Research Laboratory Attuned to Needs of Scientists: Wexner Institute for Pediatric Research," *Health Facilities Management*, vol. 2, no. 3 (March 1989), 8–9.

Laskowski-Jones, Linda. "Will Trauma Centers Become Extinct? A Review of Factors Affecting Trauma Center Financial Viability," *Emergency Nursing*, vol. 19 (1993), 121–26.

Lathrop, J. Philip. "The Patient-Focused Hospital," *Healthcare Forum Journal*, vol. 34, no. 4 (July/August 1991), 17–20.

Lave, Judith R., and Lester B. Lave. *The Hospital Construction Act: An Evaluation of the Hill-Burton Program, 1948-1973.* Washington, D.C.: American Enterprise Institute for Public Policy Research (1974).

"Lawmakers Fear Insurers Will Misuse Genetic Data," *AHA News*, vol. 32, no. 38 (September 23, 1996), 3.

Leape, Lucian L., and Donald M. Berwick. "Five Years after *To Err Is Human*: What Have We Learned?," *Journal of the American Medical Association (JAMA)*, vol. 293, no. 19 (May 18, 2005), 2384–90.

Lebovich, William L. *Design for Dignity: Accessible Environments for People with Disabilities*. New York: Wiley (1993).

Leib, Roger K. "Bed vs. Chair-Based Care," *Aesclepius* (Spring 1993), 3.

Leibrock, Cynthia. *Beautiful Barrier-Free: A Visual Guide to Accessibility*. New York: Van Nostrand Reinhold (1993).

Life Span Design of Residential Environments for an Aging Population: American Association of Retired Persons/Stein Gerontological Institute. Washington, D.C.: AARP (1993).

Levine, Jules I. "Vision Drives Planning," *Designing for Child Health: Institute for Family Centered Care*, vol. 2, no. 2 (Fall 1994), 4.

Lewin, Tamara. "Alzheimer's and Architecture: A Search for Order," *New York Times* (May 2, 1990), A9.

Liberman, Jacob. *Light: Medicine of the Future*. Santa Fe, NM: Bear (1991).

Lictig, William A. "The Integrated Agreement of Lean Project Delivery," *Construction Lawyer*, vol. 26, no. 3 (Summer 2006), 1–8.

"Light, Bright, and Beautiful: Ellerbe Becket Remodels Hospital Youth Wing with Bright Colors 30 Years Later," *Contract*, vol. 31, no. 2 (February 1989), 104–5.

Lindner, Ulrich M. "Formulas for Flexibility: Adaptability Is the Essential Ingredient in Laboratory Design—and Modular Planning Can Provide It," *The Construction Specifier*, vol. 46, no. 4 (April 1993), 53–62.

Lindsey, Mark S. "'Landlocked' Hospital Finds Room for Its MRI Unit Under the Ground," *Health Facilities Management*, vol. 5, no. 9 (September 1992), 14–15.

Linn, Charles. "Labor and Delivery Rooms Use Warm Incandescent and Fluorescent Lighting to Create a Soothing Atmosphere," *Architectural Lighting*, vol. 4, no. 6 (June 1990), 36–39.

Linton, Patrick E. "Healing Environments: Creating a Total Healing Environment," *Journal of Healthcare Design* (September 1993), 167–73.

Llewellyn, Jane G. "Short Stay Surgery: Present Practices, Future Trends," *AORN (Association of periOperative Registered Nurses) Journal*, vol. 53, no. 5 (May 1991), 1179–91.

Longinow, Lillian T., and Louise B. Rzeszewski. "The Holding Room: A Preoperative Advantage," *AORN (Association of periOperative Registered Nurses) Journal*, vol. 57, no. 4 (April 1993), 914–23.

Long-Term Care: Projected Needs of the Aging Baby Boom Generation. Washington, D.C.: U.S. General Accounting Office, 1991.

Loukin, Andrea. "Tuttleman Center: Stained Glass Murals Help Ease Patient Concerns in the Hospital by KPA Design Group," *Interior Design*, vol. 63, no. 6 (April 1992), 110–11.

Lower, Mary S., and Lois B. Nauert. "Charting: The Impact of Bedside Computers," *Nursing Management*, vol. 23, no. 7 (July 1992), 40–44.

Lubic, Ruth Watson, and Eunice M. Ernst. "The Childbearing Center: An Alternative to Conventional Care," *Nursing Outlook*, vol. 26, no. 11 (December 1978), 754–60.

Ludman, Dianne. "Emergency/Ambulatory Department—A New 'Front Door' to the Hospital," *Health Facilities Management*, vol. 1, no. 3 (November 1988), 15–16.

Lumsdon, Kevin. "The Clinical Connection: Hospitals Work to Design Information Systems That Physicians Will Use," *Hospitals* (May 5, 1993), 16.

_____. "Moving Target: Hospitals Take Careful Steps in Acquiring PET," *Hospitals*, vol. 66, no. 7 (April 5, 1992), 58–62.

Lustig, Ronald M. "One Nineteen Health and Wellness Features Spa Services," *Medical Spas Review* (September 2006).

Lutz, Sandy. "Ambulatory Care of the 1990s Stretches the Imagination," *Modern Healthcare*, vol. 20, no. 49 (December 10, 1990), 24–34.

_____. "Home-care Franchises Soar in Popularity," *Modern Healthcare*, vol. 23, no. 23 (June 7, 1993), 34–35.

_____. "Hospitals Continue Move into Home Care," *Modern Healthcare*, vol. 23, no. 4 (January 25, 1993), 28–32.

_____. "Hospitals Gird to Fight 'Disease of the Future'," *Modern Healthcare*, vol. 22, no. 49 (December 7, 1992), 22–28.

_____. "Hospitals Reassess Home-Care Ventures," *Modern Healthcare*, vol. 20, no. 37 (September 17, 1990), 23–30.

_____. "Pumping Up Profits: Hospitals Lean Toward Fitness Centers to Fatten Bottom Line," *Modern Healthcare*, vol. 21, no. 29 (July 22, 1991), 26–28.

Lyons, Rosemary E. "Cross-Training: A Richer Staff for Leaner Budgets," *Nursing Management*, vol. 23, no. 1 (January 1992), 44–46.

MacFarlane, Brian. "The Star Treatment: Dallas' Children's Medical Center Offers Disney-like On-Stage and Off-Stage Approach to Patient Care," *Medical Construction and Design* (January/February 2008), 28–35.

Mack, Alan W. "Medical/Surgical Nursing Units," *Journal of Healthcare Design*, vol. 5 (1993), 29–36.

Madden, Christine S. "Environmental Considerations in Critical Care Interiors," *Critical Care Nursing Quarterly*, vol. 14, no. 1 (1991), 43–49.

Madsen, Jana J. "Growing Old Gracefully: Today's Senior Living Environments Facilities' Quality of Life and Quality Care," *Buildings Magazine* (January 2003).

Mahnke, Frank H., and Rudolf H. Mahnke. *Color and Light in Man-Made Environments*. New York: Van Nostrand Reinhold (1993).

"Making Special Care Special: Lake Pavilion/Family Birth Center, Baptist Hospital of Miami," *Architectural Record*, vol. 178, no. 7 (June 1993), 98–101.

Malkin, Jain. *A Visual Reference for Evidence-Based Design*. San Diego: Center for Health Design (2008).

_____. "Beyond Interior Design," *Health Facilities Management*, vol. 6, no. 11 (November 1993), 18–25.

_____. "Clinic Design: The Mystery Ingredient for Profit and Productivity," *Group Practice Journal*, vol. 40, no. 4 (July/August 1991), 20–30.

_____. "Gentle Delivery: Jain Malkin Documents the Criteria for a Successful Birthing Center," *Interiors*, vol. 151, no. 12 (December 1992), 64–67.

_____. "Medical Office Design: New Possibilities," *Journal of Healthcare Design*, vol. 4 (1992), 99–108.

_____. "Medical Office Design: Theory and Types," *Journal of Healthcare Interior Design*, vol. 4 (1992), 77–85.

_____. "Medical Offices," *Journal of Healthcare Interior Design*, vol. 2 (1990), 23–28.

_____. "Wayfinding: Are Your Staff and Visitors Lost in Space?" *Health Facilities Management*, vol. 5, no. 8 (August 1992), 36, 38–41.

_____. *Hospital Interior Architecture: Creating Healing Environments for Special Patient Populations*. New York: Van Nostrand Reinhold (1992).

_____. *Medical and Dental Space Planning for the 1990s*. New York: Van Nostrand Reinhold (1990).

Mannix, Margaret. "The Case for Home Care: A New Guide by Anne Werner and James Firman Explains How Older People Can Find—and Pay For—Reliable Care at Home," *U.S. News & World Report*, vol. 114, no. 16 (April 26, 1993), 71–72.

Marsh, Barbara. "San Diego in Lead of HMO Revolution," *Los Angeles Times* (August 31, 1995), A14.

Marshall Erdman and Associates. *Planning, Designing, and Constructing Group Practice Facilities: A Practical Guidebook*. Madison, WI: Marshall Erdman and Associates (1993).

Martin, Holly. "Can Hospitals Go Green Without Spending Too Much Money?" *Health Care Design*, vol. 9, no. 5 (May 2009).

Martin, M. Caroline. "Working Out for the Best," *Healthcare Forum Journal*, vol. 36, no. 6 (November/December 1993), 57–63.

Martinsons, Jane. "The Planetree Model: Personalized Patient Care," *Trustee*, vol. 43, no. 9 (September 1990), 8–9, 17.

Maserjian, Karen. "HOK: Traditional Georgian Styling Defines an In-Patient Nursing Unit at the University of Alabama Hospital," *Cahner's Publishing Health Care Supplement to Building Design and Construction* (February 1993), S58–S61.

Mason, James O. "Healthy People 2000: The Challenge of Academic Medicine," *Academic Medicine*, vol. 66, no. 10 (October 1991), 598–99.

Matson, Theodore A. *Restructuring for Ambulatory Care: A Guide to Reorganization*. Chicago: American Hospital Publishing (1990).

Mayer, Dean. "Florida Hospital," *Healthcare Forum Journal*, vol. 35, no. 5 (September/October 1992), 75–80.

"Mayo Clinic Hospital," *Arizona Construction, Phoenix Edition* (2001).

McCarter, Debbie, and David Lenart. "A 'Most-wired' Hospital Targets Information Sharing," *IT Solutions* (September 2007), 24–26.

McConnell, Edwina A. "The Impact of Machines on the Work of Critical Care Nurses," *Critical Care Nursing Quarterly*, vol. 12, no. 4 (March 1990), 45–52.

McCoy, Chris. "Baptist Memorial Hospital for Women," *At Home in Memphis* (February 2004).

McFarlane, Brian, and Lance M. Skelley. "Comfort to All: Emory Critical Care Unit," *Medical Construction and Design* (November/December 2007), 30–36.

McGowan, Maryrose. "Restoring Choice," *The Construction Specifier*, vol. 46, no. 8 (August 1993), 62–73.

_____. "Visual Field: Wall Surfaces Are Justifiably a Major Focus of Both Specifier and Client," *The Construction Specifier*, vol. 46, no. 8 (August 1993), 96–104.

McKahan, Donald C. "Healing Environments: Healing by Design—Therapeutic Environments for Healthcare," *Journal of Healthcare Design*, vol. 5 (September 1993), 159–66.

_____. "Healthcare Facilities: Current Trends and Future Forecasts," *The Academy Journal* (of The Academy of Architecture for Health) (October 1998).

_____. "The Healing Environment of the Future," *Healthcare Forum Journal*, vol. 33, no. 4 (May/June 1990), 37–39.

McKee, Bradford. "Reforming Healthcare Design," *Architecture* (March 1994), 109–13.

McKnight, John L. "Hospitals and the Health of Their Communities," *Hospitals and Health Networks*, vol. 68, no. 1 (January 5, 1994), 40–41.

McLarney, V. James. "Health Care Reform: What to Expect, What AHA Proposes and What It Will Mean to You," *Health Facilities Management*, vol. 6, no. 3 (March 1993), 18–25.

McNamara, Peggy, et al. "Patchwork Access: Primary Care in EDs on the Rise," *Hospitals* (May 20, 1993), 44, 46.

McQuarrie, Donald G., et al. "Laminar Airflow Systems: Issues Surrounding Their Effectiveness," *AORN (Association of periOperative Registered Nurses) Journal*, vol. 51, no. 4 (April 1990), 1035–49.

"Medical Mission: Children's Hospital and Health Center Patient Care Pavilion," *Architecture*, vol. 82, no. 4 (April 1993), 76–81.

"Meditation Room Opens in San Diego," *Aesclepius*, vol. 2, no. 4 (Fall 1993), 1–2.

Meeker, Margaret Huth, and Jane C. Rothrock. *Alexander's Care of the Patient*. 9th ed. St. Louis: Mosby (1991).

Meis, J. Anthony, Rev. "A Haven for the Spirit: A Well-Designed Chapel Can Improve Nursing Home Residents' Spiritual and Psychological Health," *Health Progress*, vol. 72, no. 5 (June 1991), 56–59.

Melin, Anna-Lisa, et al. "The Cost-Effectiveness of Rehabilitation in the Home: A Study of Swedish Elderly," *American Journal of Public Health*, vol. 83, no. 3 (March 1993), 356–62.

Mellenger-Blouch, Judd. "New Diagnostic Center Brings Radiology, Lab Services into the '90s," *Health Facilities Management*, vol. 5, no. 7 (July 1992), 16–17.

Meub, Eric. "The Room and the Cure: Some Preliminary Guidelines for Architecture That Heals," *Ekriture*, vol. 3 (July 1993), 24–25.

Middleton, William G. "Homelike Setting Aids in Creation of Restraint-Free Environment," *Provider*, vol. 19, no. 5 (May 1993), 45–46.

"Midwest Medical Center, Galena, IL, Architectural Showcase Medical Center," *Medical Design*, vol. 8, no. 9 (September 2008).

"Midwest Medical Center, Galena, IL," *Modern Healthcare* (September 22, 2008).

Militello, Philip R., and Ameen I. Ramzy. "Safety by Design: Shock Trauma Center's Helipad Received Special Consideration During its Planning and Construction," *Journal of Air Medical Transport*, vol. 9, no. 8 (August 1990), 15–17.

Millenson, Michael L. "1-Day Medical Wonders on Rise—Study: Most Surgery Patients Now Skip Hospital Stay," *Chicago Tribune* (April 22, 1992), sec. 1, 11.

Miller, Richard L. "Facility Planning and Design," from *Handbook of Healthcare Delivery Systems*. Yuehwem Yih, ed. Boca Raton, FL: CRC Press (2011).

_____. "The Erector Set," *Modern Healthcare* (December 16, 2002).

_____. "When a Specialty Hospital Can Become the Right Answer," *Nashville Business Journal* (June 25–July 1, 2004).

Miller, Richard L., and Misty Chambers. "Safety Versus Aesthetics," *Healthcare Design*, vol. 6, no. 7 (November 2006).

Miller, Richard L., Harold D. Petty, and Sam W. Burnette. "The Integrated Approach: Cardiac Care as a Separate but Integral Hospital Department," *The Academy Journal* (of The Academy of Architecture for Health) (October 2001).

Miller, Richard L., and Sam W. Burnette. "Holistic Approach to Cancer Treatment Facility Design," *The Academy Journal* (of The Academy of Architecture for Health) (December 1999).

Millies, Jeff. "Platform for Success: Spacious Site Inspires Design Team's Imagination," *Health Facilities Management*, vol. 21, no. 9 (September 2008).

Milshtein, Amy. "Coming Home," *Contract Design*, vol. 36, no. 2 (February 1994), 66–70.

_____. "Going for the Gold: Azalea Trace, Pensacola," *Contract Design*, vol. 34, no. 3 (March 1992), 63–68.

_____. "One-Stop Healing: University of Nebraska Medical Center Outpatient Care Center," *Contract Design*, vol. 35, no. 10 (October 1993), 66–69.

_____. "Queens for a Day," *Contract Design*, vol. 36, no. 2 (February 1994), 72–74.

_____. "Tree of Life: St. Luke's Medical Center Outpatient Wing," *Contract Design*, vol. 35, no. 10 (October 1993), 54–57.

Modeland, Vern. "ICU: Hospital within a Hospital," *FDA Consumer*, vol. 23, no. 1 (February 1989), 31–35.

"Modern Vision: Shiley Eye Center, University of California, San Diego," *Architecture*, vol. 80, no. 7 (July 1991), 58–63.

Moeser, Shannon Dawn. "Cognitive Mapping in a Complex Building," *Environment and Behavior*, vol. 20, no. 1 (January 1988), 21–49.

Molina, Gabe. "Facility Planning, Design and Development," *SurgiStrategies* (June 2009).

Monroe, Linda K. "Feeling Good," *Buildings*, vol. 93, no. 4 (April 1999).

Monsen, Maria G., and Ulla M. Edell-Gustafsson. "Noise and Sleep Disturbance Factors Before and After Implementation of a Behavioural Modification Programme," *Intensive and Critical Care Nursing*, vol. 21, no. 4 (August 2005), 208–19.

Montague, Kimberly N. "Interview with Jeff Hill, CEO Midwest Medical Center Galena, Illinois," *Planetalk: A Newsletter for Planetree* (March 2008).

Monteleoni, Philip. "Imaging Adjacencies: Three Recent Projects Illustrate Central vs. Dedicated Specialty Planning Considerations," *European Journal of Radiology*, vol. 16 (1992), 26–29.

Montgomery, Terry, and Jane Wigle. "Children's Rehab for the 21st Century: Bloorview Kids Rehab Offers a Host of Modern Features," *Healthcare Design*, vol. 8, no. 4 (March 2008), 38–43.

Monzu, Jeffrey S. "The Holistic NICU: Designing an Environment for Every Aspect of the Patient's Development," *Medical Construction and Design* (September/October 2007), 24–26.

Mooney, Jay. "A Handy Prescription: Biometrics Safely Secures Facility Access Points with the Scan of a Hand or Fingerprint," *Healthcare Building Ideas* (April 5, 2008), 48–50.

Moore, Kim. "Critical Care Unit Design: A Collaborative Approach," *Critical Care Nursing Quarterly*, vol. 16, no. 3 (1993), 15–26.

Moore, Tod, and Nathan Larmore. "Are Health Care Facilities Ready for VoIP?," *Health Care Facilities Management* (April 2005).

Moore, Tom, and Scott Roberts. "Worlds Collide," *Health Facilities Management* (August 2005).

More, Vincent, et al., eds. *The Hospice Experiment*. Baltimore: Johns Hopkins University Press (1988).

Morrow, Lisa A. "Sick Building Syndrome and Related Workplace Disorders," *Otolaryngology—Head and Neck Surgery*, vol. 106, no. 6 (June 1992), 649–54.

Mosher, Cynthia M. "The Child Care Business: Should Hospitals Invest?," *Nursing Management*, vol. 23, no. 8 (August 1992), 50–51.

Moulas, Guy. "Bar Codes in Hospitals and Pharmacies," *Hospital Management International 1991*, 149–150.

"Mountain Design Provides Perfect Remedy for Medical Center," *Design Solutions: Journal of the Architectural Woodwork Institute* (Spring 2006), 27–31.

Mullan, Fitzhugh. "The Future of Primary Care in America," *American Family Physician*, vol. 44, no. 4 (October 1991), 1481–84.

Murayama, Koji. "Housing and the Elderly," *Ekriture*, vol. 3 (July 1993), 4–9.

Murphey, Brian. "Rating the Integrated Operating Room," *Healthcare Design*, vol. 8, no. 5 (March 2008), 55–64.

Murphy, Emmett C., and Patricia Ruflin. "How to Design a Horizontal Patient-Focused Hospital," *Health Care Strategic Management*, vol. 11, no. 5 (May 1993), 17–19.

Nanda, Upali, Kathy Hathorn, and Tali Neumann. "The Art-Cart Program." *Healthcare Design*, vol. 7, no. 9 (August 2007), 10–14.

Nasatir, Judith. "OWP&P: The Prairie Style Interior of Oak Park Hospital's ICU, CCU and Telemetry Units Treats Patients, Family and Staff in a Comfortably Familiar Home-Like Environment," *Cahner's Publishing, Healthcare Supplement to Building Design and Construction* (February 1993), S62–S65.

Neill, Harry M. "Isolation-Room Ventilation Critical to Control Disease," *Health Facilities Management*, vol. 5, no. 9 (September l992), 30–31, 34, 36, 38.

Nesmith, Lynn. "Designing for 'Special Populations'," *Architecture*, vol. 76, no. 1 (January 1987), 62–64.

Nestor, Constance. "Lean Construction: The Owner's Viewpoint," *Facility Care* (October 2007), 16–19.

"New Directions in Long Term Care," *Provider*, vol. 19, no. 8 (August 1993), 22–28.

Noble, Ann. "New Use for Old Hospital," *International Hospital Federation 1988 Official Yearbook*, 84.

"North Kansas Hospital: Employee/Visitor Cafeteria," *Food Management*, vol. 27, no. 4 (April 1992), 124.

Northrup, Scott. "Patient Monitoring," *Hospital Management International 1990*, 311–12.

"Northwestern Memorial Hospital: Cafeteria and Central Production Kitchen," *Food Management*, vol. 27, no. 4 (April 1992), 126.

Nycum, William, and James Torbet. "Planning for Coordinated Ambulatory Services," *Designing for Child Health: Institute for Family Centered Care*, vol. 2, no. 2 (Fall 1994), 1–3.

O'Hare, Patrick K., and William T. Schmidt, Jr., "Required Reading: Federal Disabilities Act Increases Litigations Risks for Providers," *Health Progress*, vol. 72, no. 4 (April 1991), 43–46.

Olds, Anita Rui. "With Children in Mind: Novel Approaches to Waiting Area and Playroom Design," *Journal of Health Care Interior Design*, vol. 3 (1991), 111–22.

Oliver, Joan Duncan. "Resorting to Water: The Curative Powers May Be Questionable, but Mineral Springs Will Certainly Soothe Your Nerves," *Health*, vol. 22, no. 4 (April 1990), 58–63.

Ollanketo, Allison, and Cara Ramsay Elsas. "No Longer an Afterthought: The Emerging Importance of Art," *Healthcare Design*, vol. 12, no. 7, 62–64.

Olmos, David R. "Some Doctors Head to Idaho, a State Without Managed Care," *Los Angeles Times* (August 29, 1995), A11.

_____. "Specialists Finding Prognosis for Good Jobs is Grimmer," *Los Angeles Times* (August 29, 1995), A10.

Olmos, David R., and Michael A. Hiltzik. "Doctors' Authority, Pay Dwindle Under HMOs," *Los Angeles Times* (August 29, 1995), A1–A5.

_____. "Family Prevails in Long Struggle With HMO," *Los Angeles Times* (August 28, 1995), A12.

Olson, Christopher. "A Place for Kids: Replacement Hospital Benefits from Experience with the Special Needs of Pediatric Burn Patients," *Building Design and Construction* (September 1993), 60–62.

O'Neill, Michael J. "Effects of Signage and Floor Plan Configuration on Wayfinding Accuracy," *Environment and Behavior*, vol. 23, no. 5 (September 1991), 553–74.

O'Reilly, Joseph Matthew. *Legal Privacy and Psychological Privacy: An Evaluation of Court Ordered Design Standards*. University of Arizona Ph.D. diss. (1985).

Orem, Helen G. "Art for Health: Emerging Trends," *Journal of Healthcare Design*, vol. 5 (September 1993), 73–81.

Ornstein, Suzyn. "First Impressions of the Symbolic Meanings Connoted by Reception Area Design," *Environment and Behavior*, vol. 24, no. 1 (January 1992), 85–110.

Orr, Robin. "Executive Forum: The Planetree Philosophy," *Journal of Healthcare Design*, vol. 4 (1992), 29–34.

————. "Health Care Environments for Healing," *Journal of Health Care Interior Design*, vol. 1 (1989), 71–76.

————. "Planetree Update," *Journal of Health Care Interior Design*, vol. 2 (1990), 181–86.

Ottolino, Rick. "Mammography Center Easily Accessible in Large, Urban Mall," *Health Facilities Management*, vol. 1, no. 2 (November 1988), 12–13.

Page, Ann, ed. *Keeping Patients Safe: Transforming the Work Environment of Nurses*. Washington, D.C.: National Academies Press (2005).

Palmer, Janice B., and Florence Nash. "Taking Shape: Environmental Art in Health Care," *North Carolina Journal of Medicine (NCMJ)*, vol. 54, no. 2 (February 1993), 101–4.

Park, Katharine, and John Henderson. "'The First Hospital Among Christians': The Ospedale di Santa Maria Nuova in Early Sixteenth-Century Florence," *Medical History*, vol. 35 (1991), 164–88.

Pearson, Clifford. "Key Players in Health Care: The Clients to Know," *Architectural Record*, vol. 186, no. 3 (March 1998), 76–81.

Perry, Linda. "Single-Room Maternity Care Begets More Utilization," *Modern Healthcare*, vol. 20, no. 5 (February 5, 1990), 46.

————. "Staff Cross-Training Caught in Cross Fire," *Modern Healthcare*, vol. 21, no. 18 (May 6, 1991), 26–29.

Persily, Nancy Alfred, ed. *Eldercare: Positioning Your Hospital for the Future*. Chicago: American Hospital Publishing (1991).

Peska, Elizabeth L., Allison M. Meisheid, and Marybeth L. O'Neil. "Educating Nurses on Genomics, *American Journal of Nursing*, vol. 108, no. 2 (February 2008), 72a–72b.

Peters, Thomas J., and Robert H. Waterman. *In Search of Excellence*. New York: MJF Books (2009).

Peterson, Kristine. "Guest Relations: Substance or Fluff?" *Healthcare Forum Journal*, vol. 31, no. 2 (March/April 1988), 23–25.

Phelps, Stephen E., Jr., and Richard B. Birrer. "Do You Know Where You Are? A Look Into One Hospital's Emergency Department," *Health Progress*, vol. 73, no. 4 (May 1992), 43–47.

————. "Traumatic Trends: Emergency Departments Abound as the Number of Trauma Centers Spirals Downward," *Health Progress*, vol. 72, no. 4 (May 1991), 48–49.

Pica-Furey, Wendy. "Ambulatory Surgery—Hospital-Based vs. Freestanding," *AORN (Association of periOperative Registered Nurses) Journal*, vol. 57, no. 5 (May 1993), 1119–26.

Piergeorge, A. R., et al. "Designing the Critical Care Unit: A Multidisciplinary Approach," *Critical Care Medicine*, vol. 11, no. 7 (July 1993), 541–45.

Planning, Design, and Construction of Health Care Facilities. Chicago: Joint Commission on Accreditation of Healthcare Organizations (2006).

Popovich, John, Jr. "Intermediate Care Units: Graded Care Options," *Chest*, vol. 99, no. 1 (January 1991), 4–5.

Port, Otis. "It's a Nano World," *Business Week, Science & Technology* (November 27, 2000).

Recommended Practices Coordinating Committee. "Proposed Recommended Practices: Traffic Patterns in the Surgical Suite," *AORN (Association of periOperative Registered Nurses) Journal*, vol. 56, no. 2 (August 1992), 312–15.

Redfer, Mark S., and Rakie Cham. "The Influence of Flooring on Standing Comfort and Fatigue," *American Industrial Hygiene Association Journal*, vol. 61 (September/October 2000), 700–8.

Redman, Melanie, Ritu Bajaj, Caroline Kelley, and Deborah Handler. "Environments for Cancer Care," *Healthcare Design*, vol. 8, no. 5 (March 2008), 45–52.

Reece, Richard L. *Innovation-Driven Health Care: 34 Key Concepts for Transformation*. Sudbury, MA: Jones and Bartlett (2007).

Reed, Gary, B.S., and Deborah Hobe Reed, B.A. "The Emerging PACS ASP Model," *Radiology Management* (November/December 2000), 50–54.

Regnier, Victor A. *Assisted Living Housing for the Elderly: Design Innovations from the United States and Europe*. New York: Van Nostrand Reinhold (1994).

Reichenthal, Jack. "Evidence-Based Design Key to Curing American Hospitals' Woes," *Healthcare Building Ideas* (June 6, 2006), 78–80.

Reid, Robert N. "Power Panels: Headwall Units Must Meet Anticipated Medical Needs at the Bedside," *The Construction Specifier*, vol. 45, no. 6 (June 1992), 108–13.

Reiling, John G. "Creating a Culture of Patient Safety Through Innovative Hospital Design," from *Advances in Patient Safety*, Kerm Henriksen et al., eds., vol. 2. Rockville, MD: Agency for Healthcare Research and Quality (2008), 425–38.

Reiling, John G., et al. "Enhancing the Traditional Hospital Design Process: A Focus on Patient Safety," *Joint Commission Journal on Quality and Safety*, vol. 30, no. 3 (March 2004), 115–24.

Reiling, John. *Safe by Design: Designing Safety in Health Care Facilities, Processes, and Culture*. Chicago: Joint Commission on Accreditation of Healthcare Organizations (2007).

Riedel, Philip. "How Safe and Efficient Are LDRs/LDRPs?," *Frontline Planning*, vol. 8, no. 12 (1990).

Rifkin, Glenn. "New Momentum for Electronic Patient Records," *New York Times* (May 2, 1993), sec. 3, 8.

Riggs, Leonard M., ed. *Emergency Department Design*. Dallas, TX: American College of Emergency Physicians (1993).

Riley, Joanne. "Cross-Training Maximizing Staffing Flexibility," *Nursing Management*, vol. 21, no. 6 (June 1990), 481–82.

Rindler, Michael. "Chapter 4: Extraordinary Success Story at Northeast Georgia Medical Center," from *Strategic Cost Reduction: Leading Your Hospital to Success*. Chicago: Health Administration (2007).

Roberts, Percy E., III. "Renovation and Addition Turn Hospital Cafeteria into Bigger Profit Center," *Health Facilities Management*, vol. 4, no. 2 (February 1991), 12–13.

Robey, Peter E., and Carrie Valiant. "The Americans with Disabilities Act: Public Accommodations Will Never Be the Same," *Group Practice Journal*, vol. 40, no. 4 (July/August 1991), 90–91.

Robinson, J. Todd, and Alan P. Richman. "Even in Today's Economy, Creative Solutions Get Hospital Projects Built," *Community and Rural Hospital Weekly* (April 30, 2010).

Rochon, Donald. "Hospital Security," *The Construction Specifier*, vol. 45, no. 6 (June 1992), 90, 94–97.

Rockey, Alexandra. "The Exceptional Environment: Preparing for Dementia Care," *Provider*, vol. 19, no. 7 (July 1993), 22–36.

Rodriguez, Glenn S., and Bruce Goldberg. "Rehabilitation in the Outpatient Setting," *Clinics in Geriatric Medicine*, vol. 9, no. 4 (November 1993), 873–81.

Roebuck, E. J., et al. "Building or Extending a Hospital Department: Radiology— A Path Through the Planning Minefield (1)," *Journal of the Royal Society of Medicine*, vol. 80 (January 1987), 40–46.

_____. "Building or Extending a Hospital Department: Radiology—A Path Through the Planning Minefield (10)," *Journal of the Royal Society of Medicine*, vol. 80 (October 1987), 640–44.

_____. "Building or Extending a Hospital Department: Radiology—A Path Through the Planning Minefield (2)," *Journal of the Royal Society of Medicine* (February 1987), 107–13.

_____. "Building or Extending a Hospital Department: Radiology—A Path Through the Planning Minefield (3)," *Journal of the Royal Society of Medicine* (March 1987), 173–79.

_____. "Building or Extending a Hospital Department: Radiology—A Path Through the Planning Minefield (4)," *Journal of the Royal Society of Medicine* (April 1987), 239–45.

_____. "Building or Extending a Hospital Department: Radiology—A Path Through the Planning Minefield (5)," *Journal of the Royal Society of Medicine*, vol. 80 (May 1987), 308–13.

_____. "Building or Extending a Hospital Department: Radiology—A Path Through the Planning Minefield (6)," *Journal of the Royal Society of Medicine*, vol. 80 (June 1987), 376–82.

_____. "Building or Extending a Hospital Department: Radiology—A Path Through the Planning Minefield (7)," *Journal of the Royal Society of Medicine*, vol. 80 (July 1987), 449–55.

_____. "Building or Extending a Hospital Department: Radiology—A Path Through the Planning Minefield (8)," *Journal of the Royal Society of Medicine*, vol. 80 (August 1987), 515–22.

_____. "Building or Extending a Hospital Department: Radiology—A Path Through the Planning Minefield (9)," *Journal of the Royal Society of Medicine*, vol. 80 (September 1987), 577–83.

Roesch, Anthony, and Julia Thomas. "Is This an Emergency?" *Contract Design*, vol. 36, no. 2 (February 1994), 63–65.

Roffe, Samantha. "Sustaining the Spirit: Backed by Hard Science, Therapeutic Gardens Strengthen the Healing Process to Deliver Compelling Outcomes," *Medical Construction and Design* (May/June 2007), 21–27.

Rogers, Pamela J. "Bedside Revolution in Robotics," *Hospital Management International 1991*, 318–21.

Ropper, Allan H. "Neurological Intensive Care," *Annals of Neurology*, vol. 32, no. 4 (October 1992), 564–69.

Rosenfeld, Erika. "Taking the Pulse of the Market," *Cahner's Publishing, Healthcare Supplement to Building Design and Construction* (February 1993), S46–S53.

Rosenthal, Samuel. "Ensuring Plant Flexibility for Telecommunications," *Health Facilities Management*, vol. 5, no. 11 (November 1992), 26, 28–31.

Ross, Kenneth, and Jeffrey Heyman. "Navigating Divergent Interests in the Timing of Technology Decisions," *Medical Construction and Design* (May/June 2008), 32–34.

Ruffin, Marshall. "Medical Informatics: The Computer-Based Patient Record Will Be the Integrated Regional Healthcare System's Most Valuable Asset," *Healthcare Forum Journal*, vol. 36, no. 2 (March/April 1993), 47–50.

Rufo, Rebecca J. Zapatochny. "Techno Advantages of the Virtual ICU," *IT Solutions* (September 2007), 16–22.

_____. "Virtual ICUs: Foundations for Healthier Environments," *Nursing Management* (February 2007), 32–39.

Russ, Mayer. "Hermanovski Lauck: More than a Spoonful of Inspiration Helps the Medicine Go Down at Children's Medical Center of Dallas," *Cahners Publishing, Healthcare Supplement to Building Design and Construction* (February 1993), S54–57.

Sabatino, Frank. "Mind and Body Medicine: A New Paradigm?," *Hospitals* (February 20, 1993), 66–71.

_____. "New Concepts of Health and Healing May Affect Hospitals' Approach to Care," *Trustee*, vol. 46, no. 3 (March 1993), 8–10.

_____. "New Products as Well as New Space Improve Gift Shop's Old Image," *Health Facilities Management*, vol. 6, no. 2 (February 1993), 14–15.

Sachner, Paul M. "A Place of Passage: Coming Home Hospice," *Architectural Record*, vol. 176, no. 13 (November 1988), 104–7.

Safaee, Massoud. "Advanced Technology: Enhancing Patient Experience," *Medical Construction and Design* (November/December 2007), 18–21.

"Saint Joseph's Hospital Emergency Dept. Addition," *Design and Cost Data* (January-March 1994), 35–36.

Salas, Eduardo, et al. "Simulation-Based Training for Patient Safety: 10 Principles that Matter," *Patient Safety*, vol. 4, no. 1 (March 2008), 3–8.

Salvin, Susan. "Creating a Home Away from Home," *Designing for Child Health: Institute for Family Centered Care*, vol. 2, no. 1 (Spring 1994), 8–10.

Sand, Barbara, et al. "Alzheimer's Disease: Special Care Units in Long-Term Care Facilities," *Journal of Gerontological Nursing*, vol. 18, no. 3 (March 1992), 28–34.

Sanders, Cindy. "Outlook on Senior Housing: Changing Economy, Changing Needs Shape Design Plans," *Nashville Medical News* (October 2009).

Sanders, Margaret. "Hospitals: The Prognosis," *The Construction Specifier*, vol. 44, no. 8 (August 1991), 46–54.

Sandrick, Karen. "Hospitals and MDs Vie for Imaging Business," *Hospitals*, vol. 67, no. 21 (November 5, 1990), 31–33.

Schaal, Dennis. "Total Computerized Care in Hospitals," *Medical World News*, vol. 34, no. 2 (February 1993), 54.

Schicht, Hans H. "Cleanroom Technology in Surgery," *Hospital Management International 1991*, 301–2.

Schneider, Edward L., and Jack M. Guralnik. "The Aging of America: Impact on Health Care Costs," *Journal Of The American Medical Association (JAMA)*, vol. 263, no. 17 (May 2, 1990), 2335–40.

Schneider, Jay W. "Healthy Sales," *Building Design and Construction* (February 2006).

Schomer, Victoria. *Interior Concerns Resource Guide: A Guide to Sustainable and Healthy Products and Educational Information for Designing and Building*. Mill Valley, CA: Interior Concerns Publications (1993).

Scott, Lisa. "Construction Key: Keep Options Open," *Modern Healthcare*, vol. 23, no. 10 (March 15, 1993), 35–44.

_____. "New and Improved: Eighth Annual Competition Honors Architectural Projects That Build on Changes in Healthcare Delivery," *Modern Healthcare*, vol. 22, no. 44 (November 1, 1993), 39–47.

Seligmann, Jean, and Laura Buckley. "A Sickroom with a View: A New Artificial Window Brightens Patients' Days," *Newsweek*, vol. 115, no. 13 (March 26, 1990), 61.

Sensmeier, Joyce. "The Future of IT? Aggressive Educational Reform," *IT Solutions*, (September 2007), 2–8.

Shapiro, Joseph P. "Growing Old in a Good Home," *U.S. News & World Report* (May 21, 2001), 57–61.

Shellner, Pamela. "E-learning Answers: Real-time Nurse Manager Orientation," *IT Solutions* (September 2007), 10–13.

Sherer, Jill L. "Retooling Leaders," *Hospitals and Health Networks*, vol. 68, no. 1 (January 5, 1994), 42–44.

Shirani, Khan Z., et al. "Effects of Environment on Infection in Burn Patients," *Archives of Surgery*, vol. 121 (January 1986), 31–35.

Shrive, Charles A. "Balancing Act: Achieving the Isolation That Is Mandatory in Laboratories Involves Balancing the Scope, Quality, and Cost of the Engineered Systems That Serve the Lab," *Health Facilities Management*, vol. 46, no. 4 (April 1993), 63–71.

Simpson, Roy L. "Automating the ICU: Facing the Realities," *Nursing Management*, vol. 23, no. 3 (March 1992), 24, 26.

Sine, David M., and James M. Hunt. *Design Guide for the Built Environment*, edition 4.0, National Association of Psychiatric Health Systems (Summer 2010).

Sison, Rebecca. "When Care is Denied, Bureaucracy and Cost Controls are the Culprits ... One Patient's Story: Assembly Line Medicine?" *Los Angeles Times* (August 27, 1995), A14.

"Six Types of Health Care Consumers Identified by Gallup," *Health Care Strategic Management*, vol. 8, no. 8 (August 1990), 3.

Slater, James M., et al. "The Proton Treatment Center at Loma Linda University Medical Center: Rationale for and Description of Its Development," *Journal of Radiation Oncology, Biology, Physics*, vol. 22, no. 2 (1992), 383–89.

Sloan, Susan Lynn. "The Hospice Movement: A Study in the Diffusion of Innovative Palliative Care," *The Journal of Hospice and Palliative Care*, vol. 9, no. 3 (May/June 1993), 24–31.

Smyth, Angela. "See the Light!," *Hospital Development* (March 1990), 17–29.

Solovy, Alden. "Health Care in the 1990s: Forecasts by Top Analysts," *Hospitals* (July 20, 1989), 34–46.

Sommers, Marilyn Sawyer, and Juanita Schackmann. "Designer Genes and Critical Care Nursing: the Future is Now," *Heart and Lung* (May/June 1995), 228–36.

Souhrada, Laura. "Imaging Devices' Shifting Uses Affect Market," *Hospitals* (November 5, 1990), 28–31.

_____. "New Rules of Success for Outpatient Facilities," *Hospitals*, vol. 65, no. 19 (October 5, 1991), 42–43.

Soule, Dan. "Information Systems in Critical Care," *Hospital Management International 1990*, 223–24.

Spector, Deborah, and Carole Runyan Price. "Fast-Tracking in Hospitals," *Healthcare Forum Journal*, vol. 31, no. 1 (January/February 1988), 26–31.

Stalder, Felix. "Designing and Building with the Handicapped," *Hospital Management International 1991*, 232–234.

Starr, Paul. *The Social Transformation of American Medicine: The Rise of a Sovereign Profession and the Making of a Vast Industry*. New York: Basic Books (1982).

Stennert, E., et al. "Incubator Noise and Hearing Loss," *Early Human Development*, vol. 1, no. 1 (June 1977), 113–15.

Stichler, Jaynette, and Ronald Stichler. "Innovative Women's Center Design Features," *Facilities Planning News*, vol. 10, no. 11 (November 1991), 3, 11–12.

Stinson, William. "On-Site Facilities," *Journal of Air Medical Transport*, vol. 9, no. 8 (August 1990), 18–19.

Stoddard, Sandol. "Hospice: Approaching the 21st Century," *American Journal of Hospice and Palliative Care*, vol. 7, no. 2 (March/April 1990), 27–30.

Stoops, Michael D. "In-House Group Builds Muir's Unique Outdoor Rehab-Therapy Garden," *Health Facilities Management*, vol. 4, no. 4 (April 1991), 12–13.

Stout, Gail. "The Best in CS: Infection Control from the Ground Up," *Infection Control Today* (January 1999).

Strange, Gary R., et al. "Use of Emergency Departments by Elderly Patients: Projections from a Multicenter Data Base," *Annals of Emergency Medicine*, vol. 21, no. 7 (July 1992), 819–24.

Strasen, Leann. "Redesigning Hospitals Around Patients and Technology," *Nursing Economics*, vol. 9, no. 4 (July/August 1991), 233–38.

Strauss, Michael J., et al. "Rationing of Intensive Care Unit Services: An Everyday Occurrence," *Journal Of The American Medical Association (JAMA)*, vol. 255, no. 9 (March 7, 1986), 1143–46.

Strawser, Robert A, and Mary M. Gregory. "Design Considerations for Heating, Air Conditioning, and Exhaust Systems in Critical Care Units," *Critical Care Nursing Quarterly*, vol. 16, no. 3 (1993), 27–30.

Struble, Becky, et al. "Recovery Care Centers," *Journal of Health Care Interior Design*, vol. 2 (1990), 14–48.

Studnicki, James. "The Medical Waste Audit," *Health Progress*, vol. 73, no. 3 (March 1992), 68–77.

Suh, Young S. "A System for the Future," *Health Progress*, vol. 74, no. 10 (December 1993), 51–60.

Suhrland, Carol. "Form Follows Function: Family-Centered Planning and Design," *Designing for Child Health: Institute for Family Centered Care*, vol. 2, no. 1 (Spring 1994), 4–7.

Swensson, Earl S. *A Passion for Design: Human-Centered Architecture and Synergenial Practice*. Rochester, NY: Zenda, Inc. (2008).

_____. "Shifting Paradigms: A New Vision for the Future," address to the American College of Greece Career Forum, Athens, Greece (March 21, 1991).

_____. "The Synergenial Suburban Village in the Year 2000," address to the 28th Annual Meeting and Exposition of the American Association of Homes for the Aging, Baltimore, MD (November 8, 1989).

Swensson, Earl S., et al. "Synergenial Design of Health Care Facilities for the Future." Report of research (March 15, 1986).

Taravella, Steve. "Hospitals Dispose of Destructive Waste Habits," *Modern Healthcare*, vol. 20, no. 1 (December 24, 1990), 26–28, 30, 42.

_____. "Recovery Centers Gaining Interest," *Modern Healthcare* (July 2, 1990), 27.

Taylor, Kathryn S. "Biotech on the Brink," *Hospitals and Health Networks*, vol. 67, no. 21 (November 5, 1993), 36–37.

_____. "Robodoc: Study Tests Robot's Use in Hip Surgery," *Hospitals*, vol. 67, no. 9 (May 5, 1993), 46.

Technique et Lumiere Vernier, France. "The Bed Head Unit," *International Hospital Federation 1988 Official Yearbook*, 275–76.

Tetlow, Karin. "Children's Scale: The Ratcliff Architects Create a Warm and Carefully Scaled Child Development Center for the Children's Hospital in Oakland," *Interiors*, vol. 150, no. 6 (January 1991), 126–27.

_____. "Defying the Skeptics, Earl Swensson Associates and Samaritan North Health Center Create a Winning Nonprofit Ambulatory Care Center," *Interiors* (June 1996), 88–93.

_____. "Design Heals: Orlando Diaz-Azcuy Brings a Fresh Perspective to Issues of Privacy and Autonomy in an Intensive Care Unit Designed for Change," *Interiors*, vol. 145, no. 5 (December 1990), 87–92.

_____. "Healing Spirit: The Newest Interiors Initiative is a Meditation Room," *Interiors*, vol. 151, no. 12 (December 1992), 52–59.

_____. "ICU Roundtable: Beyond State-of-the-Art—Health Care Professionals Discuss the 1990 Interiors Initiative," *Interiors*, vol. 150, no. 17 (December 1991), 58–59.

_____. "Neo-Natal Environments," *Interiors* (June 1992), 94.

_____. "New Home Heals: In a Stunning Transformation of a Sober House in Gloucester, Payette Associates Write a New Page for Healthcare History," *Interiors* (December 1991), 50–54.

_____. "Prototype Home: A New Respite Home and Day Care Center for Children with AIDS," *Interiors*, vol. 151, no. 12 (December 1992), 70–71.

Thames, Debby. "Valet Parking Because: 'It's the Little Things That Matter'," *Texas Hospital*, vol. 43, no. 1 (June 1987), 27.

Thiele, Jennifer. "No Bones About It: Resurgens Orthopedics," *Contract Design*, vol. 34, no. 10 (October 1992), 46–49.

Thomas, Karen A. "Design Issues in the NICU: Thermal Effects of Windows," *Neonatal Network*, vol. 9, no. 4 (December 1990), 23–26.

Thomas, Richard K. "What Hospitals Must Do," *American Demographics*, vol. 15, no. 1 (January 1993), 36–41.

Thompson, John D., and Grace Goldin. *The Hospital: A Social and Architectural History*. New Haven and London: Yale University Press (1975).

Thweatt, Albert A. "4 Basic Approaches Key to Health-Facility Design," *Health Facilities Management*, vol. 6, no. 7 (July 1991), 28–34.

Tingwald, George R., and Andrew H. Dorr. "Tale of Two Nurseries," *Designing for Child Health: Institute for Family Centered Care*, vol.3, no. 1 (Spring 1995), 1–6.

Toland, Drexel, and Susan Strong. *Hospital-Based Medical Office Buildings*. Chicago: American Hospital Publishing Company (1986).

"Tom Landry Sports Medicine and Research Center, Baylor Medical Center Campus, Dallas, TX," *Athletic Business*, vol. 15, no. 6 (June 1991), 40–41.

Topf, Margaret, and Jean E. Davis. "Critical Care Unit Noise and Rapid Eye Movement (REM) Sleep," *Heart and Lung* (May/June 1993), 252–58.

Topf, Margaret. "Effects of Personal Control over Hospital Noise on Sleep," *Research in Nursing and Health*, vol. 15 (1992), 19–28.

Topf, Margaret. "Sensitivity to Noise, Personality Hardness, and Noise-Induced Stress in Critical Care Nurses," *Environment and Behavior*, vol. 21, no. 6 (November 1989), 717–33.

Townsend, Mary B. "Patient-Focused Care: Is It for Your Hospital?" *Nursing Management*, vol. 24, no. 9 (September 1993), 74–80.

Trafford, Abigail. "America's ERs in Critical Condition," *The Washington Post* (May 1, 2001). http://stacks.msnbc.com/news/567145.asp.

Treiber, Steve. "CA Hospital 'Recycles' a 10-Year-Old Building as Urgent Care Center," *Health Facilities Management*, vol. 4, no. 10 (October 1991), 14–15.

Trofino, Joan. "Voice-Activated Nursing Documentation: On the Cutting Edge," *Nursing Management*, vol. 24, no. 7 (July 1993), 40–42.

Tully, Jane. "'Medical Home' Helps Families with Doctor Visits," *Designing for Child Health: Institute for Family Centered Care*, vol. 2, no. 2 (Fall 1994), 8–10.

Tusler, W. H., Jr., FAIA (Tib). "Evolution of the Hospital, The Next 20 Years," *The Academy Journal* (of The Academy of Architecture for Health) (October 1998).

Ullman, Dana. "The Mainstreaming of Alternative Medicine," *Healthcare Forum Journal*, vol. 36, no. 6 (November/December 1993), 24–30.

Ulrich, Roger S. "How Design Impacts Wellness," *Healthcare Forum Journal*, vol. 35, no. 2 (September/October 1992), 20–25.

_____. "Wellness by Design: 'Psychologically Supportive' Patient Surroundings," *Group Practice Journal*, vol. 40, no. 4 (July/August 1991), 10–19.

Unruh, Karen. "A Link to Life: High Technology in Long Term Care," *Provider*, vol. 19, no. 3 (March 1993), 26–43.

Urbanowicz, Gary R. "How to Store Medical Waste When Space is Tight," *Health Facilities Management*, vol. 6, no. 12 (December 1993), 56–59.

Valins, Martin S. *Primary Health Care Centres*. Harlow, Eng.: Longman, 1993.

Van Der Ryn, Sim. "Healing Environments: Environmental Awareness and Healing," *Journal of Healthcare Design*, vol. 5 (September 1993), 175–86.

VanderSteeg, Jim and Courtney Liebenrood. "Bringing Home Into the Hospital," *Aesclepius Online* (December 1999).

"Veterans Administration Outpatient Clinic," *Architectural Record*, vol. 181, no. 2 (February 1993), 100–3.

Viladas, Pilar. "The Road to Recovery: Cedars-Sinai Comprehensive Cancer Center," *Progressive Architecture*, vol. 64, no. 7 (July 1988), 67–75.

Vogel, Angeline. "Patient-Oriented Design: The Johns Hopkins Outpatient Center," *Designer's World*, vol. 40, no. 1 (November 1992), 56–59.

Vogel, Morris J. *The Invention of the Modern Hospital: Boston, 1870-1930*. Chicago: University of Chicago Press, 1980.

Vogler, Joyce H. "Birthing Centers," *Journal of Healthcare Design*, vol. 5 (1993), 121–26.

Von Gunten, Charles F., et al. "AIDS and Hospice," *The American Journal of Hospice and Palliative Care*, vol. 8, no. 4 (July/August 1991), 17–19.

Voros, Sharon V. "New Women's Center Links Traditional Care with Health Promotion," *Health Facilities Management*, vol. 2, no. 12 (December 1989), 18–19.

_____. "Psychiatric Facility—One with Nature," *Health Facilities Management*, vol. 2, no. 4 (April 1989), 14–15.

Wachter, Robert M. "The End of the Beginning: Patient Safety Five Years after 'To Err Is Human'," *Health Affairs* (November 30, 2004), 534–45.

Wagenaar, Cor, ed. *The Architecture of Hospitals*. Rotterdam: NAi (2006).

Wagner, Lynn. "Hospitals Feeling Trauma of Violence," *Modern Healthcare*, vol. 20, no. 5 (February 5, 1990), 23–24, 26, 28, 32.

Wagner, Mary. "Study Finds Stockless Inventory Saves Money, but Many Barriers Keep It From Gaining Favor," *Modern Healthcare*, vol. 20, no. 40 (October 8, 1990), 44.

_____. "Vanderbilt's Stockless System Relies on Distributors as its Materials Managers," *Modern Healthcare*, vol. 20, no. 5 (February 5, 1990), 44.

Wagner, Michael. "Healing Revolution: A New Medical/Surgical Unit Designed to Encourage Patients to Participate in Their Own Treatment," *Interiors*, vol. 150, no. 5 (December 1990), 76–77.

"A Walk Down Easy Street," *Design Solutions*, vol. 9, no. 1 (Spring 1989), 20–22.

Ward, Michael P. "NH Hospital Relocates Main Entrance, ED to Reflect Shift in Care," *Health Facilities Management*, vol. 3, no. 2 (February 1990), 10–11.

"Washington University School of Medicine/Mallinckrodt Institute of Radiology," *Ekriture*, vol. 3 (July 1993), 26–29.

Wasserman, Sue. "Eliminating Alienation," *Medical Construction and Design*, vol. 6, no. 2 (March/April 2010).

Weathersby, William, Jr. "Easy Access: A 'Medical Mall' Plan Links a Diagnostic and Treatment Center with a Professional Building and Inpatient Bed Tower," *Hospitality Design*, vol. 14, no. 4 (May 1992), 46–50.

Webb, William A. "Rights of Passage: Efforts to Establish Uniform Accessibility Requirement in the Model Codes Are Now Taking Shape," *The Construction Specifier*, vol. 43, no. 8 (August 1991), 91–95.

Weber, Chari. "Long-Term Care Design: Emerging Trends," *Journal of Healthcare Design*, vol. 5 (September 1993), 187–95.

_____. "Long-Term Care Design: The New Generation," *Journal of Healthcare Design*, vol. 5 (September 1993), 213–17.

Weber, David O. "Planetree Transplanted," *Healthcare Forum Journal*, vol. 35, no. 5 (September/October 1992), 30–37.

_____. "Rewriting the Human Prospect," *Healthcare Forum Journal*, vol. 35, no. 5 (September/October 1992), 24–33.

_____. "Six Models of Patient-Focused Care," *Healthcare Forum Journal*, vol. 34, no. 4 (July/August 1991), 23–31.

Weiland, Greg. "ED: From Reduced Wait Times to a More Home-Like Atmosphere, Emergency Departments Don't Have to Be Traumatic," *Medical Construction and Design* (January/February 2007), 19–24.

Weinhold, Virginia B. "Flooring Options: Carpet Now a Major Contender," *Health Facilities Management*, vol. 5, no. 5 (May 1992), 96–100.

Weinstein, Robert A., and Gina Pugliese. "How (and Why) to Set Up a Facilitywide TB Program," *Health Facilities Management*, vol. 7, no. 3 (March 1994), 42–46.

Weisman, Ellen. "Engineering Controls and TB: What Works? How Well?" *Health Facilities Management* (February 1994), 18–24.

_____. "Sports Medicine Attracts a Young, Healthy Market," *Hospitals* (November 20, 1990), 49.

Weiss, Rhoda. "Southern Hospitality," *Health Progress*, vol. 74, no. 10 (December 1993), 62–75.

White, Robert D. "Focusing on Individual Needs of Infants and Families," *Designing for Child Health: Institute for Family Centered Care*, vol. 3, no. 1 (Spring 1995), 9–11.

Wieland, Gregory J. ""Healthcare Exterior Design: Grounds for Healing," *Medical Construction and Design* (September/October 2007), 50–54.

Wilhelm, Karen. "Collaboration Makes Construction Lean," *Target*, vol. 23, no. 5 (2007), 4–11.

Wilkinson-West, Ann. *The Hospital Emergency Department: A Guide to Operational Excellence.* Chicago: American Hospital Publishing, Inc. (1992).

Wilson, Larkin M. "Intensive Care Delirium: The Effect of Outside Deprivation in a Windowless Unit," *Archives of Internal Medicine*, vol. 130 (August 1972), 225–26.

Winchester, Johanna P., and Hazel N. Brown. "Patient Is Discharged—But Still in the Bed! Providing a Discharge Lounge Can Be a Cost-Effective Strategy," *Nursing Management*, vol. 23, no. 10 (October 1992), 57–61.

Witzke, Anita K. "Trends in Telemedicine: The eICU Program Transforms the ICU Enabling an Intensivist-directed Model of Care," *Nursing 2006 Critical Care*, vol.1, no. 6 (November 2006), 51–60.

Wojciechowski, Jim. "Newest LEED Buildings Create Challenges in Leasing," *Nashville Business Journal* (October 2, 2009).

Wolfson, Jay, et al. "Freestanding Ambulatory Surgery: Cost-Containment Winner?" *Healthcare Financial Management*, vol. 47, no. 7 (July 1993), 27–32.

Wollaber, Debra B. "Building a Health Services Center: A Design Planner," *Nurse Educator*, vol. 33, no. 6 (December 2008).

Wuchter, Thomas B. "Four-Story Mall Helps Consolidate Obstetrics and Outpatient Services," *Health Facilities Management*, vol. 7, no. 2 (February 1994), 16–17.

Wyke, Alexandra. "The Future of Medicine," *The Economist*, vol. 330, no. 7855 (March 19, 1994), 3–18.

Yamamoto, Loren G. "Scanned Emergency Department to Emergency Department Image Transfer (SEE- IT): Implementation and Standardizing Protocols to Optimize Tertiary Referrals," *American Journal of Emergency Medicine*, vol. 11, no. 1 (January 1993), 70–75.

Yantis, Michael R. "The Quiet Hospital: HIPAA and AIA Standards Help Control Noise, Improve Heating," *Medical Construction and Design* (January/February 2006), 35–37, 66.

Yee, Roger. "What's Healthy About Health Care Design," *Contract Design*, vol. 34, no. 10 (October 1992), 41–43.

Yoders, Jeff. "Switching to BIM? User Groups Can Help Smooth the Transition," *Building Design and Construction* (June 2008), 42–45.

Young, Diony. "Family-Centered Maternity Care: Is the Central Nursery Obsolete?," *Birth*, vol. 19, no. 4 (December 1992), 183–84.

Young, Renée. "A Maturing Market," *Building Design and Construction* (April 1999).

Zablocki, Elaine. "Quality Management Targets Health Care," *Nation's Business*, vol. 81, no. 2 (February 1993), 40–41.

Zezelo, Patti Rager, Amanda Whitekettle Hansell, and Linda Thomas. "Describing the Influence of Technologies on Registered Nurses' Work," *Clinical Nurse Specialist*, vol. 22, no. 3 (2008), 132–40.

Zigmond, Jessica. "Workplace Report 2008," *Medical Healthcare* (June 2, 2008), 26–29.

Zilm, Frank. "Four Key Decisions in the Evolution of a Critical Care Unit," *Critical Care Nursing Quarterly*, vol. 14, no. 1 (1991), 9–20.

Zilm, Frank. "Planning for the Worst: Is Your Emergency Facility Ready for Epidemics and Special-Risk Patients," *Health Facilities Management Magazine* (March 2006), 39–41.

Zubatkin, Allen D. "Psychological Impact of Medical Equipment on Patients," *Journal of Clinical Engineering*, vol. 5, no. 3 (July–September 1980), 250–55.

Zun, Leslie. "Observation Units: Boom or Bust for Emergency Medicine," *Journal of Emergency Medicine*, vol. 8 (1990), 485–90.

Index

[Page numbers in *italic* refer to captions.]

CJMW Architecture, 353–55
clean-room technology, 177
Clinical Infrastructure Matrix and Operational Benchmarks, 176
clinical integration, 223, 227–30
clinical trials patients, 280–81
cloning, 364
Coe, Rodney M., 32–33
Cohen, Uriel, 333
color
    critical care unit, 200
    designs for elderly population, 334
    postanesthesia care unit, 184
    procedure room, 175–76
Columbia University Medical Center (New York, New York), *102*, 102–3, *103*
community-integrated healthcare facilities, 72, 252
computed tomography, 144–45, 154–55. *see also* imaging technology and services
Computer Motion, 368
Condell Intergenerational Day Care Center (Libertyville, Illinois), *295*
consultants, renovation, 91–92
consumer-centered healthcare market, 13, 17–18
    demands of medical technology in, 44
    implications for design, 18–19, 21–22, 53–55
    patient preferences, 63–64
continuing care retirement communities, 331, 344
    design examples, 344–55
    future of design, *362, 365, 369, 371–72, 373*
continuity of care, 56
Continuous Ambient Relaxation Environment, 263
Contract Magazine, 276
coronary care unit, 204
corridor design, 50
cost of care
    administrative costs, 39
    benefits of patient-focused care, 220
    concerns, 12
    cost-effectiveness evaluations, 25–26
    critical care facilities, 195–96
    diagnosis-related group reimbursement system, 55
    effects of exposure to arts, 220
    efforts to contain, 13
    emergency care, 118, 119
    future prospects, 361
    historical evolution of hospital design, 38, 288–89
    imaging technology, 146
    long-term care, 331
    managed care system, 16–17
    neonatal intensive care, 207
    quality of care and, 263–64
    vertical integration of services and, 56–62, 289
cost of design, 25–26
    LEED certification, 73–74, 77
cost of renovation, 91
    versus rebuilding, 85–91
Cottonwood Hospital (Salt Lake Valley, Utah), 70
Craig, Zeidler & Strong, 49
critical care units
    ceiling material, 198–99
    colors, 200
    costs, 195–96
    design examples, 208–17
    design planning, 195
    floor plans, *195*

historical evolution of designs for, 194–95
integration of services, 59–60
isolation issues, 206
levels of care, 196–97
lighting, 193–94, 200
location, 197–98
noise levels, 194, 200–201
odor control, 201
patient monitoring equipment, 199, 203
patient privacy in, 199
problems of older designs, 192–94
range of design considerations, 195–97
reality orientation of patients, 193, 198–99
significance of, in hospital mission, 192
size, 198
special care units, 197, 204–6
staff accommodations, 201–3
technology considerations in design, 203
visitor accommodations, 201
windows, 198
see also intensive care units
Cumberland at Green Hills (Nashville, Tennessee), *334*, 334–35, *335*

da Vinci Surgical System, 181, 182, 368
decontamination rooms, 123
Dekalb Medical Center (Decatur Campus), *298*, 298–99, *299*
demographic analysis, 69–70
Denmark, 44
Design Build Institute of America, 274
design of healthcare facilities, generally
    anticipation of future needs, 20
    community approach, 371–72
    conflicting needs in, 34–35
    in consumer-focused healthcare system, 18–19, 21–22
    cost considerations, 25–26
    evolution of medical technology and, 23–24, 43–44
    as expression of social order, 38–39, 42
    flexible design strategies, 46–52, 126, 147, 228, 229
    future prospects, 218, 363, 364–65, 366–67, 370–73
    healthcare system concept and, 20–21
    historical phases, 14
    hospital evolution, 32–33, 36–44
    humanizing elements, 64–65, 152, 197, 223–24
    implications of evidence-based care, 23
    medical practice considerations in, 26–27
    modernist movement, 44–45
    noninstitutional approach, 22
    paradigm shifts influencing, 18–20
    patient-centered approach, 53–55
    planning for expansion, 106–7
    population aging and, 71–72
    significance of, in healing process, 28–31, 33–34, 288, 372–73
    Synergenial® approach, 27–28
    total institution approach, 35–36
    trends influencing, 22–25, 46, 288–90, 356–61, 363, 371
    vertical integration of services and, 56–62
    wholeness in, 19–20
    see also specific design element; specific type of facility
Design Organization, Inc., 284
design process
    fast-track renovation, 94–96
    participants, 97
    renovation planning, 92–93, 97–98
    strategic and master planning, 97–98, 231–32

Naisbitt, John, 64
nanotechnology, 365–67
National Association of Children's Hospitals and Related Institutions, 315
National Electrical Code, 88
National Intrepid Center of Excellence for Traumatic Brain Injury (Bethesda, Maryland), *216*, 216–17, *217*
neonatal intensive-care units, 44, 207–9
neurological intensive care, 205
New Cancer Treatment Center/Kaiser Foundation Health Plan, Inc. (San Francisco, California), *61, 281*, 281–82, *282*
Newcastle Estates (Mequon, Wisconsin), *351*, 351–53, *352*
New Medical Center/Kaiser Foundation Health Plan, Inc. (Fresno, California), *19*
New York Hospital (New York, New York), *43*
New York–Presbyterian hospital (New York, New York), *102*, 102–3, *103*
Nightingale, Florence, 42, 194, 220–21
noise levels, 194, 200–201, 209, 213, 319
noninstitutional approach to design, 22
North Central Baptist Hospital (San Antonio, Texas), *310*, 310–11
North Florida Regional Medical Center (Gainesville, Florida), *89*
nuclear medicine department, 159
nurses
    in clinical integration of care services, 223
    future of profession, 231
    professional status, 222
    see also nursing stations
nursing homes. *see* freestanding skilled nursing facility
nursing stations, 25
    circular design, 34–35
    emergency department, 121
    Nightingale ward design, *41*, 42, 220–21

Objects of Desire: Design and Society Since 1750 (Forty), 39
obstetrics
    alternative birthing movement, 70
    future prospects, 308–10
    integration of services, 60
    see also women's healthcare facilities
Ochs, Lauren, 83
odor control, 201
One Nineteen Health and Wellness (Hoover, Alabama), *143, 286*, 286–87
operating rooms, 175–78, 182–83
organized delivery systems, 222–23
ornament, 44
OrthoColorado Hospital (Lakewood, Colorado), 236, *236*
Overlook Hospital (Summit, New Jersey), *321*, 321–22, *322*
OWP&P, *295*

Pacific Medical Center (San Francisco, California), 66
Page Southerland Page, 214–15, 300
Palladian design, *34*, 38
Paoli Hospital (Paoli, Pennsylvania), 129, *129*, 244–45, *245*
paradigm shifts, 13–14, 18–20
parking, emergency department, 120–21
Park Nicollet Melrose Institute (St. Louis Park, Minnesota), 272–73, *273*
Park Ridge Hospital (Fletcher, North Carolina), *306*
Parkwest Medical Center (Knoxville, Tennessee), *198*
Parrish Medical Center (Titusville, Florida), *165*, 165–66
patient advisory council, 53
patient-care manager, 223

patient care unit
    design examples, 233, 237–38, 244–45, 248, 249
    design for staff needs, 225–27
    floor plan, *229*
    integration of services in, 59
    robotics in, 230–31
    room arrangements, 229
    support services, 227
    in teaching hospitals, 226
    Wellness Environments design, 240–42
    see also patient rooms
patient-centered design, 53–55
    bedside diagnostics, 160–61
    clinical integration of healthcare in, 223
    design examples, 231–38
    economic benefits, 220
    historical evolution to, 220–21
    medical office building, 253
    patient room design and, 160, 227–30
    Planetree movement design, 218–19
    waiting area design, 121
patient-centered medical home, 370
patient rooms
    bed location, 203
    bedside diagnostics and monitoring, 160–61, 203, 229–30, 237
    ceiling material, 198–99
    for child care, 314
    conversion to intensive care rooms, 228
    conversion to isolation rooms, 229
    design examples, 238, 248
    design for staff needs, 225
    emergency department, 125–26
    historical evolution, 220–22
    layout strategies, 229
    lighting, 193–94, 200
    patient-centered design, 64, 160, 227–30
    Planetree movement design, 66–68, 218–19
    premium suites, 239–40
    privacy, 64, 199
    problems of older designs, 192–94
    residential model hospitals, 70
    size, 64, 227–28
    strategies for maintaining reality orientation of patients, 193, 198–99
    windows, 193, 198
    see also patient care unit
patient services, 56–57
pavilion-plan hospital, *40, 41*, 41–42
Payette, *108*, 108–9, *109*
payment system
    diagnosis-related group reimbursement, 55
    in era of provider-dominated care, 15
    historical evolution, 13, 15–16
    managed care system, 16–17
pediatric care
    ambulatory facilities, 269–70
    design of healthcare facilities, 314–27
    design of specialty medical practices, 255
    emergency departments, 117, 127, 130–31
    specialized care units, 320
Pei Cobb Feed & Partners Architects, *102*, 102–3, *103*
Pennsylvania Hospital, *34*, 38
peptic nucleic acids, 362
Peter, Laurence J., 287

specialized hospitals, 14

Spivey Station Outpatient Surgery Center (Jonesboro, Georgia), 267–68, *268*

sport medicine, 282–87

Spotsylvania Regional Medical Center (Fredericksburg, Virginia), *15*

St. Anthony Hospital (Lakewood, Colorado), *47, 48, 171, 174*

St. Anthony Medical Center (Crown Point, Indiana), *284,* 284–85, *285*

St. David's North Austin Medical Center (Austin, Texas), *297,* 297–98

St. Joseph's Hospital (St. Paul, Minnesota), 249, *249*

St. Louis Children's Hospital (St. Louis, Missouri), *31*

St. Luke's Hospital (Willowbrook, Texas), *17, 18, 26, 27*

St. Luke's Sugar Land Hospital (Sugar Land, Texas), *299,* 299–300, *300*

St. Mary-Corwin Medical Center (Pueblo, Colorado), 136, *137*

St. Vincent's (Birmingham, Alabama), *29, 125, 173, 176, 237,* 237–38, *282–83, 283*

Stanford University Hospital, 95–96

Stantec, 113

Starr, Pal, 14, 15

Staten Island University Hospital (New York), *213,* 213–14

stem cell treatments, 364

step-down units, 197, 204

Stolzman, Henry, 68–69

Stone, Marraccini, and Patterson, 49

Stonehill & Taylor, 166–67, 213

Stonehouse Hospital (Plymouth, England), 38

stormwater control, 77

Structure of Scientific Revolutions, The (Kuhn), 13–14

subacute care, 332–34

Summit at Lakeway (Lakeway, Texas), *341,* 341–43, *342, 343*

support services, 57–58

    patient care unit design, 227

surgical center

    air and temperature controls, 176–77

    angiography/surgery rooms, 153–54

    arthroscopic procedures, 179

    capacity for fetal surgery, 297

    classes of surgery performed in, 170

    clean-room technology, 177

    colors, 175–76

    components, 172

    design examples, 186–91

    design requirements, 171–72

    discharge holding area, 186

    endoscopic procedures, 178–79

    first operating room complex, 43

    floor plans, 173–74, *180, 185*

    freestanding ambulatory surgery facilities, 263–68, *265*

    future prospects, 367–68

    gamma knife procedures, 47, 180

    hospital design for ambulatory and short-stay procedures, 182–86, 264–65

    image-guided surgery, 147, 181

    integration of services, 60, 61

    isolation of, 171–72

    laser procedures, 179–80

    lighting, 177–78

    lithotripsy in, 180

    modular design, 174

    pediatric hospital, 320

    planning for design, 170–71

    preoperative holding area, 172, 183–84

    procedure room design, 175–78, 182–83

    recovery rooms, 172, 184

    restricted area, 173

    robotic technology in, 181–82, 368

    support areas, 172

    technology considerations in design of, 178–82

    three-zone layout, 172–73

Surgicenter (Phoenix, Arizona), 263

sustainable design, 74–75

Sycamore Hospital (Miamisburg, Ohio), *110,* 110–11, *111*

Synergenial® design, 27–28, 52–53, 67–68, 113–14, 373

    continuing care retirement community, *362, 365, 369, 373*

Synergenial Suburban Village, 371–72

Syska Hennessy Group Inc., 131

SystaModule, *50,* 51

teaching hospitals, 15, 226

TelePresence, 80

telomerase, 364

Texas A&M, 51

Texas Children's Hospital (Houston, Texas), *269,* 269–70, *270*

Thieriot, Angelica, 66

Three Crowns Park (Evanston, Illinois), *349,* 349–51, *350*

toilet facilities, 152, 229

    in extended-care facilities, 333

total institutions, 35–36

total quality management, 230

Toyota Motor Company, 25

transplant medicine, 44, 363–64

trauma centers, 44

typical patient, 64, 71, 308, 333

ultrasonography, 145, 155–56. *see also* imaging technology and services

universal care rooms, 228

Universal Design, 72

University of Alabama Hospital (Birmingham, Alabama), 239

University of California Hillcrest Medical Center (San Diego, California), *163,* 163–64, *164*

University of Mississippi, 51

University of Pennsylvania, 44

University of Pittsburgh Medical Center (Pittsburgh, Pennsylvania), 317–20, *319, 320*

University of Southern California, University Hospital (Los Angeles, California), *210, 211,* 211–12

U.S. Green Building Council, 72, 373

utilization

    critical care rooms, 196

    emergency department, 116, 119

    patterns and trends, 16, 71, 84, 250–51, 289

Valente, Michael, 227

Vanderbilt Bill Wilkerson Center for Otolaryngology and Communications Sciences, *260,* 260–61

Vanderbilt University Medical Center (Nashville, Tennessee), *24,* 111–12, *179, 193. see also* Monroe Carell Jr. Children's Hospital

ventilation, 40, 41

vertical integration of healthcare services, 222–23, 289

    design example, 62

    patient services, 56–57, 59–62

    rationale, 56

    support services, 57–58